Principles of Management • MGT 301

University of Massachusetts-Amherst

Third Edition

Angelo Kinicki
Arizona State University

Brian K. Williams

Luis R. Gomez-Mejia
Arizona State University

David B. Balkin
University of Colorado

Robert L. Cardy
The University of Texas at San Antonio

John A. Pearce II
College of Commerce and Finance
Villanova University

Richard B. Robinson, Jr.
Moore School of Business
University of South Carolina

Boston Burr Ridge, IL Dubuque, IA New York San Francisco St. Louis
Bangkok Bogotá Caracas Lisbon London Madrid
Mexico City Milan New Delhi Seoul Singapore Sydney Taipei Toronto

Principles of Management • MGT 301
University of Massachusetts-Amherst
Third Edition

This book is a McGraw-Hill Learning Solutions textbook and contains select material from the following sources:
Management, A Practical Introduction, Third Edition by Angelo Kinicki and Brian K. Williams. Copyright © 2008, 2006, 2003 by The McGraw-Hill Companies, Inc.
Management, People • Performance • Change, Third Edition by Luis R. Gomez-Mejia, David B. Balkin, and Robert L. Cardy. Copyright © 2008 by The McGraw-Hill Companies, Inc.
Formulation, Implementation, and Control of Competitive Strategy, Tenth Edition by John A. Pearce II and Richard B. Robinson, Jr. Copyright © 2007 by The McGraw-Hill Companies, Inc.
Reprinted with permission of the publisher. Many custom published texts are modified versions or adaptations of our best-selling textbooks. Some adaptations are printed in black and white to keep prices at a minimum, while others are in color.

1 2 3 4 5 6 7 8 9 0 QSR QSR 0 9 8 7

ISBN-13: 978-0-07-724102-5
ISBN-10: 0-07-724102-9

Custom Publishing Specialist: Bridget Iverson
Production Editor: Kathy Phelan
Printer/Binder: Quebecor World

CONTENTS

Harvard Business School

9-376-054
Rev. June 30, 1983

Note on the Structural Analysis of Industries

The essence of formulating competitive strategy is relating a company to its environment. Though the relevant environment is very broad, encompassing social as well as economic forces, the key aspect of the firm's environment is the industry or industries in which it competes. Industry structure has a strong influence in defining the competitive rules of the game as well as the strategies potentially available to the firm. Forces outside the industry are significant primarily in a relative sense; since outside forces usually affect all firms in the industry, the key is whether firms have differing abilities to deal with them.

The intensity of competition in an industry is neither a matter of coincidence nor bad luck. Rather, the nature of competition in an industry is rooted in its underlying economics and goes well beyond the established competitors already there. The state of competition in an industry depends on five basic competitive forces, which are shown in *Figure A.* The collective strength of these forces determines the ultimate profit potential in the industry, where profit potential is measured in terms of return on invested capital. Not all industries have equal potential. They differ fundamentally in their ultimate profit potential as the collective strength of the forces differs; the forces range from intense in industries like tires, paper, and steel, where no firm earns spectacular returns, to relatively mild in industries like oil field equipment and services, cosmetics, and toiletries, where high returns are quite common.

This note will be concerned with identifying the key *structural* features of industries that determine the strength of the competitive forces and hence industry profitability. The goal of competitive strategy for a business unit in an industry is to find a position in the industry where the company can best defend itself against these forces or can influence them in its favor. Since collective strength of the forces may well be painfully apparent to all competitors, the key for the strategist is to delve below the surface and analyze the sources of each. Knowledge of these underlying sources of competitive pressure highlights the critical strengths and weaknesses of the company, animates the positioning of the company in its industry, clarifies the areas where strategic changes may yield the greatest payoff, and highlights the places where industry trends promise to hold the greatest significance as either opportunities or threats. Understanding these sources will also prove to be useful in considering areas for diversification, though the primary focus here is on strategy in individual industries.

To avoid needless repetition, the term "product" rather than "product or service" will be used to refer to the output of an industry, even though both product and service businesses will be considered. These principles of structural analysis apply equally to product and service businesses.

Associate Professor ***Michael E. Porter*** *prepared this note as a basis for class discussion. The note is chapter one of* Competitive Strategy: Techniques for Analyzing Industries and Competitors *(New York: The Free Press, 1980), which contains a comprehensive framework for analyzing competition and formulating competitive strategy.*

Structural analysis also applies to diagnosing industry competition in any country or in an international market, though some of the institutional circumstances may differ.

Figure A Forces Driving Industry Competition

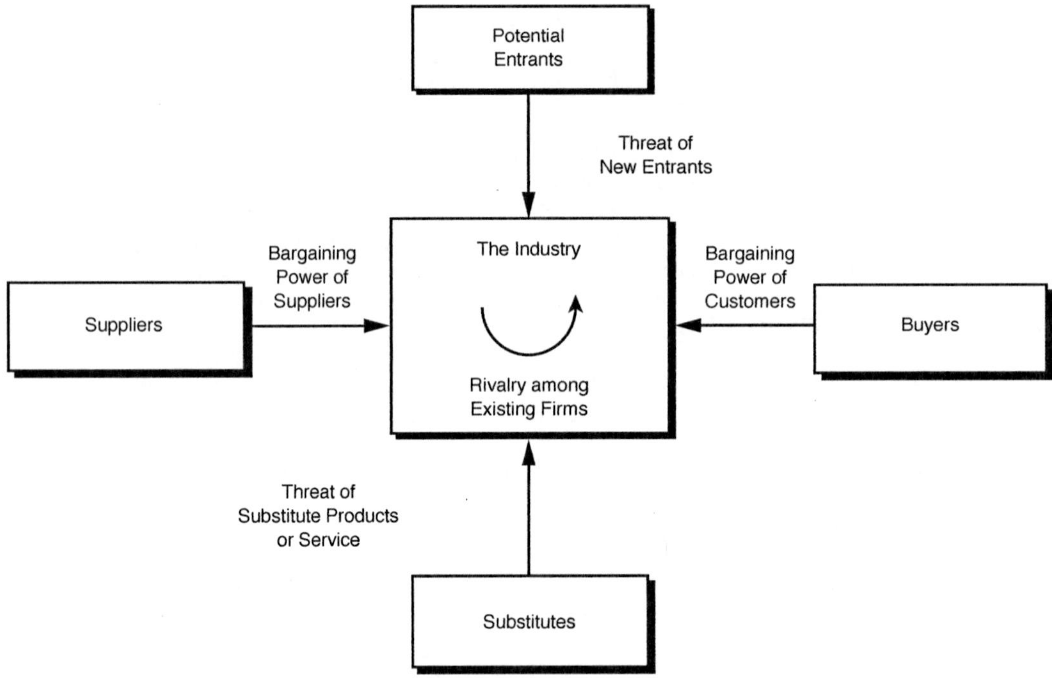

I. Structural Determinants of the Intensity of Competition

Let us adopt the working definition of an industry as the group of firms producing products that are close substitutes for each other. In practice there is often a great deal of controversy over the appropriate industry definition, centering around how close substitutability needs to be in terms of product, process, or geographic market boundaries. We will be in a better position to treat the issues in industry definition once the basic concept of structural analysis has been introduced, so it will be assumed that industry boundaries have already been drawn.

Competition in an industry continually works to drive down the rate of return on invested capital toward the competitive floor rate of return, or the return that would be earned by the economist's "perfectly competitive" industry. This competitive floor or "free market" return is approximated by capital loss. Investors will not tolerate returns below this rate in the long run because of their alternative of investing in government securities, and firms habitually earning less than this return will eventually go out of business. The presence of rates of return higher than the adjusted free market return serves to stimulate the inflow of capital into an industry either through new entry or through additional investment by existing competitors. The strength of the competitive forces in an industry determines the degree to which this inflow of investment drives the return to the free market level, and thus the ability of firms to sustain above-average returns.

The five competitive forces—entry, threat of substitution, bargaining power of buyers, bargaining power of suppliers, and rivalry among current competitors—reflect the fact that competition in an industry goes well beyond the established players. Customers, suppliers, and potential entrants are all "competitors" to firms in the industry that may be more or less prominent depending on the particular circumstances. Competition in this broader sense might be termed *extended rivalry*.

All five competitive forces jointly determine the intensity of industry competition and profitability, and the strongest force or forces are governing and become crucial from the point of view of strategy formulation. For example, even a company with a very strong market position in an industry where potential entrants are no threat will earn low returns if it faces a superior, lower-cost substitute. Even with no substitutes and blocked entry, intense rivalry among existing competitors will limit potential returns. The extreme case is the economist's perfectly competitive industry, where entry is free, existing firms have no power against suppliers and customers, and rivalry is unbridled because there are numerous firms and products all alike.

Different forces take on prominence, of course, in shaping competition in each industry. In the ocean-going tanker industry the key force is probably the buyers (the major oil companies), while in tires it is powerful OEM (original equipment manufacturer) buyers coupled with tough competitors. In the steel industry the key forces are foreign competitors and substitute materials.

The underlying structure of an industry, reflected in the strength of the competitive forces, should be distinguished from the many short-run factors that can affect competition and profitability in a transient way. For example, fluctuations in economic conditions over the business cycle influence the short-run profitability of nearly all firms in many industries, as can material shortages, strikes, spurts in demand, and the like. While such factors may have tactical significance, the focus of structural analysis is on identifying the stable, underlying characteristics of an industry rooted in its economics and technology that shape the arena in which competitive strategy must be set. Industry structure can shift over time, and firms will each have unique strengths and weaknesses in dealing with structure. Yet understanding industry structure must be the starting point for strategic analysis.

A number of key economic and technical characteristics of an industry are critical to the strength of each competitive force. These will be discussed in turn.

Threat of Entry

New entrants to an industry bring new capacity, the desire to gain market share, and often substantial resources. Prices can be bid down or costs inflated as a result, reducing profitability. Companies diversifying through acquisition into the industry from other markets often leverage their resources to cause a shake-up, as Philip Morris did with Miller beer. Thus acquisition into an industry with intent to build position should probably be viewed as entry even though no entirely new entity is created.

The threat of entry into an industry depends on the *barriers to entry* that are present, coupled with the *reaction* from existing competitors that the entrant can expect. If barriers are high and/or the newcomer can expect sharp retaliation from entrenched competitors, the threat of entry is low.

Barriers to Entry

There are six major sources of barriers to entry:

Economies of scale. Economies of scale refer to declines in unit costs of a product (or operation or function that goes into producing a product) as the absolute volume produced *per period* increases. Economies of scale deter entry by forcing the entrant to come in at large scale and risk strong reaction from existing firms or accept a cost disadvantage, both undesirable options. Scale economies can be present in nearly every function of a business, including production, research and development, marketing, service network, sales force utilization, and distribution. For example, scale economies in production, research, marketing, and service are probably the key barriers to entry in the mainframe computer industry, as Xerox and GE sadly discovered.

Scale economies may relate to an entire functional area, as in the case of a sales force, or they may stem from particular operations or activities that are part of a functional area. For example, in television set manufacturing economies of scale are large in color tube production while they are less significant in cabinet making and set assembly. It is important to examine each component of costs separately for its particular relationship between costs and scale.

Multibusiness firms may be able to reap economies similar to scale economies if they are able to *share operations or functions* subject to economies of scale with other businesses in the company. For example, the multibusiness company may manufacture small electric motors which are then used in producing industrial fans, hairdryers, and cooling systems for electronic equipment. If economies of scale in motor manufacturing extend beyond the number of motors needed in any one market, the multibusiness firm diversified in this way will reap economies in motor manufacturing that exceed those available if it only manufactured motors for use in, say, hairdryers. Thus related diversification around common operations or functions can remove volume constraints imposed by the size of a given industry.[1] The prospective entrant is forced to be diversified or face a cost disadvantage. Potentially shareable activities or functions subject to economies of scale can include sales forces, distribution systems, and so on.

A situation in which the benefits of sharing are particularly potent is the case where there are *joint costs.* Joint costs occur when a firm producing product A (or an operation or function that is part of producing A) must inherently produce product B. An example is air passenger services and air cargo. Because of technological constraints only so much space in the aircraft can be filled with passengers, leaving available cargo space and payload capacity. Many of the costs must be borne to put the plane into the air, irrespective of the quantity of passengers and freight it is carrying. Thus the firm that competes in both passenger and freight may have a substantial advantage over the firm competing in only one market. This same effect occurs in businesses that involve manufacturing processes with by-products. The entrant who cannot capture the highest incremental revenue from the by-products can face a disadvantage if incumbent firms do.

A common situation of joint costs occurs where business units can share *intangible* assets such as brand names and knowhow. The cost of creating an intangible asset need only be borne once—the asset may then be freely applied to other businesses subject only to any costs of adapting or modifying it. Thus situations where intangible assets are shared can lead to substantial economies.

A type of economies of scale entry barrier occurs when there are economies to vertical integration, or operating in successive stages of production or distribution. Here the entrant must enter integrated or face a cost disadvantage, as well as possible foreclosure of inputs or markets for its product *if* most established competitors are integrated. Foreclosure in such situations stems from the fact that most customers purchase from in-house units, or most suppliers "sell" their inputs in-house. The independent firm faces a difficult time in getting comparable prices and may get "squeezed" if integrated competitors offer different terms to it than to their captive units. The requirement to enter integrated may heighten the risks of retaliation and also elevate other entry barriers discussed below.

---

[1]For this entry barrier to be significant, it is crucial that the shared operation or function be subject to economies of scale that continue beyond the size of any one market. If this is not the case, cost savings of sharing can be illusory. A company may see its costs decline as overhead is spread, but this depends solely on the presence of excess capacity in the operation or function. These economies are short-run economies, and once capacity is fully utilized and expanded, the true cost of the shared operation will become apparent.

Product differentiation. Product differentiation means that established firms have brand identification and customer loyalties, which stem from past advertising, customer service, product differences, or simply being the first in the industry. Differentiation creates a barrier to entry by forcing entrants to spend heavily to overcome existing customer loyalties, not infrequently involving start-up losses and considerable elapsed time. Investments in building a brand name are particularly risky since they are unrecoverable.

Product differentiation is perhaps the most important entry barrier in baby care products, over-the-counter drugs, cosmetics, investment banking, and public accounting. In the brewing industry, product differentiation is coupled with economies of scale in production, marketing, and distribution to create high barriers.

Capital requirements. The need to invest large financial resources in order to compete creates a barrier to entry, particularly if the capital is required for risky or unrecoverable up-front advertising or R&D. Capital may be necessary not only for production facilities but also for things like customer credit, inventories, or covering start-up losses. Xerox created a major capital barrier to entry in copiers, for example, when it chose to rent copiers rather than sell them outright. While today's major corporations have the financial resources to enter almost any industry, the huge capital requirements in fields like computers and mineral extraction limit the pool of likely entrants. Even if capital is available on the capital markets, entry represents a risky use of that capital, which should be reflected in risk premiums charged the prospective entrant that constitute advantages for going firms.

Access to distribution channels. A barrier to entry can be created by the new entrant's need to secure distribution for its product. To the extent that logical distribution channels for the product have already been served by established firms, the new firm must persuade the channels to accept its product through price breaks, cooperative advertising allowances, and the like, which reduce profits. A new food product, for example, must displace others from the fiercely competitive supermarket shelf via promotions, intense selling efforts, heavy advertising to create consumer pull, or some other means.

The more limited the wholesale or retail channels for a product are and the more existing competitors have these tied up, obviously the tougher entry into the industry will be. Existing competitors may have ties with channels based on long relationships, high quality service, or even exclusive relationships in which the channel is solely identified with a particular manufacturer. Sometimes this barrier to entry is so high that, to surmount it, a new firm must create an entirely new distribution channel in order to get into the industry.

Cost disadvantages independent of scale. Established firms may have cost advantages not replicable by potential entrants no matter what their size and attained economies of scale. The most critical advantages are the following factors:

- Proprietary product technology: knowhow or techniques that are kept proprietary through patents or secrecy.

- Favorable access to raw materials: Established firms may have locked up the most favorable raw material sources, and/or tied up foreseeable raw material needs early at prices reflecting a lower demand for them than currently exists. For example, Frasch sulphur firms like Texas Gulf Sulphur gained control of some very favorable salt dome sulphur deposits many years ago, before mineral right-holders were aware of their value as a result of the Frasch mining technology. Discoverers of sulphur deposits were often disappointed oil companies that were exploring for oil.

- Favorable locations: Established firms may have cornered favorable locations before market forces bid up prices to capture their full value.

- Government subsidies: Preferential government subsidies may give established firms lasting advantages in some businesses.

- Learning or experience curve: In some businesses, there is an observed tendency for unit costs to decline as the firm gains more cumulative experience in producing a product. This is because workers improve their methods and get more efficient (the classic learning curve), layout improves, specialized equipment and processes are developed, better performance is coaxed from equipment, product design changes make manufacturing easier, techniques for measurement and control of operations improve, and other factors. Experience is just a name for certain kinds of technological change. As is the case with scale economies, cost declines with experience relate not to the entire firm but to the individual operations or functions that make up the firm. Experience can lower costs in marketing, distribution, and other areas as well as in production or operations within production, and each component of costs must be examined for experience effects.

Cost declines with experience seem to be the most significant in businesses involving a high labor content and/or complex assembly operations (aircraft, shipbuilding). Cost declines with experience are nearly always the most significant in the early growth phase of a product's development and later reach diminishing proportional improvements. Often economies of scale are cited as one of the reasons costs decline with experience. Economies of scale are dependent on volume per period and *not* on cumulative volume, and are very different analytically from experience, though the two often occur together and can be hard to separate. It is misleading for scale and experience to be lumped together, as will be further discussed below.

If costs decline with experience in an industry, and *if the experience can be kept proprietary by established firms,* then this leads to an entry barrier. Newly started firms, with no experience, will have inherently higher costs than established firms and must bear heavy start-up losses from below or near-cost pricing in order to gain the experience to achieve cost parity with established firms (if they ever can). Established firms, particularly the market share leader, will have higher cash flow because of their lower costs in order to invest in new equipment and techniques. However, it is important to recognize that pursuing experience curve cost declines (and scale economies) may require substantial up-front capital investment. If cost declines with volume continue to occur even as cumulative volume gets large, then new entrants may never catch up. A number of firms, notably Texas Instruments, Black and Decker, Emerson Electric, and others, have built successful strategies based on the experience curve through aggressive investments to build cumulative volume early in the development of industries, often by pricing in anticipation of future cost declines.

Cost declines due to experience can be augmented if there are diversified firms in the industry that *share* operations or functions subject to experience cost declines with other units in the company, or if there are related activities in the company from which incomplete but useful experience can be obtained. When an activity like raw material fabrication is shared by multiple business units, experience obviously accumulates faster than it would if the activity was used solely to meet the needs of one industry. Or when the corporate entity has related activities within the firm, sister units can get the benefits of their experience at little or no cost since much experience is an intangible asset. This sort of shared learning accentuates the entry barrier provided by the experience curve, provided the other conditions for its significance are met. Experience is such a widely used concept in strategy formulation that its strategic implications will be further discussed below.

Government policy. The last major source of entry barriers is government policy. Government can limit or even foreclose entry into industries with such controls as licensing requirements and limits on access to raw materials (like coal lands or mountains on which to build ski areas). Regulated industries like trucking, railroads, liquor retailing, and freight forwarding are obvious examples. More subtle government restrictions on entry can stem from controls such as air and water pollution standards, and product safety and efficacy regulations. For example, pollution control requirements can raise capital needed for entry and can increase required technological sophistication and even optimal scale of facilities. Standards for product testing, common in industries like food and in other health-related products, can impose substantial lead times on getting into an industry which not only raise the cost of entry but also give established firms ample notice of impending entry, and sometimes full knowledge of competitor products with which to formulate retaliatory strategies. Government policy in such areas certainly has direct social benefits, but it often has second-order consequences for entry which are unrecognized.

Expected Retaliation

The potential entrant's expectations about the reaction of existing competitors also will influence the threat of entry. If existing competitors are expected to respond forcefully to make the entrant's stay in the industry an unpleasant one, then entry may well be deterred. Conditions that signal strong likely retaliation to entry and hence deter it are:

- A history of vigorous retaliation to entrants;
- Established firms with substantial resources to fight back, including excess cash and unused borrowing capacity, adequate excess productive capacity to meet all likely future needs, or great leverage with distribution channels or customers;
- Slow industry growth, which limits the ability of the industry to absorb a new firm without depressing the sales and financial performance of established firms.

The Entry Deterring Price

The condition of entry facing an industry can be summarized in an important hypothetical concept called the entry deterring price. The entry deterring price is the prevailing price structure in the industry, adjusted for product quality and service, which just balances the potential rewards from entry (forecast by the potential entrant) with the expected costs of overcoming entry barriers and risking retaliation. If the current price level is higher than the entry deterring price, entrants will forecast above-average profits from entry, and entry will occur. Of course the notion of entry deterring price must reflect entrants' expectations of the future and not just current conditions.

The threat of entry into an industry can be eliminated if incumbent firms choose or are forced by competition to price below this hypothetical entry deterring price. If they price above it, gains in terms of profitability may be short-lived.

Properties of Entry Barriers

There are two additional properties of entry barriers that are crucial from a strategic standpoint. First, entry barriers can and do change as the conditions described above change. The expiration of Polaroid's basic patents on instant photography, for instance, greatly reduces its absolute cost entry barrier built by proprietary technology. It is not surprising that Kodak plunged into the market. Product differentiation in the magazine printing industry has all but disappeared, reducing barriers. Conversely, in the auto industry economies of scale increased enormously with post-World War II automation and vertical integration—virtually stopping successful new entry.

Second, while entry barriers sometimes change for reasons largely outside the firm's control, firm strategic decisions can have a major impact on entry barriers. For example, the actions of many U.S. wine producers in the 1960s to step up product introductions, raise advertising levels, and expand distribution nationally surely increased entry barriers by raising economies of scale and making access to distribution channels more difficult. Similarly, decisions by members of the recreational vehicle industry to vertically integrate in order to lower costs have greatly increased the economies of scale there and raised the capital cost barriers.

Experience and Scale as Entry Barriers

While they are often mixed together, economies of scale and experience have very different properties as entry barriers. The presence of economies of scale or sharing *always* leads to a cost advantage for the large scale or properly diversified firm over small scale or undiversified firms, presupposing that the large scale firms have the most efficient facilities, distribution systems, service organizations, and other functional units for their size. This cost advantage can only be replicated by possessing comparable scale or diversification. The large scale or diversified firm can spread the fixed costs of operating these efficient facilities over a large number of units, while the smaller firm, even if it has technologically efficient facilities, will not fully utilize them.

Some limits to economies of scale as an entry barrier, from a strategic standpoint, are as follows:

- Large scale and hence lower costs may involve tradeoffs with other potentially valuable barriers to entry such as product differentiation (scale may work against image or responsive service, for example), or the ability to rapidly develop proprietary technology.

- Technological change may penalize the large scale firm if facilities designed to reap scale economies are also more specialized and less flexible in adapting to new technologies.

- Commitment to achieving scale economies using existing technology may cloud the perception of new technological possibilities, or of other new ways of competing that are less dependent on scale.

Experience is a more ethereal entry barrier than scale, because the mere presence of an experience curve does not insure an entry barrier. Another crucial prerequisite is that the experience be proprietary, rather than available to competitors and potential entrants through (1) copying, (2) hiring competitor employees, or (3) purchasing the latest machinery from equipment suppliers or purchasing knowhow from consultants or other firms. Many times experience cannot be kept proprietary, and even when it can it may accumulate more rapidly for the second and third firms in the market than it did for the pioneer because they can observe some aspects of the pioneer's operations. In situations where experience cannot be kept proprietary, new entrants may actually have an advantage if they can buy the latest equipment or adapt to new methods unencumbered by having operated the old way in the past.

Other limits to the experience curve as an entry barrier are:

- The barrier can be nullified by product or process innovations leading to a substantially new technology and thereby creating an entirely new experience curve.2 New entrants can leapfrog the industry leaders and alight on the new experience curve, to which the leaders may be poorly positioned to jump.

---

[2]For an example of this drawn from the history of the automobile industry, see William J. Abernathy and Kenneth Wayne, "The Limits of the Learning Curve," Harvard Business Review, September–October 1974, p. 109.

- Pursuit of low cost through experience may involve tradeoffs with other valuable barriers such as product differentiation through image, or technological progressiveness. For example, Hewlett-Packard has erected substantial barriers based on technological progressiveness in industries where other firms are following strategies based on experience and scale like calculators and minicomputers.

- If more than one strong company is building its strategy on the experience curve, the consequences can be nearly fatal. By the time only one rival is left pursuing such a strategy, industry growth may have stopped and the prospects of reaping the spoils of victory may have long since evaporated.

- Aggressive pursuit of cost declines through experience may draw attention away from market developments in other areas or may cloud perception of new technologies that nullify past experience.

Intensity of Rivalry among Existing Competitors

Rivalry among existing competitors takes the familiar form of jockeying for position—using tactics like price competition, advertising battles, product introductions, and increased customer service or warranties. Rivalry occurs because one or more competitors either feels the pressure or sees the opportunity to improve position. In most industries, competitive moves by one firm have noticeable effects on its competitors and thus may incite retaliation or efforts to counter the move—that is, firms are *mutually dependent.* This pattern of action and reaction may or may not leave the initiating firm and the industry as a whole better off. If moves and countermoves escalate, then all firms in the industry may suffer and be worse off than before.

Some forms of competition, notably price competition, are highly unstable and quite likely to leave the entire industry worse off from a profitability standpoint. Price cuts are quickly and easily matched by rivals, and once they are matched they lower revenues for all firms unless industry price elasticity of demand is very great. Advertising battles, on the other hand, may well expand demand or raise the level of product differentiation in the industry for the benefit of all firms.

Rivalry in some industries is characterized by such phrases as "warlike," "bitter," or "cut-throat," while in other industries it is termed "polite" or "gentlemanly." Intense rivalry is related to the presence of a number of the following interacting structural factors.

Competitors are numerous or are roughly equal in size and power. When firms are numerous, the likelihood of mavericks is great and some firms may habitually believe they can make moves without being noticed. Even if there are relatively few firms, if they are relatively balanced in terms of size and perceived resources this creates instability because they may be prone to take each other on and have the resources for sustained and vigorous retaliation. On the other hand, when the industry is highly concentrated or dominated by one or a few firms, there is little mistaking about relative power and the leader or leaders can impose discipline as well as play a coordinative role in the industry through devices like price leadership.

In many industries, foreign competitors, either exporting into the industry or participating directly through foreign investment, play an important role in industry competition. Foreign competitors, though having some differences that will be noted below, should be treated just like national competitors for purposes of structural analysis.

Industry growth is slow. Slow industry growth turns competition into a market share game for firms seeking expansion. Market share competition is a great deal more volatile than the situation where rapid industry growth means that firms can improve results just by keeping up with the industry, and in fact all their financial and managerial resources may be consumed by expanding with the industry.

High fixed or storage costs. High fixed costs create strong pressures for all firms to fill capacity which often leads to rapidly escalating price cutting. Many basic materials like paper and aluminum suffer from this problem, for example. The key is fixed costs relative to value added, and not the absolute proportion of fixed costs. Firms purchasing a high proportion of costs in outside inputs (low value added) may feel enormous pressures to fill capacity to break even, even if the absolute proportion of fixed costs is low.

A related situation to fixed costs is when the product, once produced, is very difficult or costly to store. Here firms will also be vulnerable to temptations to shade prices in order to insure sale. This sort of pressure keeps profits low in industries like lobster fishing and certain hazardous chemicals.

The product or service lacks differentiation or switching costs. When the product or service is perceived as a commodity or near-commodity, buyer choice is based largely on price and service, and pressures for strong price and service competition result. These forms of competition are particularly volatile, as has been discussed. Differentiation, on the other hand, creates layers of insulation against competitive warfare because buyers have preferences and loyalties to particular sellers.

A related factor influencing rivalry is *switching costs.* Switching costs are one-time costs of switching brands, or switching from one competitor's product to another. Switching costs may include such things as employee retraining costs, cost of new ancillary equipment, cost and time in testing or qualifying a new source, need for technical help as a result of reliance on seller engineering help, product redesign, or even psychic costs of severing a relationship. If these switching costs are high, then competitors must offer a major improvement in cost or performance in order for the buyer to switch. For example, in intravenous (IV) solutions and kits for use in hospitals, procedures for attaching solutions to patients differ among competitive products, and the hardware for hanging the IV solution bottles is not compatible. Here switching encounters great resistance from nurses responsible for administering the treatment and requires new investments in hardware. This industry is characterized by relatively stable shares and high returns.

Capacity is normally augmented in large increments. When economics dictate that capacity must be added in large increments, capacity additions can be chronically disruptive to the industry supply/demand balance, particularly because there is a risk of bunching of capacity additions. The industry may face chronic periods of overcapacity and price cutting, like those that afflict chlorine, vinyl chloride, and ammonium fertilizer.

Competitors are diverse in strategies, origins, "personalities," and relationships to their parent companies. Diverse competitors have differing goals and differing ideas about how to compete and are continually running head-on into each other in the process. They have a hard time accurately reading each other's intentions and agreeing on a set of "rules of game" for the industry. Strategic choices that are right for one competitor will be wrong for others.

Foreign competitors often add a great deal of diversity to industries because of their differing circumstances and often differing goals. Owner-operators of small manufacturing or service firms may also, because they may be satisfied with a subnormal rate of return on their invested capital to maintain the independence of self-ownership, while such returns are unacceptable and may appear irrational to a large, publicly held competitor. In such an industry, the posture of the small firms may limit the profitability of the larger concerns. Similarly, firms viewing a market as an outlet for excess capacity (e.g., in the case of dumping) will adopt policies contrary to the profits of firms viewing the market as a main business. Finally, differences in the relationship of business units competing in an industry to their corporate parents is an important source of diversity as well. For example, a business unit that is part of a vertical chain of businesses in its corporate organization may well adopt different and perhaps contradictory goals to a freestanding firm competing in the same industry. Or a business unit that is a "cash cow" in its parent company's portfolio of businesses will behave differently than one that is being developed for long-run growth in view of a lack of other opportunities in the parent.

High strategic stakes. Industry rivalry becomes even more volatile if a number of firms in an industry have high stakes in achieving success in the particular industry. For example, a diversified firm may place great importance on achieving success in a particular industry in order to further its overall corporate strategy. Or a foreign firm like Bosch, Sony, or Philips may perceive a strong need to establish a solid position in the U.S. market in order to build global prestige or technological credibility. In such situations, the goals of high-stakes firms may not only be diverse but even more destabilizing because they are expansionary and involve potential willingness to sacrifice profitability.

Exit barriers are high. Exit barriers are economic, strategic, and emotional factors that keep companies competing in businesses even though they may be earning low or even negative returns on investment. The major sources of exit barriers are:[3]

- Specialized assets: assets highly specialized to the particular business or location have low liquidation values.
- Fixed costs of exit: such as labor agreements, resettlement costs, maintaining spare parts capabilities, and so forth.
- Strategic interrelationships: interrelationships between the business unit and others in the company in terms of image, marketing ability, access to financial markets, shared facilities, and so on. They cause the firm to perceive high strategic importance to being in the business.
- Emotional barriers: management's unwillingness to make economically justified exit decisions due to loyalty to employees, fear for their own careers, pride, and other reasons.
- Government and social restrictions: government denial or discouragement of exit due to job loss and regional economic effects. This is particularly common outside the United States.

When exit barriers are high in an industry, excess capacity does not leave the industry, and companies that lose the competitive battle do not give up. Rather they grimly hang on and, because of their weakness, have to resort to extreme tactics. The profitability of the entire industry can be destroyed as a result.

Shifting Rivalry

The factors that determine the intensity of competitive rivalry can and do change. A very common example is the change in industry growth brought about by industry maturity. As an industry matures its growth rate declines, resulting in intensified rivalry, declining profits, and (often) a shakeout. In the booming recreational vehicle industry of the early 1970s, nearly every

---

[3]For a fuller treatment see Michael E. Porter, "Please Note Location of Nearest Exit, *California Management Review,* Winter 1976, p. 21.

producer did well; but slow growth since then has eliminated the high returns, except for the strongest members, not to mention many of the weaker companies. The same story has been played out in industry after industry—snowmobiles, aerosol packaging, and sports equipment are just a few examples.

Another common change in rivalry occurs when an acquisition introduces a very different personality to an industry, as has been the case with Phillip Morris's acquisition of Miller beer, and Procter & Gamble's acquisition of Charmin Paper Company. Or technological innovation can boost the level of fixed costs in the production process and raise the volatility of rivalry, as it did in the shift from batch to continuous-line photofinishing in the 1960s.

While a company must live with many of the factors that determine the intensity of industry rivalry—because they are built into industry economics—it may have some latitude in improving matters through strategic shifts. For example, it may try to raise buyers' switching costs through providing engineering assistance to customers to design its product into their operations, or to make them dependent for technical advice. Or the firm can attempt to raise product differentiation through new kinds of service, marketing innovations, or product changes. Focusing selling efforts in the fastest-growing segments of the industry or on market areas with the lowest fixed costs can reduce the impact of industry rivalry. Or if it is feasible, a company can try to avoid confrontation with competitors having high exit barriers and can thus sidestep involvement in bitter price cutting.

Exit Barriers and Entry Barriers

While exit barriers and entry barriers are conceptually separate, their combination is an important aspect of the analysis of an industry. Often exit barriers and entry barriers move together. The presence of substantial economies of scale in production, for example, usually implies specialized assets, as does the presence of proprietary technology.

Taking the simplified case where exit barriers and entry barriers can be either high or low, there are a number of possible combinations, as shown in *Figure B.*

Figure B

Entry Barriers	Exit Barriers: Low	Exit Barriers: High
Low	Low Returns	Worst Case
High	Best Case	High Returns But Risky

The best case from the viewpoint of industry profits is when entry barriers are high but exit barriers are low. Here entry will be deterred, and unsuccessful competitors will leave the industry. When both entry and exit barriers are high, profit potential is high but is usually accompanied by more risk. Though entry is deterred, unsuccessful firms will stay and fight in the industry.

While the case of low entry and exit barriers is unexciting, the worst case is when entry barriers are low and exit barriers are high. Here entry is easy and will be attracted by upturns in economic conditions or other temporary windfalls. However, capacity will not leave the industry when results deteriorate. As a result capacity stacks up in the industry and profitability is usually chronically poor.

Pressure from Substitute Products

All firms in an industry are competing, in a broad sense, with industries producing substitute products. Substitutes limit the potential of an industry by placing a ceiling on the prices firms can charge. The more attractive the price-performance tradeoff offered by substitutes, the firmer the lid on industry profits.

Sugar producers confronted with the large-scale commercialization of high fructose corn syrup, a sugar substitute, are learning this lesson today, as are producers of acetylene and rayon facing extreme competition from alternative, lower cost materials for many of their respective applications. Substitutes not only limit profits in normal times, but they also reduce the bonanza an industry can reap in boom times. In 1978 the producers of fiberglass insulation enjoyed unprecedented demand as a result of high energy costs and severe winter weather. But the industry's ability to raise prices was tempered by the plethora of insulation substitutes, including cellulose, rock wool, and styrofoam. These substitutes are bound to become an ever stronger force once the current round of plant additions by fiberglass insulation producers has boosted capacity enough to meet demand (and then some).

Identifying substitute products is a matter of searching for other products that can perform the same *function* as the product of the industry. Sometimes this can be a subtle task, and one which takes the analyst into businesses seemingly far removed from the industry. Securities brokers, for example, are increasingly confronted with substitutes like real estate, insurance, money market funds, and other products that are alternative ways for the individual to invest capital, accentuated in importance by the poor performance of the equity markets.

Position vis-à-vis substitute products may well be a matter of *collective* industry actions. For example, while advertising by one firm in an industry does little to bolster the industry's position against a substitute, heavy and sustained advertising by all industry participants may well improve the industry's collective position against the substitute. Similar arguments apply to collective industry response in areas like product quality improvement, marketing efforts, securing greater product availability, and so on.

Substitute products that deserve most attention are those that (1) are subject to trends improving their price-performance tradeoff with the industry's product, or (2) are produced by industries earning high profits. In the latter case, substitutes often come rapidly into play if some development increases competition in their industries and causes price reduction or performance improvement. Trend analysis can be important in deciding whether to attempt to head off a substitute strategically, or plan strategy with it as inevitably a key force. In the security guard industry, for example, electronic alarm systems represent a potent substitute. Electronic systems can only become more important as a substitute since labor-intensive guard services face inevitable cost escalation, while electronic systems are highly likely to improve in performance and decline in costs. Here, the appropriate response of security guard firms is probably to offer packages of guards and electronic systems, based on a redefinition of the security guard as a skilled operator, rather than to attempt to outcompete electronic systems across the board.

Bargaining Power of Buyers

Buyers compete with the industry by forcing down prices, demanding higher quality or more services, and playing competitors off against each other—all at the expense of industry profitability. The power of each important buyer group depends on a number of characteristics of its market situation and on the relative importance of its purchases from the industry compared with its overall business. A buyer group is powerful if:

- *It is concentrated or purchases large volumes relative to seller sales:* Large volumes of purchases raise the importance of particular buyers' business in achieving firm financial results. Large volume buyers are particularly potent forces if heavy fixed costs characterize the industry—as they do in corn refining and bulk chemicals, for example—and raise the stakes to keeping capacity filled.

- *The products it purchases from the industry represent a significant fraction of its costs or purchases:* Here buyers are prone to expend the resources necessary to shop for a favorable price and purchase selectively. Where the product sold by the industry in question is a small fraction of buyers' costs, buyers are usually much less price sensitive.

- *The products it purchases from the industry are standard or undifferentiated:* Buyers, sure that they can always find alternative suppliers, may play one company against another, as they do in aluminum extrusion.

- *It faces few switching costs:* Switching costs, defined earlier, lock the buyer to particular sellers.

- *It earns low profits:* Low profits create great incentives to lower purchasing costs. Suppliers to Chrysler, for example, are complaining that they are being pressured for superior terms. Highly profitable buyers, however, are generally less price sensitive (that is, of course, if the item does not represent a large fraction of their costs).

- *Buyers pose a credible threat of backward integration:* If buyers either are partially integrated or pose a strong threat of backward integration, they are in a position to demand bargaining concessions. The major automobile producers, General Motors and Ford, are well known for using the threat of self-manufacture as a bargaining lever. They engage in the practice of *tapered integration,* or producing some of their needs for a given component in-house and purchasing the rest from outside suppliers. Not only is their threat of further integration particularly credible, but partial manufacture in-house gives them a detailed knowledge of costs which is a great aid in negotiation. Buyer power can be partially neutralized when firms in the industry offer a threat of forward integration into the buyers' industry.

- *The industry's product is unimportant to the "quality" of the buyers' products or services:* When the quality of the buyers' products is very much affected by the industry's product, buyers are generally less price sensitive. Industries in which this situation exists include oil field equipment, where a malfunction can lead to large losses (witness the enormous cost of the failure of a blowout preventor in an offshore oil well), and enclosures for electronic medical and test instruments, where the quality of the enclosure can greatly influence the user's impression about the quality of the equipment inside.

Most of these sources of buyer power can be attributed to consumers as well as to industrial and commercial buyers; only a modification of the frame of reference is necessary. For example, consumers tend to be more price sensitive if they are purchasing products that are undifferentiated, expensive relative to their incomes, and of a sort where quality is not particularly important to them.

The buyer power of wholesalers and retailers is determined by the same rules, with one important addition. Retailers can gain significant bargaining power over manufacturers when they can *influence consumers' purchasing decisions,* as they do in audio components, jewelry, appliances, sporting goods, and other goods. Similarly, wholesalers can gain bargaining power if they can influence the purchase decisions of the retailers or other firms to which they sell.

Altering Buyer Power

As the factors creating buyer power change with time or as a result of a company's strategic decisions, naturally the power of buyers rises or falls. In the ready-to-wear clothing industry, for example, as the buyers (department stores and clothing stores) have become more concentrated and control has passed to large chains, the industry has come under increasing pressure and suffered falling margins. The industry has been unable to differentiate its product or engender switching costs that lock in its buyers enough to neutralize these trends.

A company's choice of buyer groups to sell to should be viewed as a crucial strategic decision. A company can improve its strategic posture by finding buyers who possess the least power to influence it adversely—in other words, *buyer selection.* Rarely do all the buyer groups a company sells to enjoy equal power. Even if a company sells to a single industry, segments usually exist within that industry that exercise less power (and that are therefore less price sensitive) than others. For example, the replacement market for most products is less price sensitive than the OEM market.

Bargaining Power of Suppliers

Suppliers can exert bargaining power over participants in an industry by raising prices or reducing the quality of purchased goods and services. Powerful suppliers can thereby squeeze profitability out of an industry unable to recover cost increases in its own prices. By raising their prices, for example, chemical companies have contributed to the erosion of profitability of contract aerosol packagers because the packagers, facing intense competition from self-manufacture by their customers, have limited freedom to raise their prices accordingly.

The conditions making suppliers powerful are largely the inverse of those making buyers powerful. A supplier group is powerful if:

- *It is dominated by a few companies and is more concentrated than the industry it sells to:* Suppliers selling to more fragmented buyers will be able to exert considerable influence on prices, quality, and terms.

- *It is not obliged to contend with other substitute products for sale to the industry:* The power of even large, powerful suppliers can be checked if they compete with substitutes. For example, industries producing alternative sweeteners compete sharply for many applications even though individual firms are large relative to individual customers.

- *The industry is not an important customer of the supplier group:* When suppliers sell to a number of industries and a particular industry does not represent a significant fraction of sales, suppliers are much more prone to exert power. If the industry is an important customer, suppliers' fortunes will be closely tied to the industry and they will want to protect the industry through reasonable pricing and assistance in activities like R&D and lobbying.

- *The supplier group's products are differentiated or it has built up switching costs:* Differentiation or switching costs cut off buyers' options in playing one supplier against another.

- *The supplier group poses a credible threat of forward integration:* This provides a check against the industry's ability to improve the terms on which it purchases.

While we usually think of suppliers as other firms, *labor* must be recognized as a supplier as well, and one that exerts great power in many industries. There is substantial empirical evidence that scarce, highly skilled employees and/or tightly unionized labor can bargain away a significant fraction of potential profits in an industry. The principles in determining the potential power of labor as a supplier are similar to those outlined above. The key additions in assessing the power of labor are its *degree of organization,* and the ability of the supply or scarce varieties of labor to *expand.* When collective labor organization is tight and supply of scarce labor constrained from expansion, the power of labor can be high.

The conditions determining supplier power are not only subject to change but are often out of the firm's control. However, as with buyer power the firm can sometimes improve its situation through strategy. It can promote a threat of backward integration, seek to eliminate switching costs, and so forth.

Government as a Force in Industry Competition

While government has been discussed primarily in terms of its possible impact on entry barriers, in the 1970s and 1980s government at all levels must be recognized as potentially influencing many if not all aspects of industry structure both directly and indirectly. In many industries, government *is* a buyer or supplier and can influence industry competition by the policies it adopts. For example, government plays a crucial role as a buyer of defense-related products, and as a supplier of timber through the Forest Service's control of vast timber reserves in the western United States. Many times government's role as a supplier or buyer is determined more by political factors than by economic circumstances, and this is probably a fact of life. Government regulations can also set limits on the behavior of firms as suppliers or buyers.

Government can also affect the position of an industry with substitutes through regulations, subsidies, or other means. The U.S. government has strongly promoted solar heating, for example, using tax incentives and research grants. Government decontrol of natural gas has quickly eliminated acetylene as a chemical feedstock. Safety and pollution standards affect relative cost and quality of substitutes. Government can also affect rivalry among competitors by influencing industry growth, affecting the cost structure through regulations, and through other means.

Thus no structural analysis is complete without a diagnosis of how present and future government policy, at all levels, will affect structural conditions. For purposes of strategic analysis it is usually more illuminating to consider how government affects competition *through* the five competitive forces than to consider it as a force in and of itself. However, strategy may well involve treating government as an actor to be influenced.

II. Structural Analysis and Competitive Strategy

Once the forces affecting competition in an industry and their underlying causes have been diagnosed, the firm is in a position to identify its strengths and weaknesses relative to the industry. The crucial strengths and weaknesses from a strategic standpoint are the firm's posture vis-à-vis the underlying causes of each competitive force. Where does the firm stand against substitutes? Against the sources of entry barriers? In coping with rivalry from established competitors?

Competitive strategy is taking offensive or defensive action in order to create a *defendable* position against the five competitive forces. Broadly, this involves a number of possible approaches:

- Positioning the firm so that its capabilities provide the best defense against the existing array of competitive forces;
- Influencing the balance of forces through strategic moves, thereby improving the firm's relative position; or
- Anticipating shifts in the factors underlying the forces and responding to them, hopefully exploiting change by choosing a strategy appropriate to the new competitive balance before rivals recognize it.

Positioning

The first approach takes the structure of the industry as given and matches the company's strengths and weaknesses to it. Strategy can be viewed as building defenses against the competitive forces or as finding positions in the industry where the forces are weakest.

Knowledge of the company's capabilities and of the causes of the competitive forces will high-light the areas where the company should confront competition and where avoid it. If the company is a low-cost producer, for example, it may choose to confront powerful buyers while it takes care to sell them only products not vulnerable to competition from substitutes.

Influencing the Balance

When dealing with the forces that drive industry competition, a company can devise a strategy that takes the offensive. This posture is designed to do more than merely cope with the forces themselves; it is meant to alter their causes.

Innovations in marketing can raise brand identification or otherwise differentiate the product. Capital investments in large-scale facilities or vertical integration affect entry barriers. The balance of forces is partly a result of external factors and is partly within a company's control. Structural analysis can be used to identify the key factors driving competition in the particular industry and thus indicate the places where strategic action to influence the balance will yield the greatest payoff.

Exploiting Change

Industry evolution is important strategically because evolution, of course, brings with it changes in the sources of competition that have been identified. In the familiar product life-cycle pattern of industry development, for example, growth rates change, advertising is said to decline as the business becomes more mature, and the companies tend to integrate vertically.

These trends are not so important in themselves; what is critical is whether they affect the structural sources of competition. Consider vertical integration. In the maturing minicomputer industry, extensive vertical integration, both in manufacturing and in software development, has taken place. This very significant trend has greatly raised economies of scale as well as the amount of capital necessary to compete in the industry. This in turn has raised barriers to entry and could drive some smaller competitors out of the industry once growth levels off.

Obviously, the trends carrying the highest priority from a strategic standpoint are those that affect the most important sources of competition in the industry and those that bring new structural factors to the forefront. In contract aerosol packaging, for example, the trend toward less product differentiation is now dominant. It has increased buyers' powers, lowered the barriers to entry, and intensified competition.

Structural analysis can be used to predict the eventual profitability of an industry. In long-range planning the task is to examine each competitive force, forecast the magnitude of each underlying cause, and then construct a composite picture of the likely profit potential of the industry.

The outcome of such an exercise may differ a great deal from the existing industry structure. Today, for example, the solar heating business is populated by dozens and perhaps hundreds of companies, none with a major market position. Entry is easy, and competitors are battling to establish solar heating as a superior substitute for conventional heating methods.

The potential of solar heating will depend largely on the shape of future barriers to entry, the improvement of the industry's position relative to substitutes, the ultimate intensity of competition, and the power captured by buyers and suppliers. These characteristics will in turn be influenced by such factors as the likelihood of establishment of brand identities, whether significant economies of scale or experience curves in equipment manufacture will be created by technological change, what the ultimate capital costs to compete will be, and the extent of eventual fixed costs in production facilities.

Structural Analysis and Diversification Strategy

The framework for analyzing industry competition can be used in setting diversification strategy. It provides a guide for answering the extremely difficult question inherent in diversification decisions: What is the potential of this business? The framework may allow a company to spot an industry with a good future before this good future is reflected in the prices of acquisition candidates.

The framework can also help in identifying particularly valuable types of relatedness in diversification. For example, relatedness that allows the firm to overcome key entry barriers through shared functions or preexisting relationships with distribution channels can be a fruitful basis for diversification.

III. Structural Analysis and Industry Definition

A great deal of concern and attention has been directed at defining the relevant industry as a crucial step in competitive strategy formulation. Numerous writers have also stressed the need to look beyond product to function in defining a business, beyond national boundaries to potential international competition, and beyond the ranks of one's competitors today to those that may become competitors tomorrow. As a result of these urgings, the proper definition of a company's industry or industries has become an endlessly debated subject. An important motive in this debate is the fear of overlooking latent sources of competition that may someday threaten the industry.

Structural analysis, by focusing broadly on competition well beyond existing rivals, should reduce the need for debates on where to draw industry boundaries. Any definition of an industry is essentially a choice of where to draw the line between established competitors and substitute products, between existing firms and potential entrants, and between existing firms and suppliers and buyers. Drawing these lines is inherently a *matter of degree.*

If these broad sources of competition are recognized, however, and their relative impact assessed, then where the lines are actually drawn becomes more or less irrelevant to strategy formulation. Latent sources of competition will not be overlooked, nor will key dimensions of competition.

Definition of an industry is *not* the same as definition of where the firm wants to compete, however (defining *its* business). Just because the industry is defined broadly, for example, does not mean that the firm can or should compete broadly. And there may be strong benefits to competing in a group of related industries as has been discussed. Decoupling industry definition and the definition of the businesses the firm wants to be in will go far in eliminating needless confusion in drawing industry boundaries.

2 Generic Competitive Strategies

Chapter 1 described competitive strategy as taking offensive or defensive actions to create a defendable position in an industry, to cope successfully with the five competitive forces and thereby yield a superior return on investment for the firm. Firms have discovered many different approaches to this end, and the best strategy for a given firm is ultimately a unique construction reflecting its particular circumstances. However, at the broadest level we can identify three internally consistent generic strategies (which can be used singly or in combination) for creating such a defendable position in the long run and outperforming competitors in an industry. This chapter describes the generic strategies and explores some of the requirements and risks of each. Its purpose is to develop some introductory concepts that can be built upon in subsequent analysis. Succeeding chapters of this book will have much more to say about how to translate these broad generic strategies into more specific strategies in particular kinds of industry situations.

Three Generic Strategies

In coping with the five competitive forces, there are three potentially successful generic strategic approaches to outperforming other firms in an industry:

1. overall cost leadership
2 differentiation
3. focus.

Sometimes the firm can successfully pursue more than one approach as its primary target, though this is rarely possible as will be discussed further. Effectively implementing any of these generic strategies usually requires total commitment and supporting organizational arrangements that are diluted if there is more than one primary target. The generic strategies are approaches to outperforming competitors in the industry; in some industries structure will mean that all firms can earn high returns, whereas in others, success with one of the generic strategies may be necessary just to obtain acceptable returns in an absolute sense.

OVERALL COST LEADERSHIP

The first strategy, an increasingly common one in the 1970s because of popularization of the experience curve concept, is to achieve overall cost leadership in an industry through a set of functional policies aimed at this basic objective. Cost leadership requires aggressive construction of efficient-scale facilities, vigorous pursuit of cost reductions from experience, tight cost and overhead control, avoidance of marginal customer accounts, and cost minimization in areas like R&D, service, sales force, advertising, and so on. A great deal of managerial attention to cost control is necessary to achieve these aims. Low cost relative to competitors becomes the theme running through the entire strategy, though quality, service, and other areas cannot be ignored.

Having a low-cost position yields the firm above-average returns in its industry despite the presence of strong competitive forces. Its cost position gives the firm a defense against rivalry from competitors, because its lower costs mean that it can still earn returns after its competitors have competed away their profits through rivalry. A low-cost position defends the firm against powerful buyers because buyers can exert power only to drive down prices to the level of the next most efficient competitor. Low cost provides a defense against powerful suppliers by providing more flexibility to cope with input cost increases. The factors that lead to a low-cost position usually also provide substantial entry barriers in terms of scale economies or cost advantages. Finally, a low-cost position usually places the firm in a favorable position vis-à-vis substitutes relative to its competitors in the industry. Thus a low-cost position protects the firm against all five competitive forces because bargaining can only continue to erode profits until those of the next most efficient competitor are eliminated, and because the less efficient competitors will suffer first in the face of competitive pressures.

Achieving a low overall cost position often requires a high relative market share or other advantages, such as favorable access to raw materials. It may well require designing products for ease in manufacturing, maintaining a wide line of related products to spread costs, and serving all major customer groups in order to build volume. In turn, implementing the low-cost strategy may require heavy up-front capital investment in state-of-the art equipment, aggressive pricing, and start-up losses to build market share. High market share may in turn allow economies in purchasing which lower costs even further. Once achieved, the low-cost position provides high margins which can be reinvested in new equipment and modern facilities in order to maintain cost leadership. Such reinvestment may well be a prerequisite to sustaining a low-cost position.

The cost leadership strategy seems to be the cornerstone of Briggs and Stratton's success in small horsepower gasoline engines, where it holds a 50 percent worldwide share, and Lincoln Electric's success in arc welding equipment and supplies. Other firms known for successful application of cost leadership strategies to a number of businesses are Emerson Electric, Texas Instruments, Black and Decker, and Du Pont.

A cost leadership strategy can sometimes revolutionize an industry in which the historical bases of competition have been otherwise and competitors are ill-prepared either perceptually or economically to take the steps necessary for cost minimization. Harnischfeger is in the midst of a daring attempt to revolutionize the rough-terrain crane industry in 1979. Starting from a 15 percent market share,

Harnischfeger redesigned its cranes for easy manufacture and service using modularized components, configuration changes, and reduced material content. It then established subassembly areas and a conveyorized assembly line, a notable departure from industry norms. It ordered parts in large volumes to save costs. All this allowed the company to offer an acceptable quality product and drop prices by 15 percent. Harnischfeger's market share has grown rapidly to 25 percent and is continuing to grow. Says Willis Fisher, general manager of Harnischfeger's Hydraulic Equipment Division:

> We didn't set out to develop a machine significantly better than anyone else but we did want to develop one that was truly simple to manufacture and was priced, intentionally, as a low cost machine.[1]

Competitors are grumbling that Harnischfeger has "bought" market share with lower margins, a charge that the company denies.

DIFFERENTIATION

The second generic strategy is one of differentiating the product or service offering of the firm, creating something that is perceived *industrywide* as being unique. Approaches to differentiating can take many forms: design or brand image (Fieldcrest in top of the line towels and linens; Mercedes in automobiles), technology (Hyster in lift trucks; MacIntosh in stereo components; Coleman in camping equipment), features (Jenn-Air in electric ranges); customer service (Crown Cork and Seal in metal cans), dealer network (Caterpillar Tractor in construction equipment), or other dimensions. Ideally, the firm differentiates itself along several dimensions. Caterpillar Tractor, for example, is known not only for its dealer network and excellent spare parts availability but also for its extremely high-quality durable products, all of which are crucial in heavy equipment where downtime is very expensive. It should be stressed that the differentiation strategy does not allow the firm to ignore costs, but rather they are not the primary strategic target.

Differentiation, if achieved, is a viable strategy for earning above-average returns in an industry because it creates a defensible position for coping with the five competitive forces, albeit in a dif-

[1]"Harnischfeger's Dramatic Pickup in Cranes," *Business Week*, August 13, 1979.

ferent way than cost leadership. Differentiation provides insulation against competitive rivalry because of brand loyalty by customers and resulting lower sensitivity to price. It also increases margins, which avoids the need for a low-cost position. The resulting customer loyalty and the need for a competitor to overcome uniqueness provide entry barriers. Differentiation yields higher margins with which to deal with supplier power, and it clearly mitigates buyer power, since buyers lack comparable alternatives and are thereby less price sensitive. Finally, the firm that has differentiated itself to achieve customer loyalty should be better positioned vis-à-vis substitutes than its competitors.

Achieving differentiation may sometimes preclude gaining a high market share. It often requires a perception of exclusivity, which is incompatible with high market share. More commonly, however, achieving differentiation will imply a trade-off with cost position if the activities required in creating it are inherently costly, such as extensive research, product design, high quality materials, or intensive customer support. Whereas customers industrywide acknowledge the superiority of the firm, not all customers will be willing or able to pay the required higher prices (though most are in industries like earthmoving equipment where despite high prices Caterpillar has a dominant market share). In other businesses, differentiation may not be incompatible with relatively low costs and comparable prices to those of competitors.

FOCUS

The final generic strategy is focusing on a particular buyer group, segment of the product line, or geographic market; as with differentiation, focus may take many forms. Although the low cost and differentiation strategies are aimed at achieving their objectives industrywide, the entire focus strategy is built around serving a particular target very well, and each functional policy is developed with this in mind. The strategy rests on the premise that the firm is thus able to serve its narrow strategic target more effectively or efficiently than competitors who are competing more broadly. As a result, the firm achieves either differentiation from better meeting the needs of the particular target, or lower costs in serving this target, or both. Even though the focus strategy does not achieve low cost or differentiation from the perspective of the market as a whole, it does achieve one or both of these positions vis-à-vis its narrow market target. The difference among the three generic strategies are illustrated in figure 2-1.

The firm achieving focus may also potentially earn above-average returns for its industry. Its focus means that the firm either has a low cost position with its strategic target, high differentiation, or both. As we have discussed in the context of cost leadership and differentiation, these positions provide defenses against each competitive force. Focus may also be used to select targets least vulnerable to substitutes or where competitors are the weakest.

For example, Illinois Tool Works has focused on specialty markets for fasteners where it can design products for particular buyer needs and create switching costs. Although many buyers are uninterested in these services, some are. Fort Howard Paper focuses on a narrow range of industrial-grade papers, avoiding consumer products vulnerable to advertising battles and rapid introductions of new products. Porter Paint focuses on the professional painter rather than the do-it-yourself market, building its strategy around serving the professional through free paint-matching services, rapid delivery of as little as a gallon of needed paint to the worksite, and free coffee rooms designed to provide a home for professional painters at factory stores. An example of a focus strategy that achieves a low-cost

FIGURE 2-1. Three Generic Strategies

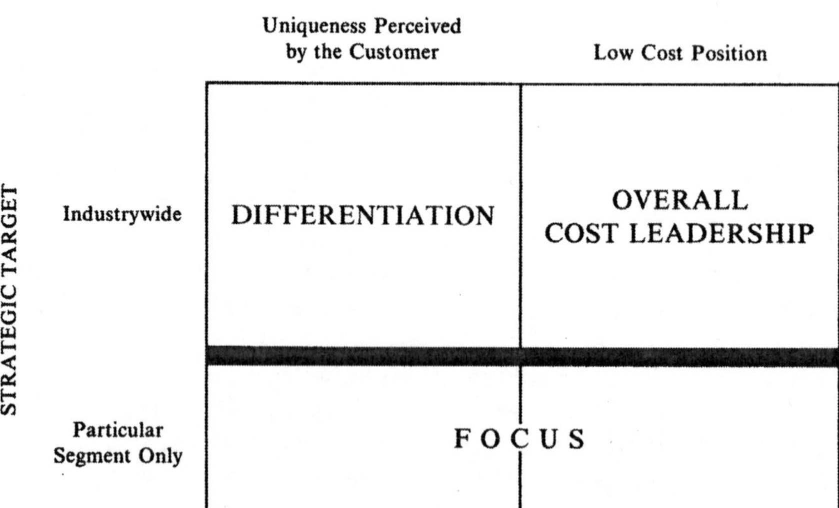

position in serving its particular target is seen in Martin-Brower, the third largest food distributor in the United States. Martin-Brower has reduced its customer list to just eight leading fast-food chains. Its entire strategy is based on meeting the specialized needs of the customers, stocking only their narrow product lines, order taking procedures geared to their purchasing cycles, locating warehouses based on their locations, and intensely controlling and computerizing record keeping. Although Martin-Brower is not the low-cost distributor in serving the market as a whole, it is in serving its particular segment. Martin-Brower has been rewarded with rapid growth and above-average profitability.

The focus strategy always implies some limitations on the overall market share achievable. Focus necessarily involves a trade-off between profitability and sales volume. Like the differentiate strategy, it may or may not involve a trade-off with overall cost position.

OTHER REQUIREMENTS OF THE GENERIC STRATEGIES

The three generic strategies differ in dimensions other than the functional differences noted above. Implementing them successfully requires different resources and skills. The generic strategies also imply differing organizational arrangements, control procedures, and inventive systems. As a result, sustained commitment to one of the strategies as the primary target is usually necessary to achieve success. Some common implications of the generic strategies in these areas are as follows:

Generic Strategy	Commonly Required Skills and Resources	Common Organizational Requirements
Overall Cost Leadership	Substained capital investment and access to capital Process engineering skills Intense supervision of labor Products designed for ease in manufacture Low-cost distribution system	Tight cost control Frequent, detailed control reports Structured organization and responsibilities Incentives based on meeting strict quantitative targets

GENERIC STRATEGY	COMMONLY REQUIRED SKILLS AND RESOURCES	COMMON ORGANIZATIONAL REQUIREMENTS
Differentiation	Strong marketing abilities Product engineering Creative flair Strong capability in basic research Corporate reputation for quality or technological leadership Long tradition in the industry or unique combination of skills drawn from other businesses Strong cooperation from channels	Strong coordination among functions in R&D, product development, and marketing Subjective measurement and incentives instead of quantitative measures Amenities to attract highly skilled labor, scientists, or creative people
Focus	Combination of the above policies directed at the particular strategic target	Combination of the above policies directed at the particular strategic target

The generic strategies may also require different styles of leadership and can translate into very different corporate cultures and atmospheres. Different sorts of people will be attracted.

Stuck in the Middle

The three generic strategies are alternative, viable approaches to dealing with the competitive forces. The converse of the previous discussion is that the firm failing to develop its strategy in at least one of the three directions—a firm that is "stuck in the middle"—is in an extremely poor strategic situation. This firm lacks the market share, capital investment, and resolve to play the low-cost game, the industrywide differentiation necessary to obviate the need for a low-cost position, or the focus to create differentiation or a low-cost position in a more limited sphere.

The firm stuck in the middle is almost guaranteed low profitability. It either loses the high-volume customers who demand low prices or must bid away its profits to get this business away from low-cost firms. Yet it also loses high-margin businesses—the cream—to the firms who are focused on high-margin targets or have achieved differentiation overall. The firm stuck in the middle also probably suffers from a blurred corporate culture and a conflicting set of organizational arrangements and motivation system.

Clark Equipment may well be stuck in the middle in the lift truck industry in which it has the leading overall U.S. and worldwide market share. Two Japanese producers, Toyota and Komatsu, have adopted strategies of serving only the high-volume segments, minimized production costs, and rock-bottom prices, also taking advantage of lower Japanese steel prices, which more than offset transportation costs. Clark's greater worldwide share (18 percent; 33 percent in the United States) does not give it clear cost leadership given its very wide product line and lack of low-cost orientation. Yet with its wide line and lack of full emphasis to technology Clark has been unable to achieve the technological reputation and product differentiation of Hyster, which has focused on larger lift trucks and spent aggressively on R&D. As a result, Clark's returns appear to be significantly lower than Hyster's, and Clark has been losing ground.[2]

The firm stuck in the middle must make a fundamental strategic decision. Either it must take the steps necessary to achieve cost leadership or at least cost parity, which usually involve aggressive investments to modernize and perhaps the necessity to buy market share, or it must orient itself to a particular target (focus) or achieve some uniqueness (differentiation). The latter two options may well involve shrinking in market share and even in absolute sales. The choice among these options is necessarily based on the firm's capabilities and limitations. Successfully executing each generic strategy involves different resources, strengths, organizational arrangements, and managerial style, as has been discussed. Rarely is a firm suited for all three.

Once stuck in the middle, it usually takes time and sustained effort to extricate the firm from this unenviable position. Yet there seems to be a tendency for firms in difficulty to flip back and forth over time among the generic strategies. Given the potential inconsistencies involved in pursuing these three strategies, such an approach is almost always doomed to failure.

These concepts suggest a number of possible relationships between market share and profitability. In some industries, the prob-

[2]See Wertheim (1977).

lem of getting caught in the middle may mean that the smaller (focused or differentiated) firms and the largest (cost leadership) firms are the most profitable, and the medium-sized firms are the least profitable. This implies a U-shaped relationship between profitability and market share, as shown in Figure 2-2. The relationship in Figure 2-2 appears to hold in the U.S. fractional horsepower electric motor business. There GE and Emerson have large market shares and strong cost positions, GE also having a strong technological reputation. Both are believed to earn high returns in motors. Baldor and Gould (Century) have adopted focused strategies, Baldor oriented toward the distributor channel and Gould toward particular customer segments. The profitability of both is also believed to be good. Franklin is in an intermediate position, with neither low cost nor focus. Its performance in motors is believed to follow accordingly. Such a U-shaped relationship probably also roughly holds in the automobile industry when viewed on a global basis, with firms like GM (low cost) and Mercedes (differentiate) the profit leaders. Chrysler, British Leyland, and Fiat lack cost position, differentiation, or focus—they are stuck in the middle.

However, the U-shaped relationship in Figure 2-2 does not hold in every industry. In some industries, there are no opportunities for focus or differentiation—it's solely a cost game—and this is true in a number of bulk commodities. In other industries, cost is relatively unimportant because of buyer and product characteristics. In these kinds of industries there is often an inverse relationship between market share and profitability. In still other industries, competition is so intense that the only way to achieve an above-average return is

FIGURE 2-2

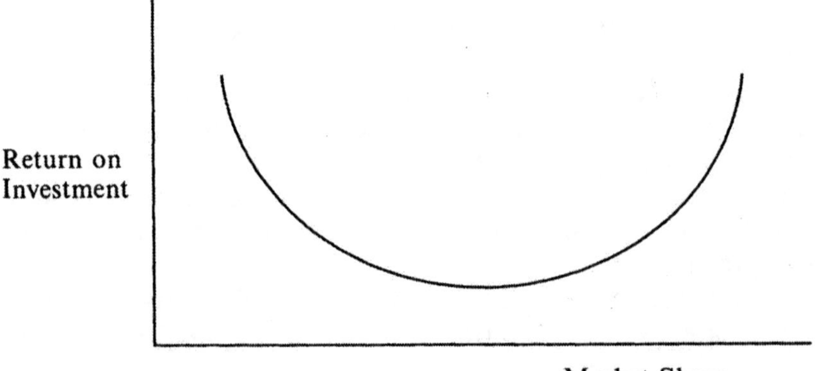

through focus or differentiation—which seems to be true in the U.S. steel industry. Finally, low overall cost position may not be incompatible with differentiation or focus, or low cost may be achievable without high share. For an example of the complex combinations that can result, Hyster is number two in lift trucks but is more profitable than several of the smaller producers in the industry (Allis-Chalmers, Eaton) who do not have the share to achieve either low costs or enough product differentiation to offset their cost position.

There is *no single relationship* between profitability and market share, unless one conveniently defines the market so that focused or differentiated firms are assigned high market shares in some narrowly defined industries and the industry definitions of cost leadership firms are allowed to stay broad (they must because cost leaders often do not have the largest share in every submarket). Even shifting industry definition cannot explain the high returns of firms who have achieved differentiation industrywide and hold market shares below that of the industry leader.

Most importantly, however, shifting the way the industry is defined from firm to firm begs the question of deciding which of the three generic strategies is appropriate for the firm. This choice rests on picking the strategy best suited to the firm's strengths and one least replicable by competitors. The principles of structural analysis should illuminate the choice, as well as allow the analyst to explain or predict the relationship between share and profitability in any particular industry. I will discuss this issue further in Chapter 7, where structural analysis is extended to consider the differing positions of firms within a particular industry.

Risks of the Generic Strategies

Fundamentally, the risks in pursuing the generic strategies are two: first, failing to attain or sustain the strategy; second, for the value of the strategic advantage provided by the strategy to erode with industry evolution. More narrowly, the three strategies are predicated on erecting differing kinds of defenses against the competitive forces, and not surprisingly they involve differing types of risks. It is important to make these risks explicit in order to improve the firm's choice among the three alternatives.

RISKS OF OVERALL COST LEADERSHIP

Cost leadership imposes severe burdens on the firm to keep up its position, which means reinvesting in modern equipment, ruthlessly scrapping obsolete assets, avoiding product line proliferation and being alert for technological improvements. Cost declines with cumulative volume are by no means automatic, nor is reaping all available economies of scale achievable without significant attention.

Cost leadership is vulnerable to the same risks, identified in Chapter 1, of relying on scale or experience as entry barriers. Some of these risks are

- technological change that nullifies past investments or learning;
- low-cost learning by industry newcomers or followers, through imitation or through their ability to invest in state-of-the-art facilities;
- inability to see required product or marketing change because of the attention placed on cost;
- inflation in costs that narrow the firm's ability to maintain enough of a price differential to offset competitors' brand images or other approaches to differentiation.

The classic example of the risks of cost leadership is the Ford Motor Company of the 1920s. Ford had achieved unchallenged cost leadership through limitation of models and varieties, aggressive backward integration, highly automated facilities, and aggressive pursuit of lower costs through learning. Learning was facilitated by the lack of model changes. Yet as incomes rose and many buyers had already purchased a car and were considering their second, the market began to place more of a premium on styling, model changes, comfort, and closed rather than open cars. Customers were willing to pay a price premium to get such features. General Motors stood ready to capitalize on this development with a full line of models. Ford faced enormous costs of strategic readjustment given the rigidities created by heavy investments in cost minimization of an obsolete model.

Another example of the risks of cost leadership as a sole focus is provided by Sharp in consumer electronics. Sharp, which has long followed a cost leadership strategy, has been forced to begin an aggressive campaign to develop brand recognition. Its ability to sufficiently undercut Sony's and Panasonic's prices was eroded by cost increases and U.S. antidumping legislation, and its strategic position was deteriorating through sole concentration on cost leadership.

RISKS OF DIFFERENTIATION

Differentiation also involves a series of risks:

- the cost differential between low-cost competitors and the differentiated firm becomes too great for differentiation to hold brand loyalty. Buyers thus sacrifice some of the features, services, or image possessed by the differentiated firm for large cost savings;
- buyers' need for the differentiating factor falls. This can occur as buyers become more sophisticated;
- imitation narrows perceived differentiation, a common occurrence as industries mature.

The first risk is so important as to be worthy of further comment. A firm may achieve differentiation, yet this differentiation will usually sustain only so much of a price differential. Thus if a differentiated firm gets too far behind in cost due to technological change or simply inattention, the low cost firm may be in a position to make major inroads. For example, Kawasaki and other Japanese motorcycle producers have been able to successfully attack differentiated producers such as Harley-Davidson and Triumph in large motorcycles by offering major cost savings to buyers.

RISKS OF FOCUS

Focus involves yet another set of risks:

- the cost differential between broad-range competitors and the focused firm widens to eliminate the cost advantages of serving a narrow target or to offset the differentiation achieved by focus;
- the differences in desired products or services between the strategic target and the market as a whole narrows;
- competitors find submarkets *within* the strategic target and outfocus the focuser.

Chapter Eight

Business Strategy

After reading and studying this chapter, you should be able to

1. Determine why a business would choose a low-cost, differentiation, or speed-based strategy.
2. Explain the nature and value of a market focus strategy.
3. Illustrate how a firm can pursue both low-cost and differentiation strategies.
4. Identify requirements for business success at different stages of industry evolution.
5. Determine good business strategies in fragmented and global industries.
6. Decide when a business should diversify.

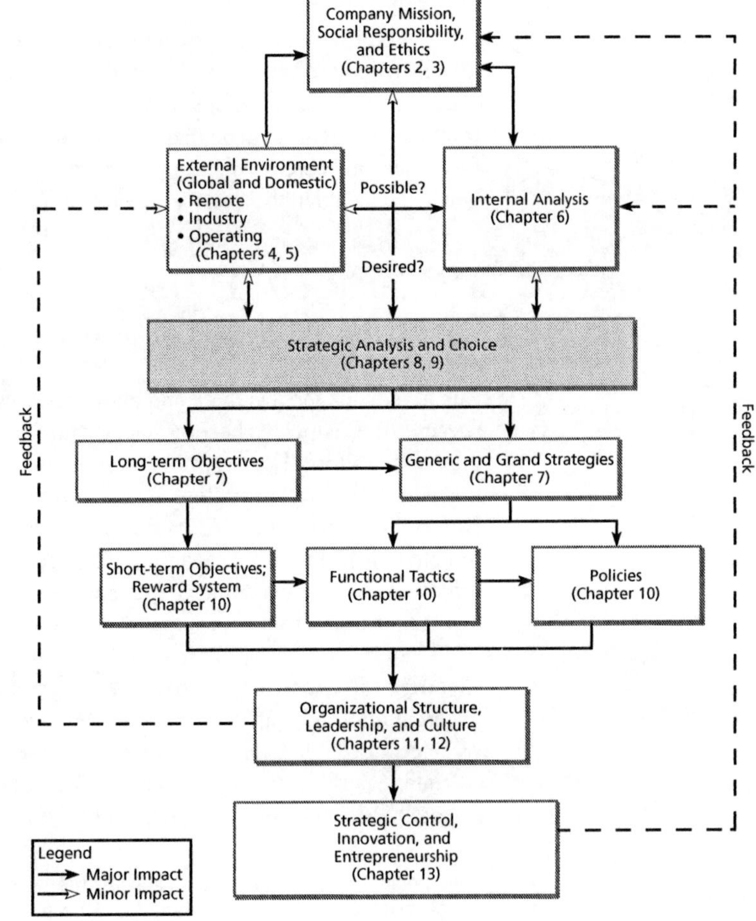

Strategic analysis and choice continue to form the phase of the strategic management process in which business managers examine and choose a business strategy that allows their business to maintain or create a sustainable competitive advantage. Their starting point is to evaluate and determine which competitive advantages provide the basis for distinguishing the firm in the customer's mind from other reasonable alternatives. Businesses with a dominant product or service line must also choose among alternate grand strategies to guide the firm's activities, particularly when they are trying to decide about broadening the scope of the firm's activities beyond its core business. This chapter examines strategic analysis and choice in single- or dominant-product/service businesses by addressing two basic issues:

1. **What strategies are most effective at building sustainable competitive advantages for single business units?** What competitive strategy positions a business most effectively in its industry? For example, Scania, the most productive truck manufacturer in the world, joins its major rival Volvo as two anchors of Sweden's economy. Scania's return on sales of 9.9 percent far exceeds Mercedes (2.6 percent) and Volvo (2.5 percent), a level it has achieved most of the last 60 years. Scania has built a sustainable competitive advantage with a strategy of focusing solely on heavy trucks, in a limited geographic area—Europe—and by providing customized trucks with standardized components (20,000 components per truck versus 25,000 for Volvo and 40,000 for Mercedes). Scania is a low-cost producer of a differentiated truck that can be custom-manufactured quickly and sold to a regionally focused market.

2. **Should dominant-product/service businesses diversify to build value and competitive advantage?** What grand strategies are most appropriate? For example, Dell and Coca-Cola managers have examined the question of diversification and apparently concluded that continued concentration on their core products and services and development of new markets for those same core products and services are best. IBM and Pepsi examined the same question and concluded that concentric diversification and vertical integration were best. Why?

EVALUATING AND CHOOSING BUSINESS STRATEGIES: SEEKING SUSTAINED COMPETITIVE ADVANTAGE

Business managers evaluate and choose strategies that they think will make their business successful. Businesses become successful because they possess some advantage relative to their competitors. The two most prominent sources of competitive advantage can be found in the business's cost structure and its ability to differentiate the business from competitors. DisneyWorld in Orlando offers theme park patrons several unique, distinct features that differentiate it from other entertainment options. Wal-Mart offers retail customers the lowest prices on popular consumer items because they have created a low-cost structure that results in a competitive advantage over most competitors.

Businesses that create competitive advantages from one or both of these sources usually experience above-average profitability within their industry. Businesses that lack a cost or differentiation advantage usually experience average or below-average profitability. Two well-recognized studies found that businesses that do not have either form of competitive advantage perform the poorest among their peers, while businesses that possess both forms of competitive advantage enjoy the highest levels of profitability within their industry.[1]

[1] R. B. Robinson and J. A. Pearce, "Planned Patterns of Strategic Behavior and Their Relationship to Business Unit Performance," *Strategic Management Journal* 9, no. 1 (1988), pp. 43–60; and G. G. Dess and G. T. Lumpkin, "Emerging Issues in Strategy Process Research," in *Handbook of Strategic Management,* M. A. Hitt, R. E. Freeman, and J. S. Harrison (eds), Oxford: Blackwell pp. 3–34. 2001.

The average return on investment for more than 2,500 businesses across seven industries looked like this:

Differentiation Advantage	Cost Advantage	Overall Average ROI across Seven Industries
High	High	35.0%
Low	High	26.0
High	Low	22.0
Low	Low	9.5

Initially, managers were advised to evaluate and choose strategies that emphasized one type of competitive advantage. Often referred to as generic strategies, firms were encouraged to become either a differentiation-oriented or low-cost-oriented company. In so doing, it was logical that organizational members would develop a clear understanding of company priorities and, as these studies suggest, likely experience profitability superior to competitors without either a differentiation or low-cost orientation.

The studies mentioned here, and the experience of many other businesses, indicate that the highest profitability levels are found in businesses that possess both types of competitive advantage at the same time. In other words, businesses that have one or more resources/capabilities that truly differentiate them from key competitors and also have resources/capabilities that let them operate at a lower cost will consistently outperform their rivals that don't. So the challenge for today's business managers is to evaluate and choose business strategies based on core competencies and value chain activities that sustain both types of competitive advantage simultaneously. Exhibit 8.1, Global Strategy in Action, shows Honda Motor Company attempting to do just this in Europe.

Evaluating Cost Leadership Opportunities

Business success built on cost leadership requires the business to be able to provide its product or service at a cost below what its competitors can achieve. And it must be a sustainable cost advantage. Through the skills and resources identified in Exhibit 8.2, a business must be able to accomplish one or more activities in its value chain activities—procuring materials, processing them into products, marketing the products, and distributing the products or support activities—in a more cost-effective manner than that of its competitors or it must be able to reconfigure its value chain so as to achieve a cost advantage. Exhibit 8.2 provides examples of such **low-cost strategies.**

low-cost strategies
Business strategies that seek to establish long-term competitive advantages by emphasizing and perfecting value chain activities that can be achieved at costs substantially below what competitors are able to match on a sustained basis. This allows the firm, in turn, to compete primarily by charging a price lower than competitors can match and still stay in business.

Strategists examining their business's value chain for low-cost leadership advantages evaluate the sustainability of those advantages by benchmarking (refer to Chapter 6 for a discussion of this comparison technique) their business against key competitors and by considering the effect of any cost advantage on the five forces in their business's competitive environment. Low-cost activities that are sustainable and that provide one or more of these advantages relative to key industry forces should become a key basis for the business's competitive strategy:

Low-cost advantages that reduce the likelihood of pricing pressure from buyers When key competitors cannot match prices from the low-cost leader, customers pressuring the leader risk establishing a price level that drives alternate sources out of business.

Truly sustained low-cost advantages may push rivals into other areas, lessening price competition Intense, continued price competition may be ruinous for all rivals, as seen occasionally in the airline industry.

Strategy in Action

Exhibit 8.1

Honda Pursues Young Buyers via Low-Cost Leadership and Differentiation Strategies

BusinessWeek

Honda is hot. In the United States, the Tokyo company can barely keep up with demand for models like the Acura MDX sport utility vehicle and the Odysssey minivan. North American sales have grown 60 percent in the last decade and its cost leadership is legendary: Honda earned $1,581 on every car sold in North America last year, versus $701 for General Motors.

But the road is not entirely smooth for the Japanese car-maker. Honda Motor Co. has suffered a serious breakdown in Europe. Honda's operations in the Old World reported a loss of nearly a billion dollars in Britain and the Continent. "A big worry for us is weak sales in Europe," said CEO Takeo Fukui.

So Honda managers have gone into overdrive to repair the European business. Their game plan includes cost leadership initiatives: boosting capacity at two plants in Britain, heeding European calls for cars with diesel engines, and implementing a hard-nosed cost-cutting program that targets parts suppliers . . . and differentiation opportunities: launching an all-new car for the subcompact market.

Honda has a reputation for tackling all of its challenges head-on. But the European problem, even against the background of record results in the United States, underscores Honda's fragility. Although less than 10 percent of Honda's global volume—and far less revenue—comes from Europe, the region has outsized importance to Fukui and his deputies. Why? Because Honda has no safe harbor if its sales in the United States begin to flag, as some analysts expect. The company earns some 90 percent of its profits in America, a far higher percentage than other Japanese carmakers. "Honda is the least globally diverse Japanese automobile manufacturer," says Chris Redl, director of equity research at UBS Warburg's office in Tokyo. "It's a minor problem for now, but with the U.S. market heading down, it could become a major problem." So a closer look at the cost leadership and differentiation approach at Honda Europe, their confident answer, is as follows:

COST LEADERSHIP

Honda's struggles in Europe today are partly the result of a key strategic error it made when it started making cars in Britain 10 years ago. Company officials didn't foresee the huge runup in the value of the British pound against Europe's single currency, the euro, which made its cars more expensive than competing models manufactured on the Continent. Subpar sales cut output in Britain last year to levels near 50 percent of capacity: It's impossible to make money at that production level. "Europe is definitely an Achilles' heel for Honda," says Toru Shimano, an analyst at Okasan Securities Co. in Tokyo.

So Honda is increasing purchases of cheaper parts from suppliers outside Britain and moving swiftly to freshen its lineup. Earlier this year, a remodeled and roomier five-door Civic hatchback with improved fuel efficiency rolled off production lines in Britain. To goose output at its British operations, Honda will start exporting perky three-door Civic sedans built at its newest plant to the United States and Japan this year. It also plans to export its British-made CR-V compact SUV to America to augment the Japan-made CR-Vs now being sold there.

DIFFERENTIATION

All of that will help, but Honda's big issue is the hole in its lineup: subcompacts. While one-liter-engine cars sell poorly in the United States, Europeans and Japanese can't get enough of them. "Honda does not have a product for Europe yet," says UBS Warburg's Redl. It missed out with its one-liter Logo. "It didn't stand out from the crowd," Yoshino admits.

So the Logo is history, and Honda's new salvation in Europe is a five-door hatchback called the Fit. At 1.3 liters, its engine outpowers Toyota's competing Vitz-class line of cars. Honda says the sporty Fit also boasts a number of nifty features. The only one it would confirm, however, is that owners will be able to flatten all four seats, including the driver's, at the flick of a switch—a selling point for youths keen to load bikes or sleep in it on long road trips.

Source: David Welch "Honda's Drive for Young Buyers," *BusinessWeek*, February 21, 2005.

EXHIBIT 8.2
Evaluating a Business's Cost Leadership Opportunities

A. Skills and Resources That Foster Cost Leadership

Sustained capital investment and access to capital
Process engineering skills
Intense supervision of labor or core technical operations
Products or services designed for ease of manufacture or delivery
Low-cost distribution system

B. Organizational Requirements to Support and Sustain Cost Leadership Activities

Tight cost control
Frequent, detailed control reports
Continuous improvement and benchmarking orientation
Structured organization and responsibilities
Incentives based on meeting strict, usually quantitative targets

C. Examples of Ways Businesses Achieve Competitive Advantage via Cost Leadership

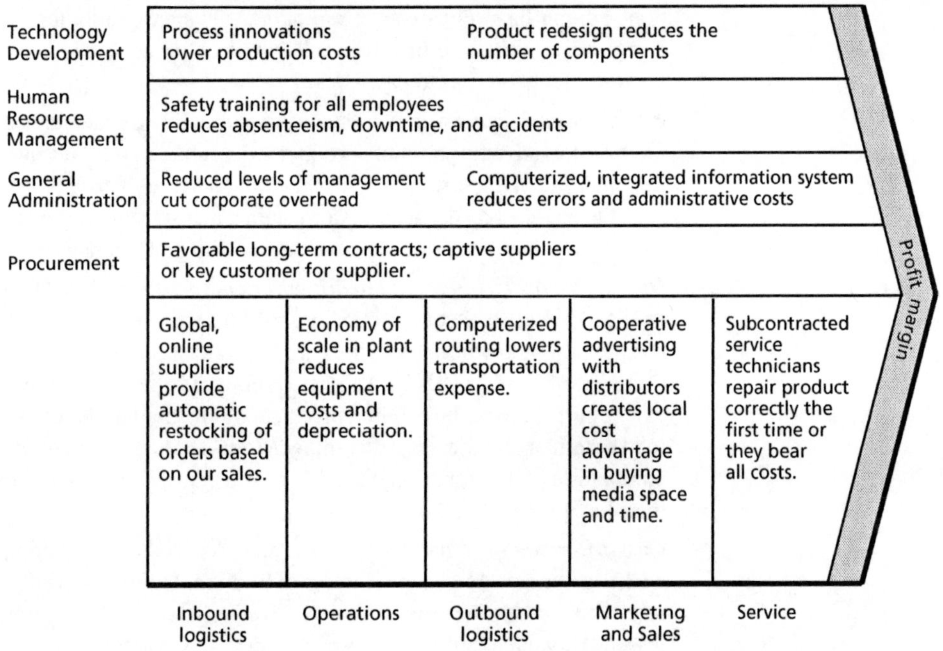

Technology Development	Process innovations lower production costs		Product redesign reduces the number of components		
Human Resource Management	Safety training for all employees reduces absenteeism, downtime, and accidents				
General Administration	Reduced levels of management cut corporate overhead		Computerized, integrated information system reduces errors and administrative costs		
Procurement	Favorable long-term contracts; captive suppliers or key customer for supplier.				
	Global, online suppliers provide automatic restocking of orders based on our sales.	Economy of scale in plant reduces equipment costs and depreciation.	Computerized routing lowers transportation expense.	Cooperative advertising with distributors creates local cost advantage in buying media space and time.	Subcontracted service technicians repair product correctly the first time or they bear all costs.
	Inbound logistics	Operations	Outbound logistics	Marketing and Sales	Service

Profit margin

Source: Based on Michael Porter, *On Competition,* 1998, Harvard Business School Press.

New entrants competing on price must face an entrenched cost leader without the experience to replicate every cost advantage easyJet, a British startup with a Southwest Airlines copycat strategy, entered the European airline market with much fanfare and low-priced, city-to-city, no-frills flights.

Analysts caution that by the time you read this, British Airways, KLM's no-frills offshoot (Buzz), and Virgin Express will simply match fares on easyJet's key routes and let high landing fees and flight delays take their toll on the British upstart.

Low-cost advantages should lessen the attractiveness of substitute products A serious concern of any business is the threat of a substitute product in which buyers can meet their original need. Low-cost advantages allow the holder to resist this happening because it allows them to remain competitive even against desirable substitutes, and it allows them to lessen concerns about price facing an inferior, lower-priced substitute.

Higher margins allow low-cost producers to withstand supplier cost increases and often gain supplier loyalty over time Sudden, particularly uncontrollable increases in the costs suppliers face can be more easily absorbed by low-cost, higher-margin producers. Severe droughts in California quadrupled the price of lettuce—a key restaurant demand. Some chains absorbed the cost; others had to confuse customers with a "lettuce tax." Furthermore, chains that worked well with produce suppliers gained a loyal, cooperative "partner" for possible assistance in a future, competitive situation.

Once managers identify opportunities to create cost advantage–based strategies, they must consider whether key risks inherent in cost leadership are present in a way that may mediate sustained success. The key risks with which they must be concerned are discussed next.

Many cost-saving activities are easily duplicated Computerizing certain order entry functions among hazardous waste companies gave early adopters lower sales costs and better customer service for a brief time. Rivals quickly adapted, adding similar capabilities with similar effects on their costs.

Exclusive cost leadership can become a trap Firms that emphasize lowest price and can offer it via cost advantages where product differentiation is increasingly not considered must truly be convinced of the sustainability of those advantages. Particularly with commodity-type products, the low-cost leader seeking to sustain a margin superior to lesser rivals may encounter increasing customer pressure for lower prices with great damage to both leader and lesser players.

Obsessive cost cutting can shrink other competitive advantages involving key product attributes Intense cost scrutiny can build margin, but it can reduce opportunities for or investment in innovation, processes, and products. Similarly, such scrutiny can lead to the use of inferior raw materials, processes, or activities that were previously viewed by customers as a key attribute of the original products. Some mail-order computer companies that sought to maintain or enhance cost advantages found reductions in telephone service personnel and automation of that function backfiring with a drop in demand for their products even though their low prices were maintained.

Cost differences often decline over time As products age, competitors learn how to match cost advantages. Absolute volumes sold often decline. Market channels and suppliers mature. Buyers become more knowledgeable. All of these factors present opportunities to lessen the value or presence of earlier cost advantages. Said another way, cost advantages that are not sustainable over a period of time are risky.

Once business managers have evaluated the cost structure of their value chain, determined activities that provide competitive cost advantages, and considered their inherent risks, they start choosing the business's strategy. Those managers concerned with differentiation-based strategies, or those seeking optimum performance incorporating both sources of competitive advantage, move to evaluating their business's sources of differentiation.

differentiation
A business strategy that seeks to build competitive advantage with its product or service by having it be "different" from other available competitive products based on features, performance, or other factors not directly related to cost and price. The difference would be one that would be hard to create and/or difficult to copy or imitate.

Evaluating Differentiation Opportunities

Differentiation requires that the business have sustainable advantages that allow it to provide buyers with something uniquely valuable to them. A successful differentiation strategy allows the business to provide a product or service of perceived higher value to buyers at a "differentiation cost" below the "value premium" to the buyers. In other words, the buyer feels the additional cost to buy the product or service is well below what the product or service is worth compared with other available alternatives.

Differentiation usually arises from one or more activities in the value chain that create a unique value important to buyers. Perrier's control of a carbonated water spring in France, Stouffer's frozen food packaging and sauce technology, Apple's control of iTunes download

EXHIBIT 8.3
Evaluating a Business's Differentiation Opportunities

A. Skills and Resources That Foster Differentiation

Strong marketing abilities
Product engineering
Creative talent and flair
Strong capabilities in basic research
Corporate reputation for quality or technical leadership
Long tradition in an industry or unique combination of skills drawn from other businesses
Strong cooperation from channels
Strong cooperation from suppliers of major components of the product or service

B. Organizational Requirements to Support and Sustain Differentiation Activities
Strong coordination among functions in R&D, product development, and marketing
Subjective measurement and incentives instead of quantitative measures
Amenities to attract highly skilled labor, scientists, and creative people
Tradition of closeness to key customers
Some personnel skilled in sales and operations—technical and marketing

C. Examples of Ways Businesses Achieve Competitive Advantage via Differentiation

Technology Development	Use cutting-edge production technology and product features to maintain a "distinct" image and actual product.			
Human Resource Management	Develop programs to ensure technical competence of sales staff and a marketing orientation of service personnel.			
General Administration	Develop comprehensive, personalized database to build knowledge of groups of customers and individual buyers to be used in "customizing" how products are sold, serviced, and replaced.			
Procurement	Maintain quality control presence at key supplier facilities; work with suppliers' new product development activities.			

Inbound logistics	Operations	Outbound logistics	Marketing and Sales	Service
Purchase superior quality, well-known components, raising the quality and image of final products.	Carefully inspect products at each step in production to improve product performance and lower defect rate.	Coordinate JIT with buyers; use own or captive transportation service to ensure timeliness.	Build brand image with expensive, informative advertising and promotion.	Allow service personnel considerable discretion to credit customers for repairs.

Profit margin

Source: Based on Michael Porter, *On Competition*, 1998, Harvard Business School Press.

software that worked solely with iPods at first, American Greeting Card's automated inventory system for retailers, and Federal Express's customer service capabilities are all examples of sustainable advantages around which successful differentiation strategies have been built. A business can achieve differentiation by performing its existing value activities or reconfiguring in some unique way. And the sustainability of that differentiation will depend on two things: a continuation of its high perceived value to buyers and a lack of imitation by competitors.

Exhibit 8.3 provides examples of the types of key skills and resources on which managers seeking to build differentiation-based strategies would base their underlying, sustainable competitive advantages. Examples of value chain activities that provide a differentiation advantage are also provided.

Strategists examining their business's resources and capabilities for differentiation advantages evaluate the sustainability of those advantages by benchmarking (refer to Chapter

6 for a discussion of this comparison technique) their business against key competitors and by considering the effect of any differentiation advantage on the five forces in their business's competitive environment. Sustainable activities that provide one or more of the following opportunities relative to key industry forces should become the basis for differentiation aspects of the business's competitive strategy:

Rivalry is reduced when a business successfully differentiates itself BMW's Z4, made in Greer, South Carolina, does not compete with Saturns made in central Tennessee. A Harvard education does not compete with an education from a local technical school. Both situations involve the same basic needs—transportation or education. However, one rival has clearly differentiated itself from others in the minds of certain buyers. In so doing, they do not have to respond competitively to that competitor.

Buyers are less sensitive to prices for effectively differentiated products The Highlands Inn in Carmel, California, and the Ventana Inn along the Big Sur charge a minimum of $600 and $900, respectively, per night for a room with a kitchen, fireplace, hot tub, and view. Other places are available along this beautiful stretch of California's spectacular coastline, but occupancy rates at these two locations remain over 90 percent. Why? You can't get a better view and a more relaxed, spectacular setting to spend a few days on the Pacific Coast. Similarly, buyers of differentiated products tolerate price increases low-cost-oriented buyers would not accept. The former become very loyal to certain brands. Harley Davidson motorcycles continue to rise in price, and its buyer base continues to expand worldwide, even though many motorcycle alternatives more reasonably priced are easily available.

Brand loyalty is hard for new entrants to overcome Many new beers are brought to market in the United States, but Budweiser continues to gain market share. Why? Brand loyalty is hard to overcome! And Anheuser-Busch has been clever to extend its brand loyalty from its core brand into newer niches, such as nonalcohol brews, that other potential entrants have pioneered.

Managers examining differentiation-based advantages must take potential risks into account as they commit their business to these advantages. Some of the more common ways risks arise are discussed next.

Imitation narrows perceived differentiation, rendering differentiation meaningless AMC pioneered the Jeep passenger version of a truck 40 years ago. Ford created the Explorer, or luxury utility vehicle, in 1990. It took luxury car features and put them inside a jeep. Ford's payoff was substantial. The Explorer has become Ford's most popular domestic vehicle. However, virtually every vehicle manufacturer offered a luxury utility in 2006, with customers beginning to be hard pressed to identify clear distinctions between lead models. Ford's Explorer managers have sought to shape a new business strategy for the next decade that relies both on new sources of differentiation and placing greater emphasis on low-cost components in their value chain.

Technological changes that nullify past investments or learning The Swiss controlled more than 95 percent of the world's watch market into the 1970s. The bulk of the craftspeople, technology, and infrastructure resided in Switzerland. U.S.-based Texas Instruments decided to experiment with the use of its digital technology in watches. Swiss producers were not interested, but Japan's SEIKO and others were. In 2007, the Swiss will make less than 5 percent of the world's watches.

The cost difference between low-cost competitors and the differentiated business becomes too great for differentiation to hold brand loyalty Buyers may begin to choose to sacrifice some of the features, services, or image possessed by the differentiated business for large cost savings. The rising cost of a college education, particularly at several "premier" institutions, has caused many students to opt for lower-cost destinations that offer very similar courses without image, frills, and professors who seldom teach undergraduate students anyway.

Evaluating Speed as a Competitive Advantage

While most telecommunication companies have used the last decade to leap aboard the information superhighway, GTE continued its impressive turnaround focusing on its core business—providing local telephone services. Long lagging behind the Baby Bells in profitability and efficiency, GTE has emphasized improving its poor customer service throughout the decade. The service was so bad in Santa Monica, California, that officials once tried to remove GTE as the local phone company. Candidly saying "we were the pits," new CEO Chuck Lee largely did away with its old system of taking customer service requests by writing them down and passing them along for resolution. Now, using personal communication services and specially designed software, service reps can solve 70 percent of all problems on the initial call—triple the success rate at the beginning of the last decade. Repair workers meanwhile plan their schedules on laptops, cutting downtime and speeding responses. CEO Lee has spent $1.5 billion on reengineering that slashed 17,000 jobs, replaced people with technology, and prioritized speed as the defining feature of GTE's business practices. Indeed Bell Atlantic was so impressed that it traveled across the United States to pay a premium in acquiring GTE with the desire to bring GTE's competitive advantage into Bell Atlantic, and subsequently Verizon.

speed-based strategies
Business strategies built around functional capabilities and activities that allow the company to meet customer needs directly or indirectly more rapidly than its main competitors.

Speed-based strategies, or rapid responses to customer requests or market and technological changes, have become a major source of competitive advantage for numerous firms in today's intensely competitive global economy. Speed is certainly a form of differentiation, but it is more than that. Speed involves the *availability of a rapid response* to a customer by providing current products quicker, accelerating new-product development or improvement, quickly adjusting production processes, and making decisions quickly. While low cost and differentiation may provide important competitive advantages, managers in tomorrow's successful companies will base their strategies on creating speed-based competitive advantages. Exhibit 8.4 describes and illustrates key skills and organizational requirements that are associated with speed-based competitive advantage. Jack Welch, the now-retired CEO who transformed General Electric from a fading company into one of Wall Street's best performers over the past 25 years, had this to say about speed:

> Speed is really the driving force that everyone is after. Faster products, faster product cycles to market. Better response time to customers. . . . Satisfying customers, getting faster communications, moving with more agility, all these things are easier when one is small. And these are all characteristics one needs in a fast-moving global environment.[2]

Speed-based competitive advantages can be created around several activities:

Customer responsiveness All consumers have encountered hassles, delays, and frustration dealing with various businesses from time to time. The same holds true when dealing business to business. Quick response with answers, information, and solutions to mistakes can become the basis for competitive advantage—one that builds customer loyalty quickly.

Product development cycles Japanese automakers have focused intensely on the time it takes to create a new model because several experienced disappointing sales growth in the last decade in Europe and North America competing against new vehicles like Ford's Explorer and Renault's Megane. VW had recently conceived, prototyped, produced, and marketed a totally new 4-wheel-drive car in Europe within 12 months. Honda, Toyota, and Nissan lowered their product development cycle from 24 months to 9 months from conception to production. This capability is old hat to 3M Corporation, which is so successful at speedy product development that one-fourth of its sales and profits each year are from products that didn't exist five years earlier.

[2] "Jack Welch: A CEO Who Can't Be Cloned," *BusinessWeek*, September 17, 2001.

EXHIBIT 8.4 Evaluating a Business's Rapid Response (Speed) Opportunities

A. Skills and Resources That Foster Speed

Process engineering skills
Excellent inbound and outbound logistics
Technical people in sales and customer service
High levels of automation
Corporate reputation for quality or technical leadership
Flexible manufacturing capabilities
Strong downstream partners
Strong cooperation from suppliers of major components of the product or service

B. Organizational Requirements to Support and Sustain Rapid Response Activities

Strong coordination among functions in R&D, product development, and marketing.
Major emphasis on customer satisfaction in incentive programs
Strong delegation to operating personnel
Tradition of closeness to key customers
Some personnel skilled in sales and operations—technical and marketing
Empowered customer service personnel

C. Examples of Ways Businesses Achieve Competitive Advantage via Speed

Technology Development	Use companywide technology sharing activities and autonomous product development teams to speed new product development.				
Human Resource Management	Develop self-managed work teams and decision making at the lowest levels to increase responsiveness.				
General Administration	Develop highly automated and integrated information processing system. Include major buyers in the "system" on a real-time basis.				
Procurement	Integrate preapproved online suppliers into production.				
	Work very closely with suppliers to include their choice of warehouse location to minimize delivery time.	Standardize dies, components, and production equipment to allow quick changeover to new or special orders.	Ensure very rapid delivery with JIT delivery plus partnering with express mail services.	Use of laptops linked directly to operations to speed the order process and shorten the sales cycle.	Locate service technicians at customer facilities that are geographically close.
	Inbound logistics	Operations	Outbound logistics	Marketing and Sales	Service

Profit margin

Product or service improvements Like development time, companies that can rapidly adapt their products or services and do so in a way that benefits their customers or creates new customers have a major competitive advantage over rivals that cannot do this.

Speed in delivery or distribution Firms that can get you what you need when you need it, even when that is tomorrow, realize that buyers have come to expect that level of responsiveness. Federal Express's success reflects the importance customers place on speed in inbound and outbound logistics.

Information Sharing and Technology Speed in sharing information that becomes the basis for decisions, actions, or other important activities taken by a customer, supplier, or partner has become a major source of competitive advantage for many businesses. Telecommunications, the Internet, and networks are but a part of a vast infrastructure that is being used by knowledgeable managers to rebuild or create value in their businesses via information sharing.

These rapid response capabilities create competitive advantages in several ways. They create a way to lessen rivalry because they have *availability* of something that a rival may not have. It can allow the business to charge buyers more, engender loyalty, or otherwise enhance the business's position relative to its buyers. Particularly where impressive customer response is involved, businesses can generate supplier cooperation and concessions because their business ultimately benefits from increased revenue. Finally, substitute products and new entrants find themselves trying to keep up with the rapid changes rather than introducing them. Exhibit 8.5, Strategy in Action, provides examples of how "speed" has become a source of competitive advantage for several well-known companies around the world.

While the notion of speed-based competitive advantage is exciting, it has risks managers must consider. First, speeding up activities that haven't been conducted in a fashion that prioritizes rapid response should only be done after considerable attention to training, reorganization, and/or reengineering. Second, some industries—stable, mature ones that have very minimal levels of change—may not offer much advantage to the firm that introduces some forms of rapid response. Customers in such settings may prefer the slower pace or the lower costs currently available, or they may have long time frames in purchasing such that speed is not that important to them.

Evaluating Market Focus as a Way to Competitive Advantage

Small companies, at least the better ones, usually thrive because they serve narrow market niches. This is usually called **market focus,** the extent to which a business concentrates on a narrowly defined market. Take the example of Soho Beverages, a business former Pepsi manager Tom Cox bought from Seagram after Seagram had acquired it and was unable to make it thrive. The tiny brand, once a healthy niche product in New York and a few other East Coast locations, languished within Seagrams because its sales force was unused to selling in delis. Cox was able to double sales in one year. He did this on a lean marketing budget that didn't include advertising or database marketing. He hired Korean- and Arabic-speaking college students and had his people walk into practically every deli in Manhattan in order to reacquaint owners with the brand, spot consumption trends, and take orders. He provided rapid stocking services to all Manhattan-area delis, regardless of size. The business has continued sales growth at more than 50 percent per year. Why? Cox says, "It is attributable to focusing on a niche market, delis; differentiating the product and its sales force; achieving low costs in promotion and delivery; and making rapid, immediate response to any deli owner request its normal practice."[3]

market focus
This is a generic strategy that applies a differentiation strategy approach, or a low-cost strategy approach, or a combination—and does so solely in a narrow (or "focused") market niche rather than trying to do so across the broader market. The narrow focus may be geographically defined or defined by product type features, or target customer type, or some combination of these.

Two things are important in this example. First, this business focused on a narrow niche market in which to build a strong competitive advantage. But focus alone was not enough to build competitive advantage. Rather, Cox created several capabilities, resources, and value chain activities that achieved differentiation, low-cost, and rapid response competitive advantages within this niche market that would be hard for other firms, particularly mass market–oriented firms, to replicate.

Market focus allows some businesses to compete on the basis of low cost, differentiation, and rapid response against much larger businesses with greater resources. Focus lets a business "learn" its target customers—their needs, special considerations they want accommodated—and establish personal relationships in ways that "differentiate" the smaller firm or make it more valuable to the target customer. Low costs can also be achieved, filling niche needs in a buyer's operations that larger rivals either do not want to bother with or cannot do as cost effectively. Cost advantage often centers around the high level of customized service the focused, smaller business can provide. And perhaps

[3]Michael Porter, *On Competition,* 1998, Harvard Business School Press, p. 57.

Strategy in Action

Exhibit 8.5

Examples of SPEED as a Source of Competitive Advantage

BusinessWeek

SPEED IN DISTRIBUTION AND DELIVERY

Clad in a blue lab coat, a technician in Singapore waves a scanner like a wand over a box of newly minted computer chips. With that simple act, he sets in motion a delivery process that is efficient and automated, almost to the point of magic. This cavernous National Semiconductor Corp. warehouse was designed and built by shipping wizards at United Parcel Service Inc. It is UPS's computers that speed the box of chips to a loading dock, then to truck, to plane, and to truck once again. In just 12 hours, the chips will reach one of National's customers, a PC maker half a world away in Silicon Valley. Throughout the journey, electronic tags embedded in the chips will let the customer track the order with accuracy down to about three feet. In the two years since UPS and National started this relationship, the team in brown has slashed National Semiconductor's inventory and shipment costs by 15 percent while reducing the time from factory floor to customer site by 60 percent.

INFORMATION SHARING AND TECHNOLOGY

Meanwhile, in the Old Economy, UPS is winning giant customers such as Ford Motor Co., which uses UPS's computerized logistics to route cars more efficiently to its dealerships. In a year, Ford has reduced delivery times by 26 percent and saved $240 million, says Frank M. Taylor, Ford's vice president for material planning and logistics. "Speed is the mindset at UPS. They'll meet a deadline at any cost," Taylor says. UPS Chairman James P. Kelly chalks it up to the company's slow-and-steady work ethic. "We've spent the past seven years studying where we should be long-term," he says.

While FedEx backpedals in logistics, UPS is in growth mode. And it has figured out how to manage distribution for many companies at one central location—a massive warehouse in Louisville, Kentucky. Here, UPS handles storage, tracking, repair, and shipping for clients such as Sprint, Hewlett-Packard, and Nike, using a mix of high- and low-tech methods. Computerized forklifts scan in new inventory while people in sneakers dash across the vast warehouse to pluck products, box them, and ship them out. In short, UPS uses expensive technology only where it cuts costs.

SPEED IN NEW-PRODUCT DEVELOPMENT AND MANAGEMENT DECISION MAKING

Recently retired Volkswagen CEO Ferdinand Piëch has every reason to feel satisfied. The Austrian engineer and scion of one of Europe's most noted automotive dynasties can boast of one of the great turnarounds in automotive history, based on his attention to new-product development combined with speed of decision making. Unlike many other auto chiefs, he called the shots on product design and engineering. And if you worked for Dr. Piëch, you had better get it right. In Wolfsburg, executives used to joke that PEP, the acronym for the product development process *(Produkt entwicklungsprozess)* really stood for *Piëch entscheidet persönlich*—Piëch decides himself. And he did it fast. He is said to have sketched out the Audi's all-wheel-drive system on the back of an envelope.

Obsession with detail and speed are key reasons VW has succeeded so brilliantly in reviving its fortunes in the United States, where the VW brand was roadkill a decade ago. Last year, VW and Audi sales in the United States jumped 14 percent, to 437,000 units, for a combined 2.5 percent market share. That's up from a microscopic 0.5 percent five years earlier. Although VW trails its Japanese rivals, it's the only European mass-market carmaker in the United States. Volkswagen's four main brands—VW, Audi, Seat, and Skoda—have taken 19 percent of the European auto market, a gain of some three points in eight years, mostly at the expense of General Motors Corp. and Ford. Not bad for a company that eight years ago suffered from quality problems and a paucity of hit models. In South America, VW vehicles account for one-quarter of car sales, and in China, one-half.

SPEED IN CUSTOMER RESPONSIVENESS

Stuart Klaskin's flight on Delta Air Lines was leaving in just 20 minutes. Although he raced through New York's LaGuardia Airport, the behind-schedule aviation consultant suspected he would make it. Why? He bypassed the long check-in lines, stopping instead at one of Delta's 670 self-service kiosks, where all he did was insert his frequent-flier card to get a boarding pass. Not only did Klaskin make his flight but, he says, "I even had time to grab a cup of coffee."

Kiosks are just the start. Delta is using everything from high-definition screens providing real-time info to direct phone access to reservation agents to speed up travel. While its rivals use similar technologies, Delta is the first airline to package it all as a comprehensive, hassle-free system. "We are pioneering significant changes in the way passengers will move through airports," says Richard W. Cordell, Delta's senior vice president for airport customer service. "In two years, 80 percent of our passengers will check in somewhere other than the old counter."

Sources: Charles Haddad, "Delta's Flight to Self-Service," *BusinessWeek,* July 7, 2003; Gail Edmondson, "VW Needs a Jump," *BusinessWeek,* May 12, 2003; Dean Foust, "Big Brown's New Bag," *BusinessWeek,* July 19, 2004; and Phillip Baggaley," Inside Delta's Low-Fare Strategy," *BusinessWeek,* January 6, 2005.

Top Strategist

Michael O'Leary, CEO of Ryanair

Exhibit 8.6

Michael O'Leary, CEO of Ryanair © AFP/Getty Images.

It was vintage Michael O'Leary. The 42-year-old CEO of Dublin-based discount airline Ryanair outfitted his staff in full combat gear, drove an old World War II tank to England's Luton airport, an hour north of London, then demanded access to the base of archrival easyJet Airline Co. With the theme to the old television series *The A-Team* blaring, O'Leary declared he was "liberating the public from easyJet's high fares." When security—surprise!—refused to let the Ryanair armor roll in, O'Leary led the troops in his own rendition of a platoon march song: "I've been told and it's no lie. easyJet's fares are way too high!"

Buffoonery? Of course. But O'Leary can get away with it. Ryanair's 31 percent operating margin dwarfs British Airways' 3.8 percent, easyJet's 8.7 percent, and the 8.6 percent of the granddaddy of discount carriers, Dallas-based Southwest Airlines. Ryanair has built up $1 billion in cash. Its $5 billion market capitalization exceeds that of British Air, Lufthansa, and Air France. Ryanair, meanwhile, is expected to post pretax profits of $308 million for the year ended March 31, up 53 percent on sales of close to $1 billion. "O'Leary and his management team are absolutely the best at adopting a focus strategy and sticking to it relentlessly," says Ryanair's chairman David Bonderman.

Ryanair's focus strategy has key differentiation, low cost, and speed elements allowing it to far outpace direct and indirect European airline competitors. They are as follows:

DIFFERENTIATION

Ryanair flies to small, secondary airports outside major European cities. Often former military bases are attractive access points to European tourists, which the airports and small towns encourage. Virtually all of its rivals, including discount rival easyJet, focus on business travelers and major international airports in Europe's largest cities. Its fares average 30 percent less than rival easyJet and are far lower than major European airlines. And Ryanair vows to lower its fares 5 percent a year for the foreseeable future, further differentiating itself from others, much like Southwest in the United States. It also offers one of Europe's leading e-tailers, Ryanair.com, which sells more than 90 percent of its tickets online and has hooked up with hotel chains, car rentals, life insurers, and mobile

(continued)

the greatest competitive weapon that can arise is rapid response. With enhanced knowledge of its customers and intricacies of their operations, the small, focused company builds up organizational knowledge about timing-sensitive ways to work with a customer. Often the needs of that narrow set of customers represent a large part of the small, focused business's revenues. Exhibit 8.6, Top Strategist, illustrates how Ireland's Ryanair has become the European leader in discount air travel via the focused application of low cost, differentiation, and speed.

The risk of focus is that you attract major competitors who have waited for your business to "prove" the market. Domino's proved that a huge market for pizza delivery existed and now faces serious challenges. Likewise, publicly traded companies built around focus strategies become takeover targets for large firms seeking to fill out a product portfolio. And perhaps the greatest risk of all is slipping into the illusion that it is focus itself, and not some special form of low cost, differentiation, or rapid response, that is creating the business's success.

Managers evaluating opportunities to build competitive advantage should link strategies to resources, capabilities, and value chain activities that exploit low cost, differentiation, and rapid response competitive advantages. When advantageous, they should consider ways to use focus to leverage these advantages. One way business managers can enhance their likelihood

Exhibit 8.6 cont.

phone companies to offer one-stop shopping to the European leisure traveler.

LOW COST

Ryanair ordered 100 new Boeing 737-800s to facilitate the company's rapid European growth plans, less than a year after placing an order for 150 next-generation 737s. Analysts estimate Boeing offered Ryanair 40 percent off list price, significantly lowering Ryanair's cost of capital, maintenance costs, and operating expenses. Ryanair's differentiation choice of flying mainly to small, secondary airports outside major European cities has led to sweetheart deals on everything from landing and handling fees to marketing support. Less congestion lets Ryanair significantly lower personnel costs and the time a plane stays on the ground compared with rivals. Ryanair grows by acquiring small, recent entrants into the discount segment that are losing money at bargain basement prices—like Buzz, the loss-making discount carrier of KLM Royal Dutch Airlines—and then reducing routes, personnel, and bloated costs by 80 percent or more. Ryanair sells snacks and rents the back of seats and overhead storage to advertisers.

SPEED

Ryanair's Ryanair.com sells more than 90 percent of its tickets quickly and conveniently for customers seeking simplicity, speed, and convenience. Its large purchases from Boeing allow it to grow to additional airports at a rate of about 30 percent annually. Its use of less congested airports allows Ryanair to get its planes back in the air in 25 minutes—half the time it takes competitors at major airports. This lets Ryanair provide significantly more frequent flights, which simplifies and adds time-saving convenience for the leisure traveler and business traveler.

FOCUS

O'Leary continues to focus like a light beam on small outlying airports and leisure travelers with speedy, low-cost services.

O'Leary's currently talking to 40 new European airports and scouting out future options in eastern Europe. When he's not traveling in Europe, he's back at headquarters at Dublin Airport, where he joins in the company's Thursday football match. He recently acquired a Mercedes taxi and driver, enabling him to speed through Dublin's notorious traffic in the bus and taxi lane. "I've always been a transport innovator," he jokes. Millions of Europeans flying Ryanair planes would agree.

Sources: Kerry Capell, "Ryanair Rising," *BusinessWeek,* June 2, 2003; Stanley Holmes, "An Updraft for Boeing and Airbus," *BusinessWeek,* October 20, 2004; and "Ryanair Down Amid Dispute with Pilots," *BusinessWeek,* March 30, 2005.

of identifying these opportunities is to consider several different "generic" industry environments from the perspective of the typical value chain activities most often linked to sustained competitive advantages in those unique industry situations. The next section discusses key generic industry environments and the value chain activities most associated with success.

Stages of Industry Evolution and Business Strategy Choices

The requirements for success in industry segments change over time. Strategists can use these changing requirements, which are associated with different stages of industry evolution, as a way to isolate key competitive advantages and shape strategic choices around them. Exhibit 8.7 depicts four stages of industry evolution and the typical functional capabilities that are often associated with business success at each of these stages.

emerging industry
An industry that has growing sales across all the companies in the industry based on growing demand for the relatively new products, technologies, and/or services made available by the firms participating in this industry.

Competitive Advantage and Strategic Choices in Emerging Industries

Emerging industries are newly formed or re-formed industries that typically are created by technological innovation, newly emerging customer needs, or other economic or sociological changes. **Emerging industries** of the last decade have been the Internet browser, fiber optics, solar heating, cellular telephone, and online services industries.

EXHIBIT 8.7 Sources of Distinctive Competence at Different Stages of Industry Evolution

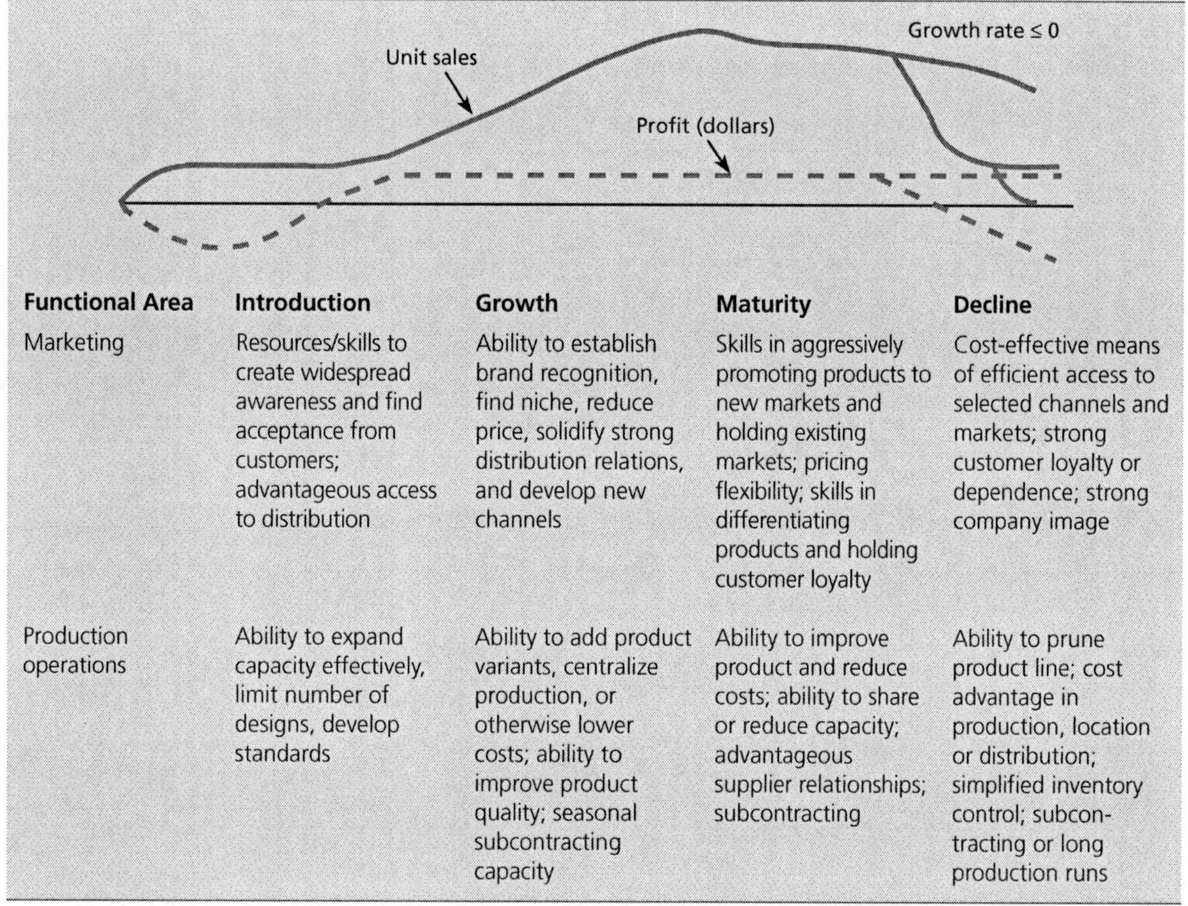

Functional Area	Introduction	Growth	Maturity	Decline
Marketing	Resources/skills to create widespread awareness and find acceptance from customers; advantageous access to distribution	Ability to establish brand recognition, find niche, reduce price, solidify strong distribution relations, and develop new channels	Skills in aggressively promoting products to new markets and holding existing markets; pricing flexibility; skills in differentiating products and holding customer loyalty	Cost-effective means of efficient access to selected channels and markets; strong customer loyalty or dependence; strong company image
Production operations	Ability to expand capacity effectively, limit number of designs, develop standards	Ability to add product variants, centralize production, or otherwise lower costs; ability to improve product quality; seasonal subcontracting capacity	Ability to improve product and reduce costs; ability to share or reduce capacity; advantageous supplier relationships; subcontracting	Ability to prune product line; cost advantage in production, location or distribution; simplified inventory control; subcontracting or long production runs

From the standpoint of strategy formulation, the essential characteristic of an emerging industry is that there are no "rules of the game." The absence of rules presents both a risk and an opportunity—a wise strategy positions the firm to favorably shape the emerging industry's rules.

Business strategies must be shaped to accommodate the following characteristics of markets in emerging industries:

- Technologies that are mostly proprietary to the pioneering firms and technological uncertainty about how product standardization will unfold.
- Competitor uncertainty because of inadequate information about competitors, buyers, and the timing of demand.
- High initial costs but steep cost declines as the experience curve takes effect.
- Few entry barriers, which often spurs the formation of many new firms.
- First-time buyers requiring initial inducement to purchase and customers confused by the availability of a number of nonstandard products.
- Inability to obtain raw materials and components until suppliers gear up to meet the industry's needs.
- Need for high-risk capital because of the industry's uncertainty prospects.

EXHIBIT 8.7 ***(continued)***

Functional Area	Introduction	Growth	Maturity	Decline
Finance	Resources to support high net cash overflow and initial losses; ability to use leverage effectively	Ability to finance rapid expansion, to have net cash outflows but increasing profits; resources to support product improvements	Ability to generate and redistribute increasing net cash inflows; effective cost control systems	Ability to reuse or liquidate unneeded equipment; advantage in cost of facilities; control system accuracy; streamlined management control
Personnel	Flexibility in staffing and training new management; existence of employees with key skills in new products or markets	Existence of an ability to add skilled personnel; motivated and loyal workforce	Ability to cost effectively, reduce workforce, increase efficiency	Capacity to reduce and reallocate personnel; cost advantage
Engineering and research and development	Ability to make engineering changes, have technical bugs in product and process resolved	Skill in quality and new feature development; ability to start developing successor product	Ability to reduce costs, develop variants, differentiate products	Ability to support other grown areas or to apply product to unique customer needs
Key functional area and strategy focus	Engineering: market penetration	Sales: consumer loyalty; market share	Production efficiency; successor products	Finance; maximum investment recovery

For success in this industry setting, business strategies require one or more of these features:

1. The ability to *shape the industry's structure* based on the timing of entry, reputation, success in related industries or technologies, and role in industry associations.
2. The ability to *rapidly improve product quality* and performance features.
3. *Advantageous relationships* with key suppliers and promising distribution channels.
4. The ability to *establish the firm's technology as the dominant one* before technological uncertainty decreases.
5. The early acquisition of *a core group of loyal customers* and then the expansion of that customer base through model changes, alternative pricing, and advertising.
6. The ability to *forecast future competitors* and the strategies they are likely to employ.

A firm that has had repeated successes with business in emerging industries is 3M Corporation. In each of the past 20 years, more than 25 percent of 3M's annual sales have come from products that did not exist five years earlier. Startup companies enhance their success by having experienced entrepreneurs at the helm, a knowledgeable management team and board of directors, and patient sources of venture capital. Steven Jobs's dramatic unveiling of Apple's iPod in 2003 came to be seen by many as the catalyst for the emergence of a new personalized digital music industry. Jobs and Apple certainly took advantage by building a strategy that shaped the industry's structure, established the firm's technology as a dominant one, endeared themselves to a core group of loyal customers, and rapidly improved the product quality and Internet-based music service.

Competitive Advantages and Strategic Choices in Growing Industries

Rapid growth brings new competitors into the industry. Oftentimes, those new entrants are large competitors with substantial resources who have waited for the market to "prove" itself before they committed significant resources. At this stage, **growth industry strategies** that emphasize brand recognition, product differentiation, and the financial resources to support both heavy marketing expenses and the effect of price competition on cash flow can be key strengths. Accelerating demand means scaling up production or service capacity to meet the growing demand. Doing so may place a premium on being able to adapt product design and production facilities to meet rapidly increasing demand effectively. Increased investment in plant and equipment, in research and development (R&D), and especially marketing efforts to target specific customer groups along with developing strong distribution capabilities place a demand on the firm's capital resources.

growth industry strategies
Business strategies that may be more advantageous for firms participating in rapidly growing industries and markets.

For success in this industry setting, business strategies require one or more of these features:

1. The ability to *establish strong brand recognition* through promotional resources and skills that increase selective demand.
2. The ability and resources to *scale up to meet increasing demand,* which may involve production facilities, service capabilities, and the training and logistics associated with that capacity.
3. *Strong product design skills* to be able to adapt products and services to scaled operations and emerging market niches.
4. The ability to *differentiate the firm's product[s]* from competitors entering the market.
5. *R&D resources and skills* to create product variations and advantages.
6. The ability to *build repeat buying from established customers* and attract new customers.
7. Strong capabilities in *sales and marketing.*

IBM entered the personal computer market—which Apple pioneered in the growth stage—and was able to rapidly become the market leader with a strategy based on its key strengths in brand awareness and possession of the financial resources needed to support consumer advertising. Many large technology companies today prefer exactly this approach: to await proof of an industry or product market and then to acquire small pioneer firms with first-mover advantage as a means to obtain an increasingly known brand, or to acquire technical know-how and experience behind which the firms can put its resources and distribution strength to build brand identify and loyalty. In 2005 as the PC market matured, IBM sold its PC division to a Chinese company and now outsources its PCs.

Competitive Advantages and Strategic Choices in Mature Industry Environments

As an industry evolves, its rate of growth eventually declines. This "transition to maturity" is accompanied by several changes in its competitive environment: Competition for market share becomes more intense as firms in the industry are forced to achieve sales growth at one another's expense. Firms working with the **mature industry strategies** sell increasingly to experienced, repeat buyers who are now making choices among known alternatives. Competition becomes more oriented to cost and service as knowledgeable buyers expect similar price and product features. Industry capacity "tops out" as sales growth ceases to cover up poorly planned expansions. New products and new applications are harder to come by. International competition increases as cost pressures lead to overseas production advantages. Profitability falls, often permanently, as a result of pressure to lower prices and the increased costs of holding or building market share.

mature industry strategies
Strategies used by firms competing in markets where the growth rate of that market from year to year has reached or is close to zero.

These changes necessitate a fundamental strategic reassessment. Strategy elements of successful firms in maturing industries often include the following:

1. *Product line* pruning, or dropping unprofitable product models, sizes, and options from the firm's product mix.
2. *Emphasis on process innovation* that permits low-cost product design, manufacturing methods, and distribution synergy.
3. *Emphasis on cost reduction* through exerting pressure on suppliers for lower prices, switching to cheaper components, introducing operational efficiencies, and lowering administrative and sales overhead.
4. *Careful buyer selection* to focus on buyers who are less aggressive, more closely tied to the firm, and able to buy more from the firm.
5. *Horizontal integration* to acquire rival firms whose weaknesses can be used to gain a bargain price and that are correctable by the acquiring firms.
6. *International expansion* to markets where attractive growth and limited competition still exist and the opportunity for lower-cost manufacturing can influence both domestic and international costs.

Business strategists in maturing industries must avoid several pitfalls. First, they must make a clear choice among the three generic strategies and avoid a middle-ground approach, which would confuse both knowledgeable buyers and the firm's personnel. Second, they must avoid sacrificing market share too quickly for short-term profit. Finally, they must avoid waiting too long to respond to price reductions, retaining unneeded excess capacity, engaging in sporadic or irrational efforts to boost sales, and placing their hopes on "new" products, rather than aggressively selling existing products.

Competitive Advantages and Strategic Choices in Declining Industries

declining industry
An industry in which the trend of total sales as an indicator of total demand for an industry's products or services among all the participants in the industry have started to drop from the last several years with the likelihood being that such a trend will continue indefinitely.

Declining industries are those that make products or services for which demand is growing slower than demand in the economy as a whole or is actually declining. This slow growth or decline in demand is caused by technological substitution (such as the substitution of electronic calculators for slide rules), demographic shifts (such as the increase in the number of older people and the decrease in the number of children), and shifts in needs (such as the decreased need for red meat).

Firms in a declining industry should choose strategies that emphasize one or more of the following themes:

1. *Focus* on segments within the industry that offer a chance for higher growth or a higher return.
2. *Emphasize product innovation and quality improvement,* where this can be done cost effectively, to differentiate the firm from rivals and to spur growth.
3. *Emphasize production and distribution efficiency* by streamlining production, closing marginal production facilities and costly distribution outlets, and adding effective new facilities and outlets.
4. *Gradually harvest the business*—generate cash by cutting down on maintenance, reducing models, and shrinking channels and make no new investment.

Strategists who incorporate one or more of these themes into the strategy of their business can anticipate relative success, particularly where the industry's decline is slow and smooth and some profitable niches remain. Penn Tennis, the nation's no. 1 maker of tennis balls, watched industrywide sales steadily decline over the last decade. In response it started marketing tennis balls as "dog toys" in the rapidly growing pet products industry. It secondly made Penn balls the official ball at major tournaments. Third, it created three different quality levels; then, as sales revived, Penn Sports sold its tennis ball business to Head Sports.

Competitive Advantage in Fragmented Industries

fragmented industry
An industry in which there are numerous competitors (providers of the same or similar products or services the industry involves) such that no single firm or small group of firms controls any significant share of the overall industry sales.

Fragmented industries are another setting in which identifiable types of competitive advantages and the strategic choices suggested by those advantages can be identified. A **fragmented industry** is one in which no firm has a significant market share and can strongly influence industry outcomes. Fragmented industries are found in many areas of the economy and are common in such areas as professional services, retailing, distribution, wood and metal fabrication, and agricultural products. The funeral industry is an example of a highly fragmented industry. Business strategists in fragmented industries pursue low-cost or differentiation strategies or focus competitive advantages in one of five ways:

Tightly managed decentralization Fragmented industries are characterized by a need for intense local coordination, a local management orientation, high personal service, and local autonomy. Recently, however, successful firms in such industries have introduced a high degree of professionalism into the operations of local managers.

"Formula" facilities This alternative, related to the previous one, introduces standardized, efficient, low-cost facilities at multiple locations. Thus, the firm gradually builds a low-cost advantage over localized competitors. Fast-food and motel chains have applied this approach with considerable success.

Increased value added The products or services of some fragmented industries are difficult to differentiate. In this case, an effective strategy may be to add value by providing more service with the sale or by engaging in some product assembly that is of additional value to the customer.

Specialization Focus strategies that creatively segment the market can enable firms to cope with fragmentation. Specialization can be pursued by

1. *Product type.* The firm builds expertise focusing on a narrow range of products or services.
2. *Customer type.* The firm becomes intimately familiar with and serves the needs of a narrow customer segment.
3. *Type of order.* The firm handles only certain kinds of orders, such as small orders, custom orders, or quick turnaround orders.
4. *Geographic area.* The firm blankets or concentrates on a single area.

Although specialization in one or more of these ways can be the basis for a sound focus strategy in a fragmented industry, each of these types of specialization risks limiting the firm's potential sales volume.

Bare bones/no frills Given the intense competition and low margins in fragmented industries, a "bare bones" posture—low overhead, minimum wage employees, tight cost control—may build a sustainable cost advantage in such industries.

Competitive Advantage in Global Industries

global industry
Industry in which competition crosses national borders.

Global industries present a final setting in which success is often associated with identifiable sources of competitive advantage. A **global industry** is one that comprises firms whose competitive positions in major geographic or national markets are fundamentally affected by their overall global competitive positions. To avoid strategic disadvantages, firms in global industries are virtually required to compete on a worldwide basis. Oil, steel, automobiles, apparel, motorcycles, televisions, and computers are examples of global industries.

Global industries have four unique strategy-shaping features:

- Differences in prices and costs from country to country due to currency exchange fluctuations, differences in wage and inflation rates, and other economic factors.
- Differences in buyer needs across different countries.
- Differences in competitors and ways of competing from country to country.
- Differences in trade rules and governmental regulations across different countries.

These unique features and the global competition of global industries require that two fundamental components be addressed in the business strategy: (1) the approach used to gain global market coverage and (2) the generic competitive strategy. Three basic options can be used to pursue global market coverage:

1. *License* foreign firms to produce and distribute the firm's products.
2. *Maintain a domestic production base* and export products to foreign countries.
3. *Establish foreign-based plants and distribution* to compete directly in the markets of one or more foreign countries.

Along with the market coverage decision, strategists must scrutinize the condition of the global industry features identified earlier to choose among four generic global competitive strategies:

1. *Broad-line global competition*—directed at competing worldwide in the full product line of the industry, often with plants in many countries, to achieve differentiation or an overall low-cost position.
2. *Global focus* strategy—targeting a particular segment of the industry for competition on a worldwide basis.
3. *National focus* strategy—taking advantage of differences in national markets that give the firm an edge over global competitors on a nation-by-nation basis.
4. *Protected niche* strategy—seeking out countries in which governmental restraints exclude or inhibit global competitors or allow concessions, or both, that are advantageous to localized firms.

Competing in global industries is an increasing reality for most U.S. firms. Strategists must carefully match their skills and resources with global industry structure and conditions in selecting the most appropriate strategy option.

DOMINANT PRODUCT/SERVICE BUSINESSES: EVALUATING AND CHOOSING TO DIVERSIFY TO BUILD VALUE

McDonald's has frequently looked at numerous opportunities to diversify into related businesses or to acquire key suppliers. Its decision has consistently been to focus on its core business using the grand strategies of concentration, market development, and product development. Rival Yum Brands, on the other hand, has chosen to diversify into related businesses and vertical integration as the best grand strategies for it to build long-term value. Both firms experienced unprecedented success during the last 20 years.

Many dominant product businesses face this question as their core business proves successful: What grand strategies are best suited to continue to build value? Under what circumstances should they choose an expanded focus (diversification, vertical integration); steady

EXHIBIT 8.8 Grand Strategy Selection Matrix

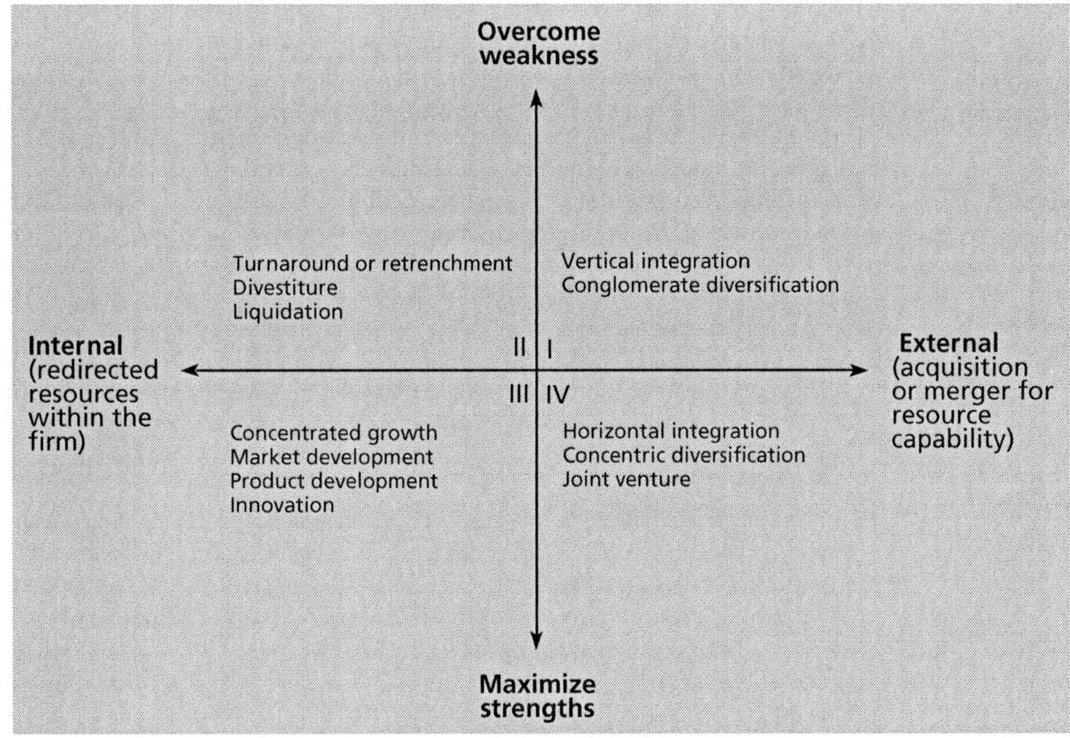

grand strategy selection matrix
A four-cell guide to strategies based upon whether the business is (1) operating from a position of strength or weakness and (2) rely on its own resources versus having to acquire resources via merger or acquisition.

vertical integration
Acquisition of firms that supply inputs such as raw materials, or customers for its outputs, such as warehouses for finished products.

continued focus (concentration, market or product development); or a narrowed focus (turnaround or divestiture)? This section examines two ways you can analyze a dominant product company's situation and choose among the 15 grand strategies identified in Chapter 7.

Grand Strategy Selection Matrix

One valuable guide to the selection of a promising grand strategy is the **grand strategy selection matrix** shown in Exhibit 8.8. The basic idea underlying the matrix is that two variables are of central concern in the selection process: (1) the principal purpose of the grand strategy and (2) the choice of an internal or external emphasis for growth or profitability.

In the past, planners were advised to follow certain rules or prescriptions in their choice of strategies. Now, most experts agree that strategy selection is better guided by the conditions of the planning period and by the company strengths and weaknesses. It should be noted, however, that even the early approaches to strategy selection sought to match a concern over internal versus external growth with a desire to overcome weaknesses or maximize strengths.

The same considerations led to the development of the grand strategy selection matrix. A firm in quadrant I, with "all its eggs in one basket," often views itself as overcommitted to a particular business with limited growth opportunities or high risks. One reasonable solution is **vertical integration,** which enables the firm to reduce risk by reducing uncertainty about inputs or access to customers. Another is **conglomerate diversification,** which provides a profitable investment alternative with diverting management attention from the original business. However, the external approaches to

conglomerate diversification
Acquiring or entering businesses unrelated to a firm's current technologies, markets, or products.

retrenchment
Cutting back on products, markets, operations because the firm's overall competitive and financial situation cannot support commitments needed to sustain or build its operations.

divestiture
The sale of a firm or a major component.

liquidation
Closing down the operations of a business and selling its assets and operations to pay its debts and distribute any gains to stockholders.

concentrated growth
Aggressive market penetration where a firm's strong position and favorable market growth allow it to "control" resources and effort for focused growth.

market development
Selling present products, often with only cosmetic modification, to customers in related marketing areas by adding channels of distribution or by changing the content of advertising or promotion.

overcoming weaknesses usually result in the most costly grand strategies. Acquiring a second business demands large investments of time and sizable financial resources. Thus, strategic managers considering these approaches must guard against exchanging one set of weaknesses for another.

More conservative approaches to overcoming weaknesses are found in quadrant II. Firms often choose to redirect resources from one internal business activity to another. This approach maintains the firm's commitment to its basic mission, rewards success, and enables further development of proven competitive advantages. The least disruptive of the quadrant II strategies is **retrenchment,** pruning the current activities of a business. If the weaknesses of the business arose from inefficiencies, retrenchment can actually serve as a *turnaround* strategy—that is, the business gains new strength from the streamlining of its operations and the elimination of waste. However, if those weaknesses are a major obstruction to success in the industry and the costs of overcoming them are unaffordable or are not justified by a cost-benefit analysis, then eliminating the business must be considered. **Divestiture** offers the best possibility for recouping the firm's investment, but even **liquidation** can be an attractive option if the alternatives are bankruptcy or an unwarranted drain on the firm's resources.

A common business adage states that a firm should build from strength. The premise of this adage is that growth and survival depend on an ability to capture a market share that is large enough for essential economies of scale. If a firm believes that this approach will be profitable and prefers an internal emphasis for maximizing strengths, four grand strategies hold considerable promise. As shown in quadrant III, the most common approach is **concentrated growth,** that is, market penetration. The firm that selects this strategy is strongly committed to its current products and markets. It strives to solidify its position by reinvesting resources to fortify its strengths.

Two alternative approaches are **market development** and **product development.** With these strategies, the firm attempts to broaden its operations. Market development is chosen if the firm's strategic managers feel that its existing products would be well received by new customer groups. Product development is chosen if they feel that the firm's existing customers would be interested in products related to its current lines. Product development also may be based on technological or other competitive advantages. The final alternative for quadrant III firms is **innovation.** When the firm's strengths are in creative product design or unique production technologies, sales can be stimulated by accelerating perceived obsolescence. This is the principle underlying the innovative grand strategy.

Maximizing a firm's strengths by aggressively expanding its base of operations usually requires an external emphasis. The preferred options in such cases are shown in quadrant IV. **Horizontal integration** is attractive because it makes possible a quick increase in output capability. Moreover, in horizontal integration, the skills of the managers of the original business often are critical in converting newly acquired facilities into profitable contributors to the parent firm; this expands a fundamental competitive advantage of the firm—its management.

Concentric diversification is a good second choice for similar reasons. Because the original and newly acquired businesses are related, the distinctive competencies of the diversifying firm are likely to facilitate a smooth, synergistic, and profitable expansion.

The final alternative for increasing resource capability through external emphasis is a **joint venture** or **strategic alliance.** This alternative allows a firm to extend its strengths into competitive arenas that it would be hesitant to enter alone. A partner's production, technological, financial, or marketing capabilities can reduce the firm's financial investment significantly and increase its probability of success.

EXHIBIT 8.9 Model of Grand Strategy Clusters

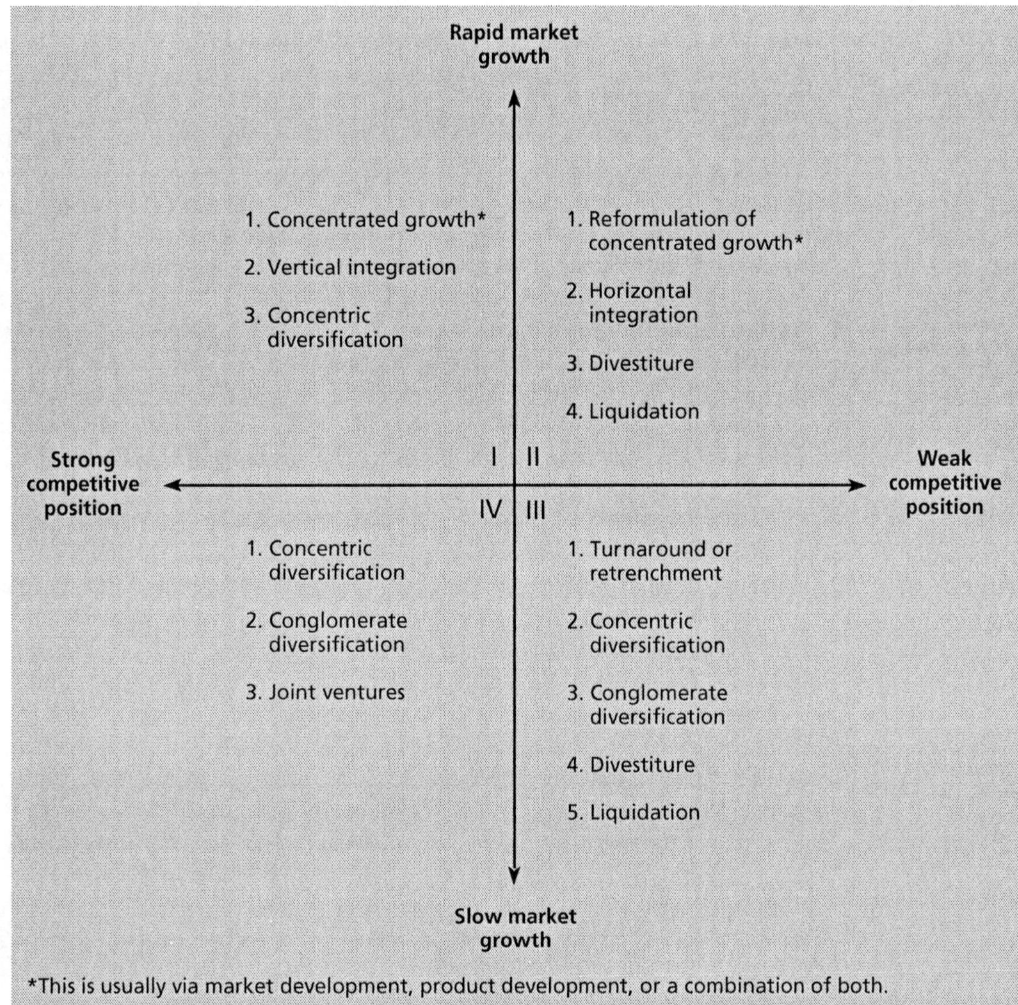

*This is usually via market development, product development, or a combination of both.

product development
The substantial modification of existing products or the creation of new but related products that can be marketed to current customers through established channels.

Model of Grand Strategy Clusters

A second guide to selecting a promising strategy is the **grand strategy cluster** shown in Exhibit 8.9. The figure is based on the idea that the situation of a business is defined in terms of the growth rate of the general market and the firm's competitive position in that market. When these factors are considered simultaneously, a business can be broadly categorized in one of four quadrants: (I) strong competitive position in a rapidly growing market, (II) weak position in a rapidly growing market, (III) weak position in a slow-growth market, or (IV) strong position in a slow-growth market. Each of these quadrants suggests a set of promising possibilities for the selection of a grand strategy.

Firms in quadrant I are in an excellent strategic position. One obvious grand strategy for such firms is continued concentration on their current business as it is currently defined. Because consumers seem satisfied with the firm's current strategy, shifting notably from it would endanger the firm's established competitive advantages. McDonald's Corporation has followed this approach for 25 years. However, if the firm has resources that exceed the demands of a concentrated growth strategy, it should consider vertical integration. Either

innovation
A strategy that seeks to reap the initially high profits associated with customer acceptance of a new or greatly improved product.

horizontal integration
Growth through the acquisition of one or more similar firms operating at the same stage of the production-marketing chain.

concentric diversification
Acquisition of businesses that are related to the acquiring firm in terms of technology, markets, or products.

joint ventures
Commercial companies created and operated for the benefit of the co-owners; usually two or more separate companies that form the venture.

strategic alliances
Partnerships that are distinguished from joint ventures because the companies involved do not take an equity position in one another.

grand strategy clusters
Strategies that may be more advantageous for firms to choose under one of four sets of conditions defined by market growth rate and the strength of the firm's competitive position.

forward or backward integration helps a firm protect its profit margins and market share by ensuring better access to consumers or material inputs. Finally, to diminish the risks associated with a narrow product or service line, a quadrant I firm might be wise to consider concentric diversification; with this strategy, the firm continues to invest heavily in its basic area of proven ability.

Firms in quadrant II must seriously evaluate their present approach to the marketplace. If a firm has competed long enough to accurately assess the merits of its current grand strategy, it must determine (1) why that strategy is ineffectual and (2) whether it is capable of competing effectively. Depending on the answers to these questions, the firm should choose one of four grand strategy options: formulation or reformulation of a concentrated growth strategy, horizontal integration, divestiture, or liquidation.

In a rapidly growing market, even a small or relatively weak business often is able to find a profitable niche. Thus, formulation or reformulation of a concentrated growth strategy is usually the first option that should be considered. However, if the firm lacks either a critical competitive element or sufficient economies of scale to achieve competitive cost efficiencies, then a grand strategy that directs its efforts toward horizontal integration is often a desirable alternative. A final pair of options involves deciding to stop competing in the market or product area of the business. A multiproduct firm may conclude that it is most likely to achieve the goals of its mission if the business is dropped through divestiture. This grand strategy not only eliminates a drain on resources but also may provide funds to promote other business activities. As an option of last resort, a firm may decide to liquidate the business. This means that the business cannot be sold as a going concern and is at best worth only the value of its tangible assets. The decision to liquidate is an undeniable admission of failure by a firm's strategic management and, thus, often is delayed—to the further detriment of the firm.

Strategic managers tend to resist divestiture because it is likely to jeopardize their control of the firm and perhaps even their jobs. Thus, by the time the desirability of divestiture is acknowledged, businesses often deteriorate to the point of failing to attract potential buyers. The consequences of such delays are financially disastrous for firm owners because the value of a going concern is many times greater than the value of its assets.

Strategic managers who have a business in quadrant III and expect a continuation of slow market growth and a relatively weak competitive position will usually attempt to decrease their resource commitment to that business. Minimal withdrawal is accomplished through retrenchment; this strategy has the side benefits of making resources available for other investments and of motivating employees to increase their operating efficiency. An alternative approach is to divert resources for expansion through investment in other businesses. This approach typically involves either concentric or conglomerate diversification because the firm usually wants to enter more promising arenas of competition than integration or concentrated growth strategies would allow. The final options for quadrant III businesses are divestiture, if an optimistic buyer can be found, and liquidation.

Quadrant IV businesses (strong competitive position in a slow-growth market) have a basis of strength from which to diversify into more promising growth areas. These businesses have characteristically high cash flow levels and limited internal growth needs. Thus, they are in an excellent position for concentric diversification into ventures that utilize their proven acumen. A previous example in this chapter described how the no. 1 tennis ball maker, Penn Racquet Sports, chose concentric diversification from humans to dogs as their best option. A second option is conglomerate diversification, which spreads investment risk and does not divert managerial attention from the present business. The final option is joint ventures, which are especially attractive to multinational firms. Through joint ventures, a domestic business can gain competitive advantages in promising new fields while exposing itself to limited risks.

Opportunities for Building Value as a Basis for Choosing Diversification or Integration

The grand strategy selection matrix and model of grand strategy clusters are useful tools to help dominant product company managers evaluate and narrow their choices among alternative grand strategies. When considering grand strategies that would broaden the scope of their company's business activities through integration, diversification, or joint venture strategies, managers must examine whether opportunities to build value are present. Opportunities to build value via diversification, integration, or joint venture strategies are usually found in market-related, operating-related, and management activities. Such opportunities center around reducing costs, improving margins, or providing access to new revenue sources more cost effectively than traditional internal growth options via concentration, market development, or product development. Major opportunities for sharing and value building as well as ways to capitalize on core competencies are outlined in the next chapter, which covers strategic analysis and choice in diversified companies.

Dominant product company managers who choose diversification or integration eventually create another management challenge. That challenge is charting the future of a company that becomes a collection of several distinct businesses. These distinct businesses often encounter different competitive environments, challenges, and opportunities. The next chapter examines ways managers of such diversified companies attempt to evaluate and choose corporate strategy. Central to their challenge is the continued desire to build value, particularly shareholder value.

Summary

This chapter examined how managers in businesses that have a single or dominant product or service evaluate and choose their company's strategy. Two critical areas deserve their attention: (1) their business's value chain, and (2) the appropriateness of 12 different grand strategies based on matching environmental factors with internal capabilities.

Managers in single-product-line business units examine their business's value chain to identify existing or potential activities around which they can create sustainable competitive advantages. As managers scrutinize their value chain activities, they are looking for three sources of competitive advantage: low cost, differentiation, and rapid response capabilities. They also examine whether focusing on a narrow market niche provides a more effective, sustainable way to build or leverage these three sources of competitive advantage.

Managers in single- or dominant-product/service businesses face two interrelated issues: (1) They must choose which grand strategies make best use of their competitive advantages. (2) They must ultimately decide whether to diversify their business activity. Twelve grand strategies were identified in this chapter along with three frameworks that aid managers in choosing which grand strategies should work best and when diversification or integration should be the best strategy for the business. The next chapter expands the coverage of diversification to look at how multibusiness companies evaluate continued diversification and how they construct corporate strategy.

Key Terms

concentrated growth, p. 253
concentric diversification, p. 255
conglomerate diversification, p. 253
declining industry, p. 249
differentiation, p. 237
divestiture, p. 253
emerging industry, p. 245
fragmented industry, p. 250
global industry, p. 250
grand strategy cluster, p. 256
grand strategy selection matrix, p. 252
growth industry strategies, p. 248
horizontal integration, p. 255
innovation, p. 255

joint ventures, p. 255
liquidation, p. 253
low-cost strategies, p. 234
market development, p. 254
market focus, p. 242
mature industry strategies, p. 248
product development, p. 255
retrenchment, p. 253
speed-based strategies, p. 240
strategic alliances, p. 255
vertical integration, p. 252

Questions for Discussion

1. What are three activities or capabilities a firm should possess to support a low-cost leadership strategy? Use Exhibit 8.2 to help you answer this question. Can you give an example of a company that has done this?
2. What are three activities or capabilities a firm should possess to support a differentiation-based strategy? Use Exhibit 8.3 to help you answer this question. Can you give an example of a company that has done this?
3. What are three ways a firm can incorporate the advantage of speed in its business? Use Exhibit 8.4 to help you answer this question. Can you give an example of a company that has done this?
4. Do you think is it better to concentrate on one source of competitive advantage (cost versus differentiation versus speed) or to nurture all three in a firm's operation?
5. How does market focus help a business create competitive advantage? What risks accompany such a posture?
6. Using Exhibits 8.8 and 8.9, describe situations or conditions under which horizontal integration and concentric diversification would be preferred strategic choices.

Chapter 7 Discussion Case

BusinessWeek

DHL's American Adventure

1 No question, those cheeky DHL ads seem to be everywhere, from the New York City subways to the World Series. In a TV pitch, a FedEx worker goes on holiday, enjoying parasailing and golf—only to see DHL trucks speeding parcels to their destinations. Then there's the bus stop poster that takes a swipe at UPS: "Yellow. It's the new Brown." And a print ad proclaims what DHL hopes is inevitable: "The Roman empire, the British empire, the FedEx empire. Nothing lasts forever."

2 In short, it's war, as DHL, the $28 billion delivery and logistics company controlled since 2002 by Deutsche Post World Net—the privatized German postal service—fights to become a credible alternative in the U.S. to FedEx Corp. and United Parcel Service Inc. DHL is the largest express carrier in Europe with a 40% share, and the largest international express carrier in Asia, also with 40%. Now DHL, whose U.S. base is in Plantation, Fla., is seeking to build its presence by expanding its trucking routes, creating air hubs, and advertising heavily to raise awareness of its brand in a country where it has only 7% of the air and ground parcel market.

3 With North American express traffic accounting for nearly half the worldwide total, no carrier with global ambitions can afford to ignore it. And DHL has set its sights on the small- and medium-size U.S. businesses that are increasingly involved in foreign trade. "It's a global economy now," says John Fellows, CEO of DHL Holdings (USA) Inc. "You have to be everywhere."

4 But taking on FedEx and UPS, which together command 78% of the U.S. parcel market, is a daunting task. It was only in May that the company won a bruising legal battle, when regulators turned aside challenges by FedEx and UPS that the planes DHL contracted to use here constituted illegal foreign control of an airline. Completing the integration of Airborne Inc., the Seattle carrier that merged with DHL last year, has been a massive job. And DHL's limited ground network has hurt its ability to attract domestic customers who want to cut costs by sending parcels overland rather than by air. In fact, until this year, DHL had almost no ground network in much of the Midwest and Rocky Mountain states.

5 The result: DHL, with $6 billion in American revenues, projects it will lose $630 million in the U.S. this year and $380 million in 2005. The company has also pushed back the breakeven date for U.S. operations by a year, to 2006. Even after reaching profitability, Fellows says that DHL's return on investment is unlikely to top 4% for the next few years.

Can DHL Deliver?
It aims to be a strong No. 3 among U.S. couriers.
How it plans to get there:

Get Better Known
This year DHL is spending $150 million annually on an ad campaign that tweaks UPS and FedEx

Improve the Infrastructure
Build stronger trucking network in Rocky Mountain and Midwest regions; open West Coast air hub

Target the Little Guy
Focus on midmarket and smaller businesses by offering more personal service

Boost Market Share
In five years, DHL wants 10% to 12% of the market, up from 7% today

CROWN JEWELS

6 It's clearly going to take a lot more than a snappy ad campaign to turn DHL into a winner. Analysts and investors are already raising substantial doubts about whether DHL can be a viable No. 3 in the U.S. Since the mid-1990s, Deutsche Post has acquired over 100 logistics, transport, and freight-forwarding services, and expertly integrated them to build its worldwide business. DHL and Airborne were to be the crown jewels, the acquisitions that extended its grasp into the world's richest economy. But Deutsche Post "underestimated the challenges," says Raimund Saxinger, a fund manager at Frankfurt Trust in Frankfurt.

7 Chief among those challenges has been the lack of ground transport capability. DHL had virtually none when it was acquired by Deutsche Post, while Airborne was just getting started. Now, with high fuel prices boosting the cost of air shipment, the parcel market in the U.S. is shifting toward ground transport, which is DHL's weakest link. So DHL is investing $1.2 billion over the next three years in sorting centers, drop-off points, and other network improvements. Nationally, for instance, DHL has only 16,000 drop-off points—about one-third FedEx's number. "It takes a lot of money and a lot of talent to build a high-quality network. That's a big hurdle," says Kurt Kuehn, senior vice-president of worldwide sales and marketing for UPS.

8 But DHL is determined to build out its network. "If we did not have an efficient pickup and delivery system in the U.S., it would be very tough for us to hold on to our No. 1 position in Europe and Asia," says Klaus Zumwinkel, chief executive of parent Deutsche Post and the mastermind behind its global strategy.

9 DHL is better situated in terms of air transport. Since 2000, it and Airborne have collectively invested $1.9 billion in the U.S. and Canada, much of it on projects such as the consolidation of air operations at its Wilmington (Ohio) hub. Construction of a West Coast hub is under way. But those outlays only begin to get DHL into the game. "It does not close the gap," says Satish Jindel, president of transportation consultant SJ Consulting Group Inc. Over the same period, he says, FedEx and UPS each spent more than $6 billion in North America.

In addition to its $150 million media campaign, DHL is counting on improved customer service to build its business. While the company knows that it won't be easy to separate customers from their UPS drivers, it's trying to mold a more customer-friendly workforce. Analysts say that task was neglected by Airborne. In one survey, DHL now rates even lower than Airborne did on customer satisfaction. To remedy that, Fellows says he's using Starbucks Corp. as a model. The coffee purveyor is known for screening workers as carefully as it screens beans. "It's training, but it's also hiring the right person," Fellows says. 10

Personalized service can be a winning pitch for some customers. Shoemaker Skechers USA Inc. already has shifted about a third of the business from its Manhattan Beach (Calif.) headquarters from FedEx to DHL, which it also uses for international shipments. "I've been responsible for shipping and receiving for 13 years, and it wasn't until this past year that I met my FedEx rep. DHL is constantly out here," says Michael Cardenas, Skechers' office services manager. He also praises DHL's hustle. "UPS and FedEx are more reluctant to go to remote locations. DHL will just do it. If their driver has to sit in the parking lot and fill out the air bills, he'll do it." 11

For now, DHL has modest goals in the U.S. The company aims just to raise market share to between 10% and 12%, Fellows says—a statement that draws derision from competitors. "I don't think that customers will turn over their mission-critical operations to a fledgling operation whose stated goal is to become the No. 3 player," says William G. Margaritis, vice-president for investor relations at FedEx. Even if DHL doesn't break even in the U.S. by 2006, don't expect it to stop trying. With a deep-pocketed corporate parent, it can keep plugging away for years. "They can afford a U.S. problem," says analyst Markus Hesse at HVB Group in Munich. Good thing, because it looks like a problem that's not going to go away soon. 12

Sources: Jack Ewing and Dean Foust, "DHL's American Adventure," *BusinessWeek,* November 29, 2004; and Jack Ewing "A Mercedes in the Parcel Industry," *BusinessWeek,* November 29, 2004.

VOICES OF INNOVATION

An Interview with Klaus Zumwinkel, CEO of DHL

DHL, a unit of Germany's Deutsche Post, is the dominant express and parcel company in Europe and also the leader in crossborder air express in Asia. In the United States, though,

DHL is still tiny compared with market leaders UPS and FedEx. Deutsche Post CEO Klaus Zumwinkel is trying to change that, in part by acquiring Airborne last year and merging it with DHL. Mr. Zumwinkel aims to be the transportation services "Mercedes" in the U.S. market.

But gaining ground in the United States is proving tougher than expected. On September 29, DHL announced that it won't break even in the United States until 2006, instead of 2005 as planned. This is partly because DHL was held up by a regulatory battle after rivals complained that the air fleet used under contract by the German outfit constituted illegal foreign control of an airline. DHL prevailed in the dispute earlier this year. Still, many analysts doubt whether even the revised profit goal is realistic.

Zumwinkel, who has overseen transformation of the German postal service into a global express-courier and logistics company, remains determined. He spoke recently with *BusinessWeek*'s Frankfurt Bureau Chief, Jack Ewing, for Pearce and Robinson, about how DHL will prove the doubters wrong.

Question: Why is the U.S. worth investing $1.2 billion in?

Zumwinkel: In an industry like ours, the network has to be complete. Customers inside the U.S. and outside are welcoming an increase in our U.S. presence. If we didn't have an efficient pickup and delivery system in the U.S., it would be very tough for us to hold onto our No. 1 position in Europe and Asia.

Question: Has the U.S. been more difficult than you expected? Have there been any surprises?

Zumwinkel: In the beginning we had a long battle with our competitors because of [regulatory issues regarding] the air fleet used by DHL. . . . We lost some time in streamlining and integrating and restructuring the whole thing. But with all of our acquisitions, we're now experts in integration. We have integrated more than 100 companies.

Question : How big a priority is DHL in the U.S. for you?

Zumwinkel: In such a big group we have several priorities. We had the IPO of Postbank [Deutsche Post's retail banking unit in Germany], and Asia is a very attractive and strong growth area. In Europe, we're integrating heavily in several key countries like Italy, the U.K., [and] France. The U.S. is one of these priorities, it's in this class.

Question : So it's not keeping you up at night?

Zumwinkel: No [laughs].

Question : The U.S. market is moving toward a ground network. Does that increase the amount of investment you have to put into the U.S.?

Zumwinkel: Yes. . . . Airborne had already established a ground-based network. Like everybody else in this industry, Airborne found that if you have a good ground network, why should the customer pay so much for air products?

This is a secular trend. We want to provide the same kind of quality our customers are used to in other parts of the world. We want to be the Mercedes in our industry.

Question : What are your profit goals for DHL in the U.S.? Will you be satisfied to break even?

Zumwinkel: Naturally, management is concentrating on [breaking even] in 2006 [and on the goals] to restructure [the U.S. business], to integrate two companies, to integrate into the worldwide network, [and] to build a ground network. That will keep everybody busy for the next two years. [If we broke even,] we would have 500 million [euros or $650 million] more profit, we would have 500 million [euros] losses less. That is only 10% of our whole group profit. That's the main objective. After that, we will see.

Question : Can you foresee that the U.S. will become a major profit center?

Zumwinkel: Sure. We have invested a lot of money in the U.S. Our competitors are earning nice profit rates, double-digit margins—something we're not used to in Europe. We won't get these margins for a while because our competitors have larger economies of scale, but with our economies of scale worldwide, I think we can [realize these margins in the long term].

Question : Is this like the Japanese carmakers coming into the U.S. decades ago where you're willing to invest for a long time in order to get a permanent foothold in the market?

Zumwinkel: I don't compare myself with Japanese carmakers. Here the game is very simple. The express game is an international game. To be international, one has to cover the largest economy in the world—the U.S. Otherwise, one is not thoroughly competitive in Asia or Europe.

We're in the U.S. for the long term. I think the globalization trend will strengthen in the next 10 years. World trade has to be transported, and we're here to provide the transport.

Discussion Questions:

1. What aspects of DHL's strategy for entering the United States reflect a low-cost strategy? A differentiation strategy?
2. Are there any aspects that appear to reflect a focus strategy?
3. How has DHL incorporated "speed" into its overall strategy?
4. What appear to be DHL's most important competitive advantages? Are they best suited to a mature industry or a growth industry? Which way would you characterize the U.S. parcel market and the global parcel market?
5. What appears to be the likelihood that DHL will succeed? What key factors will determine that?
6. DHL comes to you for advice on whether they should continue a global focus on parcels and express mail or diversify their business activities into other types of businesses. What would you advise and why?

chapter 8

Entrepreneurship and Innovation

Learning Objectives

1. Explain the economic importance of entrepreneurship.
2. Identify the key characteristics and skills of entrepreneurs.
3. Recognize the basic ingredients needed to effectively start and manage an entrepreneurial venture.
4. Differentiate among the legal forms of organizing an entrepreneurial venture.
5. Identify alternative forms of entrepreneurship.
6. Describe innovation and demonstrate why it is important for business success.
7. Apply the "Five C" management tactics to maximize innovation.

Nothing to Sneeze At

8

It might be common wisdom that doctors or scientists know best how to fight colds, but a surprisingly successful new cold product was created by a schoolteacher, and that's part of its widespread appeal.

Airborne, with its "natural formula of 17 ingredients" and sly cartoon-character packaging, is the runaway hit of the cold-and-flu aisle. The company recently logged annual sales over $120 million, and Airborne is now supported by venture capital, an experienced CEO, and a $10 million ad campaign. In some markets it outsells even Sudafed and Tylenol Cold tablets, and children's versions called Airborne Jr. and Sore Throat Gummies have been added to the product line. CEO Elise Donahue claims the product has "consumer loyalty like nothing I've ever seen before," citing product-referral rates of more than 60 percent among first-time users and nearly 100 percent among regular users.

All this success sprang from a second-grade teacher's distress at the constant colds she was picking up from the students in her Carmel, California, classroom. "All winter, I'd be sick, from one cold to the next," says Airborne's inventor and company founder Victoria Knight-McDowell. "I decided children's germs must somehow be more virulent than adults' germs."

Searching for an answer, Knight-McDowell began brewing up experimental remedies in her kitchen with vitamins C, E, and A, zinc, selenium, forsythia, ginger, isatis root, and Echinacea. When two years of using her self-treatments went by without a cold, she decided she was on to something, and she sold her first package of fizzy tablets to a local drugstore. Then she and her husband cashed out their savings to combine them with his check for writing a television screenplay and invested the money in Airborne, starting out by giving away samples in malls. "Our families thought we had gone round the bend," says Knight-McDowell. "They wanted us to do something responsible, like buy a house. They thought we were mad." But orders came in, and distribution grew. Soon the couple were leasing a warehouse and couple of order-fulfillment centers to meet demand. Knight-McDowell quit her teaching job and appeared on the "Dr. Phil" show, actor Kevin Costner endorsed the product, and the company was on its way.

Because it's marketed as a dietary supplement, Airborne did not have to be tested or approved by the Food and Drug Administration. None of its ingredients, including popular "remedies" like Echinacea and vitamin C, have been scientifically proven to prevent colds. And the packaging states that Airborne "is not intended to diagnose, treat, cure, or prevent any disease." The instructions are to take it "at the first sign of a cold symptom or before entering crowded environments," echoing the Web site's claim that "workers within our highly technological society now spend close to 90% of their time indoors" where, it warns, the EPA estimates "our exposure to pollution may be as much as five times greater . . . than outdoors!"

Controversial in some scientific circles because it's not backed by any proof of its effectiveness, Airborne nonetheless remains an extremely popular product. Positioned as a mainstream product and proud to be invented by a nonexpert, it bases its appeal on consumers' growing distrust of the very establishment that won't endorse it. "We have letters from over 40,000 consumers a year saying they swear by it," says Donahue. "People trust a schoolteacher."

Sources: www.airbornehealth.com, accessed March 13, 2006, Dana Wechsler Linden, "Nothing to Sneeze At," *Forbes* March 13, 2006, p. 41; Rob Walker, "Cold Call: Airborne," *New York Times Magazine*, www.nytimes.com, January 8, 2006; Rachel Konrad, "Out with the Cold: Teacher Serves Up Possible Remedy," *Los Angeles Daily News*, www.dailynews.com, April 24, 2003.

CRITICAL THINKING QUESTIONS

1. *What leads people to become entrepreneurs?*
2. *How can people face the risk involved in starting a new business?*
3. *Where do the ideas come from for starting a new business?*

We'll look at these questions again at the end of the chapter in our Concluding Thoughts, after you've had a chance to learn about entrepreneurs and Innovation.

Creating a new enterprise can be one of the most exciting management challenges. Numerous entrepreneurs have built successful companies by discovering and meeting unmet needs. Many kinds of people start businesses. Men, women, minorities, immigrants—all can and do become entrepreneurs. As a result, entrepreneurship is becoming a popular field of study for many university business students.

Like Lillian Vernon, Arthur Blank, Bernard Marcus, and Michael Dell, today's entrepreneurs face a variety of challenges. They must find answers to such questions as: Do I have the right skills and abilities to become a successful entrepreneur? What type of business should I start? How can I raise capital to grow the business? Which markets should my business compete in? How much growth and what rate of growth is desirable? Manager's Notebook 8.1 on page 311 presents the basic entrepreneurial skills needed to successfully launch a new business venture. This chapter explores questions and issues about starting and growing a business. The first issue is describing what entrepreneurship is and is not.

entrepreneurship

The process of creating a business enterprise capable of entering new or established markets by deploying resources and people in a unique way to develop a new organization.

entrepreneur

An individual who creates an enterprise that becomes a new entry to a market.

What Is Entrepreneurship?

The process of creating a business enterprise capable of entering new or established markets is **entrepreneurship**. Successful entrepreneurship requires deploying resources and people in unique ways to develop a new organization. An **entrepreneur** is an individual who creates an enterprise that becomes a new entry to a market. Broadly stated, an entrepreneur is anyone who undertakes some project and bears some risk.[1]

Entrepreneurship Myths

Entrepreneurs have received considerable attention from the business and popular press in recent years. Still, many misconceptions remain concerning entrepre-

SO, YOU WANT TO BECOME AN ENTREPRENEUR? KEY SKILLS FOR ENTREPRENEURIAL SUCCESS

8.1 manager's notebook

- *Opportunity Recognition Skills*. Entrepreneurs are able to identify opportunities when they develop or exist. To be successful, an entrepreneur must scan the environment, searching for opportunities and ideas. Sometimes an entrepreneur may discover a problem to be solved or find a market need that is not being filled. Other times, a person may be committed to becoming an entrepreneur and then looks for a potential business opportunity. In either case, the entrepreneur must be aware that an opportunity exists and be able to take advantage of the situation.
- *Opportunity Fit Assessment*. Not everyone can succeed at everything. To be successful, an entrepreneur must be able to evaluate whether or not his or her personality, skills, and leadership style match with the opportunity. This includes the technical and business skills that are required in addition to personal preferences and needs.
- *Implementation Skills*. Successful entrepreneurs tend to have a high need for achievement, have an internal locus of control, be risk takers, and be confident in their ability to master unforeseen challenges.
- *Networking Skills*. Networking skills are critical to obtaining financial capital, business and technical knowledge, retail shelf space, and other resources required to start a business.

Source: N. Lindsay and J. Craig, "A Framework for Understanding Opportunity Recognition: Entrepreneurs versus Private Equity Financiers," *Journal of Private Equity* 6 (2002), pp. 13–24.

neurs and what they do in order to succeed. We next consider some of these myths and contrast those with the common reality faced by most entrepreneurs.[2]

MYTH 1: ENTREPRENEURS ARE BORN, NOT MADE One common belief is that entrepreneurs possess certain innate traits that are different from regular people. In fact, many types of people with different personality characteristics have become successful entrepreneurs. Many of them studied entrepreneurship as a discipline before launching a business. Business schools offer courses in entrepreneurship that provide opportunities to learn and practice skills that are useful to entrepreneurs.

MYTH 2: IT IS NECESSARY TO HAVE ACCESS TO MONEY TO BECOME AN ENTREPRENEUR A second common myth is that only wealthy people, or those who have access to wealthy people, can start businesses. The truth is, however, that many companies have been started by people with few resources. These entrepreneurs accumulated capital by putting in long hours without pay and reinvesting the profits of the business into expansion. For example, Hewlett-Packard, the giant electronics company, was started in a Palo Alto, California, garage in 1940 by two Stanford University students with a few hundred dollars and an order for sound equipment from the Walt Disney Company.

MYTH 3: AN ENTREPRENEUR TAKES A LARGE OR IRRATIONAL RISK IN STARTING A BUSINESS Risk is part of any business venture and this reality certainly applies to entrepreneurial ventures. The costs of embracing an entrepreneurial vision in terms of personal funds and family relationships can be tremendous. However, in terms of absolute amount of financial risk, most entrepreneurs

Like many design-conscious parents, Michael and Ellen Diamant (shown here with their son Spencer) were unhappy with the clunky shapes and bland designs of the baby gear they found on the market when their son was born several years ago. Says Michael, "We decided to take products that are under the radar and turn them into objects that are beautiful to look at." So their baby-gear company Skip Hop was born. It now grosses several million dollars a year from trendy diaper bags; new products designed by award-winning professionals are already in production.

have little to risk at the outset of a new business venture. It is usually later, when trying to grow the business into a larger enterprise, that the entrepreneur can face larger risk. At this later time, the business may have developed substantial value, which means there is more to lose.

MYTH 4: MOST SUCCESSFUL ENTREPRENEURS START WITH A BREAKTHROUGH INVENTION Contrary to the idea that entrepreneurs capitalize on revolutionary change, most entrepreneurs start a new business with only a moderate or incremental change that is designed to serve a market need. Certainly, innovation and being able to distinguish your product or service from others in the marketplace is important for a start-up business. Rather than revolutionary change, however, great execution, being first in a market, or a small innovation/improvement is often enough for an entrepreneur to be successful.

MYTH 5: ENTREPRENEURS BECOME SUCCESSFUL ON THEIR FIRST VENTURE People tend to remember entrepreneurial successes. Many times, however, failure is a key part of the learning process. By failing, entrepreneurs learn lessons that eventually lead to the creation of successful ventures. Nolan Bushnell, the entrepreneur who is best remembered for starting the videogame company Atari, failed at several different businesses but he persisted and learned from his mistakes. Likewise, initial business ventures of Richard Branson, founder of Virgin Records, include a failed magazine launch.[3]

A Distinction between an Entrepreneurial Venture and a Small Business

small business

Any business that is independently owned and operated, that is small in size, and that is not dominant in its markets.

A **small business** is any company that is independently owned and operated, is small in size, and does not dominate its markets. For research purposes, the U.S. Small Business Administration defines a small business as employing fewer than 500 employees. Small businesses do not always grow into medium-sized or large businesses. Some small-business owners prefer to keep their operations modest.

One of the most important goals of an entrepreneur, on the other hand, can be growth. An entrepreneurial venture may be small during its early stages, but the goal may be to become a medium-sized firm of 100 to 499 employees or a large firm with 500 or more employees. Giant firms like Wal-Mart, Home Depot, Microsoft, and Intel started as entrepreneurships with the goal of becoming dominant companies in their markets. At the start, however, a small business and an entrepreneurial venture may be hard to tell apart. For a small business owner, stability and profitability are the ideal situation. For the entrepreneur, growth and a greater presence in the market can be important objectives.

The Importance of Entrepreneurship

According to the latest figures compiled by the U.S. Census bureau, the number of U.S. businesses increased by 10 percent between 1997 and 2002, with approximately 23 million businesses operating in the United States by the end of 2002.[4] Over 550,000 new businesses opened up in 2002.[5] The economies of the United States and many other countries depend on the creation of new enterprises. Entrepreneurship creates jobs, stimulates innovation, and provides opportunities for diverse people in society.

Job Creation

Entrepreneurship and the creation of small businesses have surprising impacts on the creation of new jobs. According to the most recent data, small businesses created three-quarters of the net new jobs in the 1999–2000 year. Over the decade of the 1990s the net job creation by small business varied between 60 and 80 percent. Young start-ups, businesses in the first two years of existence, account for nearly all of the net new jobs in the U.S. economy.[6]

Innovation

Entrepreneurships are responsible for introducing a major proportion of new and innovative products and services that reach the market. They are often started by visionary people who develop an innovative way to do something faster, better, cheaper, or with improved features. Entrepreneurships often pioneer new technologies designed to make older technologies obsolete. This was the case when Apple Computer pioneered the first commercial personal computer and challenged the computing technology of the 1970s, which was based on centralized, mainframe computers. Eventually, the personal computer became the dominant technology and spawned a huge market for computer components, software, systems, and services.

Opportunities for Diverse People

People of diverse backgrounds who have experienced frustration and blocked career paths in large corporations can improve their economic status and develop interesting careers by becoming entrepreneurs. Entrepreneurship provides an attractive alternative for women who bump up against the glass ceiling in male-dominated firms. Many female corporate executives have left their firms to become entrepreneurs to: (1) balance work and family responsibilities; (2) obtain more challenge and autonomy; and (3) avoid unpleasant organization politics.

Similarly, increasing numbers of blacks, Hispanics, and Asian Americans have launched successful entrepreneurial efforts. Entrepreneurship can provide anyone, particularly in the United States, an alternative to the corporate career path. The most recent U.S. Census Bureau data indicates that business ownership by minorities and women has increased significantly.[7] For the period 1997 to 2002, the number of black-owned businesses increased by 45 percent, Hispanic-owned businesses increased by 31 percent, and Asian-owned businesses increased by 24 percent. Female-owned businesses for the period increased by 20 percent.

LOC-In

1 Learning Objective Check-In

Jess, Carol, and Kate are all women entrepreneurs. Jess has three kids and is a single mother. Kate was a former corporate manager who worked in a male-dominated firm and was not advancing to top executive status despite years of hard work. Carol, diplomatic to a fault, simply wanted to remove herself from the cutthroat environment of the corporate world in which she worked previously to start her own company and still serve top clients.

1. *Jess removed herself from the corporate world to enter entrepreneurship in order to ______.*
   a. *make strategic decisions at a firm*
   b. *avoid unpleasant organization politics*
   c. *balance work and family responsibilities*
   d. *obtain more autonomy*
2. *Carol chose entrepreneurship because she wanted to ______.*
   a. *make strategic decisions at a firm*
   b. *obtain more autonomy and challenge at work*
   c. *balance work and family responsibilities*
   d. *avoid unpleasant organization politics*
3. *Kate chose entrepreneurship because she wanted to ______.*
   a. *avoid unpleasant organization politics*
   b. *advance beyond the "glass ceiling"*
   c. *obtain more autonomy and challenge at work*
   d. *achieve personal fulfillment through innovation*

Entrepreneurial Characteristics and Skills

There are many motives for starting a new business. Some entrepreneurs learn from successful family role models. A few stumble onto an entrepreneurial career path by inventing a new product and building a business around it, as did Steven Jobs and Steve Wozniak with the first prototype of the Apple computer. Others become dissatisfied with corporate careers and discover that entrepreneurship provides an attractive set of challenges and rewards.

Manager's Notebook 8.2 on page 315 presents basic categories that have been used to segment entrepreneurs into various types. Whatever the type of entrepreneur, there appear to be common characteristics important for success. As depicted in Figure 8.1 on page 315, key entrepreneur characteristics underlying success can be divided into categories of *personal characteristics* and *skills*. We first discuss the characteristics.

Earl G. Graves, Sr., chief executive officer of Earl G. Graves Ltd., founded Black Enterprise in 1970. His vision was to create a link of commerce and communication between the black professional class and American industry.

Characteristics of Entrepreneurs

Some key characteristics associated with entrepreneurship are a high need for achievement, an internal locus of control, the willingness to take risks, and self-confidence.

Characteristics of Successful Entrepreneurs

People with a *high need for achievement* have a strong desire to solve problems on their own. They enjoy setting goals and achieving them through their own efforts, and like receiving feedback on how they are doing. These characteristics help entrepreneurs to be more proactive and anticipate future problems, needs, or changes.

internal locus of control

A strong belief in one's own ability to succeed, so that one accepts responsibility for outcomes and tries harder after making mistakes.

external locus of control

A strong belief that luck, fate, or factors beyond one's control determine one's progress, causing feelings of helplessness and decreasing intensity of goal-seeking efforts in the face of failure.

An entrepreneur is likely to have an **internal locus of control**, with a strong belief in his or her ability to succeed. When a person with an internal locus of control fails or makes a mistake, the individual is likely to accept responsibility for the outcome and try harder, rather than searching for external reasons to explain the failure. Entrepreneurs are persistent and motivated to overcome barriers that would deter others. People with an **external locus of control** believe that what happens to them is due to luck, fate, or factors beyond their control. When people with an external locus of control fail, they are more likely to feel helpless and are less likely to sustain or intensify their goal-seeking efforts.

An entrepreneur takes on some level of risk when trying to start a new venture. In some cases, entrepreneurs may risk a substantial portion of their own capital as well as funds contributed by family, friends, and other investors. The entrepreneur may leave the security of a corporate career and still be uncertain that the new venture presents a better opportunity. However, entrepreneurs, as a group, may not face quite as much risk of failure as previously thought. A widely held belief has been that 90 percent of entrepreneurial efforts fail in the first year of operation. Current data indicates that 67 percent of new ventures are successful after four years.[8] While this percentage is certainly far from a guarantee, it is not nearly as gloomy as the high 90 percent failure rate that had been previously suggested.

AN ENTREPRENEURIAL CLASSIFICATION SYSTEM

- *The Craftsperson*—has trade or skill or overwhelming desire to do a craft.
- *The Opportunist*—commits to the entrepreneurial effort because it makes business sense.
- *The Inventor*—likes to create and bring new products to market.

These categories are not always mutually exclusive. Many entrepreneurs fit into more than one category. These general categories can still be useful for understanding the basic motives and approaches used by entrepreneurs. A craftsperson may not have a good handle on the financial realities of his/her new business venture. Likewise, an opportunist may have little understanding or concern for the skill and care that might be needed to produce the product or provide the service. Still, both have certain drives which may enable them to succeed.

Source: R. J. Kuntze, "The Dark Side of Multilevel Marketing: Appeals to the Symbolically Incomplete." Dissertation at Arizona State University, 2001.

8.2 manager's notebook

FIGURE 8.1

Key Entrepreneur Characteristics for Success

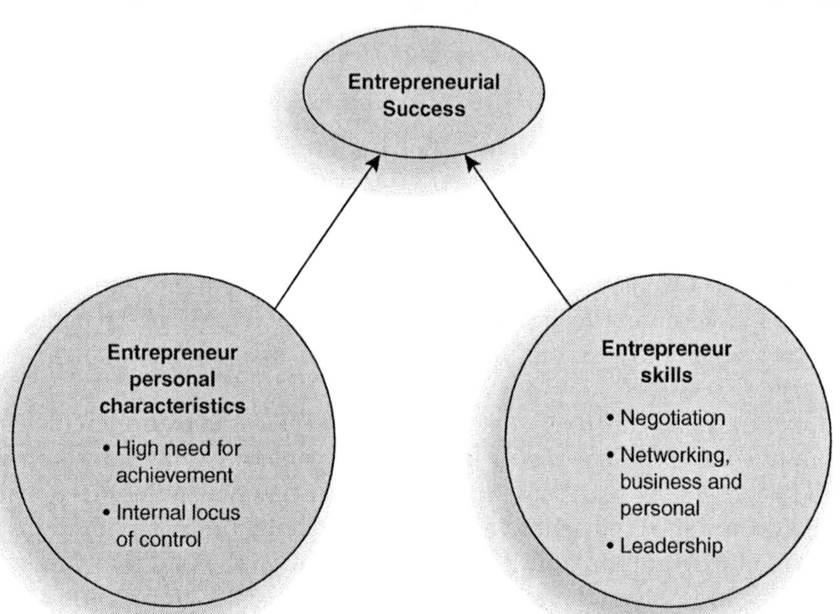

Entrepreneurs feel certain they can master the skills needed to run a business and that they can overcome unforeseen obstacles. This self-confidence can be used to energize and motivate others. Self-confidence enables entrepreneurs to improvise and find novel solutions to business problems that might discourage people who are more self-critical.

Michael Dell, the entrepreneur who founded Dell Computer, exhibits all of these characteristics. His background and reasons for launching his company are described in Management Close-Up 8.1 on page 316.

Entrepreneurs acquire these characteristics in various ways. Some learn them from family role models. Others are exposed to entrepreneurs in school, work, or social activities. Most people have opportunities to develop entrepreneurial characteristics by imitating others who have these characteristics.

8.1 MANAGEMENT CLOSE-UP

Michael Dell, Founder and CEO, Dell Computer Corporation

THEME: CUSTOMER FOCUS

Michael Dell is founder and CEO of Austin-based Dell Computer Corporation, a widely recognized U.S. computer company with over 61,000 employees and over $40 billion in revenues for 2005. With a net worth of $17 billion, he is the wealthiest person in Texas. Dell's idea was to sell computers directly to the customer by telephone, avoiding costly middlemen and saving the customer money. Rather than building computers to distribute to retail outlets and carrying large inventories of finished computers and parts to build them, he built computers to order. The company saved money by having a lean, just-in-time inventory of parts from suppliers. Michael Dell pioneered the use of the Internet as a distribution channel for selling computers, and Dell now sells more computers on the Internet than any other company.

Dell was born into a Houston family of high achievers. His father was an orthodontist, his mother a stockbroker. When Michael was 8 years old he applied for a high school equivalency exam, and by age 13 he started a mail order stamp-trading business. When Dell was 16 he started selling subscriptions to the *Houston Post* by phone and became salesman of the month shortly after. A year later he was earning $18,000 annually supervising fellow high school students as they sold subscriptions.

At a young age Dell became very interested in computers. While spending a lot of time around computer retail stores, he realized that these stores were charging up to a 40 percent markup on their products. Even though these stores were charging a high amount for their computers, their service was not very good. Dell realized that he could buy the products directly from the manufacturer, sell them cheaply to the customer, provide better service, and completely eliminate the retail store.

Dell decided to start his computer business when he was just a freshman at the University of Texas at Austin. Working out of his dorm room, Dell sold computers built to order to interested buyers. Three months later, Dell had racked up sales of $181,000. Two years later, when Dell turned 20, the company reached $34 million in sales.

Michael Dell has remained at the helm of Dell Computer from the start, becoming one of the youngest CEOs of a major U.S. corporation while still in his twenties.

Sources: A. Serwer, "Michael Dell Rocks," *Fortune*, May 11, 1998, pp. 59–70; A. Serwer, "Michael Dell Turns the PC World Inside Out," *Fortune*, September 8, 1997, pp. 76–86; D. F. Kuratko and R. M. Hodgetts, *Entrepreneurship*, 2nd ed., Fort Worth: Dryden Press, 1992, p. 72; www.dell.com.

Entrepreneurial Skills

Just as there are certain personal characteristics that are likely to be found in entrepreneurs, there are also skills which are related to success. An entrepreneur utilizes a variety of business skills to create and operate an enterprise. Among these are negotiation skills, networking skills, and leadership skills.

NEGOTIATION SKILLS Whenever an exchange of goods or services between two or more parties takes place, quality negotiation skills are helpful. A party who applies negotiation skills effectively ensures favorable terms for both parties by finding common ground. This problem-solving style of negotiation, also referred to as *win–win* negotiating, requires the individual to act in good faith to forge a relationship based on trust and cooperation. This makes it easier to discover a basis of exchange that is attractive to both parties. More information on negotiation skills is provided in Chapter 14.

Entrepreneurs use negotiation skills to obtain resources needed to launch and maintain a company. Among the situations that require negotiation skills are:

- Borrowing money from a bank at good terms to finance business expansion.
- Locking into an attractive, long-term lease to control office space expenses.
- Obtaining a low price on raw materials from a supplier to gain a cost advantage over competitors.
- Negotiating employment contracts to attract and retain key executives.

Scott Jochim turned a high school paper on auctions into his first business. He has established three successful companies since then and finds entrepreneurship to be empowering. He is currently president of Digital Tech Frontier, a technology company he started at age 23. The company provides virtual-reality technology for education, entertainment, and therapy. Scott's company has built a revenue in the six-figure range, but he says, "If I can get a cancer patient to write me and say I made chemo more bearable, that makes everything I've done worth it."

NETWORKING SKILLS Gathering information and building alliances requires quality networking skills. These are applied to both personal and business networks.

A **personal network** is based on relationships between the entrepreneur and other entrepreneurs, suppliers, creditors, investors, friends, former professors, and others. These personal contacts can help an entrepreneur make effective decisions by providing information that reduces uncertainty for the business. For example,

personal network

The relationships between an entrepreneur and other parties, including other entrepreneurs, suppliers, creditors, investors, friends, former colleagues, and others.

- A fellow entrepreneur can help locate a wealthy interested private investor (sometimes referred to as a "business angel") to provide scarce capital.
- A former professor may provide free technical consulting advice and student volunteers to help develop a marketing strategy for the new venture.
- A banker may be able to locate a skilled executive who could provide complementary management skills to the entrepreneurship at a critical stage of growth.
- Talks with fellow entrepreneurs who have been through the process of building a business from the ground up can provide invaluable feedback and emotional support.

Entrepreneurs build personal networks by actively seeking out individuals with similar interests, staying in touch with them, and looking for opportunities to make the relationship mutually satisfying. By being responsive to the needs and interests of the people in their personal networks, entrepreneurs build trust and goodwill. A personal network can be formed through participation in professional societies, business clubs, charitable organizations, trade fairs, and networks of entrepreneurs. Skills for Managing 8.1 on page 318 presents an opportunity to analyze and improve your networking skills.

8.1

NETWORKING SKILLS

Reflect on a meeting of a professional student club or organization that you have recently attended.

1. What was your purpose for attending this meeting?
2. Did you have any specific goals in mind in terms of the kinds of people you hoped to meet and how you hoped to benefit from the meeting?
3. How many people did you meet at the meeting?
4. How many of these new acquaintances did you connect with so that there was a possibility for a relationship to emerge?
5. How many people did you follow up with a phone call after the meeting?
6. What was the basis of your relationship with these new contacts?
7. Have you continued to keep in touch with these new contacts? If not, why not?

Instructions: Answer the preceding questions individually. Then form small groups of four to five students. Share your experiences in networking with each other. Then work together to answer the following questions. If time permits, attend a professional meeting after developing some network strategies and report back to the group with your experiences.

Discussion Questions

1. What are some effective practices that can be used to network with other people?
2. How can you avoid getting entangled in too many fruitless network relationships that are not mutually beneficial?
3. What are some ways to keep your network vital so that you can feel free to tap your network for opportunities when the time comes and you are in need of help?

Source: From *Entrepreneurship*, by M. J. Dollinger. Copyright © 1995 The McGraw-Hill Companies, Inc. Reprinted with permission.

business network

A firm's alliances formed with other businesses to achieve mutually beneficial goals.

Networking skills can come in handy in developing useful business alliances. A **business network** is a set of alliances forged with other businesses to achieve mutually beneficial goals. A larger company may enter a partnership with a small entrepreneurship in order to gain some of the benefits of the new and innovative product or service the entrepreneurship is developing. Through licensing agreements that provide limited access to the technology or strategic alliances to pool resources, a new company may gain access to a larger corporation's marketing and finance professionals or may obtain capital to help enter markets that are difficult to reach. This includes acquiring shelf space in Wal-Mart or having a national direct sales force call on customers.

Microsoft entered a strategic alliance with IBM in 1980 to provide DOS-based operating systems for the new IBM personal computer. This strategic alliance ensured the success of Microsoft and greatly enabled it to set the technology standard for personal computer operating systems, which resulted in huge profits for Microsoft.

LEADERSHIP SKILLS Quality leaders provide a shared vision for others to work toward common goals. As leaders, entrepreneurs inspire and motivate employees to do what is good for the enterprise, even when it is not in their short-term interests. For example, employees in a start-up company are likely to work extremely long hours for modest pay. The entrepreneur depends on leadership skills to bolster employee morale and guide the enterprise toward the objectives, overcoming obstacles that stand in the way.

MANAGEMENT IS EVERYONE'S BUSINESS 8.1

Working as an Individual Starting a new business requires a great deal of confidence. You must overcome many obstacles, weather naysayers, generate necessary funding, the list goes on and on. Unfortunately, confidence can sometimes get in the way of prudent business decisions and money is seldom sufficient when you are starting out. Here are some suggestions to help you as an entrepreneur starting a business.

- *Establish an advisory board.* Those who succeed at entrepreneurship are very confident, perhaps overconfident. A high level of confidence is generally a positive thing, but it can lead to bad business decisions based on overly optimistic assessments and failure to examine all information.
- *Keep fixed costs low.* Until there is consistent revenue, it is only rational to keep fixed costs to a minimum. Some ways to minimize fixed costs include:
  - Work out of a home office, rather than signing a lease for a commercial office.
  - Initially use consultants who are paid on the basis of completed projects, rather than hiring employees who are paid salaries.
  - Have customers pay in advance for raw materials, rather than purchasing an inventory of raw materials before you have identified a customer.

Starting a business is a difficult prospect. In addition to possessing certain personal characteristics and skills, there are steps that an entrepreneur should take to help assure the success of the new business. Management Is Everyone's Business 8.1 above offers some simple but important recommendations that should enhance your success as an individual entrepreneur.

LOC-In

2 Learning Objective Check-In

Patrick is opening his own business. He believes that he has the ability to succeed and he takes responsibility for how his life turns out. Patrick has an overwhelming desire to practice woodworking.

1. *According to the classification system of entrepreneurship, we saw in Manager's Notebook 8.2, we would say that Patrick is a(n) ______.*
   a. *craftsperson*
   b. *opportunist*
   c. *investor*
   d. *inventor*
2. *Patrick's ______ tells us that he believes he has personal responsibility for the outcomes in his life.*
   a. *entrepreneurial spirit*
   b. *negotiation skills*
   c. *external locus of control*
   d *internal locus of control*

Starting and Managing an Entrepreneurial Venture

An entrepreneurial venture begins with an idea. The next steps are developing a business plan, selecting the most appropriate type of legal structure to operate under, obtaining financing, and dealing with growth and expansion. Many entrepreneurial ventures are new businesses, rather than being franchises or spin-offs.

New Business Ideas

Entrepreneurs get ideas for new businesses from many different sources, including

- Newspapers, magazines, and trade journals that identify market trends.
- Inventions or discoveries that provide products or services faster, better, cheaper, or with more features. Corporations like the 3M Company give technologists unstructured time to experiment, hoping for the discovery of the next Post-it Notes.

8.2 MANAGEMENT CLOSE-UP

Of Kids and Mice: Making Mice Work for Children

THEME: CUSTOMER FOCUS

Many kids are being exposed to computers at a very young age. Unfortunately their fine motor skills aren't always up to the task. Moving a mouse around that is too big for your hand can be very frustrating. Why not make a mouse that fits a child's hand and is cute and engaging at the same time? That's exactly what Susan Giles thought when she saw the frustration of her 4-year-old granddaughter trying to operate a computer. Giles created a rounder and smaller mouse. She decorated each one to look like a cute bug or dinosaur and gave them cute names. The venture turned out to be so successful that she devoted herself full time to running Kidz Mouse. How successful is the company? Giles keeps numbers concerning the business to herself. She did however sign a contract with Nickelodeon to make mice based on network characters such as SpongeBob Square Pants and Blues Clues. Another indicator of success is that the mice can now be found at outlets such as CompUSA and Best Buy, among others.

Source: M. Cassidy, "Creative Marketing: The Mouse Tap," *Detroit Free Press*, December 5, 2002, accessed February 19, 2003, at www.freep.com/money/tech/mice5_20021205.htm; www.kidzmouse.com, accessed December 28, 2005.

- Trade shows and exhibitions, where new products and innovations are displayed.
- Hobbies, such as jogging, bicycling, or skiing, as was the case with new companies that marketed running shoes (Nike), mountain bicycles (Cannondale), and snowboards (Burton).
- Family members, including children, such as in the design of video games, educational toys, and the baby jogger that lets people combine jogging with taking the baby out. (See Management Close-Up 8.2 above for an example of an entrepreneur whose business was inspired by her children.)
- Entrepreneurship courses in business schools. Babson University in Wellesley, Massachusetts, sponsors a business plan contest between teams of business students who compete for prize money. Student entrepreneurs with promising business plans are likely to attract the attention of investors.

Why Entrepreneurs Fail

Entrepreneurial ventures can fail if the business idea is poorly implemented. The most common reasons for business failure include:

- *Lack of capital.* When an entrepreneur underestimates the need for capital and assumes more debt than can be repaid, the new business is in trouble. Many businesses fail because investors do not purchase enough stock during the initial public offering to cover accumulated debts.
- *Poor knowledge of the market.* An entrepreneur can miscalculate the appeal of the product or service. This often occurs when an inventor "falls in love" with an invention and expects consumers to do so as well.
- *Faulty product design.* Design or other features of a product can be rejected by consumers. This was the case with word processing products sold by Wang Computer, which were linked to mainframe computers and were

much more expensive than rival products that were driven by personal computers. Wang was unable to sell enough of its products and went out of business.

- *Human resource problems.* Entrepreneurs may select employees who do not support the goals of the business. In a family business, there is the potential for divorce or sibling rivalry to divide workers into feuding factions.
- *Poor understanding of the competition.* Entrepreneurs should study their competitors and try to understand their interests. Firmly entrenched businesses may react aggressively and use price cuts or special discounts to try to drive new competitors out of business. Any time a new grocery store opens, local competitors will make dramatic efforts to keep customers.

Sometimes businesses exit the market for reasons other than failure. An entrepreneur may sell the business to a competitor for a good price or close it because a more attractive business opportunity has come along.

LOC-In

3 Learning Objective Check-In

1. *Carlita has always had trouble using the standard adjustable headphones that come with electronic devices she has purchased in the past. They are either too stiff or too loose, or else they do not adjust to be small enough. Carlita has an idea for developing easily adjustable audio and video equipment for adults and children for use with standard electronic equipment, including video game equipment. She thinks that she might be able to turn her idea into a new business venture. The source of Carlita's idea is ______.*
   a. *newspapers, magazines, and trade journals*
   b. *inventions or discoveries*
   c. *trade shows and exhibitions*
   d. *personal hobbies or discoveries*

Business Plan

Once an entrepreneur develops an idea for a new business venture, the next critical step is to prepare a **business plan**, which is a blueprint that maps out the business strategy for entering markets and explains the business to potential investors. A business plan details the strategies and tactics needed to minimize the enterprise's risk of failure, which is highest during the early stages.

business plan

The business's blueprint that maps out its business strategy for entering markets and that explains the business to potential investors.

Key components of the business plan include:

- A description of the product or service.
- An analysis of market trends and potential competitors.
- An estimated price for the product or service.
- An estimate of the time it will take to generate profits.
- A plan for manufacturing the product.
- A plan for growth and expansion of the business.
- Sources of funding.
- A plan for obtaining financing.
- An approach for putting an effective management team in place.

A detailed outline for creating a business plan appears in Figure 8.2 on page 323.

Legal Forms

Entrepreneurs can select from three different legal forms when launching a new enterprise. The legal forms are a proprietorship, a partnership, and a corporation. An entrepreneur should consider tax implications, willingness to accept personal liability, and the ease of raising capital for the business before making this important decision.

video: THE ENTREPRENEURIAL MANAGER

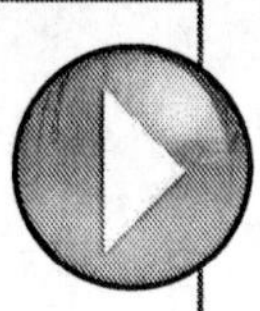

Auntie Anne's

Summary

Auntie Anne's began in Lancaster, Pennsylvania, often called the "Heart of Amish Country." In almost 15 years, the company has opened over 800 franchises worldwide. It began in the Downingtown Farmer's Market in 1988. Having no money, but wanting to help her husband open a free family resource and counseling center, Anne Beiler borrowed $6,000 to buy a concession stand in that farmer's market, selling the original Auntie Anne's pretzels, lemonade, and other goodies. Anne tasted the soft pretzel recipe and decided it just wouldn't do at first. Her husband, Jonas, helped her modify the recipe, and they were an instant success. Eventually they eliminated pizza and ice cream and focused on pretzels. At first, friends and family asked if they could sell the pretzels at other locations. By the time there were 40 different locations, Anne decided they needed to turn what they had into an official business. They considered several options, including a sole proprietorship, a partnership, and a corporation. The alternative they settled on, however, was the franchise.

The Beilers looked to outside help in setting up an official franchise. A franchise is an arrangement where there is less risk for the potential partners. The marketing assistance is another advantage. Additionally, the ownership advantages are virtually unlimited. There is high brand recognition cultivated by the franchise company. There is also good training which is managed by the larger company. Disadvantages to franchising include large start-up costs, shared profits, management regulations (also seen as an advantage for Auntie Anne's because of quality control support), coattail effects (not an issue for Auntie Anne's), restrictions on selling (owners cannot just sell the franchise to anyone), and fraudulent franchisers. Luckily for Auntie Anne's, there have been only two litigation issues in 30 years of operation.

Diversity, e-commerce, technology, and international markets are important factors for business owners today. Anne is an inspiration for many women because she serves as a good example of how to develop a company oneself and be successful. For Auntie Anne's, e-commerce is a growing area of the business, if not a very large one right now. The company operates franchises in all areas of the world.

Discussion Questions

1. How did Anne Beiler start her pretzel business? How did she get the idea to turn it into an entrepreneurial venture?
2. What legal form was right for Auntie Anne's? What are the pros and cons of this arrangement?
3. How is the company using technology to advance the business?

proprietorship

A form of business that is owned by one person.

partnership

A form of business that is an association of two or more persons acting as co-owners of a business.

PROPRIETORSHIP Many new businesses are owned by single individuals. **Proprietorships** are easy to form and require a minimum of paperwork. The owner keeps all of the profits and makes all of the important decisions without having to get the approval of co-owners.

A proprietorship is limited to one person, which restricts the owner from obtaining more than limited amounts of credit and capital. Another drawback is that the sole owner has unlimited liability, which means that the personal assets of the owner may be at stake in a lawsuit. About 74 percent of all U.S. businesses are proprietorships, though revenues and profits are relatively small compared to other forms of ownership.

PARTNERSHIP An association of two or more persons acting as co-owners of a business creates a **partnership**. Each partner provides resources and skills and shares in the profits. A partnership can raise more capital than a proprietorship

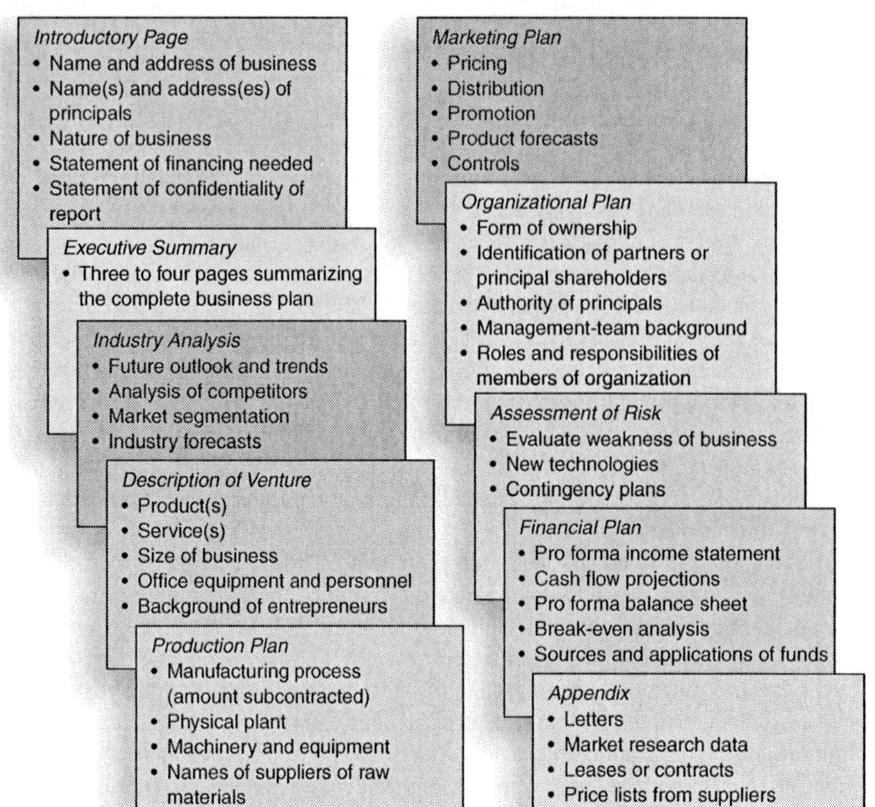

FIGURE 8.2

Outline of a Business Plan

Source: From *Entrepreneurship*, 4th ed., by R. Hisrich and M. Peters. Copyright © 1998 The McGraw-Hill Companies, Inc. Reprinted with permission.

and can provide complementary skills that can create more opportunity for the enterprise. For example, one partner of a small Los Angeles law firm is skillful at generating new clients from his extensive networks in the local bar association, while the other is skilled at providing meticulous legal research that results in a high court success rate. The synergy between these two law partners results in more profits than would be possible if each were operating alone.

While partnerships are easy to start and are subject to few government regulations, they do have some drawbacks. Each partner is responsible for the acts of the other partners. If one partner makes a bad business decision, the other partners are liable. In other words, each owner's personal assets are at risk in a lawsuit or to pay off debts. If the partners disagree about important goals of the business, the firm may become paralyzed or fail. If one of the partners dies, a partnership will be in jeopardy unless provisions for the other partners to buy out the deceased partner's share have been made. Nonetheless, some large and successful businesses use the partnership legal structure. Large accounting firms such as Arthur Andersen have more than 1,000 partners in offices around the globe.

CORPORATION A **corporation** is a legal entity separate from the individuals who own it. A corporation receives limited rights to operate from the state or government that provides its charter. A corporation is more complex and costly to form and operate than a proprietorship or a partnership. Since its activities are regulated by the government, many records must be kept and regularly filed with the government.

corporation

A form of business that is a legal entity separate from the individuals who own it.

table 8.1

Partnership and Corporation Forms of Ownership

ADVANTAGES	DISADVANTAGES
Partnership	
Ease of formation	Unlimited liability for firm's debt
Direct share of profits	Limited continuity of life of enterprise
Division of labor and management responsibility	Difficulty in obtaining capital
More capital available than in a sole proprietorship	Partners share responsibility for other partners' actions
Less governmental control and regulation	
Corporation	
Owners' liability for the firm's debt limited to their investment	Extensive government regulation of activities
Ease of raising large amounts of capital	High incorporation fees
Ease of transfer of ownership through sales of stock	Corporate capital, profits, dividends and salaries double-taxed
Life of enterprise distinct from owners	Activities limited to those stated in charter

Sources: Adapted from W. Megginson et al., *Small Business Management*, 2nd ed., New York: Irwin/McGraw-Hill, 1997, pp. 74, 78; D. F. Kuratko and R. M. Hodgetts, Entrepreneurship, 2nd ed., Fort Worth: Dryden Press, 1992, p. 208.

The benefit of forming a corporation is limited liability. If the corporation is sued, corporate assets are at risk, but the personal assets of the owners are not. A corporation is separate from the owner. When the owner dies, the corporation continues. Corporations are able to raise more capital than any of the other legal forms of enterprise. Corporations are able to raise capital through the sale of shares of stock to the public or through loans and bonds.

Besides incorporation fees and the additional record-keeping expenses, many corporations are doubly taxed by the government. The corporation pays taxes on its profits, and the owners pay taxes on their dividends. Some other countries do not have this double taxation system, and some firms find it attractive to incorporate in countries that offer advantageous tax treatment. The advantages and disadvantages of partnerships and corporations are summarized in Table 8.1 above.

Sources of Financial Resources

Entrepreneurships require capital to get started. The two principal means of obtaining the resources to fund a new business are debt financing and equity financing. Factors favoring one type of financing over the other include the value of the firm's assets, the interest rate, and the availability of investor funds.

debt financing

A means of obtaining financial resources that involves obtaining a commercial loan and setting up a plan to repay the principal and interest.

bankruptcy

A legal procedure that distributes company assets to creditors and protects the debtor from unfair demands of creditors when the debtor fails to make scheduled loan repayments.

DEBT FINANCING Commercial loans are a common form of **debt financing**. Company leaders must set up a plan to repay the principal and interest. The schedule to repay the loan may be short term, lasting less than one year, or long term. Commercial banks are the principal source of debt financing.

The bank establishes a repayment schedule for the loan and secures the loan with company assets such as inventories, equipment, and machines or real estate. Failure to make the scheduled loan repayments can lead to **bankruptcy**, a legal procedure that distributes company assets to creditors and protects the debtor from unfair demands of creditors. Bankruptcy can hurt the reputation of an entrepreneur and make it difficult to obtain future business loans.

The Kauffman Foundation's Collegiate Entrepreneurship site serves as a repository for the growing amount of information about cross-campus entrepreneurship programs. The foundation's Kauffman Campuses initiative seeks to transform the way colleges and universities make entrepreneurship education available across their campuses, enabling any student, regardless of field of study, to access entrepreneurial training.

An entrepreneur must be careful not to take on too much debt. Excessive debt will result in most of the company's positive cash flow going to retiring the debt rather than growing the business. New ventures that have uncertain cash flows during start-up may not be able to qualify for debt financing.

Other sources of debt financing for more specific purchases are:

- Equipment manufacturers (for example, a computer firm may debt finance a computer system).
- Suppliers (credit may be given on supplies for a fee).
- Credit cards (some businesses were started by overextending several of an owner's credit cards, an expensive way to obtain financing).

equity financing

A means of obtaining financial resources that involves the sale of part of the ownership of the business to investors.

venture capitalists

Financial investors who specialize in making loans to entrepreneurships that have the potential for rapid growth but are in high-risk situations with few assets and would therefore not qualify for commercial bank loans.

EQUITY FINANCING As a business grows, an entrepreneur will most likely combine a mix of debt and equity sources of capital. **Equity financing** is raising money by selling part of the ownership of the business to investors. In equity financing, the entrepreneur shares control of the business with the investors. Equity financing does not require collateral. Sources of equity financing include private investors, venture capitalists, and public offerings in which shares of stock are sold.

Early in the growth of a business, the risk of failure may be great. At this stage, private investors and venture capitalists may be willing to provide equity financing. **Venture capitalists** specialize in making loans to entrepreneurships that have the potential for rapid growth but are in high-risk situations with few assets and would therefore not qualify for commercial bank loans.

Venture capitalists manage pools of money provided by wealthy individuals and institutions seeking to invest in entrepreneurships. High-technology businesses such as software, telecommunications, and biotechnology are particularly attractive to venture capitalists because they anticipate high financial returns from their investment. Microsoft, Compaq Computer, and Intel were started with venture capital financing and made fabulous returns for early investors. Venture capitalists also provide management knowledge, contacts to hire key employees, and financial advice.

public offerings

A means of raising capital by the sale of securities in public markets such as the New York Stock Exchange and NASDAQ.

Public offerings raise capital by selling securities in public markets such as the New York Stock Exchange and NASDAQ. A public offering can provide large infusions of cash to fuel rapid internal growth or to finance a merger or acquisition. One drawback of a public offering is that publicly traded companies must disclose a great deal of information, including quarterly reports on income, balance sheet assets, and use of funds. Competitors can exploit weaknesses that are disclosed in these reports. After a public offering, management decisions are under a higher level of public scrutiny. There is a lower tolerance for management mistakes, and there is increased shareholder pressure for dividends and predictable quarterly profits. Unhappy shareholders can sell their shares, driving down the value of the company. Public offerings generally do not take place until an entrepreneurship achieves a critical mass of about $10 million to $20 million in annual revenue.

Managing Growth

Entrepreneurs manage business growth by establishing benchmarks based on market data and a thorough analysis of the firm's ability to handle increased demand without sacrificing quality. A business plan is an invaluable tool for planning growth targets. These milestones can be used to pace company expansion. The growth of a business reflects the success of the entrepreneurial effort, but can also place stress on the entrepreneur to become an effective manager. Management Is Everyone's Business 8.2 on page 327 provides some suggestions to help you successfully make the shift to managing your business.

Too much growth can put an unbearable strain on the operations of a business. A company that grows too quickly may experience the following:

- The company spends most of its available cash on expansion and has difficulty meeting obligations to creditors. The result is a cash flow crisis.
- Employees are likely to experience stress from such rapid changes as moving to new jobs without training, adjusting to new supervisors and colleagues, and making frequent changes in office locations.
- Accounting and information systems that worked well when the firm was smaller must be replaced with more complicated and sophisticated systems. Current personnel may not be capable of operating these systems, and information may not be available when it is needed.
- Management may no longer be competent to manage a larger or more diverse portfolio of business units or product lines. The board of directors may replace the chief executive officer or other key executives with more experienced managers. To make matters worse, the founder may resist stepping down. In 1985 Steve Jobs, the founder of Apple Computer, was asked to leave by its board, which felt his leadership style was not appropriate for the large company that Apple had become. (Jobs,

MANAGEMENT IS EVERYONE'S BUSINESS 8.2

Working as a Manager As an entrepreneurial business grows, the entrepreneur must adapt and manage an increasingly complex enterprise. Here are some key ideas to help make this transition a success.

- Delegation is a good thing! Many people who start a business like to be in control and it can be difficult for them to share responsibilities and duties. However, delegation is not giving away power or responsibility. It is a way to develop others and to demonstrate your trust and provide opportunity for loyal workers. In addition, delegation can free up needed time for the entrepreneur: time for the work he or she is best at and time for family and needed leisure. An entrepreneur cannot be in all places at once. The inability to delegate can actually be detrimental to the growth of the business.
- Develop formal, consistent, and fair policies for dealing with recurring business issues. As the business grows, management can't be done on an ad hoc basis any longer. Systematic approaches need to be developed so that the entrepreneur won't have to "reinvent the wheel" each time an issue comes up. Processes, such as hiring and performance appraisal, may need to be formalized so that these functions can be done effectively and fairly.
- Consider establishing a board of advisors. As the business grows, advisory board members can provide valuable advice and guidance. The board can provide a sounding board to deal with issues that arise as the business grows.

always the entrepreneur, started another company. In 1997 he returned to Apple—by then under different leadership—with the technology he had developed in the interim and sold it to Apple for $400 million.)

Unchecked growth can threaten the survival of a business venture. For example, James L. Bildner, the founder of J. Bildner & Sons Inc., a specialty food business, expanded rapidly from a single store to a chain of 20 stores after a public offering in 1986. The company ran out of cash because it had built too many stores. Employees started leaving and operations became chaotic. Too many new stores, ineffective new products, attempts to hire too many new people at once, and lack of controls made everything worse. The company experienced large losses, inventory control problems, and the departure of loyal customers. This crisis could have been avoided if the management team had pursued less aggressive growth. Sometimes managers should turn down growth opportunities in an expanding market rather than lose control of the operation.

LOC-In

4 Learning Objective Check-In

Janet's Scallops is a new business that Janet Phillips wants to start within the coming year. She will own the business herself, keeping all the profits and assuming all the risk personally. Furthermore, Janet will obtain a short-term commercial loan and will repay the principal and interest on that loan. If the company grows as she hopes it does, Janet plans to entertain the idea of another type of financing by which she will sell part of the ownership of the business to investors.

1. *Which of the following best describes the type of legal form that Janet's business will assume?*
   - *a. Proprietorship*
   - *b. Corporation*
   - *c. S-Corporation*
   - *d. Partnership*
2. *Which of the following best characterizes the type of financing Janet plans to use in the beginning of her business?*
   - *a. Equity financing*
   - *b. Public offerings*
   - *c. Venture capitalists*
   - *d. Debt financing*
3. *Which of the following represents the type of financing option Janet will entertain if the business is successful and grows in the future?*
   - *a. Debt financing*
   - *b. Venture capitalists*
   - *c. Equity financing*
   - *d. Public offerings*

Alternative Forms of Entrepreneurship

This chapter has focused on *independent entrepreneurship*. Alternatives to this form of entrepreneurship are intrapreneurship, spin-offs, and franchising. In general, these alternative forms involve smaller risks than independent entrepreneurship.

Intrapreneurship

intrapreneurship

A form of business organization in which new business units are developed within a larger corporate structure in order to deploy the firm's resources to market a new product or service; also called corporate entrepreneurship.

The development of new business units within a larger corporate structure in order to deploy the firm's resources to market a new product or service is **intrapreneurship**, or *corporate entrepreneurship*. Some large companies develop cultures that foster innovation and the nurturing of new businesses. The 3M Company maintains a corporate goal that requires over 30 percent of corporate sales to come from products less than four years old. The technical staff is encouraged to devote 15 percent of its time to experimentation in new product designs that are peripheral to the projects they have been assigned to work on. These policies support a culture of innovation that has resulted in a steady stream of internally developed new products at the 3M Company.

When Apple showed the world that there was a large market for personal computers, IBM saw the need to design its own personal computer to challenge the Apple computer. The IBM Personal Computer was developed in a separate business unit located in Florida and isolated from the rest of the company. To build, test, and market launch the IBM PC in only 12 months, the IBM Personal Computer unit used standard electronic components and systems, rather than using all-IBM manufactured components as was typical in the company.

In the 1990s the National Broadcasting Company (NBC), the television network owned by General Electric, launched CNBC, a cable television network that provided financial news 24 hours a day. The launch coincided with the 1990s bull market that generated a large demand for televised financial news. Within a few years CNBC was profitable and successful, attracting a highly desirable audience of wealthy executives and investors.

An advantage of intrapreneurship is that the company provides funding and corporate resources that an independent entrepreneur cannot gather. The intrapreneuring corporate engineer or manager does not have to abandon a corporate career to manage the new venture. On the other hand, a successful *intrapreneur* within a corporation usually does not receive the financial rewards that might be generated by an independent entrepreneurship.

Spin-Offs

spin-off

An independent entrepreneurship that produces a product or service that originated in a large company.

Sometimes a new product developed by a corporation does not fit with the company's established products. A group of managers may decide to create a new business for this product rather than forgo the opportunity to market it. A **spin-off** is an independent entrepreneurship that produces a product or service that originated in a large company. Spin-offs are typical of technology companies, which must develop a steady stream of new products to keep up with competitors. Some of the new technologies do not fit with the company's core competencies, providing the opportunity for spin-offs.

Xerox's Palo Alto Research Center (PARC) is a laboratory located in California's Silicon Valley that develops new optical imaging products that fit with the core competencies of Xerox. Occasionally, new technologies that do not fit with other Xerox products are spawned in this research laboratory. Xerox encourages

8.3 MANAGEMENT CLOSE-UP

From Outsourcing to Franchising: Capitalizing on the Entrepreneurial Spirit

THEME: DEALING WITH CHANGE

Yorkshire Electricity is an electric utility company located in the U.K. As with many utility companies around the globe, Yorkshire experienced great pressure to reduce costs and increase productivity. Government shareholder pressure resulted in the top management at Yorkshire cutting staff and looking for reengineering options. Maintenance was a major cost in the utility company since 15,000 operational sites were being maintained by a department that couldn't compete with the external marketplace in terms of productivity and cost. The immediate solution appeared to be outsourcing the maintenance function. However, there were many skilled people employed by the utility that were the best in their trade. It did not seem advisable to lose that valuable resource. Instead, the management team developed a novel approach to achieving private sector productivity and costs: They set up a franchise model.

Yorkshire Electricity established an organization called Freedom Maintenance in which people stillwork for the utility, but as franchisees, not as employees. It took two years to gain the approval of the board of directors and the union. Freedom Maintenance started with 55 franchises in 1996 and now has approximately 500 franchises.

The franchises are responsible for their own tools, vehicles, and materials. The Freedom organization helps out by handling some administrative work, such as invoicing and collection, on behalf of the franchises. The process has created hundreds of new businesses that work independently, but with some assistance from the overall organization. The model has allowed some former Yorkshire employees to exercise their skills along with an entrepreneurial spirit. One franchiser now employs eight people and relies on his former employer for less than 50 percent of his business. The self-employment model has worked well for Yorkshire Electricity. The company has realized a 20 percent savings in maintenance costs since establishing the franchise model. The model has worked so well in the United Kingdom, Freedom is promoting the approach in the electric utility industry in the United States.

Source: B. Mottram, S. Rigby, and A. Webster, "The Freedom to Call Your Own Shots," *Transmission & Distribution World* 55 (January 2003).

the formation of spin-offs when the technology has commercial potential. In some cases, Xerox forms a partnership with the managers who start the spin-off. For example, when a security product that encrypts messages for cellular phones was developed in the PARC laboratories, Xerox created a spin-off called Semaphore Communications to manufacture and market the device.

Dippin' Dots franchises sell tiny beads of "flash-frozen" ice cream in many flavors and colors. In January 2005, Dippin' Dots ranked 93rd on *Entrepreneur Magazine's* Franchise 500 list. A Dippin' Dots franchise currently costs $12,500 plus other costs.

Franchises

When a business with an established name and product is sold to additional owners along with the rights to distribute the product, a franchise operation is created. Franchising is particularly prevalent in the retail service sector of the economy, such as in the restaurant, hotel, and retail businesses. McDonald's, Taco Bell, Subway, Quality Inn, Dunkin' Donuts, Radio Shack, and Midas are well-known franchises. Franchising can also occur in unexpected situations. See Management Close-Up 8.3 above for a description of franchising in the public sector that proved effective and saved jobs from being outsourced.

In franchising, an entrepreneur assumes fewer risks because the franchise can provide: (1) a product or service with an established market and favorable image; (2) management training and assistance in operating the business; (3) economies of scale for advertising and purchasing; (4) operating and structural

LOC-In

5 Learning Objective Check-In

1. *Walton's is a large corporation in which new business units are developed within the larger corporate structure in order to deploy Walton's resources to market new products and services. This is an example of ______.*
   a. *proprietorship*
   b. *intrapreneurship*
   c. *spin-offs*
   d. *a franchise*

controls; and (5) financial assistance. The franchising company sells the distribution rights for a limited geographic area to the entrepreneur for a fee plus a share of the revenues.

Sometimes franchising companies fail to provide promised services. The franchise company may oversell franchise rights in a geographic location, making it difficult for an entrepreneur to profit. Such conflicts of interests can result in lengthy courtroom battles.

Innovation

Innovation is a key to long-term success. Exploring and developing new technologies and new ways of doing things are vital to the future viability of an organization.[9] Entrepreneurs often pursue innovative ideas in their new business ventures. They may come up with ideas and pursue them when an organization decides that the time and cost of development are just too great.

However, as pointed out earlier, entrepreneurship is often about rather modest and incremental change to a product or service, rather than a radical change. Further, larger organizations may embrace and encourage innovation. While innovation and entreprenuership are related concepts, they are basically separate and distinct issues. Whether you have entrepreneurial aspirations or want to work in a corporate environment, you are likely to find yourself in situations that call for *innovation*.

What Is Innovation?

Fundamentally, innovation is doing something differently. As Michael Tushman, professor of management at Harvard Business School, describes it,[10] innovation can involve *radical* or *incremental* change. Radical innovations often make prior technologies obsolete. For example, digital compact discs have all but replaced cassette tapes and require a compact disc player to use them. Alternatively, incremental innovations are generally improvements of existing products that usually do *not* render prior products or technologies obsolete. Examples include smaller cell phones or even Caffeine-Free Coke. So while it may be difficult to find cassette tapes in your local record store due to the radical innovation of the CD, both Coke and Caffeine-Free Coke can easily be had at your local supermarket.

Whether a change is radical or incremental, it is not just the change that is important or that defines an innovation. Certainly, the change or invention is a critical component, but an invention, by itself, does not make for innovation. A description of innovation used by 3M, a company known for innovation, is a new idea together with action or implementation that has a bottom-line impact.[11] As illustrated in Figure 8.3 on page 331, an innovation requires both a change, such as a new product or service, and implementation that results in positive impact. In other words, an innovation is more than just a novel idea or product; an innovation has to add value and somehow result in positive gain or improvement. Without adding value, a new idea or product could be just a novel invention, but would not qualify as an innovation. To be an innovator, you must find a way to

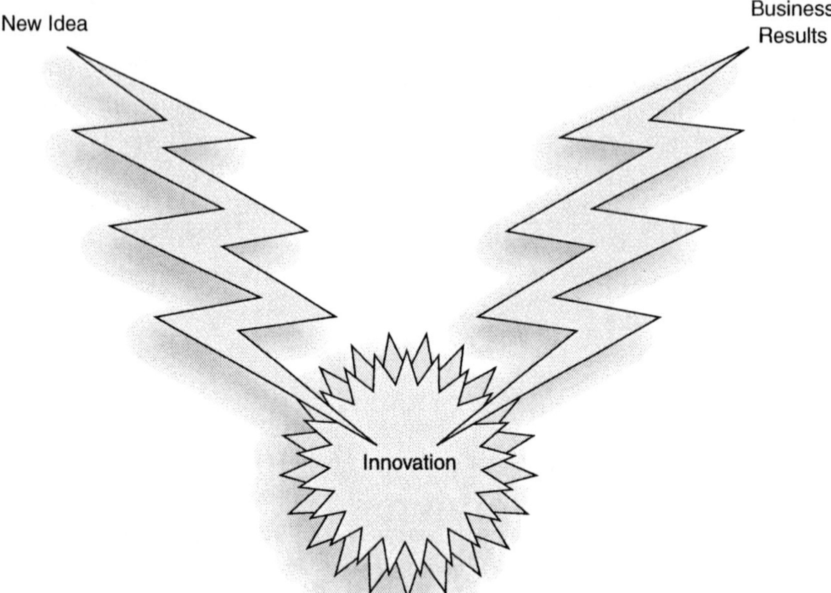

FIGURE 8.3

Innovation Requires Two Key Ingredients

implement your idea as a cost-effective or commercially viable product or service. Consider, for example, the Segway people mover. It is, no doubt, a novel invention, but a couple of years after its creation, can it be considered an innovation? At the time of its creation, Segway supporters envisioned cities being redesigned to accommodate the machine and the use of the Segway as a replacement for the automobile for short trips.[12] Today, Segways are being used in only limited situations and, chances are, you do not see any of them in regular use. The Segway is a neat invention, but it hasn't had a socioeconomic impact—it hasn't changed people's lives or what they buy. Novelty without a tangible return is not an innovation. In contrast, going from diapers to disposable diapers may have been a mundane and simple change, as inventions go, but it has proven to be major innovation.[13]

So, having ideas without the ability to execute them isn't of much business use. Management Close-Up 8.4 on page 332 presents an invention that would seem to have great innovation potential. However, the commercial viability of the product has yet to be proven. Skills for Managing 8.2 on page 333 invites you to take a closer look at the innovation and consider its current status as a potential product.

LOC-In

6 Learning Objective Check-In

1. *William thinks he has developed a composite material that could replace glass windows in houses where tornadoes are prevalent. While the material is more expensive than glass, it is 100 times more durable, and is practically shatter-proof. As an added bonus, it is naturally UV-resistant due to one of the chemicals used in producing the product. Given what you know about William's material, what kind of innovation do you think it represents for people living in tornado areas of the country?*
   a. *Incremental*
   b. *Distributive*
   c. *Radical*
   d. *New generation*

The Importance of Innovation

Innovation is playing a more important and central role in many organizations. A recent survey of senior executives from around the world concluded that innovation has become essential to success in their industries.[14] The importance

Electronic Ink: The Next Big Thing?

THEME: DEALING WITH CHANGE

E Ink is a Massachusetts Institute of Technology spin-off that, in 2002, received $25 million in fourth-round venture funding from Toppan Printing. At the end of 2005, E Ink corporation received the "Best of Small Tech" award, an honor given to companies that have made particularly noteworthy achievements. What was E Ink working on that merited that kind of investment and recognition? Electronic ink—a product that promises fundamental change in how we communicate. Electronic ink is a new way to form characters that can be presented on paper-thin screens. Monitors and handheld devices using electronic ink displays would have screens that are five times brighter and use 90 percent less energy than current displays. Perhaps the most wide-ranging application for electronic ink is a new form for books and newspapers.

Just what is electronic ink? Electronic ink is composed of millions of microcapsules, each about the diameter of a human hair. Within each microcapsule are positively charged white particles and negatively charged black particles suspended in a clear fluid. When a negative electric field is applied, the white particles move to the top of the microcapsule where they become visible to the user. At the same time, an opposite electric field pulls the black particles to the bottom of the microcapsules where they are hidden. By reversing this process, the black particles appear at the top of the capsule, which now makes the surface appear dark at that spot. E Ink laminates these microcapsules to a plastic sheet which is then sold to customers as a film product called Imaging Film.™

Because the film developed by E Ink is inherently flexible, E Ink is part of an effort by the leading electronics manufacturers to develop flexible thin-film transistors. By combining E Ink's Imaging Film with flexible TFTs, the dream of flexible electronic paper that would mimic the pages of newspapers or books can be realized.

The vision that E Ink hopes to bring to reality is the contents of books and newspapers being delivered electronically. A newspaper subscription could, for example, mean an electronic delivery of the newspaper via a radio frequency receiver attached to the electronic ink pages. The content of the paper would appear on the plastic pages until the new edition of the "paper" was delivered. Note, reading the newspaper or book would not involve scrolling down a monitor and the content would be highly portable, just as with a paper-based product. Further, the electronic paper can be reused indefinitely without cutting down any trees to make paper.

Sources: Adapted from C. T. Heun, "New 'Ink' Veers Display toward the Good Old Look," *Informationweek*, February 11, 2002, p. 18; B. Schmitt, "Growth Signs for New Ink," *ChemicalWeek* 164 (February 27, 2002), p. 46; www.eink.com, accessed December 29, 2005.

being placed on innovation may reflect a shift in the economic paradigm. In recent years the focus has been on quality and consistency of execution. However, business success may now be more tied to providing innovations that respond to customer needs. In broad terms, you might think of the current situation as shifting from quality and price as key drivers to creativity.[15] It is not that quality and price are irrelevant; it is that they are assumed. What can differentiate and underlie success in the marketplace is innovation. One of the best examples of a company that is succeeding based on creativity and innovation is Apple. The company is continually bringing new innovations to its iPod, reducing size and increasing capability to include video.

8.2

ELECTRONIC INK: FROM COOL INVENTION TO COMMERCIAL PRODUCT?

As described in Management Close-Up 8.4, electronic ink has the potential to replace paper, save trees, and disseminate information immediately. These possible outcomes, among others, as well as the potential market have probably been key to enticing venture capital to E Ink.

Discussion Questions

1. Is electronic paper a radical or incremental change? Defend your judgment.
2. Evaluate the potential market for electronic paper. Do you think it is a commercially viable innovation? Why or why not?

Internet Research Questions

1. The market for electronic paper has some competitors (such as Gyricon media applying the technology to signs and Dow Chemical working on plastic light-emitting diodes). Look for current information on these competitors and on E Ink. Do you think the market is differentiated enough that each company will have its own niche or do you think that there will be a competitive struggle for dominance in the market?
2. A key to successfully launching a new innovation is protecting the idea from possible competitors. How did E Ink protect the electronic paper technology? Do you think protecting an innovation is a necessary expense?
3. Assess the current status of E Ink. Does the company seem close to making electronic paper a commercial reality? What accomplishments/products has the company achieved to date? What recommendations, if any, would you make to E Ink?

Managing for Innovation

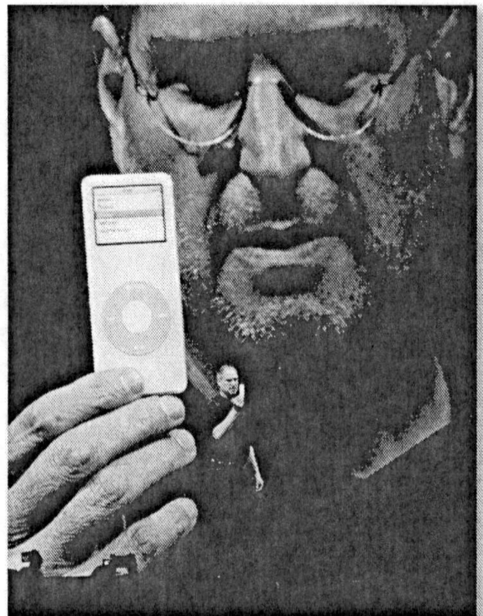

Stephen Jobs, CEO of Apple which he cofounded in 1976, is widely credited with nurturing the company's distinctive brand of creativity and innovation, blended with sleek and ground-breaking product design.

If innovation is a key to success, how can an organization be managed so that innovation is encouraged and maximized? Some notable organizations that have recently embraced innovation as a key strategy provide some lessons. First, if you want to maximize innovation, there must be measures of innovation. For example, top leaders at General Electric are being measured on how imaginative they are.[16] For GE, that means characteristics such as the courage to fund new ideas, leading teams to discover better ideas, and encouraging educated risk taking. Second, you need to get close to the customer. For example, Procter & Gamble sent out teams of people to observe how they cleaned bathrooms. In South Africa, women were observed using brooms to clean walls and showers. This customer observation resulted in the development of the Mr. Clean MagicReach, a new product with a four-foot detachable pole that was introduced to the marketplace in 2005. In terms of service, customer observation is also crucial to innovation. For example, The Gap Inc. has found social shopping, shopping in pairs or threesomes, is common in its stores. As a result, the company is making its dressing rooms bigger.[17]

The preceding examples and the lessons that can be drawn from them are general and probably leave you without a good sense of how to actually manage to increase innovativeness. There are no guaranteed and simple management

table 8.2

Management Tactics to Maximize Innovation—The Five Cs

TACTIC	FOCUS
Capability	People
Culture	Balance
Cash and recognition	Rewards
Customer orientation	Trends
Cut losses	Manage investments

techniques, but there are things that can be done to give innovation a chance to flourish.[18] We refer to these management tactics as the "Five Cs." They are summarized in Table 8.2 above.

The first management tactic listed in Table 8.2 is *capability.* Capability means having people with the skills and interests needed to generate innovative ideas. People who are smart and open and who like to try new things are more likely to create new ideas. In addition to capitalizing on these preexisting person characteristics, capability of employees can be increased by encouraging and providing opportunities for creativity. For example, the software company Intuit holds weekly free-association sessions as a means to get people to generate ideas and think about marketable changes.[19]

In addition to having the capability to generate innovation, the organizational environment should foster creativity. In most situations, organizational leaders devote most company resources to current services or products. On the other hand, giving all of the resources to the current business means that the organization may be trapped in the past. What is needed is a *culture* (the second "C") that balances routine work and innovative efforts. The appropriate *balance* depends upon the industry and on the type of managers in the organization. Whatever the balance point is, the trick is to maintain control and structure within the core process, while encouraging risk taking and experimentation outside of the everyday service or production process. Disney Corporation, for example, insists on a strict script in terms of how visitors are greeted, how rides are operated, and so on. The company also holds a monthly competitive and fun opportunity for any employee to attend and present a new idea.[20] On one side of their operation, the organization may need to limit variation. On the other side, it needs to be encouraged. It is a question of balance and making sure that people understand when each approach is appropriate. Google manages this balance with a 70/20/10 formula: 70 percent of time should be spent on the core business; 20 percent on side but related-to-the-core projects; 10 percent on unrelated new business.[21]

Establishing a culture supportive of innovation can require more than balance in terms of resources and time allocation. Innovation can sometimes be thwarted because people aren't willing to open up and risk criticism. This problem can be particularly pronounced in team settings. Management Is Everyone's Business 8.3 on page 335 offers suggestions for how team members can cultivate innovation.

The third "C" represents the tactic of *cash and recognition.* If you really want to encourage new ideas and creativity, then there should be recognition and reward for those who can deliver. Organizations can offer cash prizes for ideas

MANAGEMENT IS EVERYONE'S BUSINESS 8.3

Working as a Team Teams are common in workplaces and it is therefore often the case that innovation is expected to happen at the team level. The success of a business may hinge on the innovativeness of its teams. As a team member, here are some key suggestions/questions to maximize innovativeness.

- *Know your customer.* Whom does your team serve? Are there internal customers, external customers, or maybe both?
- *What do your customers need, expect, and want?* If possible, team observation and discussions with its customers can help identify needs and possible innovations. How well does your team provide products or services to customers? If you try an innovation, can you quickly get customer feedback on the effectiveness of the change?
- *Establish team time-lines to roll out innovations.* Also establish measures and review sessions so that the effectiveness of a change can be assessed and corrections can be made.
- *Support team creativity.* Sharing ideas in a team setting can be difficult for some, particularly if criticism, or even good-natured kidding, might result. Brainstorming, a technique for generating ideas, should occur without any criticism or editorial comments from others. This rule may need to be enforced so that all possible ideas are generated and shared with the team. A way to enforce the no-comments rule is to use an object as a prop. All team members can be told that during brainstorming they must hold the "idea object" in order to speak. Only the person with the object can speak and no other comments, no criticism, analysis, negotiation, and so on can take place. Needing the object to speak can be a simple but effective technique to set aside politics, egos, and other possible stumbling blocks to the creative process.

that are implemented and might even offer stock or other *rewards* to recognize particularly noteworthy innovations. Given incentives, people will quickly recognize that the encouragement to "think outside the box" is more than empty rhetoric.

As already discussed, *customers* are another important resource with regard to innovation. Listening to customers can provide a wealth of beneficial information. Critical customers may be the key to identifying improvements or new *trends* in products or services.

The last "C" stands for *cutting losses.* Often individuals or teams become emotionally committed to an innovative idea they have been working on. While this personal investment can increase the effort put into the project, it can also cloud judgment about what is reasonable. A process of checkoffs by people not directly involved in the project can make for an objective decision as to whether to continue investment.

LOC-In

7 Learning Objective Check-In

Gillian is a manager who wants to maximize innovation at her firm. She is trying to apply several ideas to accomplish this. For instance, she has balanced the distribution of business resources among current uses and innovation efforts. This is one way of encouraging risk taking and experimentation at the firm. On the other hand, she wants to avoid clouded judgment about what is reasonable among people who are personally invested in projects. Once individuals or teams are emotionally committed to an innovative idea they have been working on, it is difficult for them to see when they should step away from that idea. She has put in place a process that helps teams separate themselves personally from their projects and remain objective.

1. *Which of the following "Cs" represents Gillian's first idea above, "balance" in the distribution of resources?*
   a. *Culture*
   b. *Customers*
   c. *Cash and recognition*
   d. *Cutting losses*
2. *Which of the following "Cs" represents the second idea above, keeping objectivity about a project?*
   a. *Customers*
   b. *Cash and recognition*
   c. *Capability*
   d. *Cutting losses*

CONCLUDING THOUGHTS

After the story about the successful cold medicine invented by a nonexpert that opened the chapter, we posed some critical thinking questions about entrepreneurial ventures and new business ideas. Now that we have explored the topics of entrepreneurship and innovation, it's time to revisit those introductory questions. First, while some personal characteristics, such as an internal locus of control, are important, anyone with the motivation can become an entrepreneur. Victoria Knight-McDowell was motivated at first by little more than the desire to be free of cold germs! Entrepreneurs need a deep well of motivation, in addition to abilities and personal characteristics relevant to the business they would like to pursue. The source of motivation is often an internal commitment to an idea or process. The practical reality is that motivation often comes from necessity and external obstacles. For example, many people have become entrepreneurs because they were laid off or were frustrated as members of a large organization.

Second, the risk involved in entrepreneurial effort isn't as great as is typically think. The initial financial investment an entrepreneur makes might be relatively modest. It is later, when the business has grown, that the entrepreneur may have more dollars at risk. Nonetheless, in terms of psychological risk, the entrepreneur may be putting in an incredible investment at the start of a new venture.

Finally, the basis for a new business idea doesn't have to be radical change. On the contrary, entrepreneurs often capitalize on modest incremental changes to a product or service. Whether an incremental change or a radical innovation, the ideas often come from the particular skills and experiences of the entrepreneur. What may be more important than the particular idea is how it is implemented. The lack of a viable business plan can be the ruin of even a great idea.

Focusing on the Future: Using Management Theory in Daily Life

Entrepreneurship and Innovation

Dave Moore is the pastor of the New Summit Presbyterian Church—not someone most people would think of as an entrepreneur. And yet, in bringing a new church from zero members to over 300, in an environment where two-thirds of all new churches fail, he has had to use each of the five management tactics (Five "Cs") to maximize innovation described in this chapter.

Capability When Dave arrived in Lee's Summit, Missouri, he found 10 people who were interested in being part of a new church. A few of these people had been asked to be part of the new church by the Presbytery—they were "doing their duty to the denomination." Others wanted to start a new church in the area where they lived. Regardless of their initial reasons for joining, Dave recognized that he needed to build on the capabilities of each of these 10 people if the endeavor was to succeed. As he puts it, "I wanted to honor the gifts and passions of everyone involved—the first members, our emerging church leaders, and everyone else who would become part of our organization."

Based on a demographic study of the area, Dave determined that people who were likely to consider joining a new church would look at three key areas: (1) overall environment, including the structure of services and teaching; (2) music; and (3) child care. With these in mind, he asked people to consider where they could best contribute. Responses came in quickly. One member offered to do all the publicity for the new church, another to handle the technology needed in the church office and during services, another to run the day care center, and another to set up seating for services. In addition to these somewhat obvious tasks, Dave found that his other members could contribute expertise on financing and real estate development, accounting and budgetary controls, marketing, planning and the other business functions related to running any organization. One critical area remained understaffed—music. To handle this issue, Dave and the members of the church decided to hire a part-time Music Director.

As New Summit grew, new needs for people with specialized capabilities emerged. Over time, Dave and the other members of the church created a new full-time position for a church secretary. They also identified four primary "quadrants" for church activities: gather (evangelism), inspire (worship), equip (training), and send (mission work). These quadrants (and their associated teams) were developed as a direct result of Dave's reading and study of Margaret Wheatley's book *Leadership and the New Science*—a theoretical work which proposes that the "core identity" of any person or organization is more important than having policies or procedures. Each of these activities now has a leadership position associated with it. The vision for the future is that as the church grows, these leadership positions will be staffed with full-time people. Finally, 10 elders of the church serve as a "board of directors" and handle major financial and managerial decisions.

Culture Balancing innovation and tradition is not an easy job in any church, and it can be especially difficult when the church is a new venture. At first, the church services were held in a rented school auditorium. As the congregation grew, they were able to acquire a large piece of land on which to build their sanctuary. But what kind of building should go up? Tradition called for a steepled structure where people would congregate on Sundays for an hour or two. But since caring for one another and the community were integral parts of the New Summit vision and mission statements, after much deliberation, a different kind of structure was raised—a large, open space that could accommodate child care and after school activities as easily as traditional worship.

This issue was recently faced again, as the church members and elders started the process of putting up a second building. Cognizant of the fact that new buildings cost $100 to $150 a square foot in their area, the group again had to weigh the traditional with the innovative. They found that while stained glass and an organ "spoke to" people in earlier times, today's congregants speak a different language—one that is more digital and visual. Money that might have been spent on pews is now being spent on projection systems, and rather than stained glass, people respond to images of classic paintings projected on blank walls. The interesting thing about this new technology is that it allows for a marriage of tradition and innovation. For example, in one recent service, classic paintings of the crucifixion were blended with images from a current movie—Mel Gibson's "The Passion."

Dave says that he is constantly seeking ways to "talk to people in their own language." But he also realizes that this new language may not appeal to everyone. His research shows that his church is more likely to appeal to people who do not normally go to any church. It is harder to get past the expectations and past experiences of people who are "traditionally churched" because they have a different image of what church "should be." Dave challenges congregants who want a more traditional service to take responsibility for putting it together, but he also reaches out to them by trying to include at least one more traditional hymn in each service, and by retaining key elements of the service that can act as a touchstone for traditionalists.

Cash and Recognition Dave and the other leaders of New Summit have a large number of volunteer workers to motivate, and they need to be creative with rewards for those workers. While the tasks themselves can be rewarding, and there is always the promise of an eternal reward, it can be a challenge to sustain day-to-day motivational levels. Recently, Dave instituted a new program called "Kingdom Assignments." This program, created by Pastor Dennis Bellesi at the Coast Hills Community Church in Aliso Viejo, California, challenges congregants by providing them with $100 to "further the Kingdom of God" in any way they see fit. As Dave points out, the purpose of the exercise is to let people know that "the ministry that you are going to participate in has yet to be discovered, and you have a significant part in discovering it." The program is motivating both because of the recognition people receive in the church for their projects, and also because it gives people the opportunity to have complete control over a project of their own choosing. This is a key component of intrinsic motivation.

Customer Orientation Lee's Summit is a "bedroom community" of 80,000 people. Some demographers classify it as a "hopes and dreams" community. People in Lee's Summit want a meaningful career, a meaningful marriage, good relationships with friends, financial security, and a good education for their children. It is a safe community where people rarely worry about crime and drugs. But it is also a community in which people do not go to church on a regular basis. Dave asked his staff at New Summit to survey every church in the area and find out how many people the sanctuary could hold when filled to capacity. They estimated that if every sanctuary was filled to capacity twice every Sunday, there would still be 50 percent of the people in Lee's Summit who would not have a place to sit.

The survey indicated a need for a new church, but Dave had to take his customers' needs into account to attract them to that church. As he puts it, "We wanted to attract people to our services, so we said, 'Come as you are. We'll accept you, we'll speak your language, we'll take care of your kids, we'll have topics that are relevant to you, and we'll provide a place to enrich all of the relationships in your life.'" He soon found that it wasn't just Sunday morning services that attracted people, but activities they could enjoy, both as adults and as a family. Soon the new church was buzzing with everything from small group meetings to building Habitat for Humanity houses—anything and everything that might attract people and draw them away from Sunday morning soccer games and other competitors for their time and efforts.

Cut Losses When is it time to pull the plug on an innovative idea? While Dave learns as much from ideas that work as those that don't work, he watches carefully to be sure that he is not committing too many resources to a failed innovation. For example, New Summit hired a youth director at one point. It made sense at the time, because of the number of growing families, and it was a popular decision with the congregation, but it was also fraught with problems. Nationally, most youth directors are underpaid and do not stay in their jobs for more than two years. Despite Dave's best efforts to anticipate and deal with these problems, the new youth director simply didn't work out, and left after one year of service. Dave used the opportunity to reevaluate the position and decided that it would be better to put the church's resources into a full time "equipping minister" whose focus would be on training people of all ages to help them to discover their gifts.

summary of learning objectives

Entrepreneurship and innovation are critical to the continued competitiveness and economic vitality of any developed economy that hopes to remain a player in today's global marketplace. Entrepreneurship refers to the process of creating an enterprise capable of entering new or established markets. Innovation refers to the translation of knowledge into products or services that add value. Both the opportunities created through entrepreneurship and the new value and bottom-line impact of effective innovation are needed for long-term economic prosperity. This chapter's discussion should help you to promote entrepreneurship and innovation as a manager, team member, and individual employee. The chapter's learning objectives and the related chapter discussion points are summarized below.

1 Explain the economic importance of entrepreneurship.

- Entrepreneurship is responsible for much of the job creation in the U.S.
- Innovation and entrepreneurship go hand in hand bringing new products to market.
- Entrepreneurship brings opportunities to minorities and women.

2 Identify the key characteristics and skills of entrepreneurs.

- Entrepreneur's have an **internal locus of control**—a belief in one's own ability to succeed.
- Negotiation skills, networking sills, and leadership skills are critical to successful entrepreneurs.

3 Recognize the basic ingredients needed to effectively start and manage an entrepreneurial venture.

- New business ideas can come from a variety of sources.
- The business plan maps out the business strategy.
- Selecting the right form of business is crucial—**proprietorship, partnership, corporation.**
- Obtaining financing is often **debt financing** or equity financing.
- Growth must be managed.

4 Differentiate among the legal forms of organizing an entrepreneurial venture.

- Proprietorship—owned by one person.
- Partnership—association of two or more persons acting as co-owners.
- Corporation—a legal entity separate from individual owners.

5 Identify alternative forms of entrepreneurship.

- Intrapreneurship—new business units developed within a larger corporate structure.
- Spin-offs—independent entrepreneurship that originated in a large company.
- Franchises—an established business that sells distribution rights to additional owners.

6 Describe innovation and demonstrate why it is important for business success.

- Innovation
  - New Idea
  - Business Results
- Key to success in creativity-driven market

7 Apply the "Five C" management tactics to maximize innovation.

- Capability
- Culture
- Cash and recognition
- Customer orientation
- Cut losses

discussion questions

1. How does an entrepreneurial business differ from a small business? What are the similarities?
2. What are the differences between an entrepreneur and a manager?
3. What is the significance of entrepreneurship to the U.S. economy?
4. Identify the important personal characteristics of entrepreneurs. Do you think only people with these characteristics should become entrepreneurs? What problems does this approach present? What alternatives could be used to encourage people to choose an entrepreneurial path?
5. Compare and contrast debt financing and equity financing as ways of starting a new business. Does one have an overall advantage over the other? What situation is more favorable to the use of debt financing? Which situation favors equity financing?
6. Why is growth important to an entrepreneurial business? How can rapid growth be detrimental to its survival?
7. Can an individual be an entrepreneur yet work within a large corporation? Explain your answer.
8. What are the advantages of starting a franchise business (such as a McDonald's) instead of an independent entrepreneurial business? What are the disadvantages?
9. What is the purpose of a business plan for an entrepreneurial effort? Some successful businesses are started without any business plan and operate according to the gut instincts of the entrepreneur. What do you think accounts for the success of businesses that are run "by the seat of the pants" without any formal planning?
10. Describe what is meant by the statement that an invention is not necessarily an innovation. Can you provide any examples of inventions that may not be innovations?
11. Describe how you would go about setting up conditions to maximize innovativeness. Put yourself in the place of a manager and use the "Five Cs." How would you assure quality while at the same time encouraging the chaos of experimentation and creativity?

Innovation: Core Competitive Advantage or Fair Game for Outsourcing?

management minicase 8.1

Innovation has been a key to U.S. productivity and, therefore, a key to our economic strength. Further, there seems to be a belief that innovation is our forte and future. Operational details, such as executing a new design with low cost and high quality, might be left to India and China, but we will have the competitive edge in generating the innovations. This somewhat romantic belief also means that the United States will remain the home of the prestigious and high-paid professionals who create and design innovative enhancements to products and services. Unfortunately, this belief is increasingly at odds with reality.

While other countries, such as India and China, have significant cost advantages over the United States, that doesn't mean that these markets are static. U.S. companies cannot count on these countries to cheaply produce the innovative products we design. Quite to the contrary, India and China are also ramping up their ability to compete on innovation. For example, employees at a variety of Indian organizations receive training on topics such as creative thinking, customer service, managing change and innovation, and prototyping new solutions. These training topics clearly indicate that the organizational systems in other countries are not simply waiting for the next innovative development from the United States so that it can be cheaply produced. Global competition is coming, not just on price and quality, but on innovation.

Despite the competitive threats to the American capability to innovate, some organizations seem to be giving away their claim on this competence. Companies are outsourcing not just their manufacturing capabilities, but their innovation capabilities. For example, Boeing is working with India's HCL Technologies to jointly develop software for one of its upcoming jets. Procter and Gamble has an objective of increasing new product ideas generated outside of the company from the current level of 20 percent to 50 percent by 2010. Other companies are taking a more measured approach to outsourcing innovation. For example, Motorola might outsource the entire design process for its cheapest phones, but may keep in-house the development of its high-end phones.

Discussion Questions

1. Do you think innovation can be a source of competitive advantage for organizations? Why or why not?
2. If innovation can be important to organizational success, how can U.S. companies maintain a competitive edge over foreign competition?
3. Why would firms outsource innovation? What advantages could they gain? What costs or risks might they experience? (Hint: Motorola outsourced the design and manufacture of a mobile phone to a Taiwanese company. The Taiwanese company then sold the phone in the huge China market under its own brand name.)
4. Some managers contend that a line must be drawn that separates "commodity" work (that can be outsourced) from core or "mission-critical" work (that should not be outsourced). How can this line be drawn and enforced? (Hint: Motorola has a policy that limits the outsourcing of innovation. Many other approaches may be possible.)
5. Consider the following statements:
   a. Outsourcing innovation means giving away your competitive advantage.
   b. Outsourcing innovation allows you to maximize performance by capturing the creative skills of workers around the world.

   Which statement do you agree with? Explain.
6. Using the two statements in Question 5, divide into opposing teams and argue the two positions. Summarize the discussion and any resolution with the rest of the class.

Sources: Adapted from W. R. Brody, "What Happened to American Innovation?" *Chief Executive, 214* (2005), pp. 22–24; P. Engardio, B. Einhorn, M. Kripalini, A. Reinhardt, B. Nussbaum, and P. Burrows, Outsourcing Innovation, *BusinessWeek Online*, March 21 2005; R. L. Martin, "India and China: Not Just Cheap," *Business WeekOnline*, December 13, 2005.

management minicase 8.2

Nice Threads: High Tech Gets into the Fabric of Things

Fabric is gaining more capability than you may be aware of. Some of the changes include the inclusion of silver in fabrics that gives the fabric antibacterial properties. For example, Noble Biomaterials makes x-static, a silver laden fabric, that it has put into various pieces of clothing for its antibacterial properties. However, it found that an attractive feature for customers is that the material doesn't get smelly, no matter how long it is worn. In 2004 every U.S. soldier was wearing x-static socks, T-shirts, and gloves. The company will achieve approximately $50 million in sales in 2005. There are also companies that are adding microcapsules containing skin conditioners or scents that are bonded to the fibers of clothing.

While the inclusion of silver and microcapsules may be interesting developments in the fabric world, the real eye-popping changes that may be on the horizon are in an area often referred to as e-textiles. E-textiles are traditional fabrics integrated with electronics. The combination of electronics and textiles is taking a variety of forms, from garments that simply hold electronic devices to electronic devices that can be temporarily attached to special fabrics. Some of this work is at the laboratory stage, but some smart fabrics are already hitting the market. For example, Elek-Tex, an e-textile, conducts electricity when compressed. The material is being used to incorporate iPod controls into ski jackets. Textronics makes an elastic material that conducts electricity and could be used for heating or to monitor vital signs, among other possibilities. The company has just developed a sports bra that monitors heart rate and displays the information in a wrist-worn receiver. In France, a cinema has experimented with a pressure-sensitive textile on seats as a means for tracking occupancy levels. Yet another e-textile, Luminex, incorporates fiber-optic strands and has been used to make safety garments that glow.

The e-textiles or smart fabrics are taking a variety of forms and not all may prove commercially viable. Approximately 200 companies are estimated to be involved in developing e-textile products. So far, only a few companies are making a profit in this new field.

Discussion Questions

1. Lower-tech fabrics, such as x-static and the inclusion of microcapsules, are much closer to commercial reality than are e-textiles. As an entrepreneur, would you prefer to try to bring a lower-tech fabric or an e-textile to market? Why?
2. Given the discussion of innovation in this chapter, do you consider e-textiles to be inventions or innovations?
3. To the extent that e-textiles are currently more in the category of invention, what would it take to move them into the category of innovation?
4. Smart fabrics, or e-textiles, seem technologically feasible. However, e-textiles will not be commercially successful unless they serve a customer need. Can you identify customer needs that might be met with e-textiles?

Sources: V.S. Borland, "New directions for Apparel and Home Fabrics," *Textile World*, 155 (2005), 53–55; F. Byrt, "Clothes Get Wired at Digital-Edge Design Shops: Textronics Foresees T-Shirts That Monitor Heart Rates, but Market Not Yet Certain," *The Wall Street Journal*, November 17, 2005, p. B4; D. I. Lehn, C. W. Neely, K. Schoonover, T. L. Martin, M. T. Jones, "E-TAGs: e-Textile Attached Gadgets," paper presented at the Communication Networks and Distributed Systems Modeling and Simulation Conference, January 2004; S. Schubert, "The Ultimate Silver Lining: How Bill McNally turned His Idea for an Antibacterial Fabric into $50 Million Sensation," *Business 20*, *6*, (2005), 78; *The Economist*, "Threads That Think," December 10, 2005.

Running a Sole Proprietorship

individual/ collaborative learning case 8.1

The most common form of business ownership in the United States is the sole proprietorship. One such business was L. A. Nicola, a Los Angeles restaurant owned by Larry Nicola. Located away from diners' row, the restaurant attracted clientele for one major reason: great food. As with his later restaurants, Nicola made the menu choices and, in his role as chef, saw that the food was cooked to perfection. He kept on top of new industry trends and knew how to change the menu to reflect the emerging tastes of customers. For example, before health foods became a fad, L. A. Nicola had cut down on sauces and fatty foods and was offering leaner cuisine.

Nicola gets out into his restaurants and works the crowd. He ensures that everything is running smoothly, greets old customers, and welcomes new ones. From his L. A. Nicola venture he went on to open other California restaurants.

What does Nicola like best about being a sole proprietor? He says it is the freedom of choice to do things his own way. If he sees something going wrong, he can correct it. If a customer is not getting proper service, Nicola will intervene and help the waiter out or assign a second waiter to the area. If a customer's food has not been cooked to his or her taste, Nicola can send it back to the kitchen and personally supervise the preparation.

Nicola is not alone in his desire for freedom in running things his own way. In recent years more and more sole proprietorships have been formed by individuals who used to work for other companies and have now broken away and started their own businesses. In the restaurant industry, chefs with an entrepreneurial spirit often first learn the business through experience and then open their own restaurants. Since chefs are usually the people who know the most about restaurants, they have a distinct advantage in starting a new business—the operation cannot succeed without them.

Critical Thinking Questions

1. Why is the sole proprietorship business form so popular with people who want to start a business?
2. What type of liability do sole proprietors have if their business suffers a large loss?
3. If Nicola decided to raise $1 million and expand his restaurant, could he do this as a sole proprietor or would he have to form a partnership or corporation? Explain.

Collaborative Learning Exercise

One of the drawbacks of a proprietorship is that the responsibilities of operating the business are the proprietor's alone. It is difficult to take vacations, and sole proprietors tend to be workaholics who average 61 hours of work per week. Stress, burnout, and neglected families are occupational hazards. Further, there is no one in the business to provide guidance, since the business is owned and operated by one person. The business owner may make a serious blunder in the business strategy and may not become aware of it before it is too late to recover. Meet in a small group to develop tactics that would be useful to entrepreneurs for dealing with these challenges for sole proprietors.

Sources: Adapted from D. F. Kuratko and R. M. Hodgetts, *Entrepreneurship*, 2nd ed., Fort Worth: Dryden Press, 1992, pp. 220–221; R. R. Roha, "Home Alone," *Kiplinger's Personal Finance Magazine*, May 1997, pp. 85–89.

internet exercise 8.1

Freedom!

Management Close-Up 8.3 focused on the Freedom Maintenance franchise model set up in the U.K. Freedom Franchising Services has a Web site that further describes the franchising model. Explore the Freedom Franchising Web site and any related Web sites regarding this franchise.

1. What services are offered by the Freedom franchises?
2. What is needed to be a Freedom franchise? What skills or other characteristics would a franchise owner need to have in order to be successful?
3. What is the current status of the Freedom Franchise organization?
4. Would you recommend the franchise concept to U.S. electric companies? Why or why not?
5. Could the concept be successfully implemented in other industries?
6. Can you find any information on Freedom applying its franchise model in the United States?

manager's checkup 8.1

Customer-Based Innovation

A starting point for generating useful innovations, especially in regard to customer service, is to reflect on our own experiences as a customer. Try answering the following questions regarding your own experience as a customer.

1. How did I feel about the service experience (special, appreciated, annoyed, frustrated, ignored, etc.)?
2. What happened, or didn't happen, that led me to feel this way?
3. What did I learn from that service experience about what affects how a customer feels?
4. Can I apply what I learned, or some portion of it to my organizations's service?

As a manager:

5. To what extent do you encourage your workers to ask themselves the same questions?
6. Are your workers empowered to try to make innovative and positive changes to how customer are served?

Source: Adapted from D. Riddle, "Training Staff to Innovate," *International Trade Forum*, 2, (2000), pp. 28–30. Published by the International Trade Center.

video summary

Powering a Creative Economy

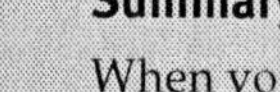

Summary

When you think of creativity, Corporate America is probably not the first thing that comes to mind, but that's changing, and it's changing fast. With millions of manufacturing jobs being outsourced, and millions of knowledge-based jobs following steadily behind them, America is turning to creativity and innovation for its new competitive edge. Companies like Procter & Gamble and General Electric are trying to model themselves more after successful innovators like Apple, which struck it rich recently with the iPod "experience," including iTunes and an array of devices that make music and video entertainment portable and interactive. The thrust of this "movement" is to generate big ideas that will give firms big margins and generate big profits. This will likely be a difficult road for these companies, because the people who work in these firms are largely engineers or process-oriented people who are used to small, incremental changes. They are now being told to take risks and think creatively, in the face of a 96 percent failure rate for all innovation attempts. However, there are ways to improve the odds of successful innovations, including cultivating the culture for innovation within a company. Consumer-centric innovation is another method by which companies can spur innovation.

Discussion Questions

1. The case presents the argument that the U.S. economy will sustain itself on innovations developed in companies like Apple, GE, and P&G. Do you think firms like P&G can change their culture to emphasize innovation, rather than just accommodate it? Why will this be difficult?
2. Is innovation "safe" from outsourcing? Can the task of innovation be outsourced to other countries, like manufacturing and knowledge-based jobs have been?
3. There is currently a 96 percent failure rate among new innovation attempts. What can managers do to maximize innovation efficiency within their firms?

chapter I

The Exceptional Manager

What You Do, How You Do It

Major Questions You Should Be Able to Answer

I.1 Management: What It Is, What Its Benefits Are
Major Question: What are the rewards of being an exceptional manager–of being a star in my workplace?

I.2 Six Challenges to Being a Star Manager
Major Question: Challenges can make one feel alive. What are six challenges I could look forward to as a manager?

I.3 What Managers Do: The Four Principal Functions
Major Question: What would I actually *do*—that is, what would be my four principal functions—as a manager?

I.4 Pyramid Power: Levels & Areas of Management
Major Question: What are the levels and areas of management I need to know to move up, down, and sideways?

I.5 Roles Managers Must Play Successfully
Major Question: To be an exceptional manager, what roles must I play successfully?

I.6 The Entrepreneurial Spirit
Major Question: Do I have what it takes to be an entrepreneur?

I.7 The Skills Star Managers Need
Major Question: To be a terrific manager, what skills should I cultivate?

THE MANAGER'S toolbox

Becoming a Star Manager: Rules for Advancing Your Career

Someday maybe you can afford to have a *personal career coach*—the kind long used by sports and entertainment figures and now adopted in the upper ranks of business. These individuals "combine executive coaching and career consulting with marketing and negotiations," says one account. "They plot career strategy, help build networks of business contacts, . . . and shape their clients' images."[1]

Because planning a career is increasingly bewildering in today's work world, in the following pages we are going to try to act much like your personal career coach. In that spirit, it is our desire *to make this book as practical as possible for you.* For instance, the **Manager's Toolbox,** like this one, which appears at the beginning of every chapter, offers practical advice appropriate to the subject matter you are about to explore.

Five Rules for Staying Ahead in Your Career The purpose of this book is to help you become a successful manager—indeed, a *star manager*—an *exceptional manager,* as this chapter's title has it, whose performance is far superior to that of other managers. The first thing star managers learn is how to stay ahead in their careers.

The following strategies for staying ahead in the workplace of tomorrow are adapted from rules offered by professional career counselor Richard L. Knowdell, president of Career Research and Testing in San Jose, California.[2]

- **Take charge of your career and avoid misconceptions:** Because you, not others, are in charge of your career, and it's an ongoing process, you should develop a career plan and base your choices on that plan. When considering a new job or industry, find out how that world *really* works, not what it's reputed to be. When considering a company you might want to work for, find out its corporate "style" or culture by talking to its employees.
- **Develop new capacities:** "Being good at several things will be more advantageous in the long run than being excellent at one narrow specialty," says Knowdell. "A complex world will not only demand *specialized knowledge* but also *general and flexible skills.*"
- **Anticipate and adapt to, even embrace, changes:** Learn to analyze, anticipate, and adapt to new circumstances in the world and in your own life. For instance, as technology changes the rules, *embrace* the new rules.
- **Keep learning:** "You can take a one- or two-day course in a new subject," says Knowdell, "just to get an idea of whether you want to use those specific skills and to see if you would be good at it. Then, if there is a match, you could seek out an extended course."
- **Develop your people and communications skills:** No matter how much communication technology takes over the workplace, there will always be a strong need for effectiveness in interpersonal relationships. In particular, learn to listen well.

For Discussion Which of these five rules do you think is the most important—and why?

forecast

What's Ahead in This Chapter

We describe the rewards, benefits, and privileges managers might expect. We also describe the six challenges to managers in today's world—not only staying ahead of rivals but also managing for diversity, globalization, information technology, ethical standards, and personal happiness and life goals. You'll be introduced to the four principal functions of management—planning, organizing, leading, and controlling—and levels and areas of management. Then we consider the contributions of entrepreneurship. Finally, we describe the three types of roles (interpersonal, informational, and decisional) and three skills (technical, conceptual, and human) required of a manager.

major question

What are the rewards of being an exceptional manager—of being a star in my workplace?

THE BIG PICTURE

Management is defined as the pursuit of organizational goals efficiently and effectively. Organizations, or people who work together to achieve a specific purpose, value managers because of the multiplier effect: Good managers have an influence on the organization far beyond the results that can be achieved by one person acting alone. Managers are well paid, with the CEOs and presidents of even small and midsize businesses earning good salaries and many benefits.

Judy McGrath, from a blue-collar Irish neighborhood in Scranton, Pennsylvania, was 26 when she arrived in New York in 1978 with an English degree. After a period of writing articles for women's magazines, she was hired to create promotional materials for MTV. Today at age 53 she is chief executive officer (CEO) of MTV Networks, which was launched in 1981 as a music video channel but now comprises TV channels, Web sites, and wireless services reaching 440 million households in 169 countries. What brought about her rise to the top of this $7 billion company?

One quality she brought to her job is a strong sense of community. If she has been "smart or lucky at one thing," she says, "it has been [picking] good people." Another quality is perseverance. "It's a really undervalued asset," she points out, "but if you really want something, you've got to hang in there." A third quality: encouraging an anything-is-possible spirit by creating an atmosphere in which people feel safe and are not afraid to fail. "Falling flat is a great motivator, " she says. "So is accident."[3]

In an era of broadband, iPods, and an "Always On" online generation, MTV faces a slew of threats. The company will now have to deliver services across new broadband channels, over cell phones, and via video games. Two important rules in the McGrath playbook, therefore, are "Make change part of your DNA" and "Companies don't innovate, people do."

Being prepared for surprises and change is important to any manager's survival, and continuing change—in the world and in the workplace—is a major theme of this book.

MTV in New York City. The sprawl of the MTV empire includes multiple online communities for various geographical locations, shops such as this one in the Big Apple, and, of course, TV channels. As CEO, Judy McGrath must understand the unique needs of customers from Stockholm to Toronto to Chicago, as well as how to reach them with MTV's offerings. If you were in her shoes, what would you consider to be the key component of managerial success? A strong sense of community? Perseverance? Making people not afraid to fail?

The Art of Management Defined

Is being an exceptional manager—a star manager—a gift, like a musician having perfect pitch? Not exactly. But in good part it may be an art. Fortunately, it is one that is teachable.

Management, said one pioneer of management ideas, is "the art of getting things done through people."[4]

Getting things done. Through people. Thus, managers are task oriented, achievement oriented, and people oriented. And they operate within an ***organization*****—a group of people who work together to achieve some specific purpose.**

More formally, ***management*** **is defined as (1) the pursuit of organizational goals efficiently and effectively by (2) integrating the work of people through (3) planning, organizing, leading, and controlling the organization's resources.**

Note the words *efficiently* and *effectively,* which basically mean "doing things right."

- ***Efficiency—the means.*** Efficiency is the means of attaining the organization's goals. **To be *efficient* means to use resources—people, money, raw materials, and the like—wisely and cost-effectively.**
- ***Effectiveness—the ends.*** Effectiveness is the organization's ends, the goals. **To be *effective* means to achieve results, to make the right decisions and to successfully carry them out so that they achieve the organization's goals.**

Good managers are concerned with trying to achieve both qualities. Often, however, organizations will erroneously strive for efficiency without being effective.

Why Organizations Value Managers: The Multiplier Effect

Some great achievements of history, such as scientific discoveries or works of art, were accomplished by individuals working quietly by themselves. But so much more has been achieved by people who were able to leverage their talents and abilities by being managers. For instance, of the top 10 great architectural wonders of the world named by the American Institute of Architects, none was built single-handedly by one person. All were triumphs of management, although some reflected the vision of an individual.

Example

Efficiency versus Effectiveness: Won't Someone Answer the Phone—*Please?*

We're all now accustomed to having our calls to companies answered not by people but by a recorded "telephone menu" of options. Certainly this arrangement is *efficient* for the companies, since they no longer need as many telephone receptionists. But it's not *effective* if it leaves us, the customers, fuming and not inclined to continue doing business.

The cost for self-service via an automated phone system averages $1.85, whereas the cost of using a live customer-service representative is $4.50, according to the Gartner Group, an information technology analyst.[5] Nevertheless, automated technologies often don't allow completion of transactions, because of customer confusion and technological glitches, so this leads to "ping-ponging"—customers calling back trying to find a live representative or other means of contacting the company.

Effective? How often do you encounter organizations using their telephone systems more efficiently than effectively?

Thus, Scott Broetzmann, president of CustomerCare Measurement Consulting, a firm that does surveys on customer service, says that 90% of consumers say they want nothing to do with an automated telephone system. "They just don't like it," he says. The most telling finding is that 50% of those surveyed had become so aggravated that they were willing to pay an additional charge for customer service that avoids going through an automated phone system.[6]

Richard Shapiro, head of a firm that evaluates the experiences of customers calling in to toll-free call centers, says that companies "create more value through a dialogue with a live agent. A call is an opportunity to build a relationship, to encourage a customer to stay with the brand. There can be a real return on this investment."[7]

Your Call

Paul English, chief technology officer for a travel search engine business, was so fed up with automated voice services and other awful customer service that he started Get Human to "change the face of customer service." The Web site, **www.gethuman.com,** publishes the unpublicized codes for reaching a company's human operators, a list of the best and worst companies, and cut-through-automation tips.[8] What recent unpleasant customer experience would you want to post on this Web site?

(The wonders are the Great Wall of China, the Great Pyramid, Machu Picchu, the Acropolis, the Coliseum, the Taj Mahal, the Eiffel Tower, the Brooklyn Bridge, the Empire State Building, and Frank Lloyd Wright's Falling Water house in Pennsylvania.)

Good managers create value. The reason is that in being a manager you have a *multiplier effect:* your influence on the organization is multiplied far beyond the results that can be achieved by just one person acting alone. Thus, while a solo operator such as a salesperson might accomplish many things and incidentally make a very good living, his or her boss could accomplish a great deal more—and could well earn two to seven times the income. And the manager will undoubtedly have a lot more influence.

Star managers are in high demand. "The scarcest, most valuable resource in business is no longer financial capital," says a recent *Fortune* article. "It's talent. If you doubt that, just watch how hard companies are battling for the best people. . . . Talent of every type is in short supply, but the greatest shortage of all is skilled, effective managers.[9]

Lee Raymond. The former ExxonMobil CEO earned about $144,573 a day in the years before retirement-equivalent to the yearly salary of a well-paid middle manager. The company's shares rose an average of 13% a year on Raymond's watch. What do you think your chances are of making $400 million, as Raymond did in his final year?

Financial Rewards of Being a Star Manager

How well compensated are managers? According to the U.S. Bureau of Labor Statistics, the median weekly wage in 2004 for American workers of all sorts was $638, or $33,176 a year. Education pays: The average 2003 income for full-time workers with a bachelor's degree was $43,000 and with a master's degree was $53,000. (For high-school graduates, it was $26,000.)

The business press frequently reports on the astronomical earnings of top chief executive officers such as Lee R. Raymond, chairman and chief executive of the oil giant ExxonMobil, who was compensated more than $686 million from 1993 to 2005, which works out to $144,573 a day.[10] However, this kind of compensation isn't common. In 2005, the median pay of CEOs running the nation's 100 largest companies was $17.9 million.[11] Another 2005 survey found that the median CEO salary and bonus of 350 big public companies was $2.4 million.[12] More usual is the take-home pay for the head of a small business: in 2000 (the latest year for which data are available), the chief executive of a $3 million firm had an average base salary of $159,543 plus about $30,000 in cash incentives, and the chief executive of a $10 million company had a total compensation of $268,092.[13] (As for nonprofits, the Council on Foundations reported that the median annual salary for CEOs and chief giving officers of nonprofits in 2004 was $110,000.)[14]

Managers farther down in the organization usually don't make this much, of course; nevertheless, they do fairly well compared to most workers. At the lower rungs, managers may make between $25,000 and $50,000 a year; in the middle levels, between $35,000 and $110,000.

There are also all kinds of fringe benefits and status rewards that go with being a manager, ranging from health insurance to stock options to large offices. And the higher you ascend in the management hierarchy, the more privileges may come your way: personal parking space, better furniture, lunch in the executive dining room, on up to—for those on the top rung of big companies—company car and driver, corporate jet, and even executive sabbaticals (months of paid time off to pursue alternative projects).

What Are the Rewards of Studying & Practicing Management?

Are you studying management but have no plans to be a manager? Or are you trying to learn techniques and concepts that will help you be an exceptional management practitioner? Either way there are considerable rewards.

The Rewards of Studying Management Students sign up for the introductory management course for all kinds of reasons. Many, of course, are planning business careers, but others are taking it to fulfill a requirement or an elective or just to fill a hole in their course schedule. Some students are in technical fields, such as accounting, finance, computer science, and engineering, and never expect to have to supervise other people.

Here are just a few of the payoffs of studying management as a discipline:

- **You will understand how to deal with organizations from the outside.** Since we all are in constant interaction with all kinds of organizations, it helps to understand how they work and how the people in them make decisions. Such knowledge may give you some defensive skills that you can use in dealing with organizations from the outside, as a customer or investor, for example.
- **You will understand how to relate to your supervisors.** Since most of us work in organizations and most of us have bosses, studying management will enable you to understand the pressures managers deal with and how they will best respond to you.
- **You will understand how to interact with co-workers.** The kinds of management policies in place can affect how your co-workers behave. Studying management can give you the understanding of teams and teamwork, cultural differences, conflict and stress, and negotiation and communication skills that will help you get along with fellow employees.
- **You will understand how to manage yourself in the workplace.** Management courses in general, and this book in particular, give you the opportunity to realize insights about yourself—your personality, emotions, values, perceptions, needs, and goals. We help you build your skills in areas such as self-management, listening, handling change, managing stress, avoiding groupthink, and coping with organizational politics.

The Rewards of Practicing Management It's possible you are planning to be a manager. Or it's possible you will start your career practicing a narrow specialty but find yourself tapped for some sort of supervisory or leadership position. However you become a management practitioner, there are many rewards—apart from those of money and status—to being a manager:

- **You and your employees can experience a sense of accomplishment.** Every successful goal accomplished provides you not only with personal satisfaction but also with the satisfaction of all those employees you directed who helped you accomplish it.
- **You can stretch your abilities and magnify your range.** Every promotion up the hierarchy of an organization stretches your abilities, challenges your talents and skills, and magnifies the range of your accomplishments.
- **You can build a catalog of successful products or services.** Every product or service you provide—the personal Eiffel Tower or Empire State Building you build, as it were—becomes a monument to your accomplishments. Indeed, studying management may well help you in running your own business.

Finally, points out Odette Pollar, who owns Time Management Systems, a productivity-improvement firm in Oakland, California, "Managers are able to view the business in a broader context, to plan and grow personally. Managers can play more of a leadership role than ever before. This is an opportunity to counsel, motivate, advise, guide, empower, and influence large groups of people. These important skills can be used in business as well as in personal and volunteer activities. If you truly like people and enjoy mentoring and helping others to grow and thrive, management is a great job."[15] ●

Mentoring. Being a manager is an opportunity "to counsel, motivate, advise, guide, empower, and influence" other people. Does this sense of accomplishment appeal to you?

1.2 SIX CHALLENGES TO BEING A STAR MANAGER

major question Challenges can make one feel alive. What are six challenges I could look forward to as a manager?

THE BIG PICTURE

Six challenges face any manager: You need to manage for competitive advantage—to stay ahead of rivals. You need to manage for diversity in race, ethnicity, gender, and so on, because the future won't resemble the past. You need to manage for the effects of globalization and of information technology. You always need to manage to maintain ethical standards. Finally, you need to manage for the achievement for your own happiness and life goals.

The ideal state that many people seek is an emotional zone somewhere between boredom and anxiety, in the view of psychologist Mihaly Csikzentmihalyi.[16] Boredom, he says, may arise because skills and challenges are mismatched: You are exercising your high level of skill in a job with a low level of challenge, such as licking envelopes. Anxiety arises when one has low levels of skill but a high level of challenge.

As a manager, could you achieve a balance between these two states? Certainly managers have enough challenges to keep their lives more than mildly interesting. Let's see what they are.

Challenge #1: Managing for Competitive Advantage—Staying Ahead of Rivals

Competitive advantage **is the ability of an organization to produce goods or services more effectively than competitors do, thereby outperforming them.** This means an organization must stay ahead in four areas: (1) being responsive to customers, (2) innovation, (3) quality, and (4) efficiency.

1. Being Responsive to Customers The first law of business is: *take care of the customer.* Without customers—buyers, clients, consumers, shoppers, users, patrons, guests, investors, or whatever they're called—sooner or later there will be no organization. Nonprofit organizations are well advised to be responsive to their "customers," too, whether they're called citizens, members, students, patients, voters, rate-payers, or whatever, since they are the justification for the organizations' existence.

2. Innovation **Finding ways to deliver new or better goods or services is called *innovation*.** No organization, for-profit or nonprofit, can allow itself to become complacent—especially when rivals are coming up with creative ideas. "Innovate or die" is an important adage for any manager.

We discuss innovation in Chapter 3.

3. Quality If your organization is the only one of its kind, customers may put up with products or services that are less than stellar (as they have with some airlines whose hub systems give them a near-monopoly on flights out of certain cities), but only because they have no choice. But if another organization comes along and offers a better-quality travel experience, TV program, cut of meat, computer software, or whatever, you may find your company falling behind. Making improvements in quality has become an important management idea in recent times, as we shall discuss.

Example

Losing Competitive Advantage: Network Television Battles "On-Demand" Technologies

The four major television networks—ABC, CBS, NBC, and Fox—have felt extreme pressure on revenues as the mass audience they used to take for granted has fragmented, causing the networks to lose their competitive advantage. Indeed, during the past dozen years, their share of the viewing audience has fallen from 72% to 46%. This has been caused by three developments, says television critic David Friend.[17]

First has been the rise of cable television, supported by its two revenue streams, advertisers and subscribers, and its offerings, which, says Friend, "made even the best network shows look strangely antique." Examples have been the HBO hits "The Sopranos" and "Deadwood," Comedy Central's "South Park," and FX's "The Shield." The major networks responded by premiering shows not just in the fall but throughout the year, by putting on serial dramas and reality shows, and by running shows in short series of only 10 or 12 episodes. However, these tactics adversely affected the ability of the networks to sell hit shows into syndication (reruns), causing them to lose further revenues.

Second has been further audience fragmentation occasioned by the change from a "linear" viewing model to an "on-demand" model. In the linear model, according to Friend, people watch a show at the time the network airs it, such as "Desperate Housewives" at 9 P.M. on ABC. In the on-demand model, viewers tune in whenever they want to, using ad-skipping digital video-recorders (TiVo systems), iPods, personal computers, and cell phones. This has two results: on-demand viewers frequently become distracted by other offerings (including "grassroots" content, such as skateboard wipeouts created by sk8hed), and they frequently skip or delete commercials. By the end of 2007, 20–40% of viewers could be in a position to zap ads.[18] This phenomenon has forced the networks to resort to more "product (or brand) integration," in which products are placed in scenes visible to viewers and advertisers are given roles in plots of shows, such as "a desperate housewife showing off a Buick at a shopping mall," in one description.[19]

Third has been the networks' obsession with beating other hit shows, moving successful shows around to different time slots in order to try to outdraw rivals. "By obsessing about whether 'Chicago Hope' will beat 'ER,'" says Friend, "the execs are making a classic *Time* vs. *Newsweek* . . . mistake: grappling with their longtime rival, oblivious of their surroundings, they all fall over the cliff together."

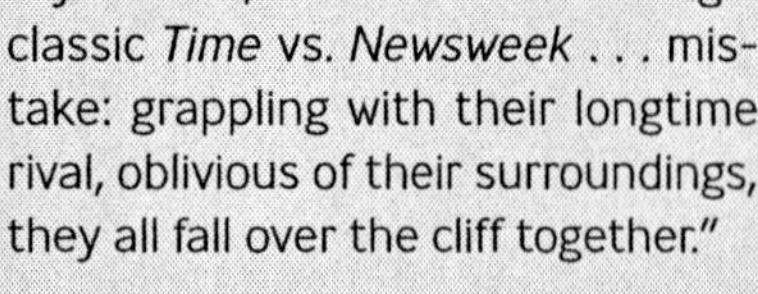

Your Call

As the networks go, will cable follow? What do you think the effect will be of iPods, DVRs, HDTV, video-on-demand, and the like on the cable industry?[20]

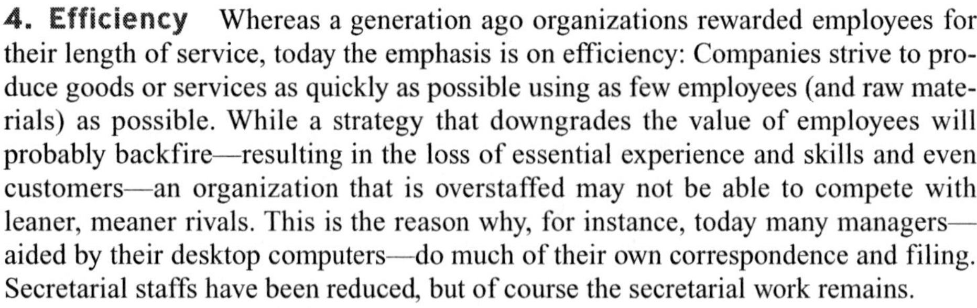

4. Efficiency Whereas a generation ago organizations rewarded employees for their length of service, today the emphasis is on efficiency: Companies strive to produce goods or services as quickly as possible using as few employees (and raw materials) as possible. While a strategy that downgrades the value of employees will probably backfire—resulting in the loss of essential experience and skills and even customers—an organization that is overstaffed may not be able to compete with leaner, meaner rivals. This is the reason why, for instance, today many managers—aided by their desktop computers—do much of their own correspondence and filing. Secretarial staffs have been reduced, but of course the secretarial work remains.

Challenge #2: Managing for Diversity—The Future Won't Resemble the Past

During the next half-century, the mix of American racial or ethnic groups will change considerably, with the U.S. becoming half minority. Nonhispanic whites are projected to decrease from 69% of the population at the turn of the 21st century to 50% in 2050.

The famous golden arches. This McDonald's store in Beijing is an example of globalization.

African Americans will increase from 13% to 15%, Asians and Pacific Islanders from 4% to 8%, and Hispanics (who may be of any race) from 13% to 24%.[21] In addition, in the coming years there will be a different mix of women, immigrants, and older people in the general population, as well as in the workforce.

Clearly, the challenge to the manager of the near future is to maximize the contributions of employees diverse in gender, age, race, and ethnicity. We discuss this matter in more detail in Chapter 3.

Challenge #3: Managing for Globalization—The Expanding Management Universe

"In Japan it is considered rude to look directly in the eye for more than a few seconds," says a report about teaching Americans how to behave abroad, "and in Greece the hand-waving gesture commonly used in America for goodbye is considered an insult."[22]

The point: gestures and symbols don't have the same meaning to everyone throughout the world. Not understanding such differences can affect how well organizations manage globally.

American firms have been going out into the world in a major way. At the same time, the world has been coming to us. Indeed, despite political outcries about white-collar jobs disappearing overseas to places such as India, foreigners actually send far more office work to the U.S. than American companies send abroad.[23] Managing for globalization will be a complex, ongoing challenge, as we discuss at length in Chapter 4.

Challenge #4: Managing for Information Technology

The challenge of managing for information technology, not to mention other technologies affecting your business, will require your unflagging attention. Perhaps most important is the ***Internet,*** **the global network of independently operating but interconnected computers, linking hundreds of thousands of smaller networks around the world.**

By 2008, according to International Data Corp., Internet trade between businesses will surpass $650 billion in the United States and $1 trillion worldwide, representing a compound annual growth of 52%.[24] This kind of ***e-commerce,*** **or electronic commerce—the buying and selling of goods or services over computer networks**—is reshaping entire industries and revamping the very notion of what a company is. More important than e-commerce, the information technology has facilitated ***e-business,*** **using the Internet to facilitate *every* aspect of running a business.** As one article puts it, "at bottom, the Internet is a tool that dramatically lowers the cost of communication. That means it can radically alter any industry or activity that depends heavily on the flow of information."[25]

Some of the implications of e-business that we will discuss throughout the book are as follows:

- **Far-ranging e-management and e-communication.** Using wired and wireless telephones, fax machines, electronic mail, or ***e-mail*****—text messages and documents transmitted over a computer network**—as well as ***project management software*****—programs for planning and scheduling the people, costs, and resources to complete a project on time**—21st-century managers will find themselves responsible for creating, motivating, and leading teams of specialists all over the world. This will require them to be masters of organizational communication, able to create concise, powerful e-mail and voice-mail messages.
- **Accelerated decision making, conflict, and stress.** The Internet not only speeds everything up, it also, with its huge, interconnected ***databases*****—computerized collections of interrelated files**—can overwhelm us with information, much of it useful, much of it not. The result affects the pace and quality of managerial decision making: one survey of 479 managers found that 77% reported making more decisions, and 43% said they had less time in

which to make decisions.[26] Among the unavoidable by-products are increased conflict and stress, although, as we will show, these can be managed.

- **Changes in organizational structure, jobs, goal setting, and knowledge management.** With computers and telecommunications technology, organizations and teams become "virtual"; they are no longer as bound by time zones and locations. Employees, for instance, may ***telecommute,*** **or work from home or remote locations using a variety of information technologies.** Meetings may be conducted via ***videoconferencing,*** **using video and audio links along with computers to let people in different locations see, hear, and talk with one another.** In addition, ***collaborative computing,*** **using state-of-the-art computer software and hardware, will help people work better together.** Goal setting and feedback will be conducted via Web-based software programs such as eWorkbench, which enables managers to create and track employee goals. All such forms of interaction will require managers and employees to be more flexible, and there will be an increased emphasis on ***knowledge management*****—the implementing of systems and practices to increase the sharing of knowledge and information throughout an organization.**

Challenge #5: Managing for Ethical Standards

With the pressure to meet sales, production, and other targets, managers can find themselves confronting ethical dilemmas. What do you do when you learn an employee dropped a gyroscope but put it in the helicopter anyway in order to hold the product's delivery date? How much should you allow your sales reps to knock the competition? (Rivals could sue for confusing or deceptive statements, according to one attorney.)[27] How much leeway do you have in giving gifts to prospective clients in a foreign country to try to land a contract? (American companies need to walk a fine line between observing the realities of the local business culture and complying with the Foreign Corrupt Practices Act, which prohibits bribery.)

Ethical behavior is not just a nicety, it is a very important part of doing business. This was made clear during the period 2003–2004 as executives from Enron, Tyco, WorldCom, Adelphia, and other companies were paraded in handcuffs before television cameras. Not since sociologist Edwin Sutherland invented the term "white-collar crime" in the 1930s were so many top-level executives being hauled into court. We consider ethics in Chapter 3 and elsewhere in the book.

Cuffed. Former Merrill Lynch & Co. executive Daniel Bayly leaves the FBI offices in Houston to go to the federal courthouse in September 2003. Bayly was charged with helping Enron Corp. appear to have met earnings targets with a loan wrongly booked as a sale. If you're tempted to stretch your ethics in order to pass a college course, do you think you'd do the same in business, where the pressures can be even worse?

Challenge #6: Managing for Your Own Happiness & Life Goals

Ann Garcia had the view that good managers push decision making down, spread the compliments, and take the blame, but after being given a team to manage at her technology company, she gave it up. "I'm just not a big enough person all the time to want to do that," she said. "Many of us realize that we don't want the career path that corporate America has to offer."[28]

Regardless of how well paid you are, you have to consider whether in meeting the organization's challenges you are also meeting the challenge of realizing your own happiness. Many people simply don't find being a manager fulfilling. They may complain that they have to go to too many meetings, that they can't do enough for their employees, that they are caught in the middle between bosses and subordinates. They may feel, at a time when Dilbert cartoons have created such an unflattering portrayal of managers, that they lack respect.[29] They may decide that, despite the greater income, money cannot buy happiness, as the adage goes.

In the end, however, recall what Odette Pollar said: "If you truly like people and enjoy mentoring and helping others to grow and thrive, management is a great job." And it helps to know, as she points out, that "one's experience in management is greatly affected by the company's culture."[30] Culture, or style, is indeed an important matter, because it affects your happiness within an organization, and we discuss it in detail in Chapter 8. ●

2.1 EVOLVING VIEWPOINTS: HOW WE GOT TO TODAY'S MANAGEMENT OUTLOOK

major question What's the payoff in studying different management perspectives, both yesterday's and today's?

THE BIG PICTURE

Management began as an art but is evolving into a science. Two principal perspectives are the *historical* and the *contemporary.* Studying management theory provides a guide to action, a source of new ideas, clues to the meaning of your managers' decisions, and clues to the meaning of outside events.

"These days, there aren't any hot, new trends, just a lot of repackaged ones from the past," writes *Wall Street Journal* columnist Carol Hymowitz.[4] "Executives have been treated to an overdose of management guides that mostly haven't delivered what they promised. Many bosses have adopted them all, regardless of their company's business model, balance sheet, competition, employee bench strength, or any other unique qualities. They have become copycat managers, trying to find a one-stop, fix-it-all answer to their various problems."

How will you know whether the next "fit-it-all" book to hit the business bestseller list is simply a recycling of old ideas? The answer is: you have to have studied history—hence the reason for this chapter.

Is Management an Art or a Science?

There's no question that the practice of management can be an art. Judy McGrath, CEO of MTV Networks, has a background in English and journalism, not business. Bill Gates, the founder of Microsoft Corp. and today the richest man in the world, had no training in management—in fact, he was a college dropout (from Harvard) with a background in computer science. Great managers, like great painters or actors, are those who have the right mix of intuition, judgment, and experience.

But management is also a science. That is, rather than being performed in a seat-of-the-pants, trial-and-error, make-it-up-as-you-go-along kind of way—which can lead to some truly horrendous mistakes—management can be approached deliberately, rationally, systematically. That's what the scientific method is, after all—a logical process, embodying four steps:

1. You observe events and gather facts.
2. You pose a possible solution or explanation based on those facts.
3. You make a prediction of future events.
4. You test the prediction under systematic conditions.

This process is now known as *evidence-based management.* Throughout the book, we describe various scientific tools that managers use to solve problems.

Two Overarching Perspectives about Management & Five Practical Reasons for Studying Them

In this chapter, we describe two overarching perspectives about management:

- **Historical. The *historical perspective* includes three viewpoints—*classical, behavioral,* and *quantitative.***

- **Contemporary. The *contemporary perspective* also includes three viewpoints—*systems, contingency,* and *quality-management.***

This is supposed to be a practical book. But what could be more practical than studying different approaches to management to see which seem to work best? After all, as philosopher George Santayana said, "Those who cannot remember the past are condemned to repeat it."

Indeed, there are five good reasons for studying theoretical perspectives:

1. **Understanding of the present.** When you view current management practices, an understanding of history will help you understand why they are still in favor, whether for the right reasons or the wrong ones.
2. **Guide to action.** Knowing management perspectives helps you develop a set of principles, a blueprint, that will guide your actions.
3. **Source of new ideas.** Being aware of various perspectives can also provide new ideas when you encounter new situations.
4. **Clues to meaning of your managers' decisions.** It can help you understand the focus of your organization, where the top managers are "coming from."
5. **Clues to meaning of outside events.** Finally, it may allow you to understand events outside the organization that could affect it or you. ●

Example

How Understanding Theory Can Help You: Is the Pyramid Hierarchy Useful or Useless?

Is there a reason for having the kind of management hierarchy that we described in Chapter 1? The idea that the company is shaped like a pyramid, with the CEO at the top and everybody else in layers below, is a legacy with strong roots in the military bureaucracy. German sociologist Max Weber thought bureaucracy was actually a rational approach to organizations, and in his day it probably was an improvement over the organizational arrangements then in place, as we'll discuss. The traditional pyramid hierarchy and bureaucracy have had a past history of great success in large corporations such as the Coca-Cola Company.

Knowing what you know about the pyramid hierarchy, can you think of any problems posed by the traditional organization chart? Could a hierarchy of boxes with lines showing who works in what department and who reports to whom actually become a corporate straitjacket?

That's what Lars Kolind, CEO of Danish digital hearing-aid producer Oticon, thought. In the early 1990s, he took Oticon's organization chart and simply threw it away. "He unilaterally abolished the old pyramid," says one account. In the new "spaghetti organization," as it came to be called, there was "no formal organization, no departments, no functions, no paper, no permanent desks."[5] All employees worked at mobile workstations, all desks were on wheels, and everybody worked on projects that were always subject to reorganization. Why such deliberate disorganization? Because if you want to have a company that is fast, agile, and innovative, as CEO Kolind did, you might want to have a flexible organizational structure that allows for fast reaction time. And it worked. By 1993, Oticon achieved the greatest profits since it was founded in 1904.

Your Call

Kolind says that the spaghetti organization structure has four characteristics: a much broader job definition, less formal structure, more open and informal physical layouts to facilitate communications, and management based on values (in Oticon's case, to help people achieve a better quality of life with the hearing they have) rather than on command-and-control mechanisms.[6] Do you think a spaghetti organization could be applied to a factory with hundreds or thousands of employees, such as a Coca-Cola bottling plant or a Ford assembly plant?

2.2 CLASSICAL VIEWPOINT: SCIENTIFIC & ADMINISTRATIVE MANAGEMENT

major question If the name of the game is to manage work more efficiently, what can the classical viewpoint teach me?

THE BIG PICTURE

The *three historical management viewpoints* we will describe include (1) the classical, described in this section; (2) the behavioral; and (3) the quantitative. The classical viewpoint, which emphasized ways to manage work more efficiently, had two approaches: (a) scientific management and (b) administrative management. *Scientific management,* pioneered by Frederick W. Taylor and Frank and Lillian Gilbreth, emphasized the scientific study of work methods to improve the productivity of individual workers. *Administrative management,* pioneered by Henry Fayol and Max Weber, was concerned with managing the total organization.

Bet you've never heard of a "therblig," although it may describe some physical motions you perform from time to time—perhaps when you have to wash dishes. A made-up word you won't find in most dictionaries, *therblig* was coined by Frank Gilbreth and is, in fact, "Gilbreth" spelled backward, with the "t" and the "h" reversed. It refers to 1 of 17 basic motions. By identifying the therbligs in a job, as in the tasks of a bricklayer (which he had once been), Frank and his wife, Lillian, were able to eliminate motions while simultaneously reducing fatigue.

The Gilbreths were a husband-and-wife team of industrial engineers who were pioneers in one of the classical approaches to management, part of the historical perspective. As we mentioned, there are *three historical management viewpoints* or approaches. *(See Figure 2.1, opposite page.)* They are

- Classical
- Behavioral
- Quantitative

In this section, we describe the classical perspective of management, which originated during the early 1900s. **The *classical viewpoint,* which emphasized finding ways to manage work more efficiently, had two branches—*scientific* and *administrative***—each of which is identified with particular pioneering theorists. In general, classical management assumes that *people are rational.* Let's compare the two approaches.

Scientific Management: Pioneered by Taylor & the Gilbreths

The problem for which scientific management emerged as a solution was this: In the expansive days of the early 20th century, labor was in such short supply that managers were hard pressed to raise the productivity of workers. ***Scientific management* emphasized the scientific study of work methods to improve the productivity of individual workers.** Two of its chief proponents were **Frederick W. Taylor** and the team of **Frank and Lillian Gilbreth.**

Frederick Taylor & the Four Principles of Scientific Management No doubt there are some days when you haven't studied, or worked, as efficiently as you could. This could be called "underachieving," or "loafing," or what Taylor called

① **Classical Viewpoint**
Emphasis on ways to manage work more efficiently

Scientific management
Emphasized scientific study of work methods to improve productivity of individual workers

Proponents:
Frederick W. Taylor
Frank and Lillian Gilbreth

Administrative management
Concerned with managing the total organization

Proponents:
Henri Fayol
Max Weber

② **Behavioral Viewpoint**
Emphasis on importance of understanding human behavior and motivating and encouraging employees toward achievement

Early behaviorists

Proponents:
Hugo Munsterberg
Mary Parker Follet
Elton Mayo

Human relations movement
Proposed better human relations could increase worker productivity

Proponents:
Abraham Maslow
Douglas McGregor

Behavioral science approach
Relies on scientific research for developing theory to provide practical management tools

③ **Quantitative Viewpoint**
Applies quantitative techniques to management

Management science
Focuses on using mathematics to aid in problem solving and decision making

Operations management
Focuses on managing the production and delivery of an organization's products or services more effectively

figure 2.1

THE HISTORICAL PERSPECTIVE

Three viewpoints are shown.

it—*soldiering,* deliberately working at less than full capacity. Known as "the father of scientific management," Taylor was an American engineer from Philadelphia who believed that managers could eliminate soldiering by applying four principles of science:

1. Evaluate a task by scientifically studying each part of the task (not use old rule-of-thumb methods).
2. Carefully select workers with the right abilities for the task.
3. Give workers the training and incentives to do the task with the proper work methods.
4. Use scientific principles to plan the work methods and ease the way for workers to do their jobs.

Taylor based his system on *motion studies,* in which he broke down each worker's job at a steel company, say, into basic physical motions and then trained workers to use the methods of their best-performing co-workers. In addition, he suggested employers institute a *differential rate system,* in which more efficient workers earned higher wages.

Frederick W. Taylor. Called the father of scientific management, Taylor published *The Principles of Scientific Management* in 1911.

Lillian and Frank Gilbreth. These industrial engineers pioneered time and motion studies. If you're an athlete, you would appreciate how small changes could make you efficient.

Although "Taylorism" met considerable resistance from employees fearing that working harder would lead to lost jobs except for the highly productive few, Taylor believed that by raising production both labor and management could increase profits to the point where they no longer would have to quarrel over them. If used correctly, the principles of scientific management can enhance productivity, and such innovations as motion studies and differential pay are still used today.

Frank & Lillian Gilbreth & Industrial Engineering As mentioned, Frank and Lillian Gilbreth were a husband-and-wife team of industrial engineers who lectured at Purdue University in the early 1900s. Their experiences in raising 12 children—to whom they applied some of their ideas about improving efficiency (such as printing the Morse Code on the back of the bathroom door so that family members could learn it while doing other things)—later were popularized in a book, two movies, and a TV sitcom, *Cheaper by the Dozen*. The Gilbreths expanded on Taylor's motion studies—for instance, by using movie cameras to film workers at work in order to isolate the parts of a job.

Lillian Gilbreth, who received a PhD in psychology, was the first woman to be a major contributor to management science.

Administrative Management: Pioneered by Fayol & Weber

Scientific management is concerned with the jobs of individuals. ***Administrative management* is concerned with managing the total organization.** Among the pioneering theorists were **Henri Fayol** and **Max Weber.**

Test Your Knowledge Exercise: *"Managerial Functions"*

Henri Fayol & the Functions of Management Fayol was not the first to investigate management behavior, but he was the first to systematize it. A French engineer and industrialist, he became known to American business when his most important work, *General and Industrial Management,* was translated into English in 1930.

Fayol was the first to identify the major functions of management (p. 12)—planning, organizing, leading, and controlling, as well as coordinating—the first four of which you'll recognize as the functions providing the framework for this and most other management books.

Max Weber & the Rationality of Bureaucracy In our time, the word "bureaucracy" has come to have negative associations: impersonality, inflexibility, red tape, a molasseslike response to problems. But to German sociologist Max Weber, a *bureaucracy* was a rational, efficient, ideal organization based on principles of logic. After all, in Weber's Germany in the late 19th century, many people were in positions of authority (particularly in the government) not because of their abilities but because of their social status. The result, Weber wrote, was that they didn't perform effectively.

A better-performing organization, he felt, should have five positive bureaucratic features:

1. A well-defined hierarchy of authority.
2. Formal rules and procedures.
3. A clear division of labor.
4. Impersonality.
5. Careers based on merit.

Weber's work was not translated into English until 1947, but, as we mentioned in the box on page 41, it came to have an important influence on the structure of large corporations, such as the Coca-Cola Company.

The Problem with the Classical Viewpoint: Too Mechanistic

The essence of the classical viewpoint was that work activity was amenable to a rational approach, that through the application of scientific methods, time and motion studies, and job specialization it was possible to boost productivity. Indeed, these concepts are still in use today, the results visible to you every time you visit McDonald's or Pizza Hut.

The flaw in the classical viewpoint, however, is that it is mechanistic: it tends to view humans as cogs within a machine, not taking into account the importance of human needs. Behavioral theory addressed this problem, as we explain next. ●

Scientific management. Car makers have broken down automobile manufacturing into its constituent tasks. This reflects the contributions of the school of scientific management. Is there anything wrong with this approach? How could it be improved?

2.3 BEHAVIORAL VIEWPOINT: BEHAVIORISM, HUMAN RELATIONS, & BEHAVIORAL SCIENCE

major question To understand how people are motivated to achieve, what can I learn from the behavioral viewpoint?

THE BIG PICTURE

The second of the three historical management perspectives was the *behavioral* viewpoint, which emphasized the importance of understanding human behavior and of motivating employees toward achievement. The behavioral viewpoint developed over three phases: (1) *Early behaviorism* was pioneered by Hugo Munsterberg, Mary Parker Follett, and Elton Mayo. (2) The *human relations movement* was pioneered by Abraham Maslow (who proposed a hierarchy of needs) and Douglas McGregor (who proposed a Theory X and Theory Y view to explain managers' attitudes toward workers). (3) The *behavioral science approach* relied on scientific research for developing theories about behavior useful to managers.

The ***behavioral viewpoint*** **emphasized the importance of understanding human behavior and of motivating employees toward achievement.** The behavioral viewpoint developed over three phases: (1) early behaviorism, (2) the human relations movement, and (3) behavioral science.

Early Behaviorism: Pioneered by Munsterberg, Follett, & Mayo

The three people who pioneered behavioral theory were **Hugo Munsterberg, Mary Parker Follett,** and **Elton Mayo.**

Mary Parker Follett. She proposed that managers and employees should work together cooperatively.

Hugo Munsterberg & the First Application of Psychology to Industry

Called "the father of industrial psychology," German-born Hugo Munsterberg had a PhD in psychology and a medical degree and joined the faculty at Harvard University in 1892. Munsterberg suggested that psychologists could contribute to industry in three ways. They could:

1. Study jobs and determine which people are best suited to specific jobs.
2. Identify the psychological conditions under which employees do their best work.
3. Devise management strategies to influence employees to follow management's interests.

His ideas led to the field of *industrial psychology,* the study of human behavior in workplaces, which is still taught in colleges today.

Mary Parker Follett & Power Sharing among Employees & Managers

A Massachusetts social worker and social philosopher, Mary Parker Follett was lauded on her death in 1933 as "one of the most important women America has yet produced in the fields of civics and sociology." Instead of following the usual hierarchical arrangement of managers as order givers and employees as order takers,

Follett thought organizations should become more democratic, with managers and employees working cooperatively.

The following ideas were among her most important:

1. Organizations should be operated as "communities," with managers and subordinates working together in harmony.
2. Conflicts should be resolved by having managers and workers talk over differences and find solutions that would satisfy both parties—a process she called *integration*.
3. The work process should be under the control of workers with the relevant knowledge, rather than of managers, who should act as facilitators.

With these and other ideas, Follett anticipated some of today's concepts of "self-managed teams," "worker empowerment," and "interdepartmental teams"—that is, members of different departments working together on joint projects.

Elton Mayo & the Supposed "Hawthorne Effect" Do you think workers would be more productive if they thought they were receiving special attention? This was the conclusion drawn by a Harvard research group in the late 1920s.

Conducted by Elton Mayo and his associates at Western Electric's Hawthorne (Chicago) plant, what came to be called the *Hawthorne studies* began with an investigation into whether workplace lighting level affected worker productivity. (This was the type of study that Taylor or the Gilbreths might have done.) In later experiments, other variables were altered, such as wage levels, rest periods, and length of workday. Worker performance varied but tended to increase over time, leading Mayo and his colleagues to hypothesize what came to be known as the *Hawthorne effect*—namely, that employees worked harder if they received added attention, if they thought that managers cared about their welfare and that supervisors paid special attention to them.

Hawthorne. Western Electric's Hawthorne plant, where Elton Mayo and his team conducted their studies in the 1920s. Do you think you'd perform better in a robotlike job if you thought your supervisor cared about you and paid more attention to you?

Ultimately, the Hawthorne studies were faulted for being poorly designed and not having enough empirical data to support the conclusions. Nevertheless, they succeeded in drawing attention to the importance of "social man" (social beings) and how managers using good human relations could improve worker productivity. This in turn led to the so-called human relations movement in the 1950s and 1960s.

The Human Relations Movement: Pioneered by Maslow & McGregor

The two theorists who contributed most to the ***human relations movement*****—which proposed that better human relations could increase worker productivity**—were Abraham Maslow and Douglas McGregor.

Abraham Maslow & the Hierarchy of Needs What motivates you to perform: Food? Security? Love? Recognition? Self-fulfillment? Probably all of these, Abraham Maslow would say, although some needs must be satisfied before others. The chairman of the psychology department at Brandeis University and one of the earliest researchers to study motivation, in 1943 Maslow proposed his famous *hierarchy of human needs:* physiological, safety, social, esteem, and self-actualization[7] (as we discuss in detail in Chapter 12).

Douglas McGregor & Theory X versus Theory Y Having been for a time a college president (at Antioch College in Ohio), Douglas McGregor came to realize that it was not enough for managers to try to be liked; they also needed to be aware of their attitudes toward employees.[8] Basically, McGregor suggested in a 1960 book, these attitudes could be either "X" or "Y."

Theory X represents a pessimistic, negative view of workers. In this view, workers are considered to be irresponsible, to be resistant to change, to lack ambition, to hate work, and to want to be led rather than to lead.

Theory Y? Debra Stark (third from left) built her Concord, Massachusetts–based Debra's Natural Gourmet store into a $2.5 million business by assigning each of her 26 employees, whom she calls "co-workers," a management role, such as monitoring product turnover. Each quarter, Stark distributes 20% of her after-tax profits among everyone, divided according to not only hours worked and salary level but also "how I see they're interacting with customers, each other, and me."

Theory Y represents the outlook of human relations proponents—an optimistic, positive view of workers. In this view, workers are considered to be capable of accepting responsibility, self-direction, and self-control and of being imaginative and creative.

The principal contribution offered by the Theory X/Theory Y perspective is that it can help managers avoid falling into the trap of the *self-fulfilling prophecy*. This is the idea that if a manager expects a subordinate to act in a certain way, the worker may, in fact, very well act that way, thereby confirming the manager's expectations: The prophecy that the manager made is fulfilled.

The Behavioral Science Approach

The human relations movement was a necessary correction to the sterile approach used within scientific management, but its optimism came to be considered too simplistic for practical use. More recently, the human relations view has been superseded by the behavioral science approach to management. ***Behavioral science*** **relies on scientific research for developing theories about human behavior that can be used to provide practical tools for managers.** The disciplines of behavioral science include psychology, sociology, anthropology, and economics. ●

Example

Application of Behavioral Science Approach: Which Is Better—Competition or Cooperation?

A widely held assumption among American managers is that "competition brings out the best in people." From an economic standpoint, business survival depends on staying ahead of the competition. But from an interpersonal standpoint, critics contend competition has been overemphasized, primarily at the expense of cooperation.[9]

One strong advocate of greater emphasis on cooperation, Alfie Kahn, reviewed the evidence and found two reasons for what he sees as competition's failure.

First, he said, "success often depends on sharing resources efficiently, and this is nearly impossible when people have to work against one another." Competition makes people suspicious and hostile toward each other. Cooperation, by contrast, "takes advantage of all the skills represented in a group as well as the mysterious process by which that group becomes more than the sum of its parts."

Second, Kahn says, competition does not promote excellence, "because trying to do well and trying to beat others simply are two different things." Kahn points out the example of children in class who wave their arms to get the teacher's attention, but when they are finally recognized they then seem befuddled and ask the teacher to repeat the question—because they were more focused on beating their classmates than on the subject matter.[10]

What does the behavioral science research suggest about the question of cooperation versus competition? One team of researchers reviewed 122 studies encompassing a wide variety of subjects and settings and came up with three conclusions: (1) Cooperation is superior to competition in promoting achievement and productivity. (2) Cooperation is superior to individualistic efforts in promoting achievement and productivity. (3) Cooperation without intergroup competition promotes higher achievement and productivity than cooperation with intergroup competition.[11]

Your Call

What kind of office layout do you think would encourage more cooperation—a system of private offices or an open-office configuration with desks scattered about in a small area with no partitions?

chapter 12

Motivating Employees

Achieving Superior Performance in the Workplace

Major Questions You Should Be Able to Answer

12.1 Motivating for Performance
Major Question: What's the motivation for studying motivation?

12.2 Content Perspectives on Employee Motivation
Major Question: What kinds of needs motivate employees?

12.3 Process Perspectives on Employee Motivation
Major Question: Is a good reward good enough? How do other factors affect motivation?

12.4 Job Design Perspectives on Motivation
Major Question: What's the best way to design jobs—adapt people to work or work to people?

12.5 Reinforcement Perspectives on Motivation
Major Question: What are the types of incentives I might use to influence employee behavior?

12.6 Using Compensation & Other Rewards to Motivate
Major Question: How can I use compensation and other rewards to motivate people?

THE MANAGER'S toolbox

Managing for Motivation: The Flexible Workplace

Can a company slice and dice the 24 hours in a day, the 7 days a week, in ways that can better motivate employees?

With the parents of so many two-paycheck families, single parents, and other diverse kinds of employees in the workforce, employers have begun to develop the so-called *flexible workplace* as a way of recruiting, retaining, and motivating employees. Among the types of alternative work schedules available:

- **Part-time work-less than 40 hours:** Part-time work is any work done on a schedule less than the standard 40-hour workweek. Some part-time workers—so-called temporary workers or contingency workers—do want to work 40 hours or more but can't find full-time jobs. Others, however, work part time by choice. Today an organization can hire not only part-time clerical help, for instance, but also part-time programmers, market researchers, lawyers, even part-time top executives.
- **Flextime-flexible working hours:** Flextime, or flexible time, consists of flexible working hours or any schedule that gives one some choices in working hours. If, for example, an organization's normal working hours are 9 A.M. to 5 P.M., a flextime worker might be allowed to start and finish an hour earlier or an hour later—for instance, to work from 8 A.M. to 4 P.M. The main requirement is that the employee be at work during certain "core" hours, so as to be available for meetings, consultations, and so on. By offering flextime hours, organizations can attract and keep employees with special requirements such as the need to take care of children or elderly parents. It also benefits employees who wish to avoid commuting during rush hour.
- **Compressed workweek-40 hours in four days:** In a compressed workweek, employees perform a full-time job in less than 5 days of standard 8- (or 9-) hour shifts. The most common variation is a 40-hour week performed in 4 days of 10 hours each, which gives employees three (instead of two) consecutive days off. The benefits are that organizations can offer employees more leisure time and reduced wear and tear and expense from commuting. The disadvantages are possible scheduling problems, unavailability of an employee to co-workers and customers, and fatigue from long workdays.
- **Job sharing-two people split the same job:** In job sharing, two people divide one full-time job. Usually, each person works a half day, although there can be other arrangements (working alternate days or alternate weeks, for example). As with a compressed workweek, job sharing provides employees with more personal or leisure time. The disadvantage is that it can result in communication problems with co-workers or customers.
- **Telecommuting & other work-at-home schedules:** There have always been some employees who have had special full-time or part-time arrangements whereby they are allowed to work at home, keeping in touch with their employers and co-workers by mail and phone. The fax machine, the personal computer, the Internet, and overnight-delivery services have now made work-at-home arrangements much more feasible.

Working at home with telecommunications between office and home is called *telecommuting*. The advantage to employers is increased productivity because telecommuters experience less distraction at home and can work flexible hours.

For Discussion Which of these alternative work schedules most appeals to you? Why?

forecast

What's Ahead in This Chapter

This chapter discusses how to motivate people to perform well. We consider motivation from four perspectives: content (covering theories by Maslow, McClelland, and Herzberg); process (covering equity, expectancy, and goal-setting theories); job design; and reinforcement. Finally, we apply these perspectives to compensation and other rewards for motivating performance.

12.1 MOTIVATING FOR PERFORMANCE

major question

What's the motivation for studying motivation?

THE BIG PICTURE

Motivation is defined as the psychological processes that arouse and direct people's goal-directed behavior. The model of how it works is that people have certain needs that motivate them to perform specific behaviors for which they receive rewards, both extrinsic and intrinsic, that feed back and satisfy the original need. The three major perspectives on motivation are need-based, process, and reinforcement.

What would make you rise a half hour earlier than usual to ensure you got to work on time—and to perform your best once there?

A new leased car? Help with college tuition? Bringing your dog to work? Onsite laundry, gym, or childcare? Free lunch? Really nice bosses?

Believe it or not, these are among the perks available to some lucky employees—and not just high-level managers.[1] Especially when employment rates are high, companies are desperate to attract, retain, and motivate key people. But even in tough economic times, there are always industries and occupations in which employers feel they need to bend over backward to retain their "human capital."

Motivation: What It Is, Why It's Important

Why do people do the things they do? The answer is this: they are mainly motivated to fulfill their wants, their needs.

What Is Motivation & How Does It Work? ***Motivation*** **may be defined as the psychological processes that arouse and direct goal-directed behavior.**[2] Motivation is difficult to understand because you can't actually see it or know it in another person; it must be *inferred* from one's behavior. Nevertheless, it's imperative that you as a manager understand the process of motivation if you are to guide employees in accomplishing your organization's objectives.

The way motivation works actually is complex. However, in a simple model of motivation, people have certain *needs* that *motivate* them to perform specific *behaviors* for which they receive *rewards* that *feed back* and satisfy the original need. *(See Figure 12.1.)*

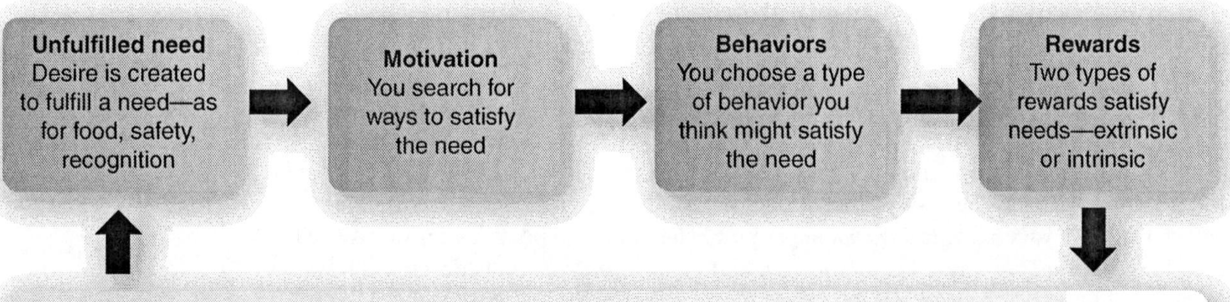

figure 12.1

A SIMPLE MODEL OF MOTIVATION

For example, you find you are hungry (need), which impels you to seek food (motive). You make a sandwich and eat it (behavior), which provides satisfaction (reward) and informs you (feedback loop) that sandwiches will reduce hunger and so should be used in the future. Or as an hourly worker you desire more money (need), which impels you (motivates you) to work more hours (behavior), which provides you with more money (reward) and informs you (feedback loop) that working more hours will fulfill your need for more money in the future.

Rewards (as well as motivation itself) are of two types—*extrinsic* and *intrinsic.*[3] Managers can use both to encourage better work performance.

Group Exercise: What Motivates You?

- **Extrinsic rewards—satisfaction in the payoff from others.** An ***extrinsic reward*** **is the payoff, such as money, a person receives from others for performing a particular task.** An extrinsic reward is an external reward; the payoff comes from pleasing others.

  Example: In performing your job as a maker of custom sailboats, you get your principal satisfaction from receiving the great amount of money buyers pay you for a boat—an extrinsic reward.
- **Intrinsic rewards—satisfaction in performing the task itself. An *intrinsic reward* is the satisfaction, such as a feeling of accomplishment, a person receives from performing the particular task itself.** An intrinsic reward is an internal reward; the payoff comes from pleasing yourself.

  Example: In making custom sailboats, you derive satisfaction—warm feelings of accomplishment and heightened self-esteem—from the process of building a sailboat.

Why Is Motivation Important? It seems obvious that organizations would want to motivate their employees to be more productive. Actually, though, there are five reasons why you as a manager will find knowledge of motivation important.[4] In order of importance, you want to motivate people to . . .

- ***Join your organization.*** You need to instill in talented prospective workers the desire to come to work for you.
- ***Stay with your organization.*** Whether you are in good economic times or bad, you always want to be able to retain good people.
- ***Show up for work at your organization.*** In many organizations, absenteeism and lateness are tremendous problems.[5]
- ***Perform better for your organization.*** Some employees do just enough to avoid being fired.[6] But what you really want is employees who will give you high productivity.
- ***Do extra for your organization.*** You hope your employees will perform extra tasks above and beyond the call of duty (be organizational "good citizens").

The Four Major Perspectives on Motivation: Overview

There is no theory accepted by everyone as to what motivates people. In this chapter, therefore, we present the four principal perspectives. From these, you may be able to select what ideas seem most workable to you. The four perspectives on motivation are (1) *content,* (2) *process,* (3) *job design,* and (4) *reinforcement,* as described in the following four main sections. ●

12.2 CONTENT PERSPECTIVES ON EMPLOYEE MOTIVATION

major question

What kinds of needs motivate employees?

THE BIG PICTURE

Content perspectives are theories emphasizing the needs that motivate people. Needs are defined as physiological or psychological deficiencies that arouse behavior. The content perspective includes three theories: Maslow's hierarchy of needs, McClelland's acquired needs theory, and Herzberg's two-factor theory.

Content perspectives, **also known as** ***need-based perspectives,*** **are theories that emphasize the needs that motivate people.** Content theorists ask, "What kind of needs motivate employees in the workplace?" ***Needs*** **are defined as physiological or psychological deficiencies that arouse behavior.** They can be strong or weak, and, because they are influenced by environmental factors, they can vary over time and from place to place.

In addition to McGregor's Theory X/Theory Y (see Chapter 2), content perspectives include three theories:

- Maslow's hierarchy of needs theory
- McClelland's acquired needs theory
- Herzberg's two-factor theory

Maslow's Hierarchy of Needs Theory: Five Levels

In 1943, Brandeis University psychology professor **Abraham Maslow,** one of the first researchers to study motivation, put forth his ***hierarchy of needs theory,*** **which proposes that people are motivated by five levels of needs: (1) physiological, (2) safety, (3) belongingness, (4) esteem, and (5) self-actualization.**[7]

Self-actualization. No one has to engage in volunteerism, as this teacher is doing with a young girl at a Garden Grove, California, after-school reading program. But for some people, according to Maslow's theory, it represents the kind of realization of the best life has to offer-after other needs are satisfied. What activity or experience within your lifetime would represent self-fulfillment for you, the best that would realize your potential?

The Five Levels of Needs In proposing this hierarchy of five needs, ranging from basic to highest level, Maslow suggested that needs are never completely satisfied. That is, our actions are aimed at fulfilling the "deprived" needs, the needs that remain unsatisfied at any point in time. Thus, for example, once you have achieved security, which is the second most basic need, you will then seek to fulfill the third most basic need—belongingness.

In order of ascendance, from bottom to top, the five levels of needs are as follows. *(See Figure 12.2.)*

figure 12.2

MASLOW'S HIERARCHY OF NEEDS

1. Physiological Needs These are the most basic human physical needs, in which one is concerned with having food, clothing, shelter, and comfort and with self-preservation.

2. Safety Needs These needs are concerned with physical safety and emotional security, so that a person is concerned with avoiding violence and threats.

3. Belongingness Needs Once basic needs and security are taken care of, people look for love, friendship, and affection.

4. Esteem Needs After they meet their social needs, people focus on such matters as self-respect, status, reputation, recognition, and self-confidence.

5. Self-Actualization Needs The highest level of need, self-actualization is self-fulfillment—the need to develop one's fullest potential, to become the best one is capable of being.

Example

Higher-Level Needs: One Man Finds a Way to Measure Integrity

Software engineer Firinn Taisdeal of Walnut Creek, California, designed a social event database, now called LinkUp Central, that offers its 19,000 San Francisco Bay-area members 12,000 events per year, from rock climbing to theater, for $5 a month. But he discovered early on that events were being ruined and hosts disappointed by people who didn't show up. "Flakes," he calls them.

So he modified the database to chart patterns of flakiness—an accountability system. Thus, if a person RSVPs for events but doesn't show up 50% of the time, his or her "reliability threshold" goes down. With some events, such as restaurant dinners, guests can sign up only if they have a reliability index of 50% or more. "By changing their behavior over time," says one report, "people can improve their ratings."[9]

Driven to raise the level of integrity in the culture, Taisdeal is an example of a "cultural creative," a term coined by sociologists Paul Ray and Sherry Ruth Anderson to describe people who long to create deep and meaningful change in their lives and in the world.[10] Another name for people like Taisdeal is "tempered radical," the term that Stanford organizational behavior professor Debra Meyerson uses to describe people who work to strike a balance between what they believe in and what the system expects.[11] In this way, they fulfill their safety needs while also striving to fulfill their self-actualization needs.

Your Call

What kind of higher-level needs do you think you could fulfill through your work?

Research does not clearly support Maslow's theory, although it remains popular among managers. "There are still very few studies that can legitimately confirm (or refute) it," one scholar writes. "It may be that the dynamics implied by Maslow's theory of needs are too complex to be operationalized and confirmed by scientific research."[8]

Using the Hierarchy of Needs Theory to Motivate Employees For managers, the importance of Maslow's contribution is that he showed that workers have needs beyond that of just earning a paycheck. To the extent the organization permits, managers should first try to meet employees' level 1 and level 2 needs, of course, so that employees won't be preoccupied with them. Then, however, they need to give employees a chance to fulfill their higher-level needs in ways that also advance the goals of the organization.

McClelland's Acquired Needs Theory: Achievement, Affiliation, & Power

David McClelland, a well-known psychologist, investigated the needs for affiliation and power and as a consequence proposed the ***acquired needs theory,* which states that three needs—achievement, affiliation, and power—are major motives determining people's behavior in the workplace.**[12] McClelland believes that we are not born with our needs; rather we learn them from the culture—from our life experiences.

The Three Needs Managers are encouraged to recognize three needs in themselves and others and to attempt to create work environments that are responsive to them. The three needs, one of which tends to be dominant in each of us, are as follows. *(See Figure 12.3, at right.)*

- **Need for achievement—"I need to excel at tasks."** This is the desire to excel, to do something better or more efficiently, to solve problems, to achieve excellence in challenging tasks.
- **Need for affiliation—"I need close relationships."** This is the desire for friendly and warm relations with other people.
- **Need for power—"I need to control others."** This is the desire to be responsible for other people, to influence their behavior or to control them.[13]

McClelland identifies two forms of the need for power.

The negative kind is the need for *personal power,* as expressed in the desire to dominate others, and involves manipulating people for one's own gratification.

The positive kind, characteristic of top managers and leaders, is the desire for *institutional power,* as expressed in the need to solve problems that further organizational goals.

Using Acquired Needs Theory to Motivate Employees McClelland associates the three needs with different sets of work preferences, as follows:[14]

- **Need for achievement.** If you (or an employee) are happy with accomplishment of a task being its own reward, don't mind or even prefer working alone, and are willing to take moderate risks, then you probably have a *high need for achievement.* That being the case, you (or your employee) would probably

figure 12.3

McCLELLAND'S THREE NEEDS

A "well-balanced" individual: achievement, affiliation, and power are of equal size

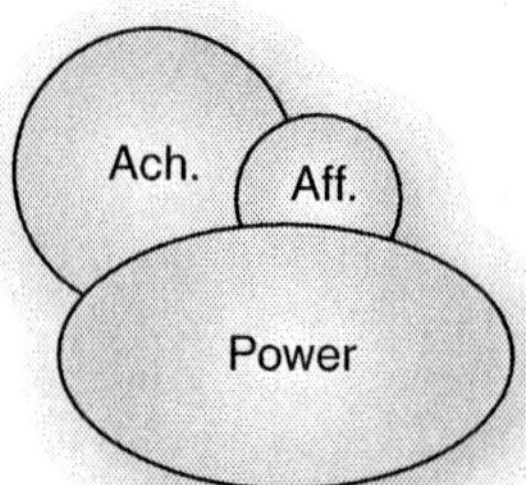

A "control freak" individual: achievement is normal, but affiliation is small and power is large

Example

Acquired Needs Theory: The Need for Power of an Ad Agency CEO

In their book *The 100-Mile Walk: A Father and Son on a Quest to Find the Essence of Leadership,* Sander A. Flaum and his son, Jonathan, describe the generational values that divide them.[16] Sander, 69, became CEO of health care ad agency Robert A. Becker Euro RSCG in New York, a $1.7 billion business with 975 employees. Jonathan, 38, started his own public/corporate relations firm, WriteMind Communications, in Asheville, North Carolina, and hires people by the project. Sander learned to be diligent and loyal and to put work ahead of family, which led to his divorce. Jonathan grew up to be self-reliant, skeptical, and determined to balance work and family.

When the two decided to coauthor a book on leadership, they arranged to walk a combined total of 100 miles together in various places, from New York City to pre-Hurricane Katrina New Orleans, during which they talked about their views of the workplace. The book offers a comparison of their outlooks. Sander's view: "Show company loyalty." Jonathan's view: "Move on if recognition and growth opportunities are absent." Sander: "Young people in India and China are not talking about work/life balance or . . . worrying about how to spend more time at home." Jonathan: "Work without adequate time for intimate connection and personal time has long-term degenerative effects." Sander: "I think you should be attuned to the knowledge that, at any time, every competitor of yours is out to recruit your best people, steal your ideas, take over your customers, and reinvent and improve your products." Jonathan: "Paranoia works . . . sometimes. But it robs us of fully enjoying those times when everything is just fine."

Your Call

In acquired needs theory, Sander would seem to embody the need for power. What needs do you think Jonathan embodies?

prefer doing the kind of work that offers feedback on performance, challenging but achievable goals, and individual responsibility for results. People high in need for achievement tend to advance in technical fields requiring creativity and individual skills.[15]

- **Need for power.** If you, like most effective managers, have a *high need for power,* that means you enjoy being in control of people and events and being recognized for this responsibility. Accordingly, your preference would probably be for work that allows you to control or have an effect on people and be publicly recognized for your accomplishments.
- **Need for affiliation.** If you tend to seek social approval and satisfying personal relationships, you may have a *high need for affiliation.* In that case, you may not be the most efficient manager because at times you will have to make decisions that will make people resent you. Instead, you will tend to prefer work, such as sales, that provides for personal relationships and social approval.

Herzberg's Two-Factor Theory: From Dissatisfying Factors to Satisfying Factors

Frederick Herzberg arrived at his needs-based theory as a result of a landmark study of 203 accountants and engineers, who were interviewed to determine the factors responsible for job satisfaction and dissatisfaction.[17] Job satisfaction was more frequently associated with achievement, recognition, characteristics of the work, responsibility, and advancement. Job dissatisfaction was more often associated with working conditions, pay and security, company policies, supervisors, and interpersonal relationships. The result was Herzberg's ***two-factor theory,*** **which proposed that work satisfaction and dissatisfaction arise from two different factors—work satisfaction from so-called *motivating factors* and work dissatisfaction from so-called *hygiene factors.***

Hygiene Factors versus Motivating Factors

In Herzberg's theory, the hygiene factors are the lower-level needs, the motivating factors are the higher-level needs. The two areas are separated by a zone in which employees are neither satisfied nor dissatisfied. *(See Figure 12.4, opposite page.)*

- **Hygiene factors—"Why are my people dissatisfied?"** The lower-level needs, ***hygiene factors,*** **are factors associated with job *dissatisfaction*—such as salary, working conditions, interpersonal relationships, and company policy—all of which affect the job *context* in which people work.**

  An example of a hygiene factor is the temperature in a factory that's not air-conditioned during the summer. Installing air-conditioning will remove a cause of job dissatisfaction. It will not, however, spur factory workers' motivation and make them greatly satisfied in their work. Because motivating factors are absent, workers become, in Herzberg's view, merely neutral in their attitudes toward work—neither dissatisfied nor satisfied.
- **Motivating factors—"What will make my people satisfied?"** The higher-level needs, ***motivating factors,*** **or simply *motivators,* are factors associated with job *satisfaction*—such as achievement, recognition, responsibility, and advancement—all of which affect the job content or the rewards of work performance.** Motivating factors—challenges, opportunities, recognition—must be instituted, Herzberg believed, to spur superior work performance.

  An example of a motivating factor would be to give factory workers more control over their work. For example, instead of repeating a single task over

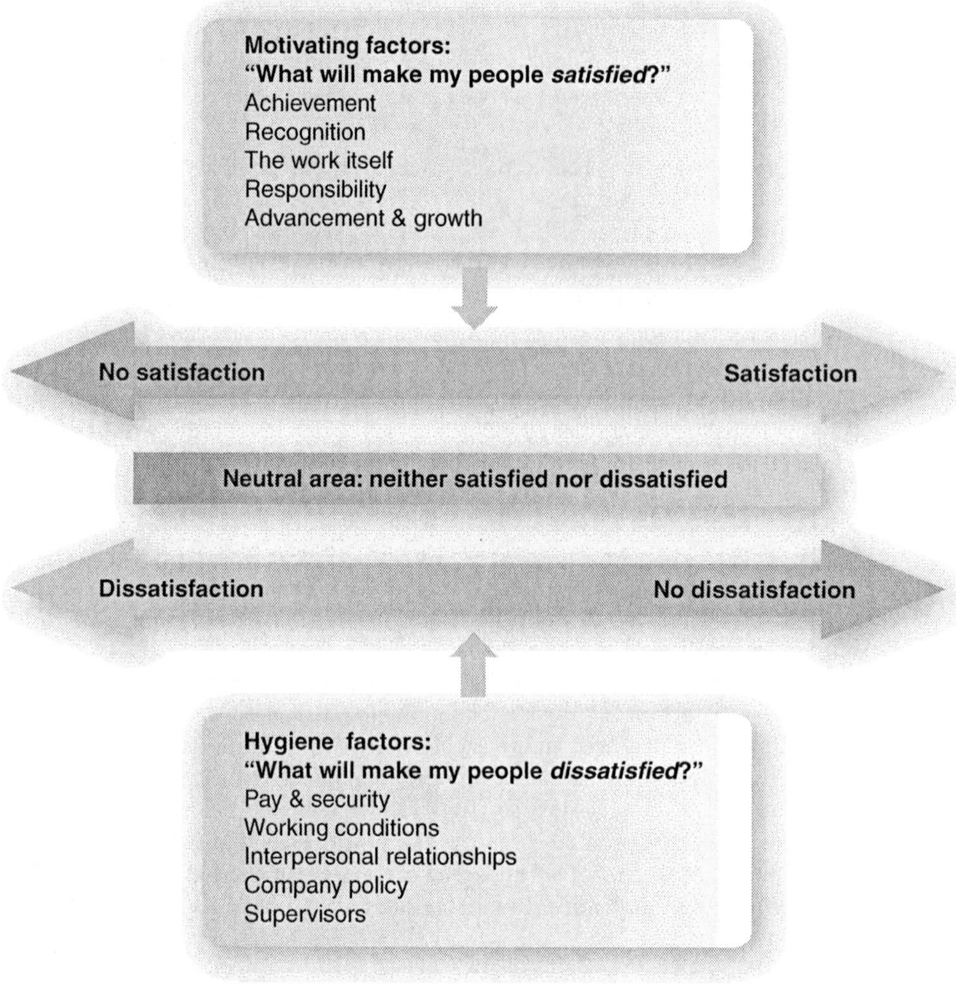

Motivating factors:
"What will make my people *satisfied*?"
Achievement
Recognition
The work itself
Responsibility
Advancement & growth

No satisfaction — **Satisfaction**

Neutral area: neither satisfied nor dissatisfied

Dissatisfaction — **No dissatisfaction**

Hygiene factors:
"What will make my people *dissatisfied*?"
Pay & security
Working conditions
Interpersonal relationships
Company policy
Supervisors

figure 12.4

HERZBERG'S TWO-FACTOR THEORY: SATISFACTION VERSUS DISSATISFACTION

and over, a worker might join with other workers in a team in which each one does several tasks. This is the approach that Swedish automaker Volvo has taken in building cars.

Using Two-Factor Theory to Motivate Employees The basic lesson of Herzberg's research is that managers should first eliminate dissatisfaction, making sure that working conditions, pay levels, and company policies are reasonable. They should then concentrate on spurring motivation by providing opportunities for achievement, recognition, responsibility, and personal growth.

The three needs theories are compared below. *(See Figure 12.5.)* ●

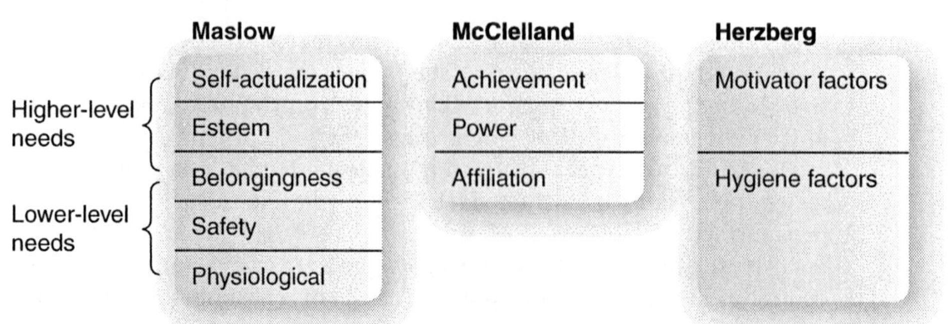

figure 12.5

A COMPARISON OF NEEDS THEORIES: MASLOW, McCLELLAND, AND HERZBERG. McClelland has no classification for lower-level needs.

12.3 PROCESS PERSPECTIVES ON EMPLOYEE MOTIVATION

major question Is a good reward good enough? How do other factors affect motivation?

THE BIG PICTURE

Process perspectives, which are concerned with the thought processes by which people decide how to act, have three viewpoints: equity theory, expectancy theory, and goal-setting theory.

Process perspectives **are concerned with the thought processes by which people decide how to act**—how employees choose behavior to meet their needs. Whereas need-based perspectives simply try to understand employee needs, process perspectives go further and try to understand why employees have different needs, what behaviors they select to satisfy them, and how they decide if their choices were successful.

In this section we discuss three process perspectives on motivation:

- Equity theory
- Expectancy theory
- Goal-setting theory

Equity Theory: How Fairly Do You Think You're Being Treated in Relation to Others?

Fairness—or, perhaps equally important, the *perception* of fairness—can be a big issue in organizations. For example, if you received a 10% bonus from Circuit City for doubling your sales, would that be enough? What if other Circuit City salespeople received 15%?

Equity theory **focuses on employee perceptions as to how fairly they think they are being treated compared to others.** Developed by psychologist **J. Stacy Adams,** equity theory is based on the idea that employees are motivated to see fairness in the rewards they expect for task performance.[18] Clearly, this is an important matter. The U.S. Department of Commerce estimates that employee theft, for example, costs American business about $50 billion a year. This may represent employees' attempts to even the score when they feel that they haven't been treated fairly by their organizations.[19]

The Elements of Equity Theory: Comparing Your Inputs & Outputs with Those of Others The key elements in equity theory are *inputs, outputs (rewards),* and *comparisons.* *(See Figure 12.6, opposite page.)*

- **Inputs—"What do you think you're putting into the job?"** The inputs that people perceive they give to an organization are their time, effort, training, experience, intelligence, creativity, seniority, status, and so on.
- **Outputs or rewards—"What do you think you're getting out of the job?"** The outputs are the rewards that people receive from an organization: pay, benefits, praise, recognition, bonuses, promotions, status perquisites (corner office with a view, say, or private parking space), and so on.
- **Comparison—"How do you think your ratio of inputs and rewards compares with those of others?"** Equity theory suggests that people

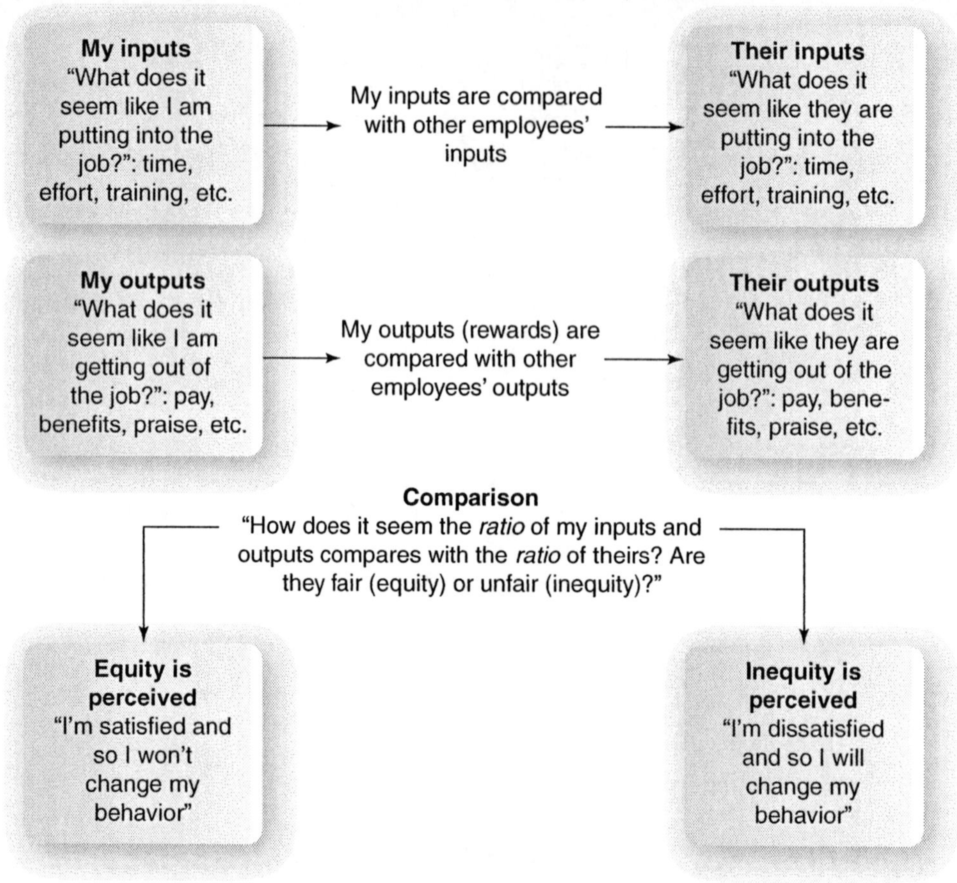

My inputs
"What does it seem like I am putting into the job?": time, effort, training, etc.

My inputs are compared with other employees' inputs

Their inputs
"What does it seem like they are putting into the job?": time, effort, training, etc.

My outputs
"What does it seem like I am getting out of the job?": pay, benefits, praise, etc.

My outputs (rewards) are compared with other employees' outputs

Their outputs
"What does it seem like they are getting out of the job?": pay, benefits, praise, etc.

Comparison
"How does it seem the *ratio* of my inputs and outputs compares with the *ratio* of theirs? Are they fair (equity) or unfair (inequity)?"

Equity is perceived
"I'm satisfied and so I won't change my behavior"

Inequity is perceived
"I'm dissatisfied and so I will change my behavior"

figure 12.6

EQUITY THEORY

How people perceive they are being fairly or unfairly rewarded

compare the *ratio* of their own outcomes to inputs against the *ratio* of someone else's outcomes to inputs. When employees compare the ratio of their inputs and outputs (rewards) with those of others—whether co-workers within the organization or even other people in similar jobs outside it—they then make a judgment about fairness. Either they perceive there is *equity*—they are satisfied with the ratio and so they don't change their behavior. Or they perceive there is *inequity*—they feel resentful and act to change the inequity.

To get a sense of your own reaction to equity differences, see the Self-Assessment at the end of this chapter.

Using Equity Theory to Motivate Employees Adams suggests that employees who feel they are being underrewarded will respond to the perceived inequity in one or more negative ways, as by reducing their inputs, trying to change the outputs or rewards they receive, distorting the inequity, changing the object of comparison, or leaving the situation. *(See Table 12.1, next page.)*

By contrast, employees who think they are treated fairly are more likely to support organizational change, more apt to cooperate in group settings, and less apt to turn to arbitration and the courts to remedy real or imagined wrongs.

Three practical lessons that can be drawn from equity theory are as follows.

1. Employee Perceptions Are What Count Probably the most important result of research on equity theory is this: no matter how fair managers think the organization's policies, procedures, and reward system are, each employee's *perception* of those factors is what counts.

table 12.1

SOME WAYS EMPLOYEES TRY TO REDUCE INEQUITY

- **They will reduce their inputs:** They will do less work, take long breaks, call in "sick" on Mondays, leave early on Fridays, and so on.
- **They will try to change the outputs or rewards they receive:** They will lobby the boss for a raise, or they will pilfer company equipment.
- **They will distort the inequity:** They will exaggerate how hard they work so they can complain they're not paid what they're worth.
- **They will change the object of comparison:** They may compare themselves to another person instead of the original one.
- **They will leave the situation:** They will quit, transfer, or shift to another reference group.

2. Employee Participation Helps Managers benefit by allowing employees to participate in important decisions. For example, employees are more satisfied with their performance appraisal when they have a "voice" during their appraisal review.[20]

3. Having an Appeal Process Helps When employees are able to appeal decisions affecting their welfare, it promotes the belief that management treats them fairly. Perceptions of fair treatment promote job satisfaction and commitment and reduce absenteeism and turnover.[21]

Expectancy Theory: How Much Do You Want & How Likely Are You to Get It?

Introduced by **Victor Vroom, *expectancy theory* suggests that people are motivated by two things: (1) how much they want something and (2) how likely they think they are to get it.**[22] In other words, assuming they have choices, people will make the choice that promises them the greatest reward if they think they can get it.

The Three Elements: Expectancy, Instrumentality, Valence What determines how willing you (or an employee) are to work hard at tasks important to the success of the organization? The answer, says Vroom, is: You will do what you *can* do when you *want* to.

Your motivation, according to expectancy theory, involves the relationship between your *effort,* your *performance,* and the desirability of the *outcomes* (such as pay or recognition) of your performance. These relationships, which are shown in the accompanying drawing, are affected by the three elements of *expectancy, instrumentality,* and *valence. (See Figure 12.7, opposite page.)*

1. Expectancy—"Will I be able to perform at the desired level on a task?" ***Expectancy* is the belief that a particular level of effort will lead to a particular level of performance.** ***This is called the** effort-to-performance expectancy.*

Example: If you believe that putting in more hours working at Circuit City selling videogame machines will

How much do you want? Would a well-appointed office represent the tangible realization of managerial success for you? How likely do you think you are to get it? The answers to these questions represent your important motivations, according to expectancy theory.

figure 12.7

EXPECTANCY THEORY: THE MAJOR ELEMENTS

result in higher sales, then you have high effort-to-performance expectancy. That is, you believe that your efforts will matter. You think you have the ability, the product knowledge, and so on so that putting in extra hours of selling can probably raise your sales of videogame machines.

2. Instrumentality—"What outcome will I receive if I perform at this level?" ***Instrumentality*** **is the expectation that successful performance of the task will lead to the outcome desired.** This is called the *performance-to-reward expectancy.*

Group Exercise:
What Rewards Motivate Student Achievement?

Example: If you believe that making higher sales will cause Circuit City to give you a bonus, then you have high performance-to-reward expectancy. You believe *if* you can achieve your goals, the outcome will be worthwhile. This element is independent of the previous one—you might decide you don't have the ability to make the extra sales, but if you did, you'll be rewarded. (Lately, because of constant shareholder complaints about overpaid top executives, boards of directors have made stronger efforts to tie CEO pay more tightly to performance.)[23]

3. Valence—"How much do I want the outcome?" ***Valence*** **is value, the importance a worker assigns to the possible outcome or reward.**

Example: If you assign a lot of importance or a high value to Circuit City's prospective bonus or pay raise, then your valence is said to be high.

For your motivation to be high, you must be high on all three elements—expectancy, instrumentality, and valence. If any element is low, you will not be motivated. Your effort-to-performance expectancy might be low, for instance, because you doubt making an effort will make a difference (because retail selling has too much competition from Internet sellers). Or your performance-to-reward expectancy might be low because you don't think Circuit City is going to give you a bonus for being a star at selling. Or your valence might be low because you don't think the bonus or raise is going to be high enough to justify working evenings and weekends.

Using Expectancy Theory to Motivate Employees The principal problem with the expectancy theory is that it is complex. Even so, the underlying logic is understandable, and research seems to show that managers are not following its principles.[24]

When attempting to motivate employees, managers should ask the following questions:

- **What rewards do your employees value?** As a manager, you need to get to know your employees and determine what rewards (outcomes) they value, such as pay raises or recognition.

Champions. Members of Italy's football (soccer) team celebrate winning the 2006 World Cup. For sports teams, performance seems easily measured by a simple outcome-whether you win or not. Do you think performance can be as clearly measured in the business world?

- **What are the job objectives and the performance level you desire?** You need to clearly define the performance objectives and determine what performance level or behavior you want so that you can tell your employees what they need to do to attain the rewards.
- **Are the rewards linked to performance?** You want to reward high performance, of course. If high-performing employees aren't rewarded, they may

Example

Use of Expectancy Theory: Tying Teacher Pay to Student Achievement in the Denver Public Schools

The concept of instrumentality can be seen in practice by considering the debate over pay-for-performance compensation for teachers. Many educational and political leaders have been promoting the idea of providing financial rewards to teachers for improving the achievement of students, as a way to improve both student achievement and teacher quality in public schools.

A landmark 4-year study sponsored jointly by the Denver public schools and the Denver Classroom Teachers Association of a pay-for-performance program found that linking teacher compensation to student achievement can trigger fundamental improvements in school systems.[26] In the pilot program, which was implemented in 13% of the district schools, teachers developed two annual objectives for the achievement of their students that required the approval of the principal. Teachers received additional compensation if they met their objectives. The study found that students whose teachers had excellent objectives achieved higher scores, on average, than other students. The findings held true at elementary, middle, and high school levels.

Since then, similar programs have been initiated in other states, including California, Florida, Kentucky, Louisiana, Minnesota, Texas, and Wisconsin.[27] Previous pay-for-performance programs have been unsuccessful because they were based on the belief that compensation is the primary incentive for teachers to perform at high levels or they were designed to punish teachers who were labeled as underperforming. The study referred to above notes that for the program to work, school districts need to align and improve the quality of the curriculum, instructional delivery, and supervision and training. In addition, districts need to be sure they have high-quality assessments that can measure student progress based on what teachers are being asked to teach.

Your Call

Do you think a pay-for-performance program can work if it is simply imposed on teachers without the teachers' collaboration? If you were a teacher, what would you recommend?

leave or slow down and affect the performance of other employees. Thus, employees must be aware that X level of performance within Y period of time will result in Z kinds of rewards.[25]

- **Do employees believe you will deliver the right rewards for the right performance?** Your credibility is on the line here. Your employees must believe that you have the power, the ability, and the will to give them the rewards you promise for the performance you are requesting.

Goal-Setting Theory: Objectives Should Be Specific & Challenging but Achievable

Goal-setting theory **suggests that employees can be motivated by goals that are specific and challenging but achievable.** According to psychologists **Edwin Locke** and **Gary Latham,** who developed the theory, it is natural for people to set and strive for goals; however, the goal-setting process is useful only if people *understand* and *accept* the goals. Thus, the best way to motivate performance is to set the right objectives in the right ways.[28]

Self-Assessment Exercise: *Assessing How Personality Type Impacts Your Goal-Setting Skills*

The benefits of setting goals is that a manager can tailor rewards to the needs of individual employees, clarify what is expected of them, provide regular reinforcement, and maintain equity.

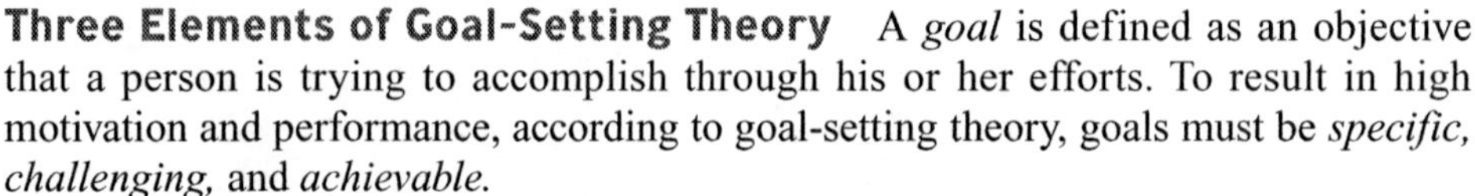

Three Elements of Goal-Setting Theory

A *goal* is defined as an objective that a person is trying to accomplish through his or her efforts. To result in high motivation and performance, according to goal-setting theory, goals must be *specific, challenging,* and *achievable.*

1. Goals Should Be Specific Goals such as "Sell as many cars as you can" or "Be nicer to customers" are too vague and therefore have no effect on motivation. Instead, goals need to be specific—usually meaning *quantitative.* As a manager, for example, you may be asked to boost the revenues of your unit by 25% and to cut absenteeism by 10%, all specific targets.

2. Goals Should Be Challenging Goal theory suggests you not set goals that a lot of people can reach, since this is not very motivational. Rather you should set goals that are challenging, which will impel people to focus their attention in the right place and to apply more effort or inputs toward their jobs—in other words, motivate them toward higher performance.

3. Goals Should Be Achievable Goals can't be unattainable, of course. You might ask data-entry clerks to enter 25% more names and addresses an hour into a database, but if they don't have touch-typing skills, that goal won't be attainable. Thus, managers need to make sure employees have additional training, if necessary, to achieve difficult goals.

Small business. Do employees in small businesses, such as this worker in a bakery, need the same kind of motivational goals as employees in large corporations? Is setting goals in small businesses, where there's apt to be less specialization, more or less difficult than in large organizations?

Using Goal-Setting Theory to Motivate Employees

In addition, when developing employee goals, you need to follow the recommendation made in Chapter 5 that goals should be SMART—that is, Specific, Measurable, Attainable, Results-oriented, and have Target dates. It is also important to make sure that employees have the abilities and resources to accomplish their goals.

Finally, make sure that you give feedback so that employees know of their progress—and don't forget to reward people for doing what they set out to do. ●

12.4 JOB DESIGN PERSPECTIVES ON MOTIVATION

major question What's the best way to design jobs—adapt people to work or work to people?

THE BIG PICTURE

Job design, the division of an organization's work among employees, applies motivational theories to jobs to increase performance and satisfaction. The traditional approach to job design is to fit people to the jobs; the modern way is to fit the jobs to the people, using job enlargement and enrichment. The job characteristics model offers five job attributes for better work outcomes.

Job design **is (1) the division of an organization's work among its employees and (2) the application of motivational theories to jobs to increase satisfaction and performance.** There are two different approaches to job design, one traditional, one modern, that can be taken in deciding how to design jobs. The traditional way is *fitting people to jobs;* the modern way is *fitting jobs to people.*

Fitting people to jobs is based on the assumption that people will gradually adapt to any work situation. Even so, jobs must still be tailored so that nearly anyone can do them. This is the approach often taken with assembly-line jobs and jobs involving routine tasks. For managers the main challenge becomes *"How can we make the worker most compatible with the work?"*

One technique is ***job simplification,*** **the process of reducing the number of tasks a worker performs.** When a job is stripped down to its simplest elements, it enables a worker to focus on doing more of the same task, thus increasing employee efficiency and productivity. This may be especially useful, for instance, in designing jobs for mentally disadvantaged workers, such as those run by Goodwill Industries. However, research shows that simplified, repetitive jobs lead to job dissatisfaction, poor mental health, and a low sense of accomplishment and personal growth.[29]

Fitting Jobs to People

Fitting jobs to people is based on the assumption that people are underutilized at work and that they want more variety, challenges, and responsibility. This philosophy, an outgrowth of Herzberg's theory, is one of the reasons for the popularity of work teams in the United States. The main challenge for managers is *"How can we make the work most compatible with the worker so as to produce both high performance and high job satisfaction?"* Two techniques for this type of job design include (1) *job enlargement* and (2) *job enrichment.*

Job Enlargement: Putting More Variety into a Job The opposite of job simplification, ***job enlargement*** **consists of increasing the number of tasks in a job to increase variety and motivation.** For instance, the job of installing television picture tubes could be enlarged to include installation of the circuit boards.

Although proponents claim job enlargement can improve employee satisfaction, motivation, and quality of production, research suggests job enlargement by itself won't have a significant and lasting positive effect on job performance. After all, working at two boring tasks instead of one doesn't add up to a challenging job. Instead, job enlargement is just one tool of many that should be considered in job design.[30]

Job Enrichment: Putting More Responsibility & Other Motivating Factors into a Job Job enrichment is the practical application of Frederick Herzberg's two-factor motivator-hygiene theory of job satisfaction.[31] Specifically, ***job enrichment***

consists of building into a job such motivating factors as responsibility, achievement, recognition, stimulating work, and advancement.

However, instead of the job-enlargement technique of simply giving employees additional tasks of similar difficulty (known as *horizontal loading*), with job enrichment employees are given more responsibility (known as *vertical loading*). Thus, employees take on chores that would normally be performed by their supervisors. For example, one department store authorized thousands of its sales clerks to handle functions normally reserved for store managers, such as handling merchandise-return problems and approving customers' checks.[32]

The Job Characteristics Model: Five Job Attributes for Better Work Outcomes

Developed by researchers **J. Richard Hackman** and **Greg Oldham,** the job characteristics model of design is an outgrowth of job enrichment.[33] **The *job characteristics model* consists of (a) five core job characteristics that affect (b) three critical psychological states of an employee that in turn affect (c) work outcomes—the employee's motivation, performance, and satisfaction.** The model is illustrated below. *(See Figure 12.8.)*

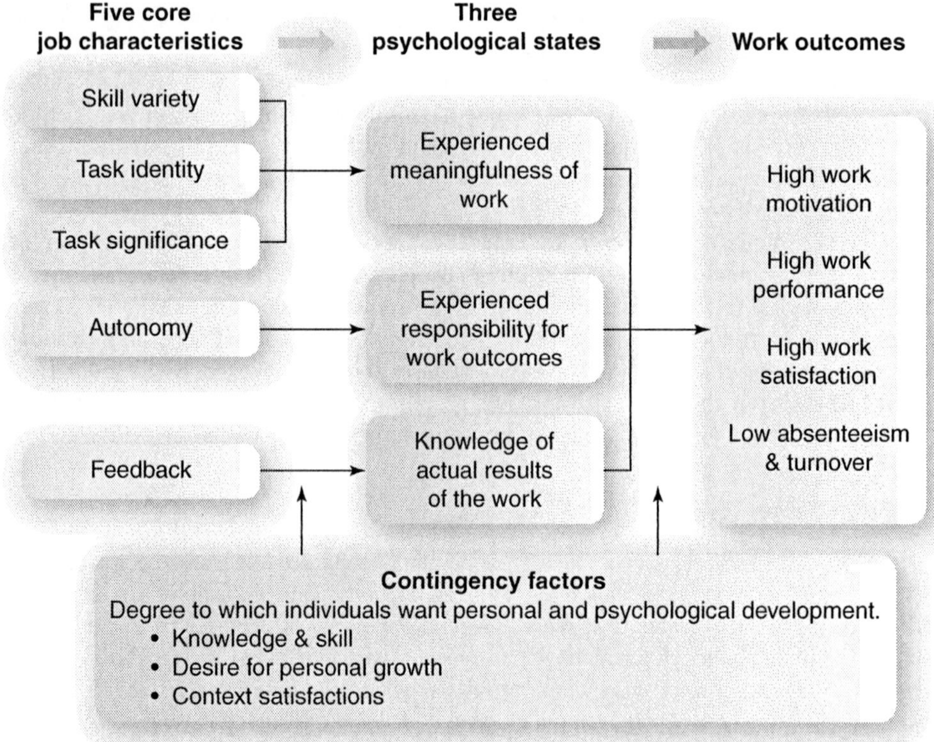

figure 12.8

THE JOB CHARACTERISTICS MODEL

Source: Adapted from J. R. Hackman and G. R. Oldham, *Work Redesign* (Reading, MA: Addison-Wesley, 1980), p. 90.

Five Job Characteristics The five core job characteristics are as follows.

1. Skill Variety—How Many Different Skills Does Your Job Require?" *Skill variety* describes the extent to which a job requires a person to use a wide range of different skills and abilities.

Example: The skill variety required by a rocket scientist is higher than that for a short-order cook.

2. Task Identity—How Many Different Tasks Are Required to Complete the Work?" *Task identity* describes the extent to which a job requires a worker to perform all the tasks needed to complete the job from beginning to end.

Example: The task identity for a craftsperson who goes through all the steps to build a hand-made acoustic guitar is higher than it is for an assembly-line worker who just installs windshields on cars.

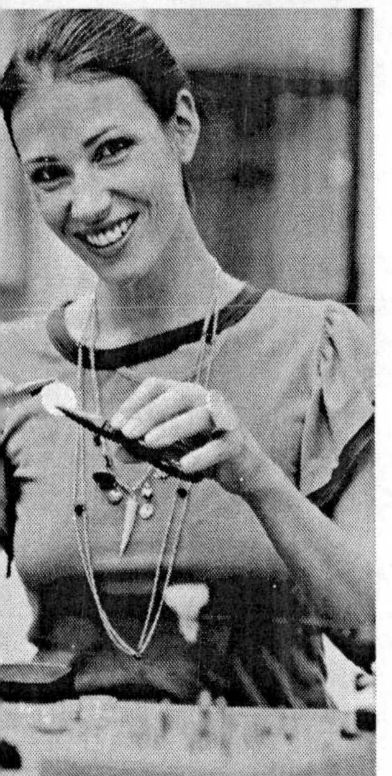

Skill variety. Being a jewelry designer~~or~~ airline pilot, building contractor, physician, or orchestra conductor—requires a greater number of skills than, say, driving a truck. Do highly skilled employees typically make good managers? What skills do jewelry designers have that would make them effective managers in other kinds of work?

3. Task Significance—How Many Other People Are Affected by Your Job?" *Task significance* describes the extent to which a job affects the lives of other people, whether inside or outside the organization.

Example: A technician who is responsible for keeping a hospital's electronic equipment in working order has higher task significance than does a person wiping down cars in a carwash.

4. Autonomy—How Much Discretion Does Your Job Give You?" *Autonomy* describes the extent to which a job allows an employee to make choices about scheduling different tasks and deciding how to perform them.

Example: College-textbook salespeople have lots of leeway in planning which campuses and professors to call on. Thus, they have higher autonomy than do toll-takers on a bridge, whose actions are determined by the flow of vehicles.

5. Feedback—How Much Do You Find Out How Well You're Doing?" *Feedback* describes the extent to which workers receive clear, direct information about how well they are performing the job.

Example: Professional basketball players receive immediate feedback on how many of their shots are going into the basket. Engineers working on new weapons systems may go years before learning how effective their performance has been.

How the Model Works According to the job characteristics model, these five core characteristics affect a worker's motivation because they affect three critical psychological states: *meaningfulness of work, responsibility for results,* and *knowledge of results.* (Refer to Figure 12.8 again.) That is, the more that workers (1) feel that they are doing meaningful work, (2) feel that they are responsible for outcomes of the work, and (3) have knowledge of the actual results of the work and how they affect others, then the more likely they are to have favorable work outcomes: *high motivation, high performance, high satisfaction,* and *low absenteeism and turnover.*

One other element—shown at the bottom of Figure 12.8—needs to be discussed: *contingency factors.* This refers to the degree to which a person wants personal and psychological development. Job enrichment will be more successful for employees with high growth-need strength. Not everyone will respond well to enriched jobs. To be motivated, a person must have three attributes: (1) necessary knowledge and skill, (2) desire for personal growth, and (3) context satisfactions—that is, the right physical working conditions, pay, and supervision.

Applying the Job Characteristics Model There are three major steps to follow when applying the model.

- **Diagnose the work environment to see whether a problem exists.** Hackman and Oldham developed a self-report instrument for managers to use called the *job diagnostic survey.* This will indicate whether an individual's so-called motivating potential score (MPS)—the amount of internal work motivation associated with a specific job—is high or low.
- **Determine whether job redesign is appropriate.** If a person's MPS score is low, an attempt should be made to determine which of the core job characteristics is causing the problem. You should next decide whether job redesign is appropriate for a given group of employees. Job design is most likely to work in a participative environment in which employees have the necessary knowledge and skills.
- **Consider how to redesign the job.** Here you try to increase those core job characteristics that are lower than national norms.

  Example: At one time, the 470 workers at Alexander Doll Co. individually produced parts for dolls. Based on input from the workers, owners organized employees into seven- or eight-person teams, each responsible for completing about 300 doll or wardrobe assemblies a day. The result: orders can now be filled in 1 or 2 weeks instead of 8.[34] ●

12.5 REINFORCEMENT PERSPECTIVES ON MOTIVATION

What are the types of incentives I might use to influence employee behavior?

THE BIG PICTURE

Reinforcement theory suggests behavior will be repeated if it has positive consequences and won't be if it has negative consequences. There are four types of reinforcement: positive reinforcement, negative reinforcement, extinction, and punishment. This section also describes how to use some reinforcement techniques to modify employee behavior.

Test Your Knowledge: *Reinforcing Performance*

Reinforcement evades the issue of people's needs and thinking processes in relation to motivation, as we described under the need-based and process perspectives. Instead, the reinforcement perspective, which was pioneered by **Edward L. Thorndike** and **B. F. Skinner,** is concerned with how the consequences of a certain behavior affect that behavior in the future.[35]

Skinner was the father of *operant conditioning,* the process of controlling behavior by manipulating its consequences. Operant conditioning rests on Thorndike's *law of effect,* which states that behavior that results in a pleasant outcome is likely to be repeated and behavior that results in unpleasant outcomes is not likely to be repeated.

From these underpinnings has come ***reinforcement theory,*** **which attempts to explain behavior change by suggesting that behavior with positive consequences tends to be repeated, whereas behavior with negative consequences tends not to be repeated.** The use of reinforcement theory to change human behavior is called *behavior modification.*

The Four Types of Reinforcement: Positive, Negative, Extinction, & Punishment

Reinforcement **is anything that causes a given behavior to be repeated or inhibited,** whether praising a child for cleaning his or her room or scolding a child for leaving a tricycle in the driveway. There are four types of reinforcement: (1) *positive reinforcement,* (2) *negative reinforcement,* (3) *extinction,* and (4) *punishment.* *(See Figure 12.9, next page.)*

Positive Reinforcement: Giving Rewards ***Positive reinforcement*** **is the use of positive consequences to encourage desirable behavior.**

Example: A supervisor who's asked an insurance salesperson to sell more policies might reward successful performance by saying, "It's great that you exceeded your quota, and you'll get a bonus for it. Maybe next time you'll sell even more and will become a member of the Circle of 100 Top Sellers and win a trip to Paris as well." Note the rewards: praise, more money, recognition, awards. Presumably this will *strengthen* the behavior and the sales rep will work even harder in the coming months.

Negative Reinforcement: Avoiding Unpleasantness ***Negative reinforcement*** **is the removal of unpleasant consequences following a desired behavior.**

Example: A supervisor who has been nagging a salesperson might say, "Well, so you exceeded your quota" and stop the nagging. Note the neutral statement; there is no

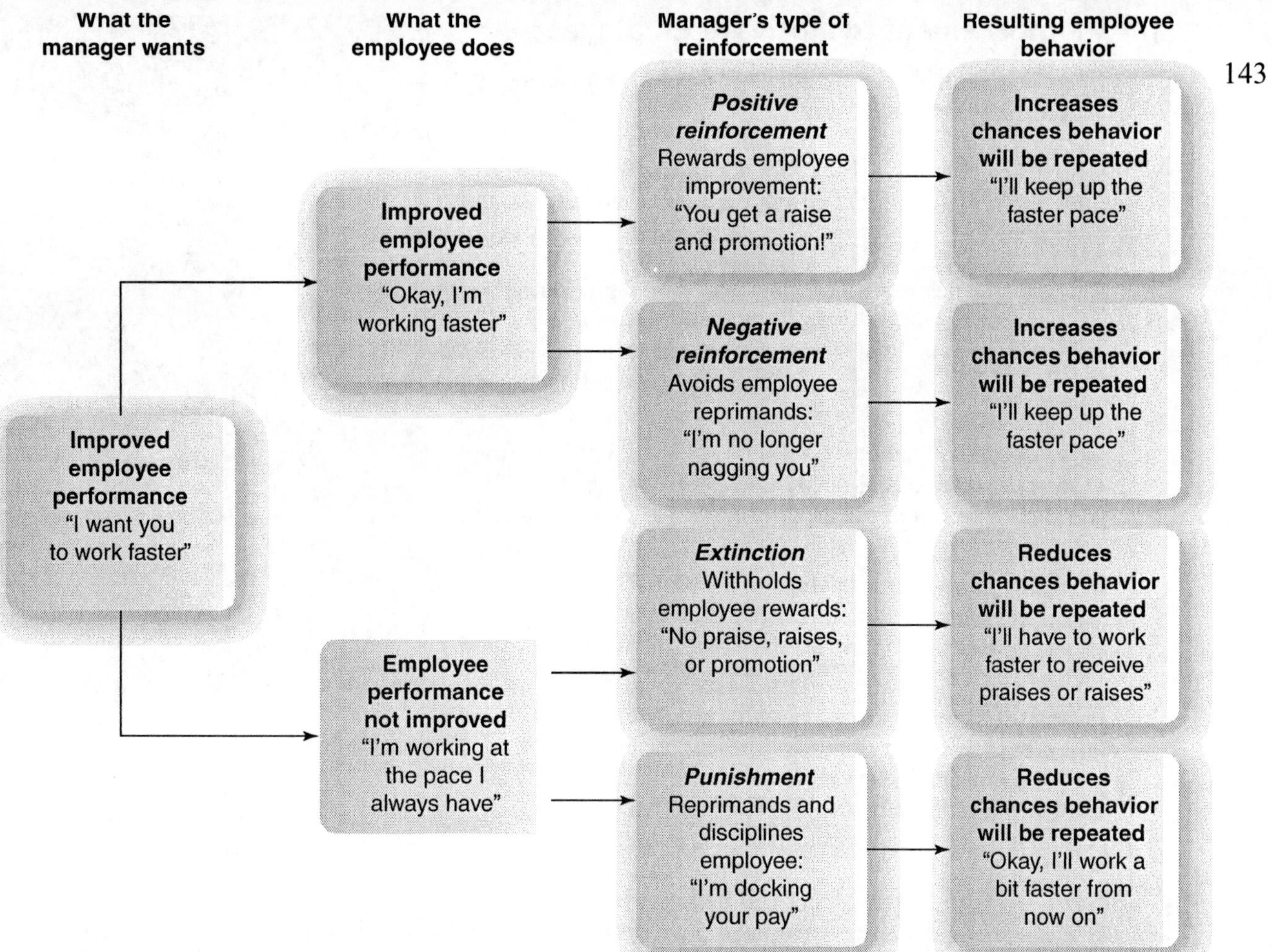

figure 12.9

FOUR TYPES OF REINFORCEMENT

These are different ways of changing employee behavior.

praise but also no longer any negative statements. This could cause the sales rep to *maintain* his or her existing behavior.

Extinction: Withholding Rewards ***Extinction* is the withholding or withdrawal of positive rewards for desirable behavior, so that the behavior is less likely to occur in the future.**

Example: A supervisor might tell a successful salesperson, "I know you exceeded your quota, but now that our company has been taken over by another firm, we're not giving out bonuses any more." Presumably this will *weaken* the salesperson's efforts to perform better in the future.

Punishment: Applying Negative Consequences ***Punishment* is the application of negative consequences to stop or change undesirable behavior.**

Example: A supervisor might tell an unsuccessful salesperson who's been lazy about making calls to clients and so didn't make quota, "Well, if this keeps up, you'll probably be let go." This could *inhibit* the salesperson from being so lackadaisical about making calls to clients.

Using Reinforcement to Motivate Employees

 The following are some guidelines for using two types of reinforcement—positive reinforcement and punishment.

Positive Reinforcement There are several aspects of positive reinforcement, which should definitely be part of your toolkit of managerial skills:

Punishment. Does getting a wallet-busting traffic violation ticket change your behavior? What if it happens several times? Yet consider also other, presumably stronger forms of governmental punishment that are supposed to act as deterrents to bad behavior. Does the possibility of the death punishment really deter homicides? Why or why not?

- **Reward only desirable behavior.** You should give rewards to your employees only when they show *desirable* behavior. Thus, for example, you should give praise to employees not for showing up for work on time (an expected part of any job) but for showing up early.
- **Give rewards as soon as possible.** You should give a reward as soon as possible after the desirable behavior appears. Thus, you should give praise to an early-arriving employee as soon as he or she arrives, not later in the week.
- **Be clear about what behavior is desired.** Clear communication is everything. You should tell employees exactly what kinds of work behaviors are desirable and you should tell everyone exactly what they must do to earn rewards.
- **Have different rewards and recognize individual differences.** Recognizing that different people respond to different kinds of rewards, you should have different rewards available. Thus, you might give a word of praise verbally to one person, shoot a line or two by e-mail to another person, or send a hand-scrawled note to another.

Punishment Unquestionably there will be times when you'll need to threaten or administer an unpleasant consequence to stop an employee's undesirable behavior. Sometimes it's best to address a problem by combining punishment with positive reinforcement. Some suggestions for using punishment are as follows.

- **Punish only undesirable behavior.** You should give punishment only when employees show frequent *undesirable* behavior. Otherwise, employees may come to view you negatively as a tyrannical boss. Thus, for example, you should reprimand employees who show up, say, a half hour late for work but not 5 or 10 minutes late.
- **Give reprimands or disciplinary actions as soon as possible.** You should mete out punishment as soon as possible after the undesirable behavior occurs. Thus, you should give a reprimand to a late-arriving employee as soon as he or she arrives.
- **Be clear about what behavior is undesirable.** Tell employees exactly what kinds of work behaviors are undesirable and make any disciplinary action or reprimand match the behavior. A manager should not, for example, dock an hourly employee's pay if he or she is only 5 or 10 minutes late for work.
- **Administer punishment in private.** You would hate to have your boss chew you out in front of your subordinates, and the people who report to you also shouldn't be reprimanded in public, which would lead only to resentments that may have nothing to do with an employee's infractions.
- **Combine punishment and positive reinforcement.** If you're reprimanding an employee, be sure to also say what he or she is doing right and state what rewards the employee might be eligible for. For example, while reprimanding someone for being late, say that a perfect attendance record over the next few months will put that employee in line for a raise or promotion. ●

Test Your Knowledge: *Reinforcement Theory*

12.6 USING COMPENSATION & OTHER REWARDS TO MOTIVATE

major question How can I use compensation and other rewards to motivate people?

THE BIG PICTURE

Compensation, the main motivator of performance, includes pay for performance, bonuses, profit sharing, gain sharing, stock options, and pay for knowledge. Other nonmonetary incentives address needs that aren't being met, such as work-life balance, growth in skills, and commitment.

Perhaps the first thing that comes to mind when you think about motivating performance is compensation—how much money you or your employees can make. But consider how motivation worked for software engineer Firinn Taisdeal, mentioned previously. In 2003, he walked away from a job just before a historic public offering that probably would have made him rich. Why? Because the people he worked with repelled him. "They were not just greedy," he says. "They had no integrity."[36] Or consider Mary Morse, another software engineer, who turned down several offers from other Silicon Valley firms, at least one of which would have made her wealthy, in order to stay with the computer-aided design firm Autodesk. The reason? She liked her bosses.[37]

Morse in particular demonstrates the truth of a Gallup Organization poll that found that most workers rate having a caring boss higher than they value monetary benefits.[38] Clearly, then, motivating doesn't just involve dollars.

Motivation & Compensation

Most people are paid an hourly wage or a weekly or monthly salary. Both of these are easy for organizations to administer, of course. But by itself a wage or a salary gives an employee little incentive to work hard. Incentive compensation plans try to do so, although no single plan will boost the performance of all employees.

Motivation as a small business owner. Susan Brown of Golden, Colorado, had dreamed of opening her own business since she was a child. However, she invented the Boppy, a simple pillow stuffed with foam, almost accidentally, when her daughter's day care center asked parents to bring in pillows to prop up infants who couldn't sit up on their own. Today the Boppy Co. has annual sales of $15 million to $25 million. For some people, like Brown, the only way to merge motivation and compensation is to own and manage their own business. What factors or incentives motivate you to work hard?

Characteristics of the Best Incentive Compensation Plans In accordance with most of the theories of motivation we described earlier, for incentive plans to work, certain criteria are advisable, as follows. (1) Rewards must be linked to performance and be measurable. (2) The rewards must satisfy individual needs. (3) The rewards must be agreed on by manager and employees. (4) The rewards believable, and achievable by employees.

Popular Incentive Compensation Plans How would you like to be rewarded for your efforts? Some of the most well-known incentive compensation plans are *pay for performance, bonuses, profit sharing, gainsharing, stock options,* and *pay for knowledge.*

- **Pay for performance.** Also known as *merit pay,* ***pay for performance*** **bases pay on one's results.** Thus, different salaried employees might get different pay raises and other rewards (such as promotions) depending on their overall job performance.[39]

  Examples: One standard pay-for-performance plan, already mentioned, is payment according to a ***piece rate,*** **in which employees are paid according to how much output they produce,** as is often used with farmworkers picking fruit and vegetables. Another is the ***sales commission,*** **in which sales representatives are paid a percentage of the earnings the company made from their sales,** so that the more they sell, the more they are paid. We discussed teacher pay for performance under expectancy theory. A good deal of the criticism of excessive executive pay is that it has not been tied to company performance.[40]
- **Bonuses.** ***Bonuses*** **are cash awards given to employees who achieve specific performance objectives.**

  Example: Nieman Marcus, the department store, pays its salespeople a percentage of the earnings from the goods they sell.
- **Profit sharing.** ***Profit sharing*** **is the distribution to employees of a percentage of the company's profits.**

  Example: In one T-shirt and sweatshirt manufacturing company, 10% of pretax profits are distributed to employees every month, and more is given out at the end of the year. Distributions are apportioned according to such criteria as performance, attendance, and lateness for individual employees.
- **Gainsharing.** ***Gainsharing*** **is the distribution of savings or "gains" to groups of employees who reduced costs and increased measurable productivity.**

  Example: There are different types of gainsharing plans, but in one known as the *Scanlon plan,* developed in the 1920s by a steel-industry union leader named Joseph Scanlon, a portion of any cost savings, usually 75%, are distributed back to employees; the company keeps the other 25%.[41]
- **Stock options.** With ***stock options,*** **certain employees are given the right to buy stock at a future date for a discounted price.** The motivator here is that employees holding stock options will supposedly work hard to make the company's stock rise so that they can obtain it at a cheaper price. By giving stock options to all employees who work 20 or more hours a week, Starbucks Corp. has been able to hold its annual turnover rate to 60%—in an industry (fast food and restaurants) in which 300% is not unheard of.[42] (The use of stock options has been criticized recently because many companies allowed "backdating"—permitting their executives to buy company stock at low purchase prices from previous days or weeks. As one writer points out, this is sort of like being able to make a fortune by betting on a Kentucky Derby whose outcome you've known for some time.[43])

- **Pay for knowledge.** Also known as *skill-based pay*, ***pay for knowledge*** **ties employee pay to the number of job-relevant skills or academic degrees they earn.**

  Example: The teaching profession is a time-honored instance of this incentive, in which elementary and secondary teachers are encouraged to increase their salaries by earning further college credit. However, firms such as FedEx also have pay-for-knowledge plans.

Nonmonetary Ways of Motivating Employees

Employees who can behave autonomously, solve problems, and take the initiative are apt to be the very ones who will leave if they find their own needs aren't being met—namely:[44]

- **The need for work-life balance.** A PricewaterhouseCoopers survey of 2,500 university students in 11 countries found that 57% named as their primary career goal "attaining a balance between personal life and career."[45] A 25-year study of values in the United States found that "employees have become less convinced that work should be an important part of one's life or that working hard makes one a better person."[46]
- **The need to expand skills.** Having watched their parents undergo downsizing, younger workers in particular are apt to view a job as a way of gaining skills that will enable them to earn a decent living in the future.
- **The need to matter.** Workers now want to be with an organization that allows them to feel they matter. They want to commit to their profession or fellow team members rather than have to profess a blind loyalty to the corporation.

There is a whole class of nonmonetary incentives to attract, retain, and motivate employees. The foremost example is the *flexible workplace*—including part-time work, flextime, compressed workweek, job sharing, and telecommuting. Other incentives can be expressed simply as *treat employees well,* some examples of which follow.

Thoughtfulness: The Value of Being Nice A study by Walker Information, an Indianapolis-based research firm, found that employers spend too little time showing workers they matter, as manifested in lack of communication and lack of interest in new ideas and contributions.[47] A majority of employees feel underappreciated, according to a 1999 survey. Forty percent of employees who rated their boss's performance as poor said they were likely to look for a new job; only 11% of those who rated it excellent said they would.[48] "Being nice" to employees means, for example, reducing criticism, becoming more effusive in your praise, and writing thank-you notes to employees for exceptional performance.[49]

The No. 1 reason people quit their jobs, it's believed, is their dissatisfaction with their supervisors, not their paychecks. Thus, industrial psychologist B. Lynn Ware suggests that if you learn valued employees are disgruntled, you should discuss it with them.[50] "It's extraordinary how often it is the small and often banal gestures that are the most meaningful," says another expert. "People will often say things like, 'I'm not really happy, but not yet prepared to jump ship because my boss was really good to me when my mother was sick.'"[51] Employers can promote personal relationships, which most employees are concerned about on the job, by offering breaks or other opportunities in which people can mix and socialize.

Work-Life Benefits Work-life benefits, according to Kathie Lingle, are programs "used by employers to increase productivity and commitment by removing certain barriers that make it hard for people to strike a balance between their work and personal lives."[52]

Lingle, who is national work-life director for KPMG, an accounting and consulting firm, emphasizes that work-life benefits "are not a reward, but a way of getting work done." After all, some employees are low performers simply because of a lack of life-work balance, with great demands at home. "If you only give these 'rewards' to existing high performers," says Lingle, "you're cutting people off who could, with some support, be high performers." Nevertheless, handing out extra time off can be used to reward performance and prevent burnout.[53]

Besides alternative scheduling, work-life benefits include helping employees with daycare costs or even establishing on-site centers; domestic-partner benefits; job-protected leave for new parents; and provision of technology such as mobile phones and laptops to enable parents to work at home.[54]

Surroundings The cubicle, according to new research, is stifling the creativity and morale of many workers, and the bias of modern-day office designers for open spaces and neutral colors is leading to employee complaints that their workplaces are too noisy or too bland.

"There is no such thing as something that works for everybody," says Alan Hedge, a professor of environmental analysis at Cornell University.[55] An 8-foot-by-8-foot cubicle may not be a good visual trigger for human brains, and companies wanting to improve creativity and productivity may need to think about giving office employees better things to look at.

Skill-Building & Educational Opportunities Learning opportunities can take two forms. Managers can see that workers are matched with co-workers from whom they can learn, allowing them, for instance, to "shadow" workers in other jobs or be in interdepartmental task forces. There can also be tuition reimbursement for part-time study at a college or university.[56]

Sabbaticals Intel and Apple understand that in a climate of 80-hour weeks people need to recharge themselves. But even McDonald's offers sabbaticals to longtime employees, giving a month to a year of paid time off in which to travel, learn, and pursue personal projects. The aim, of course, is to enable employees to recharge themselves but also, it is hoped, to cement their loyalty to the organization.[57] ●

Cubicle culture. It might be too difficult to design a setup in which everyone has an office with a view. But would it be possible to design a layout in which everyone has a private office? Do you think it would better motivate employees?

chapter 14

Power, Influence, & Leadership

From Becoming a Manager to Becoming a Leader

Major Questions You Should Be Able to Answer

14.1 The Nature of Leadership: Wielding Influence
Major Question: I don't want to be just a manager; I want to be a leader. What's the difference between the two?

14.2 Trait Approaches: Do Leaders Have Distinctive Personality Characteristics?
Major Question: What does it take to be a successful leader?

14.3 Behavioral Approaches: Do Leaders Show Distinctive Patterns of Behavior?
Major Question: Do effective leaders behave in similar ways?

14.4 Contingency Approaches: Does Leadership Vary with the Situation?
Major Question: How might effective leadership vary according to the situation at hand?

14.5 The Full-Range Model: Uses of Transactional & Transformational Leadership
Major Question: What does it take to truly inspire people to perform beyond their normal levels?

14.6 Six Additional Perspectives
Major Question: If there are many ways to be a leader, which one would describe me best?

THE MANAGER'S toolbox

How to Become a Star in the Workplace

People who are stars at work "are made, not born," says Carnegie Mellon professor Robert E. Kelley. "They have a fundamentally different conception of what work is."

Here are nine "star strategies" Kelly has identified, which average performers can adopt to become star performers—even leaders, the subject of this chapter.[1]

- **Initiative:** Initiative, says Kelley, is doing something outside your regular job that makes a difference to the company's core mission—doing something beyond your job description that helps other people. Initiative means you need to see the activity through to the end and you may need to take some risks.
- **Networking:** Star performers use networking to multiply their productivity, to do their current jobs better. "Average performers wait until they need some information, then cold-call someone to get it," Kelley says. "Stars know that you can't get work done today without a knowledge network and that you've got to put it in place beforehand."
- **Self-management:** Stars know how to get ahead of the game instead of waiting for the game to come to them. They look at the big picture and think about managing their whole life at work. They understand who they are and how they work best.
- **Perspective:** Average performers tend to see things just from their own points of view, says Kelley. Star performers try to think how things look through the eyes of their boss, co-workers, clients, and competitors. That depth of perspective can lead to better solutions.
- **Followership:** Stars know not only how to stand out but also how to help out—to be a follower as well as a leader. The idea is that if you help out others, they will later look out for you.
- **Leadership:** Star performers lead by understanding other people's interests and by using persuasion to bring out the best in people. People want leaders who are knowledgeable, who bring energy to a project and create energy in other people, and who pay close attention to the needs of everyone involved in the project.
- **Teamwork:** Stars join only workplace teams in which they think they will make a difference, and they become very good participants. They "make sure, once the team is put together, that it actually gets the job done," says Kelley.
- **Organizational savvy:** Average performers think of office politics as being dirty. Stars avoid getting needlessly involved in office melodramas, but they learn how to manage competing interests to achieve their work goals. They learn that not just one perspective is right, but that there are different perspectives.
- **Show and tell:** In both formal and informal meetings, stars learn how to craft their messages and to time them so that people pay attention. To excel at "show and tell," they learn to match the language of their communication to the language that people speak, then deliver the message in a way that works for them.

The good news is that these nine strategies can be learned. Like improving yourself in a sport, you identify the areas in which you need to improve and then practice those improvements every day. Take a look at yourself, then at the star performers you know. Then become a student of the stars—do what they do.

For Discussion Which two of these qualities do you think you need to work on most in order to develop into a star performer?

forecast

What's Ahead in This Chapter

Are there differences between managers and leaders? This chapter considers this question. We discuss the sources of a leader's power and how leaders use persuasion to influence people. We then consider the following approaches to leadership: trait, behavioral, contingency, full-range, and six additional perspectives.

14.1 THE NATURE OF LEADERSHIP: WIELDING INFLUENCE

major question I don't want to be just a manager; I want to be a leader. What's the difference between the two?

THE BIG PICTURE

Being a manager and being a leader are not the same. A leader is able to influence employees to voluntarily pursue the organization's goals. Leadership is needed for organizational change. We describe five sources of power leaders may draw on. Leaders use the power of persuasion or influence to get others to follow them. Five approaches to leadership are described in the next five sections.

Leadership. What is it? Is it a skill anyone can develop?

***Leadership* is the ability to influence employees to voluntarily pursue organizational goals.**[2] In an effective organization, leadership is present at all levels, say Tom Peters and Nancy Austin in *A Passion for Excellence,* and it represents the sum of many things. Leadership, they say, "means vision, cheerleading, enthusiasm, love, trust, verve, passion, obsession, consistency, the use of symbols, paying attention as illustrated by the content of one's calendar, out-and-out drama (and the management thereof), creating heroes at all levels, coaching, effectively wandering around, and numerous other things."[3]

Managers & Leaders: Not Always the Same

Group Exercise: *What Kind of Leader Do You Prefer?*

Group Exercise: *What Is Your Motivation to Lead?*

You see the words "manager" and "leader" used interchangeably all the time. However, as one leadership expert has said, "leaders manage and managers lead, but the two activities are not synonymous."[4]

Retired Harvard Business School professor **John Kotter** suggests that one is not better than the other, that in fact they are complementary systems of action. The difference is that . . .

- *Management* is about coping with *complexity,*
- *Leadership* is about coping with *change.*[5]

Let's consider these differences.

Being a Manager: Coping with Complexity Management is necessary because complex organizations, especially the large ones that so much dominate the economic landscape, tend to become chaotic unless there is good management.

According to Kotter, companies manage complexity in three ways:

- **Determining what needs to be done—planning and budgeting.** Companies manage complexity first by *planning and budgeting*—setting targets or goals for the future, establishing steps for achieving them, and allocating resources to accomplish them.
- **Creating arrangements of people to accomplish an agenda—organizing and staffing.** Management achieves its plan by *organizing and staffing,* Kotter says—creating the organizational structure and hiring qualified individuals to fill the necessary jobs, then devising systems of implementation.
- **Ensuring people do their jobs—controlling and problem solving.** Management ensures the plan is accomplished by *controlling and problem solving,* says

Kotter. That is, managers monitor results versus the plan in some detail by means of reports, meetings, and other tools. They then plan and organize to solve problems as they arise.

Being a Leader: Coping with Change As the business world has become more competitive and volatile, doing things the same way as last year (or doing it 5% better) is no longer a formula for success. More changes are required for survival—hence the need for leadership.

Leadership copes with change in three ways:

- **Determining what needs to be done—setting a direction.** Instead of dealing with complexity through planning and budgeting, leaders strive for constructive change by *setting a direction.* That is, they develop a vision for the future, along with strategies for realizing the changes.
- **Creating arrangements of people to accomplish an agenda—aligning people.** Instead of organizing and staffing, leaders are concerned with *aligning people,* Kotter says. That is, they communicate the new direction to people in the company who can understand the vision and build coalitions that will realize it.
- **Ensuring people do their jobs—motivating and inspiring.** Instead of controlling and problem solving, leaders try to achieve their vision by *motivating and inspiring.* That is, they appeal to "basic but often untapped human needs, values, and emotions," says Kotter, to keep people moving in the right direction, despite obstacles to change.

Do Kotter's ideas describe real leaders in the real business world? Certainly many participants in a seminar convened by *Harvard Business Review* appeared to agree. "The primary task of leadership is to communicate the vision and the values of an organization," Frederick Smith, chairman and CEO of FedEx, told the group. "Second, leaders must win support for the vision and values they articulate. And third, leaders have to reinforce the vision and the values."[6]

Managers have legitimate power (as we'll describe) that derives from the formal authority of the positions to which they have been appointed. This power allows managers to hire and fire, reward and punish. Managers plan, organize, and control, but they don't necessarily have the characteristics to be leaders.

Whereas management is a process that lots of people are able to learn, leadership is more visionary. As we've said, leaders inspire others, provide emotional support, and try to get employees to rally around a common goal. Leaders also play a role in creating a vision and strategic plan for an organization, which managers are then charged with implementing.[7]

Do you have what it takes to be a leader? To learn more about the skills required and to assess your own leadership ability, try the Self-Assessment at the end of this chapter.

Amazing Amazon. Jeffrey Bezos, founder and CEO of online retailer Amazon.com, has done nearly everything Kotter suggests. For instance, Bezos's "culture of divine discontent" permits employees to plunge ahead with new ideas even though they know that most will probably fail.

Five Sources of Power

To really understand leadership, we need to understand the concept of power and authority. *Authority* is the right to perform or command; it comes with the job. In contrast, *power* is the extent to which a person is able to influence others so they respond to orders.

People who pursue ***personalized power*—power directed at helping oneself**—as a way of enhancing their own selfish ends may give the word power a bad name. However, there is another kind of power, ***socialized power*—power directed at helping others.**[8] This is the kind of power you hear in expressions such as "My goal is to have a powerful impact on my community."

Within organizations there are typically five sources of power leaders may draw on: *legitimate, reward, coercive, expert,* and *referent.*

1. Legitimate Power: Influencing Behavior Because of One's Formal Position ***Legitimate power,*** **which all managers have, is power that results from managers' formal positions within the organization.** All managers have legitimate power over their employees, deriving from their position, whether it's a construction supervisor, ad account supervisor, sales manager, or CEO. This power may be exerted both positively or negatively—as praise or as criticism, for example.

2. Reward Power: Influencing Behavior by Promising or Giving Rewards ***Reward power,*** **which all managers have, is power that results from managers' authority to reward their subordinates.** Rewards can range from praise to pay raises, from recognition to promotions.

Example: Lloyd D. Ward, former CEO of Maytag and among the highest-ranking African Americans in corporate America, skillfully uses praise to reward positive behavior both on and off the job. For instance, while teaching karate moves during a workout with a reporter, he used such phrases as "You got it. Cool!" and "Outstanding! . . . Go! Go, David!"[9]

3. Coercive Power: Influencing Behavior by Threatening or Giving Punishment ***Coercive power,*** **which all managers have, results from managers' authority to punish their subordinates.** Punishment can range from verbal or written reprimands to demotions to terminations. In some lines of work, fines and suspensions may be used. Coercive power has to be used judiciously, of course, since a manager who is seen as being constantly negative will produce a lot of resentments among employees. But there have been many leaders who have risen to the top of major corporations—such as Disney's Michael Eisner, Miramax's Harvey Weinstein, and Hewlett-Packard's Carly Fiorina—who have been abrasive and intimidating.[10]

4. Expert Power: Influencing Behavior Because of One's Expertise ***Expert power*** **is power resulting from one's specialized information or expertise.** Expertise, or special knowledge, can be mundane, such as knowing the work schedules and assignments of the people who report to you. Or it can be sophisticated, such as having computer or medical knowledge. Secretaries may have expert power because, for example, they have been in a job a long time and know all the necessary contacts. CEOs may have expert power because they have strategic knowledge not shared by many others.

5. Referent Power: Influencing Behavior Because of One's Personal Attraction ***Referent power*** **is power deriving from one's personal attraction.** As we will see later in this chapter (under the discussion of transformational leadership), this kind of power characterizes strong, visionary leaders who are able to persuade their followers by dint of their personality, attitudes, or background. Referent power may be associated with managers, but it is more likely to be characteristic of leaders.

Leadership & Influence: Using Persuasion to Get Your Way at Work

What would you do if you discovered your car stolen from the parking lot? Here's what Doug Dusenberg, a Houston, Texas, businessman, did on noticing his Jeep Cherokee missing. He telephoned the number of his car phone, and when one of the pair of young

Example

A Strong Leader: Andy Grove, Former CEO of Intel Corp.

Symbolic of his ability to reinvent himself, Andy Grove has had three different names in his life. Born in 1936 as a Hungarian Jew, he was known as Andras Istvan Grof until 1944, when the Nazis invaded Hungary, at which point his mother changed his name to the Slavic Andras Malesevics. The following year, when the communists arrived, he changed back to Andras Grof. Nauseated by Communism, he escaped and arrived in the U.S. in 1957, where he enrolled at City College of New York and changed his name to Andrew Stephen Grove.

In 1968, with a PhD in chemical engineering, Grove joined two engineering colleagues in starting Intel Corporation in Mountain View, California, where at age 32 he found himself in the role of leader in a manufacturing startup. It was then that he began to teach himself about management. "Grove succeeded where others didn't," says historian Richard Tedlow, "in part, by approaching management as a discipline unto itself. There's a real urgency in his efforts to school himself: He never lost his Hungarian refugee's apprehension of the risk of imminent failure."[12]

By 1983, Intel was a $1.1 billion maker of memory chips and Grove had become its president. But something was about to happen that would reinforce in him a lesson he would later write about in his book *Only the Paranoid Survive*—namely, that in business you often don't see the cliff until you've already walked off it.[13] In the mid-1980s, Intel woke up to find that Japanese companies had mastered the industry it had invented and were turning memory chips into a commodity, so that in a single year Intel profits plunged from $198 million to $2 million.

A key to Grove's leadership was that he seemed to be one of the original practitioners of what we in this text have described as "evidence-based management." His management style was "direct and confrontational," says *BusinessWeek*. "His shouts echoed down company halls."[14] Adds Tedlow, "At Intel he fostered a culture in which 'knowledge power' would trump 'position power.' Anyone could challenge anyone else's idea, so long as it was about the idea and not the person—and so long as you were ready for the demand 'Prove it.' That required data. Without data, an idea was only a story—a representation of reality and thus subject to distortion."[15]

It was at that point that Grove made the painful decision to abandon Intel-the-memory-chip-company, firing some 8,000 people, and to stake its future on the microprocessor. The personal computer was just coming into being, and once IBM chose to base its PCs on Intel's processor chip, the former memory company started a successful 11-year run. In 1986, it took a chance when launching the Intel 386 microprocessor to license it not just to IBM but to other computer makers as well. With the success of Microsoft's smash-hit Windows 3.0, designed to work on 386-chip machines, Intel began a compound annual growth rate of nearly 30%.

Andy Grove is celebrated as a leader because, as Tedlow says, he "was willing to let go of his instincts—since they could be wrong—and view himself as a student might: from outside, peering down with the wide-angle, disinterested perspective of the observer. . . . It is the singular ability to inhabit both roles at once—subject and object, actor and audience, master and student—that sets Grove apart."

Your Call

Which of the five sources of leadership power do you think Grove represents? Do you think you could follow Grove's example?

joyriders answered, he talked them into returning the car in exchange for keeping $20 that was in the glove compartment.[11]

Dusenberg probably would be considered to have leadership skills because of his powers of persuasion, or *influence.* Influence is the ability to get others to follow your wishes. There are nine general tactics for trying to influence others, but some work better than others. In one pair of studies, employees were asked in effect, "How do you get your boss, coworker, or subordinate to do something you want?" The nine answers—ranked from most used to least used tactics—were as follows.[16]

1. Rational Persuasion Trying to convince someone by using reason, logic, or facts.
Example: "You know, all the cutting-edge companies use this approach."

2. Inspirational Appeals Trying to build enthusiasm or confidence by appealing to others' emotions, ideals, or values.
Example: "If we do this as a goodwill gesture, customers will love us."

3. Consultation Getting others to participate in a decision or change.
Example: "Wonder if I could get your thoughts about this matter."

4. Ingratiating Tactics Acting humble or friendly or making someone feel good or feel important before making a request.
Example: "I hate to impose on your time, knowing how busy you are, but you're the only one who can help me."

5. Personal Appeals Referring to friendship and loyalty when making a request.
Example: "We've known each other a long time, and I'm sure I can count on you."

6. Exchange Tactics Reminding someone of past favors or offering to trade favors.
Example: "Since I backed you at last month's meeting, maybe you could help me this time around."

7. Coalition Tactics Getting others to support your effort to persuade someone.
Example: "Everyone in the department thinks this is a great idea."

8. Pressure Tactics Using demands, threats, or intimidation to gain compliance.
Example: "If this doesn't happen, you'd better think about cleaning out your desk."

9. Legitimating Tactics Basing a request on one's authority or right, organizational rules or policies, or express or implied support from superiors.
Example: "This has been green-lighted at the highest levels."

These influence tactics are considered *generic* because they are applied in all directions—up, down, and sideways within the organization. The first five influence tactics are considered "soft" tactics because they are considered friendlier than the last four "hard," or pressure, tactics. As it happens, research shows that of the three possible responses to an influence tactic—enthusiastic commitment, grudging compliance, and outright resistance—commitment is most apt to result when the tactics used are consultation, strong rational persuasion, and inspirational appeals.[17]

Knowing this, do you think you have what it takes to be a leader? To answer this, you need to understand what factors produce people of leadership character. We consider these in the rest of the chapter.

Five Approaches to Leadership

The next five sections describe five principal approaches or perspectives on leadership, which have been refined by research. They are (1) *trait,* (2) *behavioral,* (3) *contingency,* (4) *full-range,* and (5) *six additional. (See Table 14.1.)* ●

table 14.1

FIVE APPROACHES TO LEADERSHIP

1. **Trait approaches**
   - *Kouzes & Posner's five traits*—honest, competent, forward-looking, inspiring, intelligent
   - *Bossidy*—ability to execute, career runway, team orientation, multiple experiences
   - *Judge & colleagues*—two meta-analyses: importance of extroversion, conscientiousness, and openness; importance of personality over intelligence
   - *Gender studies*—motivating others, fostering communication, producing high-quality work, and so on
   - *Leadership lessons from the GLOBE project*—visionary and inspirational charismatic leaders who are good team builders are best worldwide

2. **Behavioral approaches**
   - *Michigan model*—two leadership styles: job-centered and employee-centered
   - *Ohio State model*—two dimensions: initiating-structure behavior and consideration behavior

3. **Contingency approaches**
   - *Fiedler's contingency model*—task-oriented style and relationship-oriented style—*and three dimensions of control:* leader-member, task structure, position power
   - *House's path*-goal revised leadership model—clarifying paths for subordinates' goals—and employee characteristics and environmental factors that affect leadership behaviors
   - *Hersey & Blanchard's situational leadership model*—adjusting leadership style to employee readiness

4. **Full-range approach**
   - *Transactional leadership*—clarify employee roles and tasks and provide rewards and punishments
   - *Transformational leadership*—transform employees to pursue organizational goals over self-interests, using inspirational motivation, idealized influence, individualized consideration, intellectual stimulation

5. **Six additional perspectives**
   - *Leader-member exchange (LMX) model*—leaders have different sorts of relationships with different subordinates
   - *Shared leadership*—mutual influence process in which people share responsibility for leading
   - *Greenleaf's servant leadership model*—providing service to others, not oneself
   - *Loyalty*—Reichheld's six principles: preach what one practices, pay win-win, be picky, keep it simple, reward right results, listen hard and talk straight
   - *Collins's Level 5 Leadership*—leader has humility plus fearless will to succeed, plus four other capabilities
   - *E-Leadership*—using information technology for one-to-one, one-to-many, and between group and collective interactions

14.2 TRAIT APPROACHES: DO LEADERS HAVE DISTINCTIVE PERSONALITY CHARACTERISTICS?

major question

What does it take to be a successful leader?

THE BIG PICTURE

Trait approaches attempt to identify distinctive characteristics that account for the effectiveness of leaders. We describe (1) two trait perspectives expressed by Kouzes and Posner and by Bossidy; (2) Judge's research on traits; (3) some results of gender studies; and (4) leadership lessons from the GLOBE project.

Consider two high-powered leaders of the late 20th century. Each "personifies the word 'stubborn,'" says a *Fortune* magazine account. Both "are piercingly analytical thinkers who combine hands-on technical smarts with take-no-prisoners business savvy. Both absolutely hate to lose."[18]

Who are they? They are two of the most successful former CEOs in American business—Bill Gates of Microsoft and Andy Grove of Intel. Do they have distinctive personality traits that might teach us something about leadership? Perhaps they do. They would seem to embody the traits of (1) dominance, (2) intelligence, (3) self-confidence, (4) high energy, and (5) task-relevant knowledge.

These are the five traits that researcher **Ralph Stogdill** in 1948 concluded were typical of successful leaders.[19] Stogdill is one of many contributors to ***trait approaches to leadership,*** **which attempt to identify distinctive characteristics that account for the effectiveness of leaders.** Indeed, over the past 70 years, over 300 trait studies have been done.[20]

Trait theory is the successor to what used to be thought of as the "great man" approach to leadership, which held that leaders such as Napoleon Bonaparte and Abraham Lincoln were supposed to have some inborn ability to lead. Trait theorists believed that leadership skills were not innate, that they could be acquired through learning and experience. Today traits still often play a central role in how we perceive leaders, and organizations may find it beneficial to consider selected leadership traits when choosing among candidates for leadership positions. Gender, race, and ethnicity should not be used as any of these traits.

Two Trait Perspectives: Kouzes & Posner, & Bossidy

Two examples of trait approaches are those represented in the perspectives presented by Kouzes and Posner and by Larry Bossidy.

Kouzes & Posner's Research: Is Honesty the Top Leadership Trait? During the 1980s, **James Kouzes** and **Barry Posner** surveyed more than 7,500 managers throughout the United States as to what personal traits they looked for and admired in their superiors.[21] The respondents suggested that a credible leader should have five traits. He or she should be (1) honest, (2) competent, (3) forward-looking, (4) inspiring, and (5) intelligent. The first trait, honesty, was considered particularly important, being selected by 87% of the respondents, suggesting that people want their leaders to be ethical.

Although this research does reveal the traits preferred by employees, it has not, however, been able to predict which people might be successful leaders.

Bossidy's Observations: A Working CEO Tells How to Find & Develop Great Leaders We mentioned **Larry Bossidy** earlier in Chapter 6 (Section 6.5) in conjunction with execution. Bossidy became CEO of AlliedSignal in 1991, when the company was suffering from low everything—morale, stock price, operating margins, and return on equity. Based on his experience of 34 years at General Electric, he realized that AlliedSignal's "inattention to leadership was a major problem."[22] He thereupon began a 2-year program of devoting up to 40% of his time to the task of hiring and developing leaders, a successful effort to which he attributes the company's turnaround.

Bossidy's approach represents the kinds of judgments that working top managers have to practice when they go about the empirical job of finding people who can be groomed into future leaders. The four qualities he looks for when interviewing and evaluating job candidates are (1) the ability to execute, (2) a career runway, (3) a team orientation, and (4) multiple experiences. *(See Table 14.2.)* Bossidy claims a 70% success rate in hiring leaders, and his approach contributed to a ninefold return for AlliedSignal shareholders from 1991 to 1999.

table 14.2

THE LEADERSHIP TRAITS BOSSIDY LOOKS FOR IN JOB CANDIDATES

1. ***Ability to execute.*** Look for a demonstrated history of real accomplishment and execution. Are you honest?	3. ***A team orientation.*** Someone able to work with other people has better potential than someone who's an individual contributor.
2. ***A career runway.*** Leaders have "plenty of runway" left in their careers, with the perspective to go beyond the present job.	4. ***Multiple experiences.*** People with significant responsibility in two or three different industries or companies have a range of good experience.

Judge's Research: Is Personality More Important Than Intelligence in Leadership?

Timothy Judge and his colleagues recently published the results of two meta-analyses that bear on the subject of traits and leaderships. **A *meta-analysis* is a statistical pooling technique that permits behavioral scientists to draw general conclusions about certain variables from many different studies.**

The Importance of Extroversion, Conscientiousness, & Openness The Big Five personality dimensions, you'll recall (from Chapter 11, Section 11.3), are extroversion, agreeableness, conscientiousness, emotional stability, and openness to experience. Judge and his group examined the Big Five personality traits and their relationship to leadership in 94 studies. Their conclusion: extroversion was most consistently and positively related to both leadership emergence and leadership effectiveness. Conscientiousness and openness to experience also were positively related to leadership effectiveness.[23]

The Importance of Personality over Intelligence In the second meta-analysis, which involved 151 samples, Judge and his colleagues found that intelligence was modestly related to leadership effectiveness. The study concluded that in the selection of leaders personality is more important than intelligence.[24] This conclusion is supported by research that found that managers who were leadership failures showed several personality flaws, including being overly controlling, irritable, exploitative, arrogant, abrasive, selfish, and lacking in emotional intelligence.[25]

Gender Studies: Do Women Have Traits That Make Them Better Leaders?

WOMEN ASPIRE TO BE CHIEF AS MUCH AS MEN DO, declared the headline in *The Wall Street Journal.* A study by a New York research firm found that 55% of women and 57% of men aspire to be CEO, challenging the notion that more women aren't at the top because they don't want to be there.[26] And, in fact, it's possible that women may have traits that make them better managers—indeed, better leaders—than men.

A number of management studies conducted in the United States for companies ranging from high-tech to manufacturing to consumer services were reviewed by *BusinessWeek*.[27] By and large, the magazine reports, the studies showed that "women executives, when rated by their peers, underlings, and bosses, score higher than their male counterparts on a wide variety of measures—from producing high-quality work to goal-setting to mentoring employees." Researchers accidentally stumbled on these findings about gender differences while compiling hundreds of routine performance evaluations and analyzing the results. In one study of 425 high-level executives, women won higher ratings on 42 of the 52 skills measured.[28]

What are the desirable traits in which women excel? Among those traits mentioned are teamwork and partnering, being more collaborative, seeking less personal glory, being motivated less by self-interest than in what they can do for the company, being more stable, and being less turf-conscious. Women were also found to be better at producing quality work, recognizing trends, and generating new ideas and acting on them. A gender comparison of skills is summarized below. *(See Table 14.3.)*

table 14.3

WHERE FEMALE EXECUTIVES DO BETTER: A SCORECARD

The check mark denotes which group scored higher on the respective studies. The asterisk indicates that in one study women's and men's scores in these categories were statistically even.

Skill	Men	Women
Motivating others		√√√√√
Fostering communication		√√√√*
Producing high-quality work		√√√√√
Strategic planning	√√	√√*
Listening to others		√√√√√
Analyzing issues	√√	√√*

Source: Data from Hagberg Consulting Group, Management Research Group, Lawrence A. Pfaff, Personnel Decisions International Inc., and Advanced Teamware Inc., in table in R. Sharpe, "As Leaders, Women Rule," *BusinessWeek*, November 20, 2000, p. 75.

Why, then, aren't more women in positions of leadership? Males and females disagree about this issue. A team of researchers asked this question of 461 executive women holding titles of vice president or higher in Fortune 100 companies and all the male Fortune 100 CEOs. CEOs believed that women are not in senior leadership positions because (1) they lack significant general management experience and (2) women have not been in the executive talent pool long enough to get selected. Women, by contrast, believed that (1) male stereotyping and (2) exclusion from important informal networks are the biggest barriers to promotability.[29]

There are two additional possible explanations. First, as we suggested earlier in the book, there are many women who, though hard working, simply aren't willing to compete as hard as most men are or are not willing to make the required personal sacrifices.[30] (As Jamie Gorelick, former vice chair of Fannie Mae but also mother of two children ages 10 and 15, said when declining to be considered for CEO: "I just don't want that pace in my life.")[31] Second, women have a tendency to be overly modest and to give credit to others rather than taking it for themselves, which can undermine opportunities for promotions and raises.[32]

Leadership Lessons from the GLOBE Project

Project GLOBE (Global Leadership and Organizational Behavior Effectiveness), you'll recall from Chapter 4, is a massive and ongoing attempt to develop an empirically based theory to "describe, understand, and predict the impact of specific cultural variables on leadership and organizational processes and the effectiveness of these processes."[33] Surveying 17,000 middle managers working for 951 organizations across 62 countries, the researchers determined that certain attributes of leadership were universally liked or disliked. *(See Table 14.4.)* Visionary and inspirational *charismatic leaders* who are good team builders generally do the best. *Self-centered leaders* seen as loners or face-savers generally receive a poor reception worldwide. ●

table 14.4

LESSONS FROM GLOBE: LEADERSHIP ATTRIBUTES UNIVERSALLY LIKED AND DISLIKED ACROSS 62 NATIONS

Universally positive leader attributes	Universally negative leader attributes
Trustworthy	Loner
Just	Asocial
Honest	Noncooperative
Foresight	Irritable
Plans ahead	Nonexplicit
Encouraging	Egocentric
Positive	Ruthless
Dynamic	Dictatorial
Motive arouser	
Confidence builder	
Motivational	
Dependable	
Intelligent	
Decisive	
Effective bargainer	
Win-win problem solver	
Administrative skilled	
Communicative	
Informed	
Coordinator	
Team builder	
Excellence oriented	

Source: Excerpted and adapted from P. W. Dorfman, P. J. Hanges, and F. C. Brodbeck, "Leadership and Cultural Variation: The Identification of Culturally Endorsed Leadership Profiles," in R. J. House, P. J. Hanges, M. Javidan, P. W. Dorfman, and V. Gupta eds., *Culture, Leadership and Organizations: The GLOBE Study of 62 Societies* (Thousand Oaks, CA: Sage, 2004), Tables 21.2 and 21.3, pp. 677–678.

14.3 BEHAVIORAL APPROACHES: DO LEADERS SHOW DISTINCTIVE PATTERNS OF BEHAVIOR?

major question

Do effective leaders behave in similar ways?

THE BIG PICTURE

Behavioral leadership approaches try to determine the distinctive styles used by effective leaders. Two models we describe are the University of Michigan model and the Ohio State model.

Printing press. What kind of leadership behavior is appropriate for directing these kinds of workers?

Maybe what's important to know about leaders is not their *personality traits* but rather their *patterns of behavior* or *leadership styles.* This is the line of thought pursued by those interested in ***behavioral leadership approaches,*** **which attempt to determine the distinctive styles used by effective leaders.** By *leadership styles,* we mean the combination of traits, skills, and behaviors that leaders use when interacting with others.

What all models of leadership behavior have in common is the consideration of *task orientation versus people orientation.* Two classic studies came out of the universities of Michigan and Ohio State.

The University of Michigan Leadership Model

In the late 1940s, researchers at the University of Michigan came up with what came to be known as the **University of Michigan Leadership Model.** A team led by **Rensis Likert** began studying the effects of leader behavior on job performance, interviewing numerous managers and subordinates.[34] The investigators identified two forms of leadership styles: *job-centered* and *employee-centered.*

- **Job-centered behavior—"I'm concerned more with the needs of the job."** In *job-centered behavior,* managers paid more attention to the job and work procedures. Thus, their principal concerns were with achieving production efficiency, keeping costs down, and meeting schedules.
- **Employee-centered behavior—"I'm concerned more with the needs of employees."** In *employee-centered behavior,* managers paid more attention to employee satisfaction and making work groups cohesive. By concentrating on subordinates' needs they hoped to build effective work groups with high-performance goals.

The Ohio State Leadership Model

A second approach to leadership research was begun in 1945 at Ohio State University under **Ralph Stogdill** (mentioned in the last section). Hundreds of dimensions of leadership behavior were studied, resulting in what came to be known as the **Ohio State**

Leadership Model.[35] From surveys of leadership behavior, two major dimensions of leader behavior were identified, as follows.

- **Initiating structure—"What do I do to get the job done?"** *Initiating structure* is leadership behavior that organizes and defines what group members should be doing. It consists of the efforts the leader makes to get things organized and get the job done. This is much the same as Likert's "job-centered behavior."
- **Consideration—"What do I do to show consideration for my employees?"** *Consideration* is leadership behavior that expresses concern for employees by establishing a warm, friendly, supportive climate. This behavior, which resembles Likert's "employee-centered behavior," is sensitive to subordinates' ideas and feelings and establishes mutual trust.

All in all, one management expert concluded from the Michigan and Ohio studies that effective leaders (1) tend to have supportive or employee-centered relationships with employees, (2) use group rather than individual methods of supervision, and (3) set high performance goals.[36] ●

Practical Action

Transition Problems on Your Way Up: How to Avoid the Pitfalls

Before you can become a good leader you need to become a good manager. Making the leap from individual contributor to a manager of several employees "is one of the most difficult in peoples' careers," suggests *Wall Street Journal* columnist Hal Lancaster.

Although corporations and managements may make noises about training and mentoring support, newly promoted managers may not see any of this and may simply be expected to know what to do. And, as managers move up the ladder, they may encounter other problems that they have not anticipated. How can you avoid some pitfalls as you make your ascent? Some suggestions:[37]

- **Have realistic expectations.** New managers often focus on the rights and privileges of their new jobs and underestimate the duties and obligations.
- **Don't forget to manage upward and sideways as well as downward.** You not only need to manage your subordinates but also the perceptions of your peers and your own managers above you.
- **Stay in touch with managers in other departments.** In addition, you need to have good relationships with managers in other departments—and be perceptive about their needs and priorities—since they have resources you need to get your job done. Don't make the mistake of thinking your own department is the center of the universe.
- **Think about what kind of manager or leader you want to be.** Make a list of all your previous bosses and their good and bad attributes. This may produce a list of dos and don'ts that can serve you well.
- **Get guidance from other managers.** You may not get advice on how to manage from your own manager, who may have promoted you to help reduce his or her workload, not add to it by expecting some coaching. If this is the case, don't be shy about consulting other managers as well as people in professional organizations.
- **Resist isolation.** If you're promoted beyond supervisor of a small team and you have to manage hundreds rather than dozens, or thousands rather than hundreds, you may find the biggest surprise is isolation. The way to stay in touch is to talk daily with your senior managers, perhaps have "town meetings" with staffers several times a year, and employ "management by walking around"—bringing teams together to talk.

14.4 CONTINGENCY APPROACHES: DOES LEADERSHIP VARY WITH THE SITUATION?

major question How might effective leadership vary according to the situation at hand?

THE BIG PICTURE

Effective leadership behavior depends on the situation at hand, say believers in the three contingency approaches: Fiedler's contingency leadership model, House's path-goal leadership model, and Hersey and Blanchard's situational leadership model.

Perhaps leadership is not characterized by universally important traits or behaviors. Perhaps there is no one best style that will work in all situations. This is the point of view of proponents of the ***contingency approach*** **to leadership, who believe that effective leadership behavior depends on the situation at hand.** That is, as situations change, different styles become appropriate.

Let's consider three contingency approaches: (1) the *contingency leadership model* by Fiedler, (2) the *path-goal leadership model* by House, and (3) the *situational leadership model* by Hersey and Blanchard.

I. The Contingency Leadership Model: Fiedler's Approach

The oldest model of the contingency approach to leadership was developed by **Fred Fiedler** and his associates in 1951.[38] **The *contingency leadership model* determines if a leader's style is (1) task-oriented or (2) relationship-oriented and if that style is effective for the situation at hand.** Fiedler's work was based on 80 studies conducted over 30 years.

Two Leadership Orientations: Tasks versus Relationships

Are you task-oriented or relationship-oriented? That is, are you more concerned with task accomplishment or with people?

To find out, you or your employees would fill out a questionnaire (known as the least preferred co-worker, or LPC, scale), in which you think of the co-worker you least enjoyed working with and rate him or her according to an eight-point scale of 16 pairs of opposite characteristics (such as friendly/unfriendly, tense/relaxed, efficient/inefficient). The higher the score, the more the relationship-oriented the respondent; the lower the score, the more task-oriented.

Tile style. Do successful entrepreneurs or small-business managers need to be task-oriented, relationship-oriented, or both? What style of leadership model would best suit a small tile manufacturing business in which employees need to work with a great deal of independence?

The Three Dimensions of Situational Control

Once the leadership orientation is known, then you determine *situational control*—how much control and influence a leader has in the immediate work environment.

There are three dimensions of situational control: *leader-member relations, task structure,* and *position power.*

- **Leader-member relations—"Do my subordinates accept me as a leader?"** This dimension, the most important component of situational control, reflects the extent to which a leader has or doesn't have the support, loyalty, and trust of the work group.
- **Task structure—"Do my subordinates perform unambiguous, easily understood tasks?"** This dimension refers to the extent to which tasks are routine, unambiguous, and easily understood. The more structured the jobs, the more influence a leader has.

- **Position power—"Do I have power to reward and punish?"** This dimension refers to how much power a leader has to make work assignments and reward and punish. More power equals more control and influence.

For each dimension, the amount of control can be *high*—the leader's decisions will produce predictable results because he or she has the ability to influence work outcomes. Or it can be *low*—he or she doesn't have that kind of predictability or influence. By combining the three different dimensions with different high/low ratings, we have eight different leadership situations.

Which Style Is Most Effective? Neither leadership style is effective all the time, Fiedler's research concludes, although each is right in certain situations.

- **When task-oriented style is best.** The task-oriented style works best in either *high-control* or *low-control* situations.

  Example of *high-control* situation (leader decisions produce predictable results because he or she can influence work outcomes): Suppose you were supervising parking-control officers ticketing cars parked illegally in expired meter zones, bus zones, and the like. You have (1) high leader-member relations because your subordinates are highly supportive of you and (2) high task structure because their jobs are clearly defined. (3) You have high position control because you have complete authority to evaluate their performance and dole out punishment and rewards. Thus, a task-oriented style would be best.

  Example of *low-control* situation (leader decisions can't produce predictable results because he or she can't really influence outcomes): Suppose you were a high school principal trying to clean up graffiti on your private-school campus, helped only by students you can find after school. You might have (1) low leader-member relations because many people might not see the need for the goal. (2) The task structure might also be low because people might see many different ways to achieve the goal. And (3) your position power would be low because the committee is voluntary and people are free to leave. In this low-control situation, a task-oriented style would also be best.
- **When relationship-oriented style is best.** The relationship-oriented style works best in situations of *moderate control.*

  Example: Suppose you were working in a government job supervising a group of firefighters fighting wildfires. You might have (1) low leader-member relations if you were promoted over others in the group but (2) high task structure, because the job is fairly well defined. (3) You might have low position power, because the rigidity of the civil-service job prohibits you from doing much in the way of rewarding and punishing. Thus, in this moderate-control situation, relationship-oriented leadership would be most effective.

Test Your Knowledge: *Fiedler's Contingency Model of Leadership*

What do you do if your leadership orientation does not match the situation? Then, says Fiedler, it's better to try to move leaders into suitable situations rather than try to alter their personalities to fit the situations.[39]

2. The Path–Goal Leadership Model: House's Approach

A second contingency approach, advanced by **Robert House** in the 1970s and revised by him in 1996, is the ***path-goal leadership model*****, which holds that the effective leader makes available to followers desirable rewards in the workplace and increases their motivation by clarifying the *paths,* or behavior, that will help them achieve those *goals* and providing them with support.** A successful leader thus helps followers by tying meaningful rewards to goal accomplishment, reducing barriers, and providing support, so as to increase "the number and kinds of personal payoffs to subordinates for work-goal attainment."[40]

Numerous studies testing various predictions from House's original path–goal theory provided mixed results.[41] As a consequence, he proposed a new model, a graphical version, shown below. *(See Figure 14.1.)*

figure 14.1

GENERAL REPRESENTATION OF HOUSE'S REVISED PATH–GOAL THEORY

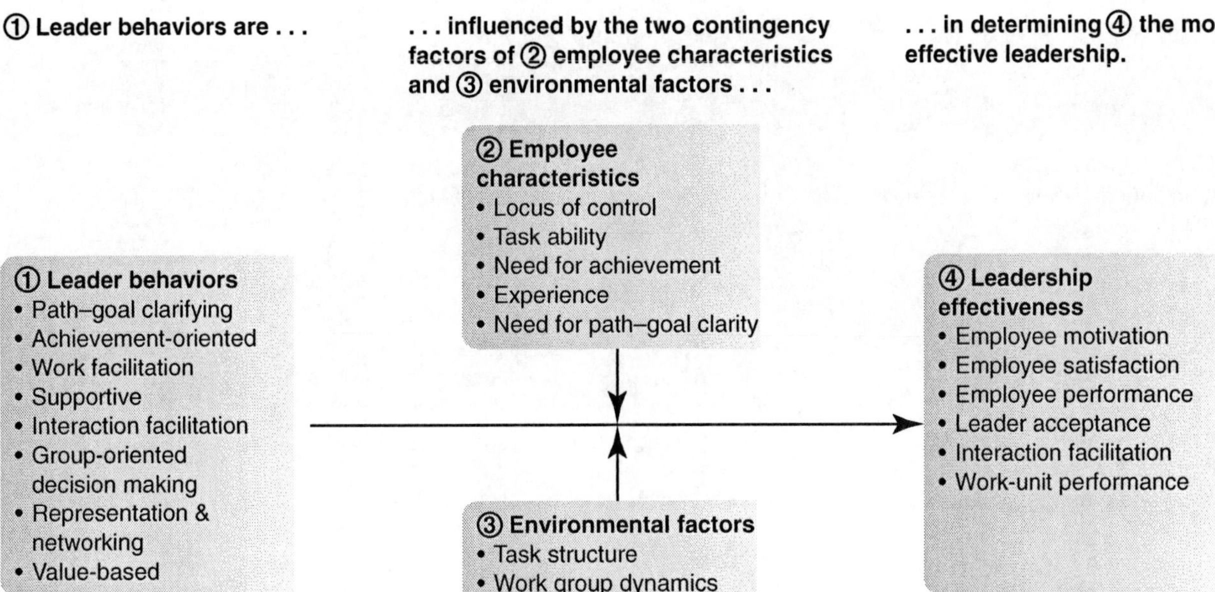

What Determines Leadership Effectiveness: Employee Characteristics & Environmental Factors Affect Leader Behavior As the drawing indicates, two contingency factors, or variables—*employee characteristics* and *environmental factors*—cause some *leadership behaviors* to be more effective than others.

- **Employee characteristics.** Five employee characteristics are locus of control (described in Chapter 11), task ability, need for achievement, experience, and need for path–goal clarity.
- **Environmental factors.** Two environmental factors are task structure (independent versus interdependent tasks) and work group dynamics.
- **Leader behaviors.** Originally House proposed that there were four leader behaviors, or leadership styles—*directive* ("Here's what's expected of you and here's how to do it"), *supportive* ("I want things to be pleasant, since everyone's about equal here"), *participative* ("I want your suggestions in order to help me make decisions"), and *achievement-oriented* ("I'm confident you can accomplish the following great things"). The revised theory expands the number of leader behaviors from four to eight. *(See Table 14.5, opposite.)*

Thus, for example, employees with an internal locus of control are more likely to prefer achievement-oriented leadership or group-oriented decision making (formerly participative) leadership because they believe they have control over the work environment. The same is true for employees with high task ability and experience.

Employees with an external locus of control, however, tend to view the environment as uncontrollable, so they prefer the structure provided by supportive or path–goal clarifying (formerly directive) leadership. The same is probably true of inexperienced employees.

Besides expanding the styles of leader behavior from four to eight, House's revision of his theory also puts more emphasis on the need for leaders to foster intrinsic motivation

table 14.5

EIGHT LEADERSHIP STYLES OF THE REVISED PATH-GOAL THEORY

Style of leader behaviors	Description of behavior toward employees
1. Path-goal clarifying ("Here's what's expected of you and here's how to do it")	Clarify performance goals. Provide guidance on how employees can complete tasks. Clarify performance standards and expectations. Use positive and negative rewards contingent on performance.
2. Achievement-oriented ("I'm confident you can accomplish the following great things")	Set challenging goals. Emphasize excellence. Demonstrate confidence in employee abilities.
3. Work facilitation ("Here's the goal, and here's what I can do to help you achieve it")	Plan, schedule, organize, and coordinate work. Provide mentoring, coaching, counseling, and feedback to assist employees in developing their skills. Eliminate roadblocks. Provide resources. Empower employees to take actions and make decisions.
4. Supportive ("I want things to be pleasant, since everyone's about equal here")	Treat as equals. Show concern for well-being and needs. Be friendly and approachable.
5. Interaction facilitation ("Let's see how we can all work together to accomplish our goals")	Emphasize collaboration and teamwork. Encourage close employee relationships and sharing of minority opinions. Facilitate communication, resolve disputes.
6. Group-oriented decision making ("I want your suggestions in order to help me make decisions")	Pose problems rather than solutions to work group. Encourage members to participate in decision making. Provide necessary information to the group for analysis. Involve knowledgeable employees in decision making.
7. Representation & networking ("I've got a great bunch of people working for me whom you'll probably want to meet")	Present work group in positive light to others. Maintain positive relationships with influential others. Participate in organization-wide social functions and ceremonies. Do unconditional favors for others.
8. Value-based ("We're destined to accomplish great things")	Establish a vision, display passion for it, and support its accomplishment. Communicate high performance expectations and confidence in others' abilities to meet their goals. Give frequent positive feedback. Demonstrate self-confidence.

Source: Adapted from R. J. House, "Path-Goal Theory of Leadership: Lessons, Legacy, and a Reformulated Theory," *Leadership Quarterly*, Autumn 1996, pp. 323–352.

through empowerment. Finally, his revised theory stresses the concept of shared leadership, the idea that employees do not have to be supervisors or managers to engage in leader behavior but rather may share leadership among all employees of the organization.

Does the Revised Path–Goal Theory Work? There have not been enough direct tests of House's revised path–goal theory using appropriate research methods and statistical procedures to draw overall conclusions. Research on charismatic leadership, however, which is discussed in Section 14.5, is supportive of the revised model.[42]

Although further research is needed on the new model, it offers two important implications for managers:

Test Your Knowledge: *Path-Goal Theory*

- ***Use more than one leadership style.*** Effective leaders possess and use more than one style of leadership. Thus, you are encouraged to study the eight styles

Cranium's grand poo-bah and chief noodler. Richard Tait (left), responsible for business operations and marketing for the 14-person, Seattle-based game company Cranium, takes the unorthodox title of grand poo-bah. Whit Alexander, who focuses on product development, editorial content, and manufacturing, is called chief noodler. In devising the board game Cranium, the two entrepreneurs decided to adopt the acronym CHIFF—for "clever, high quality, innovative, friendly, and fun"—as the criterion by which all decisions would be guided. "Our survival and success will come from optimizing fun, focus, passion, and profits," says Tait. Which one of the eight path-goal leadership styles would you expect to find dominating this organization?

offered in path–goal theory so that you can try new leader behaviors when a situation calls for them.

- ***Modify leadership style to fit employee and task characteristics.*** A small set of employee characteristics (ability, experience, and need for independence) and environmental factors (task characteristics of autonomy, variety, and significance) are relevant contingency factors, and managers should modify their leadership style to fit them.[43]

3. The Situational Leadership Theory Model: Hersey & Blanchard's Approach

A third contingency approach has been proposed by management writers **Paul Hersey** and **Kenneth Blanchard.**[44] **In their *situational leadership theory,* leadership behavior reflects how leaders should adjust their leadership style according to the readiness of the followers.** The model suggests that managers should be flexible in choosing a leadership behavior style and be sensitive to the readiness level of their employees. ***Readiness* is defined as the extent to which a follower possesses the ability and willingness to complete a task.** Subordinates with high readiness (with high ability, skills, and willingness to work) require a different leadership style than do those with low readiness (low ability, training, and willingness).

The appropriate leadership style is found by cross-referencing follower readiness (low–high) with one of four leaderships styles. *(See Figure 14.2, opposite.)*

How the Situational Leadership Model Works

Let's see what the illustration means.

- **Leadership styles—relationship behavior plus task behavior.** The upper part of the drawing shows the leadership style, which is based on the combination of relationship behavior (vertical axis) and task behavior (horizontal axis).

  Relationship behavior is the extent to which leaders maintain personal relationships with their followers, as in providing support and keeping communication open.

  Task behavior is the extent to which leaders organize and explain the role of their followers, which is achieved by explaining what subordinates are to do and how tasks are to be accomplished.

- **Four leadership styles—telling, selling, participating, delegating.** The bell-shaped curve indicates when each of the four leadership styles—telling (S1), selling (S2), participating (S3), and delegating (S4)—should be used.
- **When a leadership style should be used—depends on the readiness of the followers.** How do you know which leadership style to employ? You need to have an understanding of the *readiness* of your followers, as represented by the scale at the bottom of the drawing, where R1 represents low readiness and R4 represents high readiness.

  Let's consider which leadership style to apply when.

  Telling represents the guiding and directing of performance. This leadership style works best for followers with a low level of readiness—that is, subordinates are neither willing nor able to take responsibility.

  Selling is explaining decisions and persuading others to follow a course of action. Because it offers both direction and support, this leadership style is most suitable for followers who are unable but willing to assume task responsibility.

  Participating involves encouraging followers to solve problems on their own. Because it shares decision making, this leadership style encourages subordinates in performing tasks. Thus, it is most appropriate for followers whose readiness is in the moderate to high range.

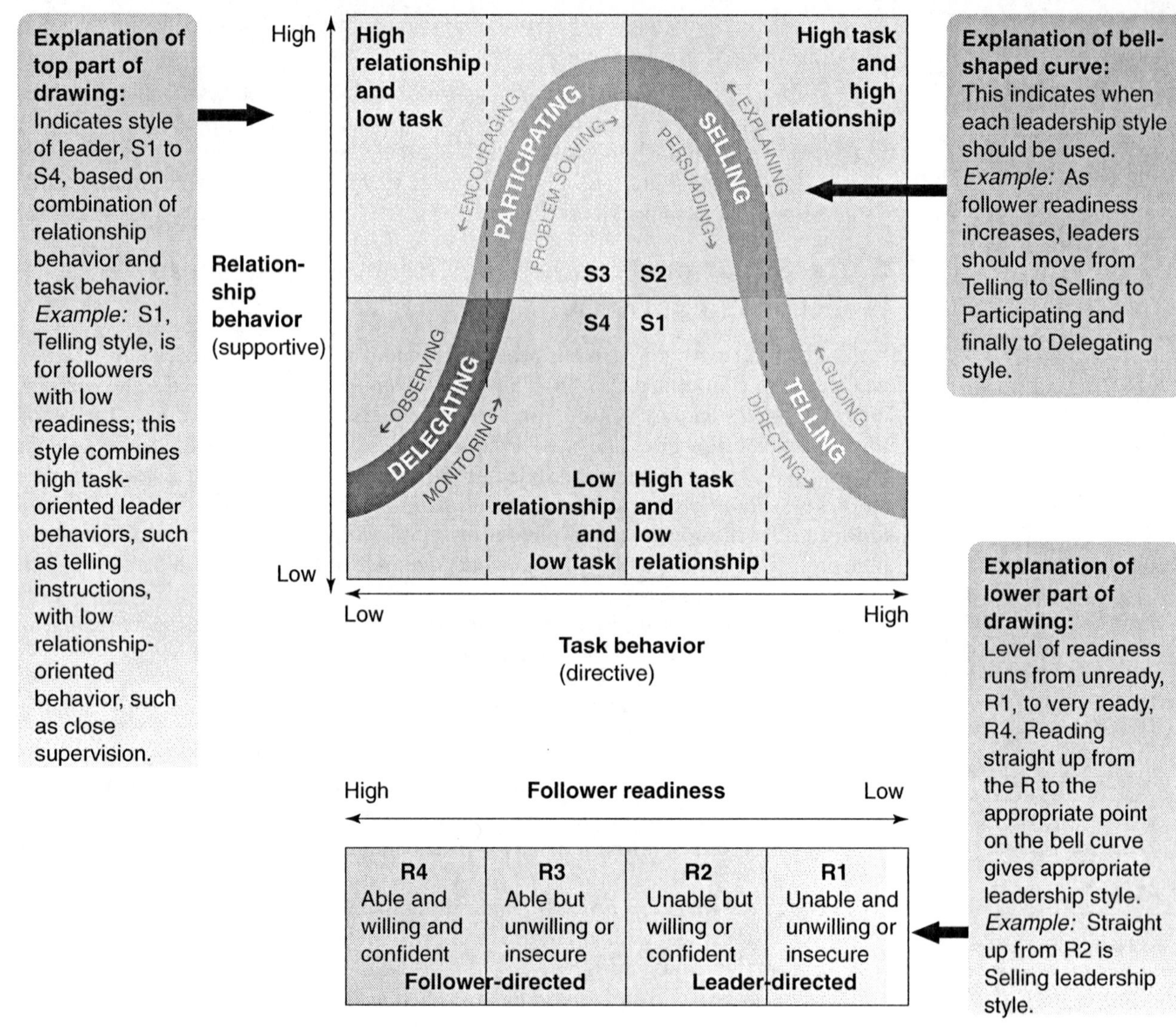

figure 14. 2

HERSEY AND BLANCHARD'S SITUATIONAL LEADERSHIP MODEL

Source: Adapted from P. Hersey, K. H. Blanchard, and D. E. Johnson, *Management of Organizational Behavior: Leading Human Resources,* 8th ed. (Upper Saddle River, NJ: Prentice Hall, 2000). Situational leadership® is a registered trademark of the Center for Leadership Studies, Inc.

Delegating is providing subordinates with little support or direction. As such, the leader's role is to observe and monitor. This leadership style is best for followers who have a high level of readiness, both able and willing to perform tasks.

Does the Hersey-Blanchard Model Work? The situational leadership model is widely used as a training tool, but it is not strongly supported by scientific research. For instance, a study of 459 salespeople found that leadership effectiveness was not attributable to the predicted interaction between follower readiness and leadership style.[45] This is consistent with another study, in which 57 chief nurse executives were found not to delegate in accordance with situational leadership theory.[46] Researchers also have concluded that the self-assessment instrument used to measure leadership style and follower readiness is inaccurate.[47] In sum, managers should exercise discretion when using prescriptions from this model. ●

14.5 THE FULL-RANGE MODEL: USES OF TRANSACTIONAL & TRANSFORMATIONAL LEADERSHIP

major question What does it take to truly inspire people to perform beyond their normal levels?

THE BIG PICTURE

Full-range leadership describes leadership along a range of styles, with the most effective being transactional/transformational leaders. Four key behaviors of transformational leaders in affecting employees are they inspire motivation, inspire trust, encourage excellence, and stimulate them intellectually.

We have considered the major traditional approaches to understanding leadership—the trait, behavioral, and contingency approaches. But newer approaches seem to offer something more by trying to determine what factors inspire and motivate people to perform beyond their normal levels.

One recent approach proposed by **Bernard Bass and Bruce Avolio,** known as ***full range leadership,*** **suggests that leadership behavior varies along a full range of leadership styles, from take-no-responsibility (*laissez-faire*) "leadership" at one extreme, through transactional leadership, to transformational leadership at the other extreme.**[48] Not taking responsibility can hardly be considered leadership (although it often seems to be manifested by CEOs whose companies got in trouble, as when they say "I had no idea about the criminal behavior of my subordinates"). Transactional and transformational leadership behaviors, however, are both positive aspects of being a good leader.

Transactional versus Transformational Leaders

Plans, budgets, schedules. Would you expect management in the construction field to focus more on the nonpeople aspects of work?

Jim McNerney, chairman and CEO of 3M, is able to be both a transactional and a transformational leader. Let us consider the differences.

Transactional Leadership As a manager, your power stems from your ability to provide rewards (and threaten reprimands) in exchange for your subordinates' doing the work. When you do this, you are performing ***transactional leadership,*** **focusing on clarifying employees' roles and task requirements and providing rewards and punishments contingent on performance.** Transactional leadership also encompasses the fundamental managerial activities of setting goals and monitoring progress toward their achievement.[49]

"[3M's] McNerney's secret to success is elementary," says a *BusinessWeek* article. "He sets high goals that can be measured, such as business-unit sales or the rate of product introductions, and demands that his managers meet them. Granted, many CEOs do that today. But like a dedicated teacher or coach, McNerney also works with his team day in, day out, to help them make the grade."[50]

We shouldn't think of a transactional leader as being a mediocre leader—indeed, competent transactional leaders are badly needed. But transactional leaders are best in stable situations. What's needed in rapidly changing situations, as is often the case in many organizations today, is a transformational leader.

Transformational Leadership ***Transformational leadership*** **transforms employees to pursue organizational goals over self-interests.** Transformational leaders, in one description, "engender trust, seek to develop leadership in others, exhibit self-sacrifice, and serve as moral agents, focusing themselves and followers on objectives that transcend the more immediate needs of the work group."[51] Whereas transactional leaders try to get people to do *ordinary things,* transformational leaders encourage their people to do *exceptional* things—significantly higher levels of intrinsic motivation, trust, commitment, and loyalty—that can produce significant organizational change and results.

Transformational leaders are influenced by two factors:

- **Individual characteristics.** The personalities of such leaders tend to be more extroverted, agreeable, and proactive than nontransformational leaders. (Female leaders tend to use transformational leadership more than male leaders do.)[52]
- **Organizational culture.** Adaptive, flexible organizational cultures are more likely than are rigid, bureaucratic cultures to foster transformational leadership.

The Best Leaders Are Both Transactional & Transformational

It's important to note that transactional leadership is an essential *prerequisite* to effective leadership, and the best leaders learn to display both transactional and transformational styles of leadership to some degree. Indeed, research suggests that transformational leadership leads to superior performance when it "augments" or adds to transactional leadership.[53]

This is apparent in the case of 3M CEO McNerney. "Some people think you either have a demanding, command-and-control management style or you have a nurturing, encouraging style," he says. "I believe you can't have one without the other." *BusinessWeek* points out that McNerney is praised for being an inspirational leader who is comfortable speaking either one-on-one or to large groups. He also is quick to attribute the company's achievements to the entire organization and praises employees for their work ethic.[54]

Four Key Behaviors of Transformational Leaders

Whereas transactional leaders are dispassionate, transformational leaders excite passion, inspiring and empowering people to look beyond their own interests to the interests of the organization. They appeal to their followers' self-concepts—their values and personal identity—to create changes in their goals, values, needs, beliefs, and aspirations.

Transformational leaders have four key kinds of behavior that affect followers.[55]

1. Inspirational Motivation: "Let Me Share a Vision That Transcends Us All" Transformational leaders have ***charisma*** **("kar-*riz*-muh"), a form of interpersonal attraction that inspires acceptance and support.** Such leaders inspire motivation

Sir Branson. One of today's most flamboyant businessmen, Britain's Richard Branson (middle), is shown here in May 2003 in Sydney Australia, with Paul Pester (right), CEO for the Virgin Money Group Ltd (UK) at the launch of the new Virgin credit card (shown behind them). Branson left school at 16 to start a 1960s counterculture magazine. By 2006, he was heading a $5 billion-plus empire ~~the~~ Virgin Group ~~that~~ includes airlines, entertainment companies, car dealerships, railroads, bridal gowns, soft drinks, financial services, a space tourism company, and his latest venture, Virgin Fuel. Knighted in 2000 ~~which~~ entitles him to be called 'Sir' Branson, who is dyslexic, says he is not for scrutinizing spreadsheets and plotting strategies based on estimates of market share. 'In the end,"he says, 'It is your own gut and your own experience of running businesses."Do you think charismatic business leaders like Sir Branson are able to be more successful than more conventional and conservative managers?

by offering an agenda, a grand design, an ultimate goal—in short, a *vision,* "a realistic, credible, attractive future" for the organization, as leadership expert Burt Nanus calls it. The right vision unleashes human potential, says Nanus, because it serves as a beacon of hope and common purpose. It does so by attracting commitment, energizing workers, creating meaning in their lives, establishing a standard of excellence, promoting high ideals, and bridging the divide between the organization's problems and its goals and aspirations.[56]

Examples: Civil rights leader Martin Luther King Jr. had a vision—a "dream," as he put it—of racial equality. United Farm Workers leader Cesar Chavez had a vision of better working conditions and pay for agricultural workers. Candy Lightner, founder of Mothers Against Drunk Driving, had a vision of getting rid of alcohol-related car crashes. Apple Computer's Steve Jobs had a vision of developing an "insanely great" desktop computer.

2. Idealized Influence: "We Are Here to Do the Right Thing" Transformational leaders are able to inspire trust in their followers because they express their integrity by being consistent, single-minded, and persistent in pursuit of their goal. Not only do they display high ethical standards and act as models of desirable values, but they are also able to make sacrifices for the good of the group.[57]

Examples: In 1982, when seven people died consuming cyanide-laced Tylenol capsules, Johnson & Johnson CEO James Burke retained consumer confidence by his actions in taking the drug off the market. Anita Roddick of The Body Shop cosmetics company has been a model for her beliefs in fair trade, environmental awareness, animal protection, and respect for human rights.

3. Individualized Consideration: "You Have the Opportunity Here to Grow & Excel" Transformational leaders don't just express concern for subordinates' well-being. They actively encourage them to grow and to excel by giving them challenging work, more responsibility, empowerment, and one-on-one mentoring.

Example: Curt "Curre" Linström as head coach of the Finnish national ice hockey team was able to be the caring, fatherly figure to his athletes that enabled them to trust his leadership—and to go from gloomy failure to world championship victory in 1995.

4. Intellectual Stimulation: "Let Me Describe the Great Challenges We Can Conquer Together" These leaders are gifted at communicating the organization's strengths, weaknesses, opportunities, and threats so that subordinates develop a new sense of purpose. Employees become less apt to view problems as insurmountable or "that's not my department." Instead they learn to view them as personal challenges that they are responsible for overcoming, to question the status quo, and to seek creative solutions.

Example: Ben Cohen, co-founder of Ben & Jerry's, was able to communicate his vision that making ice cream shouldn't be just about profits but also about using some profits for good works.

Implications of Transformational Leadership for Managers

The research shows that transformational leadership yields several positive results. For example, it is positively associated with (1) measures of organizational effectiveness;[58] (2) measures of leadership effectiveness and employee job satisfaction;[59] (3) more employee identification with their leaders and with their immediate work groups;[60] and (4) higher levels of intrinsic motivation, group cohesion, work engagement, and setting of goals consistent with those of the leader.[61]

Besides the fact that, as we mentioned, the best leaders are *both* transactional and transformational, there are three important implications of transformational leadership for managers, as follows.

1. It Can Improve Results for Both Individuals & Groups You can use the four types of transformational behavior just described to improve results for individuals—such as job satisfaction, organizational commitment, and performance. You can also use them to improve outcomes for groups—an important matter in today's organization, where people tend not to work in isolation but in collaboration with others.

2. It Can Be Used to Train Employees at Any Level Not just top managers but employees at any level can be trained to be more transactional and transformational.[62] This kind of leadership training among employees should be based on a corporate philosophy, however. Johnson & Johnson, for instance, bases its training on seven principles of leadership development. *(See Table 14.6.)*

table 14.6

SEVEN PRINCIPLES OF LEADERSHIP DEVELOPMENT

These were developed by Johnson & Johnson.

1. Leadership development is a key business strategy.
2. Leadership excellence is a definable set of standards.
3. People are responsible for their own development.
4. Johnson & Johnson executives are accountable for developing leaders.
5. Leaders are developed primarily on the job.
6. People are an asset of the corporation; leadership development is a collaborative, corporation-wide process.
7. Human resources are vital to the success of leadership development.

Source: Excerpted from R. M. Fulmer, "Johnson & Johnson: Framework for Leadership," *Organizational Dynamics*, Winter 2001, p. 214.

3. It Can Be Used by Both Ethical & Unethical Leaders Ethical transformational leaders help employees to enhance their self-concepts. Unethical leaders may select or produce obedient, dependent, and compliant followers. To better ensure positive results from transformational leadership, top managers should do the following:[63]

- **Employ a code of ethics.** The company should create and enforce a clearly stated code of ethics.
- **Choose the right people.** Recruit, select, and promote people who display ethical behavior.
- **Make performance expectations reflect employee treatment.** Develop performance expectations around the treatment of employees; these expectations can be assessed in the performance-appraisal process.
- **Emphasize value of diversity.** Train employees to value diversity.
- **Reward high moral conduct.** Identify, reward, and publicly praise employees who exemplify high moral conduct. ●

14.6 SIX ADDITIONAL PERSPECTIVES

major question If there are many ways to be a leader, which one would describe me best?

THE BIG PICTURE

We consider six other kinds of leadership. The *leader–member exchange model* emphasizes that leaders have different sorts of relationships with different subordinates. In *shared leadership,* people share responsibility for leading with others. In *servant leadership,* leaders provide service to employees and the organization. *Loyalty leaders* inspire others by their integrity in words and deeds. *Level 5 leaders* possess the paradoxical qualities of humility and fearless will to succeed. *E-leadership* involves leader interactions with others via information technology.

Six additional kinds of leadership deserve discussion: (1) *leader–member exchange (LMX) model of leadership,* (2) *shared leadership,* (3) *servant leadership,* (4) *loyalty leadership,* (5) *Level 5 leadership,* and (6) *e-leadership.*

Leader–Member Exchange (LMX) Leadership

Self-Assessment Exercise: *Assessing Your Leader–Member Exchange*

Proposed by **George Graen and Fred Dansereau, the *leader–member exchange (LMX) model of leadership* emphasizes that leaders have different sorts of relationships with different subordinates.**[64] Unlike other models we've described, which focus on the behaviors or traits of leaders or followers, the LMX model looks at the quality of relationships between managers and subordinates. Also, unlike other models, which presuppose stable relationships between leaders and followers, the LMX model assumes each manager-subordinate relationship is unique (what behavioral scientists call a "vertical dyad").

In-Group Exchange versus Out-Group Exchange The unique relationship, which supposedly results from the leader's attempt to delegate and assign work roles, can produce two types of leader–member exchange interactions:[65]

- **In-group exchange.** In the *in-group exchange,* the relationship between leader and follower becomes a partnership characterized by mutual trust, respect and liking, and a sense of common fates. Subordinates may receive special assignments and may also receive special privileges.
- **Out-group exchange.** In the *out-group exchange,* leaders are characterized as overseers who fail to create a sense of mutual trust, respect, or common fate. Subordinates receive less of the manager's time and attention than those in in-group exchange relationships.

Is the LMX Model Useful? It is not clear why a leader selects particular subordinates to be part of the in-group, but presumably the choice is made for reasons of compatibility and competence. Certainly, however, a positive (that is, in-group) leader–member exchange is positively associated with goal commitment, trust between managers and employees, work climate, satisfaction with leadership, and—important to any employer—job performance and job satisfaction.[66] The type of leader–member exchange also was found to predict not only turnover among nurses and computer analysts but also career outcomes, such as promotability, salary level, and receipt of bonuses, over a 7-year period.[67]

Shared Leadership

Which is better—leadership in a single chain of command or shared leadership responsibility among two or more individuals? Perhaps, it's suggested, shared leadership is more optimal.[68] ***Shared leadership* is a simultaneous, ongoing, mutual influence process in which people share responsibility for leading.** It is based on the idea that people need to share information and collaborate to get things done. This kind of leadership is most likely to be needed when people work in teams, are involved in complex projects, or are doing knowledge work—work requiring voluntary contributions of intellectual capital by skilled professionals.[69] Researchers are beginning to explore the process of shared leadership, and the results are promising. For example, shared leadership in teams has been found to be positively associated with group cohesion, group citizenship, and group effectiveness.[70]

Example

Shared Leadership: Tech Companies Spread the Power

All kinds of organizations are run with shared leadership. The famed Mayo Clinic, for example, which employs more than 42,000 employees in various hospitals and clinics, relies on shared leadership to provide high-quality health care and customer service.[71] For a while, Ford Motor Company was run by three individuals at the top.[72] At Dell, founder and chairman Michael Dell shares power with Chief Executive Officer and President Kevin Rollins.[73] At Google, cofounders Sergey Brin, President, Technology, and Larry Page, President, Products, are part of a triumvirate with Eric Schmidt, Chief Executive Officer.[74]

The fastest-growing Web site on the planet, with 100 million "friends," is MySpace.com. The founders, Tom Anderson and Chris DeWolfe, who live in Los Angeles, created the site, according to *Fortune*, "to promote local acts and connect fans and friends . . . who connected friends . . . who connected friends. . . . The two had a friendship based on business, then they—quite literally—founded a business based on friendship." When News Corp. CEO Rupert Murdoch offered $580 million for MySpace's parent company, they accepted the deal but remained on as the top executives, with DeWolfe as CEO and Anderson as President. DeWolfe is the business brain, the smart person with the compelling vision; Anderson is the "soul" of the enterprise, the one who understands the users.[75]

Your Call

If you were leading a business with a friend of yours, which role do you think would suit you best—the "business brain" or the "soul"?

Servant Leadership: Meeting the Goals of Followers & the Organization, Not of Oneself

The term *servant leadership,* coined in 1970 by **Robert Greenleaf,** reflects not only his one-time background as a management researcher for AT&T but also his views as a lifelong philosopher and devout Quaker.[76] ***Servant leaders* focus on providing increased service to others—meeting the goals of both followers and the organization—rather than to themselves.**

Former UCLA coach John Wooden, described as "a humble, giving person who wants nothing in return but to see other people succeed," is one such example. Wooden led the university's men's basketball teams to 10 national championships.[77] Wal-Mart's Sam Walton believed that leadership consisted of providing employees with the products, training, and support needed to serve customers and then standing back and letting them do their jobs.[78] Max De Pree, former chairman of furniture maker Herman Miller Inc., promoted a "covenant" with his employees. Leaders, he wrote, should give employees "space so that we can both give and receive such beautiful things as ideas, openness, dignity, joy, healing, and inclusion."[79] Starbucks CEO Howard Schultz is also cited as being one of the foremost practitioners of servant-style leadership. Schultz has made sure his employees have health insurance and work in a positive environment and as a result Starbucks has a strong brand following.[80]

Servant leadership is not a quick-fix approach to leadership. Rather, it is a long-term, transformational approach to life and work. Ten characteristics of the servant leader are shown below. *(See Table 14.7.)* One can hardly go wrong by trying to adopt these characteristics.

table 14.7

TEN CHARACTERISTICS OF THE SERVANT LEADER

1. Focus on listening.
2. Ability to empathize with others' feelings.
3. Focus on healing suffering.
4. Self-awareness of strengths and weaknesses.
5. Use of persuasion rather than positional authority to influence others.
6. Broad-based conceptual thinking.
7. Ability to foresee future outcomes.
8. Belief they are stewards of their employees and resources.
9. Commitment to the growth of people.
10. Drive to build community within and outside the organization.

Source: L. C. Spears, "Introduction: Servant-Leadership and the Greenleaf Legacy," in L. C. Spears, ed., *Reflections on Leadership: How Robert K. Greenleaf's Theory of Servant-Leadership Influenced Today's Top Management* (New York: John Wiley & Sons, 1995), pp. 1–14. Reprinted with permission of John Wiley & Sons, Inc.

Leading for Loyalty: Six Principles for Generating Faithful Employees, Customers, & Investors

Frederick F. Reichheld, former director of Bain & Company in Boston, is the author of books on loyalty, the latest being *The Loyalty Effect: The Hidden Force Behind Growth, Profits, and Lasting Value.*[81] After a dozen years of research, he has concluded that companies that are most successful in winning and retaining the allegiance of employees, customers, and investors are those that inspire loyalty. And outstanding loyalty, he suggests, "is the direct result of the words and deeds—the decisions and practices—of committed top executives who have personal integrity."[82]

Loyalty leader companies are quite diverse, ranging from Enterprise Rent-A-Car to Harley-Davidson to Northwestern Mutual. But what all have in common, says Reichheld, are six principles designed to engender and retain loyalty—principles that begin with executives at the top of the organization and affect all the relationships within it. *(See Table 14.8, opposite page.)* Let's consider them.

1. Preach What You Practice "Many business leaders are vaguely embarrassed by the idea of trumpeting their deepest values," says Reichheld. They feel that their actions should speak louder than their words.

table 14.8

SIX PRINCIPLES OF THE LOYALTY LEADER

These are the six bedrock principles of loyalty or commitment upon which leaders build enduring enterprises.

1. Preach what you practice. Explain your principles, then live by them.
2. Play to win/win. Never profit at the expense of partners. It's a short-cut to a dead end.
3. Be picky. Membership must be a privilege.
4. Keep it simple. Complexity is the enemy of speed and responsiveness.
5. Reward the right results. Worthy partners deserve worthy goals.
6. Listen hard, talk straight. Insist on honest, two-way communication and learning.

Source: Adapted from F. F. Reichheld and T. Teal, *The Loyalty Effect: The Hidden Force Behind Growth, Profits, and Lasting Value* (Boston: Harvard Business School Press, 2001); F. F. Reichheld, *Loyalty Rules! How Today's Leaders Build Lasting Relationships* (Boston: Harvard Business School Press, 2001). Copyright © 2001 by the Harvard Business School Publishing Coporation. Reprinted by permission of Harvard Business School Press; all rights reserved.

Loyalty leaders realize that more is required—that they need to constantly preach the importance of loyalty in clear, powerful terms to fight beliefs that today loyalty is irrelevant to success. Scott Cook, CEO of personal-finance software maker Intuit, constantly delivers the message to employees that the company's mission is to treat customers right.

2. Play to Win-Win "In building loyalty, it's not enough that your competitors lose," says Reichheld. "Your partners must win." It is not a good strategy, he suggests, to browbeat employees, unions, and suppliers to make concession after concession or to tolerate dealers who abuse customers, as U.S. carmakers used to do. By treating employees right, loyalty leaders inspire them to deliver superior value to their customers.

Harley-Davidson, for example, has respectful dealings with its unions, and both labor and management have such good relations with customers that many even tattoo the company's logo on their bodies.

3. Be Picky "Arrogance is thinking your company can be all things to all customers," says Reichheld. "A truly humble company knows it can satisfy only certain customers, and it goes all out to keep them happy." Enterprise Rent-A-Car has become successful by satisfying its existing customer base, not chasing after frequent travelers in every air terminal.

Loyalty leaders are also picky about their employees. Not everyone can get a job with Southwest Airlines, which accepts only 4% of its applicants. As a result, Southwest is known for both service and customer loyalty.

4. Keep It Simple In a complex world, people need simple rules to guide their decision making, and they work better in small teams that simplify responsibility and accountability. Simplicity also helps companies deal with fast-changing business demands. And small teams help keep customers from getting lost in a faceless bureaucracy.

Northwestern Mutual CEO Jim Ericson piloted the insurance company through a "brutally complex business," Reichheld says, "by keeping his company on one simple rule: Do whatever is in the customer's best interest."

5. Reward the Right Results Many companies reward the wrong customer or employee, Reichheld points out. For example, they may reward employees who work for short-term profits rather than for long-term value and customer loyalty.

Enterprise Rent-A-Car CEO Andy Taylor devised a pay system that balanced profit inducements with incentives for building long-term employee and customer loyalty, as reflected in a survey measuring customer satisfaction and repeat business.

6. Listen Hard, Talk Straight "Long-term relationships require honest, two-way communication and learning," writes Reichheld. "True communication promotes trust, which in turn engenders loyalty. Communication also enables businesses to clarify their priorities and coordinate responses to problems and opportunities as they develop."

Dell Computer, for instance, posts all costs on a Web site, so customers are never confused about prices. It also grades its vendors on a publicly posted online supplier report card, so that suppliers can see how their performance measures against other vendors.

The High Road "Low-road" companies can survive for some time—maybe even generate impressive financial returns in the short run—by taking advantage of customers, employees, and vendors when they are vulnerable. Ultimately, however, such companies fail to anticipate market shifts or are blindsided by competitors.

Leaders of "high-road" companies realize that high standards of decency and consideration don't diminish profitability. Rather they enable it. Loyalty leaders, says Reichheld, show "they believe that business is not a zero-sum game, that an organization thrives when its partners and customers thrive."

Example

A Leader Who Bucked Conventional Wisdom: Scott McNealy of Sun Microsystems

Considered one of Silicon Valley's highest profile but also most colorful and controversial CEOs, Scott McNealy stepped down from that position at computer maker Sun Microsystems in Santa Clara, California, in April 2006, although continuing in his role as chairman of the board. McNealy, who had cofounded Sun in 1982, was famously combative, honing his competitive business strategy through a passion for ice hockey and golf.

A great innovator, in the 1980s McNealy bucked conventional wisdom by overruling his own executives and launching several Sun initiatives (selling machines based on a chip and an operating system of Sun's own design and putting Java software into Sun's servers when the Internet boom took off). Those strategies paid off hugely.[83] In the 1990s, he offered consumers alternatives to rivals IBM, Hewlett-Packard, and Dell, which offered computers based on industry standard chips and operating systems such as Windows and Linux. As a result, says one writer, McNealy "led Sun during a glorious run in the dot-com years, when every Internet startup seemed to rely on an army of Sun server computers."[84] But many companies considered Sun's machines too expensive, and the company reported frequent losses over the past 5 years.[85]

Still, McNealy tried to restore growth and profit without slashing spending on research and development.[86] He also spoke of his sense of responsibility toward Sun's roughly 39,000 employees and had strongly resisted Wall Street's push to make steep job cuts.

"He was a powerful visionary and a determined business person," says marketing professor Peter Sealey at the Haas School of Business at the University of California, Berkeley. His failure, however, was that "he was not able to adjust to a profoundly changed marketplace."[87]

Tough call. Scott McNealy led Sun with a determination not to cut jobs even when times were difficult. Faced with similar circumstances, do you think you would choose similarly?

Your Call

After McNealy stepped down, a business columnist wrote: "I know that the company needs to do something to right the ship, but I think it's worth tipping the hat to a guy that's passionate about his company and has done everything possible to maintain jobs. It's a downright rarity in modern American business."[88] Despite his failures, do you think McNealy has been a strong loyalty leader?

Level 5 Leadership

Can a good company become a great company, and, if so, how? That was the question that **Jim Collins** asked, who then proceeded to perform a longitudinal research study to find the answer. The results were summarized in his 2001 bestseller *Good to Great.*[89]

Collins and his team identified a set of companies that shifted from "good" performance to "great" performance, defined as "fifteen-year cumulative stock returns at or below the general stock market, punctuated by a transition point, then cumulative returns at least three times the market over the next fifteen years."[90] From a sample of 1,435 Fortune 500 companies from 1965 to 1995, 11 good-to-great companies were identified: Abbot, Circuit City, Fannie Mae, Gillette, Kimberly-Clark, Kroger, Nucor, Philip Morris, Pitney Bowes, Walgreens, and Wells Fargo. These companies were then compared with a targeted set of direct-comparison companies to uncover the drivers of the good-to-great transformations. One of the key drivers was that the successful companies had what Collins called Level 5 leadership. Collins' research data revealed "all the good-to-great companies had Level 5 leadership at a time of transition. Furthermore, the absence of Level 5 leadership showed up as a consistent pattern in comparison companies."[91]

Level 5 Leadership: What Is It? ***Level 5 leadership* means an organization is led by a person, a Level 5 executive, who possesses the paradoxical characteristics of humility and a fearless will to succeed, as well as the capabilities associated with levels 1-4.** *(See Figure 14.3.)*

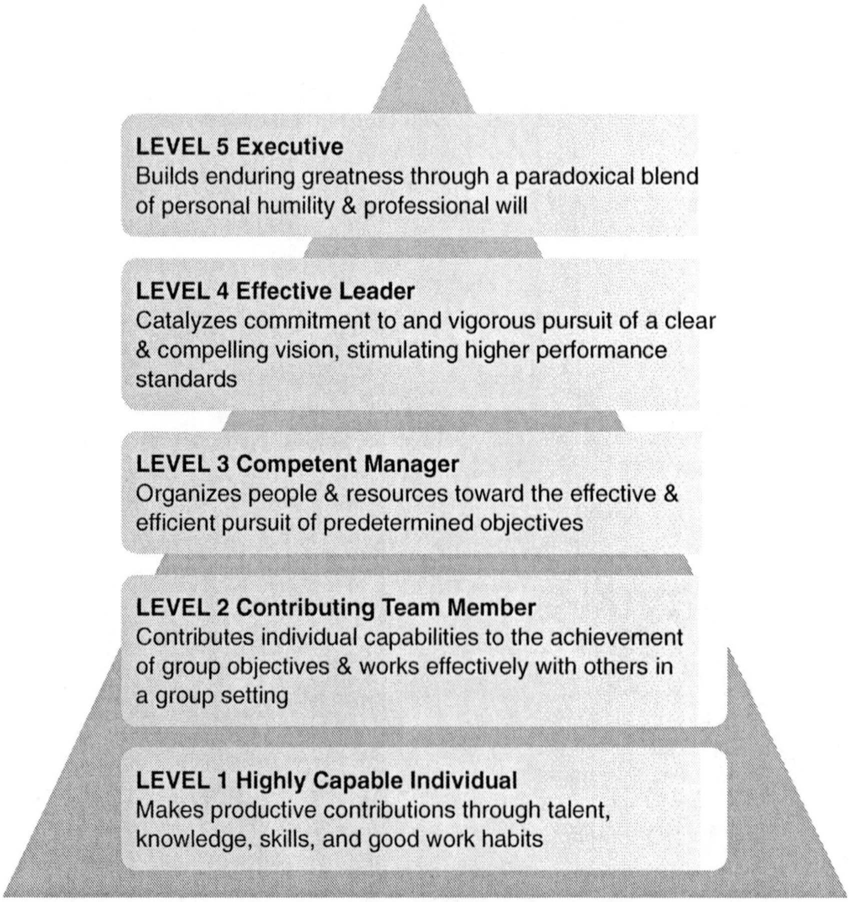

LEVEL 5 Executive
Builds enduring greatness through a paradoxical blend of personal humility & professional will

LEVEL 4 Effective Leader
Catalyzes commitment to and vigorous pursuit of a clear & compelling vision, stimulating higher performance standards

LEVEL 3 Competent Manager
Organizes people & resources toward the effective & efficient pursuit of predetermined objectives

LEVEL 2 Contributing Team Member
Contributes individual capabilities to the achievement of group objectives & works effectively with others in a group setting

LEVEL 1 Highly Capable Individual
Makes productive contributions through talent, knowledge, skills, and good work habits

figure 14.3

THE LEVEL 5 HIERARCHY

Source: Jim Collins, *Good to Great* (New York: Harper Business, 2001), p. 20. Copyright © 2001 by Jim Collins.

An example of a Level 5 executive was President Abraham Lincoln, who, though humble, soft spoken, and shy, possessed great will to keep the American Republic united during the Civil War of 1861–1865, despite a loss of 250,000 Confederate and 360,000 Union soldiers. Like other Level 5 leaders, however, Lincoln also possessed the capabilities of the other four levels of the hierarchy, ranging upward from being a highly capable individual, to a contributing team member, to a competent manager, to an effective leader. Although a Level 5 leader does not move up the hierarchy, he or she must possess the capabilities of levels 1–4 before being able to use the Level 5 characteristics to transform an organization.

Note the resemblances to Level 5 theory and other leadership theories we've discussed. For example, Level 1 is consistent with research on trait theory, which suggests that leaders are intelligent and possess the personality characteristics of extraversion, conscientiousness, and openness to experience. Levels 3 and 4 seem to contain behaviors associated with transactional and transformational leadership. But what is a novel contribution of Level 5 theory is that good-to-great leaders are not only transactional and transformational but, most importantly, are also humble and fiercely determined.

Three Observations about Level 5 Theory There are three points to keep in mind about Level 5 leadership.

- **Additional drivers.** Collins notes that, besides having a Level 5 leader, additional drivers are required to take a company from good to great.[92] Level 5 leadership, however, enables the implementation of these additional drivers.
- **Further research needed.** To date there has been no additional testing of Collins's conclusions. Future research is clearly needed to confirm the Level 5 hierarchy.
- **Hindrances.** Collins believes that some people will never become Level 5 leaders because their narcissistic and boastful tendencies do not allow them to subdue their own ego and needs to the greater good of others.

E-Leadership: Managing for Global Networks

The Internet and other forms of advanced information technology have led to new possible ways for interacting within and between organizations (e-business) and with customers and suppliers (e-commerce). Leadership within the context of this electronic technology, called ***e-leadership,*** **can involve one-to-one, one-to-many, and within- and between-group and collective interactions via information technology.**[93]

An e-leader doesn't have to be a tech guru, but he or she does have to know enough about information technology to overhaul traditional corporate structures. E-leaders, says one writer, "have a global mind-set that recognizes that the Internet is opening new markets and recharging existing ones. They don't bother fighting mere battles with competitors because they're too busy creating businesses that will surround and destroy them."[94] Harvard Business School professor D. Quinn Mills, author of *E-Leadership,* suggests that individual companies will be replaced by much broader global networks that a single CEO will not be able to manage. Thus, while 20th-century management emphasized competition, he says, future organizations will run on knowledge sharing and open exchange.[95]

These observations suggest that e-leadership means having to deal with quite a number of responsibilities, some of which are suggested opposite. *(See Table 14.9.)* Some of these responsibilities are developing business opportunities through cooperative relationships, restructuring a company into global networks, decentralizing the company's organization, and energizing the staff.[96] ●

table 14.9

SIX SECRETS OF SUCCESSFUL E-LEADERS

These tips are offered by Don MacRae, president of the Lachlan Group, Toronto.

1. **Create the future rather than a better status quo.** No matter how successful your business is now, it can be wiped out overnight by the swiftness of the Internet economy. Pay attention to new possibilities rather than simply reacting to today's problems.
2. **Create a "teachable vision."** When Steve Jobs started Apple Computer, his teachable vision was to develop a computer that was as simple to use as a bicycle. Think about how your organization needs to act differently in order to stay at the top of your industry. Have the best and brightest stars in your company investigate how your traditional markets are shifting and what new opportunities might be up for grabs.
3. **Follow a strategy your customers set, not you.** Get over your love affair with your own products and services. What matters most is whether your customers love them. Talk to them about their needs and how you could serve them better. Let them set corporate direction.
4. **Foster a collaborative culture.** E-leaders don't give orders from the top. They let teams form organically in their organizations and encourage people to question the way things are done. Be open to unorthodox strategies.
5. **Think globally.** Technology allows you to build ties with customers, suppliers, and strategic partners all over the world. Don't neglect the opportunity. Be disciplined about finding the best places to do business and seeing opportunities where they exist.
6. **Thrive on information.** This means all kinds of information: overnight sales figures, customer-satisfaction scores, employee turnover, on-time delivery rates, canceled orders, and so on. Technology allows e-leaders to track their companies by every conceivable detail. Without taking a 360-degree view of what's going on in your business—and adjusting your strategy accordingly—you can forget about leading for much longer.

Source: Adapted from D. MacRae, *BusinessWeek online*, September 6, 2001, www.businessweek.com/technology/content/sep2001/tc2001096_619.htm, accessed August 15, 2004.

key terms used in this chapter

behavioral leadership approaches 458
charisma 467
contingency approach 460
contingency leadership model 460
coercive power 450
e-leadership 476
expert power 450
full-range leadership 466
leader–member exchange (LMX) model 470
leadership 448
legitimate power 450
Level 5 leadership 475
meta-analysis 455
path–goal leadership model 461
personalized power 449
readiness 464
referent power 450
reward power 450
servant leaders 471
shared leadership 471
situational leadership theory 464
socialized power 449
trait approaches to leadership 454
transactional leadership 466
transformational leadership 467

chapter 13

Groups & Teams

Increasing Cooperation, Reducing Conflict

Major Questions You Should Be Able to Answer

13.1 **Groups versus Teams**
Major Question: How is one collection of workers different from any other?

13.2 **Stages of Group & Team Development**
Major Question: How does a group evolve into a team?

13.3 **Building Effective Teams**
Major Question: How can I as a manager build an effective team?

13.4 **Managing Conflict**
Major Question: Since conflict is a part of life, what should a manager know about it in order to deal successfully with it?

Dealing with Disagreements

Even if you're at the top of your game as a manager, working with groups and teams of people—the subject of this chapter—will now and then put you in the middle of disagreements, sometimes even destructive conflict. How can you deal with it?

There are five conflict-handling styles, or techniques, a manager can use for handling disagreements with individuals, as follows:[1]

- **Avoiding—"Maybe the problem will go away."** *Avoiding* involves ignoring or suppressing a conflict. Avoidance is appropriate for trivial issues, when emotions are high and a cooling-off period is needed, or when the cost of confrontation outweighs the benefits of resolving the conflict. It is not appropriate for difficult or worsening problems.

  The benefit of this approach is that it buys time in unfolding and ambiguous situations. The weakness is that it provides only a temporary fix and sidesteps the underlying problem.
- **Accommodating—"Let's do it your way."** An accommodating manager is also known as a "smoothing" or "obliging" manager. *Accommodating* is allowing the desires of the other party to prevail. As one writer describes it, "An obliging [accommodating] person neglects his or her own concern to satisfy the concern of the other party."[2] Accommodating may be an appropriate conflict-handling strategy when it's possible to eventually get something in return or when the issue isn't important to you. It's not appropriate for complex or worsening problems.

  The advantage of accommodating is that it encourages cooperation. The weakness is that once again it's only a temporary fix that fails to confront the underlying problem.
- **Forcing—"You have to do it my way."** Also known as "dominating," *forcing* is simply ordering an outcome, when a manager relies on his or her formal authority and power to resolve a conflict. Forcing is appropriate when an unpopular solution must be implemented and when it's not important that others be committed to your viewpoint.

  The advantage of forcing is speed: It can get results quickly. The disadvantage is that in the end it doesn't resolve personal conflict—if anything, it aggravates it by breeding hurt feelings and resentments.
- **Compromising—"Let's split the difference."** In *compromising,* both parties give up something in order to gain something. Compromise is appropriate when both sides have opposite goals or possess equal power. But compromise isn't workable when it is used so often that it doesn't achieve results—for example, continual failure to meet production deadlines.

  The benefit of compromise is that it is a democratic process that seems to have no losers. However, since so many people approach compromise situations with a win-lose attitude, they may be disappointed and feel cheated.
- **Collaborating—"Let's cooperate to reach a win-win solution that benefits both of us."** *Collaborating* strives to devise solutions that benefit both parties. Collaboration is appropriate for complex issues plagued by misunderstanding. It is inappropriate for resolving conflicts rooted in opposing value systems.

  The strength of collaborating is its longer lasting effect: it deals with the underlying problem, not just its symptoms. Its weakness is that it's very time-consuming. Nevertheless, collaboration is the best approach for dealing with groups and teams of people.

For Discussion Which kind of conflict-handling style are you most likely to use, based on your experience? Which kind do you feel comfortable trying?

forecast

What's Ahead in This Chapter

In this chapter, we consider groups versus teams and discuss different kinds of teams. We describe how groups evolve into teams and discuss how managers can build effective teams. We also consider the nature of conflict, both good and bad.

13.1 GROUPS VERSUS TEAMS

major question How is one collection of workers different from any other?

THE BIG PICTURE

Teamwork promises to be a cornerstone of future management. A team is different from a group. A group typically is management-directed, a team self-directed. Groups may be formal, created to do productive work, or informal, created for friendship. Work teams, which engage in collective work requiring coordinated effort, may be organized according to four basic purposes: advice, production, project, and action. Two types of teams are quality circles and self-managed teams.

The year 2006 was not a good one for American men's sports teams on the world stage. The U.S. soccer team failed to muster one victory at the World Cup. The U.S. baseball team was defeated by Mexico, Korea, and Canada at the World Baseball Classic and did not even make it to the semifinals. And at the World Basketball Championship, the U.S. men's team—in a sport invented by Americans—failed for the third straight year to bring home the gold.[3] What went wrong?

Take the basketball team, which despite having such NBA stars as Dwyane Wade and LeBron James nevertheless lost to Greece 101–95 in the semifinals. Team USA players had been together for more than a year, but, says one account, "the lack of experience—and familiarity with each other—was glaringly obvious against a Greek squad that has been together three years."[4] But perhaps there was more to it than that. "Our best male athletes have regressed as team players—as *teammates,*" writes Michael Sokolove. "A couple of decades of free agency and lavish salaries freed the players from the grips of owners but also unbound them from one another. . . . If our greatest young athletes don't care enough about one another to commit to effort and team play, that can't be a good thing."[5]

More Teamwork: The Change Today's Employees Need to Make

"You lead today by building teams and placing others first," says General Electric CEO Jeffrey Immelt. "It's not about you."[6] According to management philosopher Peter Drucker, tomorrow's organizations will not only be flatter and information-based but also organized around teamwork.[7] "We have this mythology in America about the lone genius," says Tom Kelley, general manager of Ideo, an industrial design company in Palo Alto, California, that helped create the Apple mouse and the Palm V handheld computer. "We love to personify things. But Michelangelo didn't paint the Sistine Chapel alone, and Edison didn't invent the light bulb alone."[8]

There are many reasons why teamwork is now the cornerstone of progressive management, as the table opposite shows. *(See Table 13.1.)* Regardless, when you take a job in an organization, the chances are you won't be working as a lone genius or even as a lone wolf. You'll be working with others in situations demanding teamwork.

table 13.1

The improvements	Example
Increased productivity	At one GE factory, teamwork resulted in a workforce that was 20% more productive than comparable GE workforces elsewhere.
Increased speed	Guidant Corp., maker of life-saving medical devices, halved the time it took to get products to market.
Reduced costs	Boeing used teamwork to develop the 777 at costs far less than normal.
Improved quality	Westinghouse used teamwork to improve quality performance in its truck and trailer division and within its electronic components division.
Reduced destructive internal competition	Men's Wearhouse fired a salesman who wasn't sharing walk-in customer traffic, and total clothing sales volume among all salespeople increased significantly.
Improved workplace cohesiveness	Cisco Systems told executives they would gain or lose 30% of their bonuses based on how well they worked with peers and in 3 years had record profits.

Groups & Teams: How Do They Differ?

Aren't a group of people and a team of people the same thing? By and large, no. One is a collection of people, the other a powerful unit of collective performance. One is typically management-directed, the other self-directed.

Consider the differences.

What a Group Is: Collection of People Performing as Individuals A ***group*** **is defined as two or more freely interacting individuals who share collective norms, share collective goals, and have a common identity.**[9] A group is different from a crowd, a transitory collection of people who don't interact with one another, such as a crowd gathering on a sidewalk to watch a fire. And it is different from an organization, such as a labor union, which is so large that members also don't interact.[10]

An example of a work group would be a collection of, say, 10 employees meeting to exchange information about various companies' policies on wages and hours.

What a Team Is: Collection of People with Common Commitment McKinsey & Company management consultants Jon R. Katzenbach and Douglas K. Smith say it is a mistake to use the terms *group* and *team* interchangeably. Successful teams, they say, tend to take on a life of their own. Thus, a ***team*** **is defined as a small group of people with complementary skills who are committed to a common purpose, performance goals, and approach for which they hold themselves mutually accountable.**[11] "The essence of a team is common commitment," say Katzenbach and Smith. "Without it, groups perform as individuals; with it, they become a powerful unit of collective performance."[12]

An example of a team would be a collection of 2–10 employees who are studying industry pay scales with the goal of making recommendations for adjusting pay grades within their own company.

Formal versus Informal Groups

Groups may be either formal or informal.

- **Formal groups—created to do productive work. A *formal group* is a group established to do something productive for the organization and is headed by a leader.** A formal group may be a division, a department, a work group, or a committee. It may be permanent or temporary. In general, people are assigned to them according to their skills and the organization's requirements.
- **Informal groups—created for friendship. An *informal group* is a group formed by people seeking friendship and has no officially appointed leader, although a leader may emerge from the membership.** An informal group may be simply a collection of friends who hang out with one another, such as those who take coffee breaks together, or it may be as organized as a prayer breakfast, a bowling team, a service club, or other voluntary organization.

What's important for you as a manager to know is that informal groups can advance or undercut the plans of formal groups. The formal organization may make efforts, say, to speed up the plant assembly line or to institute workplace reforms. But these attempts may be sabotaged through the informal networks of workers who meet and gossip over lunch pails and after-work beers.[13]

However, interestingly, informal groups can also be highly productive—even more so than formal groups.

Example

Informal Groups Can Help with Informal Learning: Worker Chitchat "Is Not Goofing Off, It's Training"

As a manager, what would you think when you saw employees making brief exchanges near the coffeepot? "The assumption was made," said Barry Blyston, director of training at a plant in Wendell, North Carolina, where managers wondered how to stop workers from gathering so often in the cafeteria, "that this was chitchat, talking about their golf game. But there was a whole lot of work activity."[14]

Or so a 2-year $1.6 million study by the Center for Workplace Development discovered.[15] At Siemens Power Transmission and Distribution, as well as companies such as Motorola and Boeing, the study found that 70% of workplace learning is informal, despite the $60 billion organizations spend on formal training programs every year.[16]

Your Call

Following the study, Siemens managers placed overhead projectors and empty pads of paper in the lunchroom to facilitate informal meetings. They also alerted supervisors about the informal gatherings. What other things would you do to encourage employees to informally learn from each other?

Talking it out. Ever worked in a job in which you got a lot of informal training through conversations over coffee?

Work Teams for Four Purposes: Advice, Production, Project, & Action

The names given to different kinds of teams can be bewildering. We have identified some important ones. *(See Table 13.2.)*

table 13.2

VARIOUS TYPES OF TEAMS

These teams are not mutually exclusive. Work teams, for instance, may also be self-managed, cross-functional, or virtual.

Cross-functional team	Members composed of people from different departments, such as sales and production, pursuing a common objective
Problem-solving team	Knowledgeable workers who meet as a temporary team to solve a specific problem and then disband
Quality circle	Volunteers of workers and supervisors who meet intermittently to discuss workplace and quality-related problems
Self-managed team	Workers are trained to do all or most of the jobs in a work unit, have no direct supervisor, and do their own day-to-day supervision
Top-management team	Members consist of the CEO, president, and top department heads and work to help the organization achieve its mission and goals
Virtual team	Members interact by computer network to collaborate on projects
Work team	Members engage in collective work requiring coordinated effort; purpose of team is advice, production, project, or action *(see text discussion)*

You will probably benefit most by understanding the various types of work teams distinguished according to their purpose. Work teams, which engage in collective work requiring coordinated effort, are of four types, which may be identified according to their basic purpose: *advice, production, project,* or *action.*[17]

1. Advice Teams *Advice teams* are created to broaden the information base for managerial decisions. Examples are committees, review panels, advisory councils, employee involvement groups, and quality circles (as we'll discuss).

2. Production Teams *Production teams* are responsible for performing day-to-day operations. Examples are mining teams, flight-attendant crews, maintenance crews, assembly teams, data processing groups, and manufacturing crews.

3. Project Teams *Project teams* work to do creative problem solving, often by applying the specialized knowledge of members of a ***cross-functional team,*** **which is staffed with specialists pursuing a common objective.** Examples are task forces, research groups, planning teams, architect teams, engineering teams, and development teams.

4. Action Teams *Action teams* work to accomplish tasks that require people with (1) specialized training and (2) a high degree of coordination, as on a baseball team, with specialized athletes acting in coordination. Examples are hospital surgery teams, airline cockpit crews, mountain-climbing expeditions, police SWAT teams, and labor contract negotiating teams.

Self-Managed Teams: Workers with Own Administrative Oversight

To give you an idea of how teams work, consider self-managed teams. These kinds of teams have emerged out of ***quality circles,*** **which consist of small groups of volunteers or workers and supervisors who meet intermittently to discuss workplace- and quality-related problems.** Typically a group of 10–12 people will meet for 60–90 minutes once or twice a month, with management listening to presentations and the important payoff for members usually being the chance for meaningful participation and skills training.[18]

In many places, such as the Texas Instruments electronics factory in Malaysia, the quality circles have evolved into a system made up almost entirely of self-managed teams, with routine activities formerly performed by supervisors now performed by team members. "Self-managed" does not, however, mean simply turning workers loose to do their own thing. ***Self-managed teams*** **are defined as groups of workers who are given administrative oversight for their task domains.** Administrative oversight involves delegated activities such as planning, scheduling, monitoring, and staffing. Nearly 70% of *Fortune* 1000 companies have created self-managed work teams.[19]

Self-managed teams are an outgrowth of a blend of behavioral science and management practice.[20] The goal has been to increase productivity and employee quality of work life. The traditional clear-cut distinction between manager and managed is being blurred as nonmanagerial employees are delegated greater authority and granted increased autonomy.

A Volvo team. This Volvo assembly plant in Torslanda, Sweden, makes cars by using team-based portable assembly platforms rather than a single constantly moving assembly line. Volvo puts the names of team members on every engine they build to instill pride in their work. Although teams have been used since the Egyptians built the pyramids, the idea didn't really gain currency in the workplace until it was promoted by management theorists such as Frederick Taylor and Douglas McGregor. In the 1930s, teams were adopted in factories to streamline manufacturing. In the 1960s, teams gained popularity as ways to improve worker satisfaction. Ironically, Volvo was acquired in 1999 by the company that was instrumental in using the assembly-line concept in manufacturing-Ford Motor Company.

In creating self-managed teams, both technical and organizational redesign are necessary. Self-managed teams may require special technology. Volvo's team-based auto assembly plant, for example, relies on portable assembly platforms rather than traditional assembly lines. Structural redesign of the organization must take place because self-managed teams are an integral part of the organization, not patched onto it, as is the case with quality circles. Personnel and reward systems need to be adapted to encourage teamwork. Staffing decisions may shift from management to team members who hire their own co-workers. Individual bonuses must give way to team bonuses. Supervisory development workshops are needed to teach managers to be facilitators rather than order givers.[21] Finally, extensive team training is required to help team members learn more about technical details, the business as a whole, and how to be team players.[22] ●

Practical Action

The Challenge of Managing Virtual Teams: Reaching across Time & Space

Once upon a time, managers subscribed to the so-called Fifty-Foot Rule—namely, "If people are more than 50 feet apart, they are not likely to collaborate." That is no longer true in today's era of virtual teams. Virtual teams are groups of people who use information technology—computers and telecommunications—to collaborate across space, time, and organizational boundaries.[23]

Teams are generally defined as consisting of 2–16 people. But virtual collaborations may be even larger. For instance, NCR Corp. created a virtual "team" (group) of more than 1,000 people working at 17 locations to develop a next-generation computer system. Using a high-bandwidth audio-video-data telecommunications network, members completed the project on budget and ahead of schedule.[24] And Hong Kong–based Cathay Pacific Airlines designed a network, called GalaCXy, appropriate for a company where employees are never in one place for very long but need to be able to communicate intelligently wherever they go. "GalaCXy users can set up meetings with each other without calling to check one another's schedules," says one account. "They can access one another's schedules to see when they're available and then suggest a time by e-mail."[25]

As technology has made it easier for workers to function from remote places, it has posed challenges for managers. Following are some suggestions for managing virtual workers, especially those working at home:[26]

- **Take baby steps.** When trying out virtual arrangements with new employees, take it slow. Let them show they can handle the challenge.
- **State expectations.** Nip problems in the bud by letting virtual workers know what you expect from them. With home-based workers, for example, go over the terms of your virtual arrangement—whether, for example, you want them to carry an office cell phone—and tell them if there are specific ways you want the job done.
- **Write it down.** Record directions, project changes, and updates in writing, by sending an e-mail or fax or using Web-based services that allow for sharing calendars and tracking projects.
- **Communicate.** Whether your virtual workers take an occasional day away or work from home full-time, make sure they're reachable during business hours. Phone call, e-mail, fax, and chat all work well—but they have to be able to reach you, too.
- **Manage by results.** Focus on what's accomplished, not whether your employee is working from her patio or at 10 P.M. Set interim deadlines on projects and stick to them.
- **Meet regularly.** Human contact still matters. When possible, schedule periodic and regular meetings at which all team members can discuss current projects, and telecommuters can catch up on office gossip. Fly out-of-towners in at least quarterly, so they can develop working friendships with your in-office staff.

13.2 STAGES OF GROUP & TEAM DEVELOPMENT

major question

How does a group evolve into a team?

THE BIG PICTURE

Groups may evolve into teams by going through five stages of development: forming, storming, norming, performing, and adjourning.

Elsewhere in this book we have described how products and organizations go through stages of development. Groups and teams go through the same thing. One theory proposes five stages of development: *forming, storming, norming, performing, adjourning.*[27] *(See Figure 13.1.)* Let us consider these stages in which groups may evolve into teams—bearing in mind that the stages aren't necessarily of the same duration or intensity.

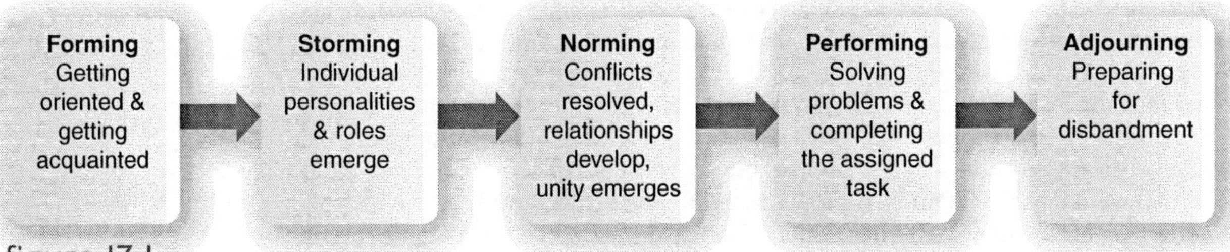

figure 13.1

FIVE STAGES OF GROUP AND TEAM DEVELOPMENT

Stage 1: Forming—"Why Are We Here?"

Hot Seat DVD Applications:
Working in Teams: Cross-Functional Dysfunction

The first stage, ***forming,*** **is the process of getting oriented and getting acquainted.** This stage is characterized by a high degree of uncertainty as members try to break the ice and figure out who is in charge and what the group's goals are. For example, if you were to become part of a team that is to work on a class project, the question for you as an individual would be "How do I fit in here?" For the group, the question is "Why are we here?"[28]

At this point, mutual trust is low, and there is a good deal of holding back to see who takes charge and how. If the formal leader (such as the class instructor or a supervisor) does not assert his or her authority, an emergent leader will eventually step in to fill the group's need for leadership and direction.

What the Leader Should Do Leaders typically mistake this honeymoon period as a mandate for permanent control, but later problems may force a leadership change. During this stage, leaders should allow time for people to become acquainted and socialize.

Stage 2: Storming—"Why Are We Fighting Over Who Does What & Who's in Charge?"

The second stage, ***storming,*** **is characterized by the emergence of individual personalities and roles and conflicts within the group.** For you as an individual, the question is "What's my role here?" For the group, the issue is "Why are we fighting over who does what and who's in charge?" This stage may be of short duration or painfully long, depending on the goal clarity and the commitment and maturity of the members.

This is a time of testing. Individuals test the leader's policies and assumptions as they try to determine how they fit into the power structure.[29] Subgroups take shape, and subtle forms of rebellion, such as procrastination, occur. Many groups stall in stage 2 because power politics may erupt into open rebellion.

What the Leader Should Do In this stage, the leader should encourage members to suggest ideas, voice disagreements, and work through their conflicts about tasks and goals.

Stage 3: Norming—"Can We Agree on Roles & Work as a Team?"

In the third stage, ***norming,*** **conflicts are resolved, close relationships develop, and unity and harmony emerge.** For individuals, the main issue is "What do the others expect me to do?" For the group, the issue is "Can we agree on roles and work as a team?" Note, then, that the *group* may now evolve into a *team.*

Teams set guidelines related to what members will do together and how they will do it. The teams consider such matters as attendance at meetings, being late, and missing assignments as well as how members treat one another.

Groups that make it through stage 2 generally do so because a respected member other than the leader challenges the group to resolve its power struggles so something can be accomplished. Questions about authority are resolved through unemotional, matter-of-fact group discussion. A feeling of team spirit is experienced because members believe they have found their proper roles. ***Group cohesiveness,*** **a "we feeling" binding group members together,** is the principal by-product of stage 3. (We discuss cohesiveness next, in Section 13.3.)

What the Leader Should Do This stage generally does not last long. Here the leader should emphasize unity and help identify team goals and values.

Stage 4: Performing—"Can We Do the Job Properly?"

In ***performing,*** **members concentrate on solving problems and completing the assigned task.** For individuals, the question here is "How can I best perform my role?" For the group/team, the issue is "Can we do the job properly?"

What the Leader Should Do During this stage, the leader should allow members the empowerment they need to work on tasks.

Stage 5: Adjourning—"Can We Help Members Transition Out?"

In the final stage, ***adjourning,*** **members prepare for disbandment.** Having worked so hard to get along and get something done, many members feel a compelling sense of loss. For the individual, the question now is "What's next?" For the team, the issue is "Can we help members transition out?"

What the Leader Should Do The leader can help ease the transition by rituals celebrating "the end" and "new beginnings." Parties, award ceremonies, graduations, or mock funerals can provide the needed punctuation at the end of a significant teamwork project. The leader can emphasize valuable lessons learned in group dynamics to prepare everyone for future group and team efforts. ●

13.3 BUILDING EFFECTIVE TEAMS

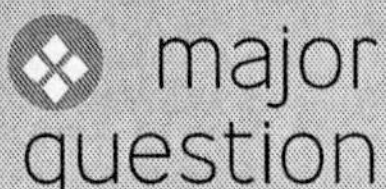

major question

How can I as a manager build an effective team?

THE BIG PICTURE

Two types of change are reactive and proactive. Forces for change may consist of forces outside the organization—demographic characteristics, market changes, technological advancements, and social and political pressures. Or they may be forces inside the organization—employee problems and managers' behavior.

Within an organization, you may hear managers loosely (and incorrectly) use the word *team* to describe any collection of people that have been pulled together. But because traditional managers are often reluctant to give up control, no thought is given to providing the "team" (really just a group) with training and support. That is, no attempt is made to sharpen communication skills, reward innovation, or encourage independence without group members running away and losing control.[30]

Thus, as a manager, the first thing you have to realize is that building a high-performance team is going to require some work. But the payoff will be a stronger, better-performing work unit.

The considerations in building a group into an effective team are (1) *performance goals and feedback,* (2) *motivation through mutual accountability,* (3) *size,* (4) *roles,* (5) *norms,* (6) *cohesiveness,* and (7) *groupthink.*

Learning teamwork from a NASCAR pit crew. Randy Darcy, chief technical officer for cereal maker General Mills, was given the challenge of cutting $1 billion out of the company's supply chain, Darcy's approach was to adapt lessons in efficiency and high performance learned elsewhere-watching Air Force mechanics fix Stealth bombers, participating in predawn raids with a U.S. Marshals Service SWAT team, and getting time- and money-saving ideas by observing a NASCAR pit crew. Learning how the pit crew was able to work with blinding speed through better team organization, the cereal company was able to cut the time workers changed a production line for a Betty Crocker product from 4.5 hours to just 12 minutes.

1. Performance Goals & Feedback

As an individual, you no doubt prefer to have measurable goals and to have feedback about your performance. The same is true with teams. Teams are not just collections of individuals. They are individuals organized for a collective purpose. That purpose needs to be defined in terms of specific, measurable performance goals with continual feedback to tell team members how well they are doing.

An obvious example are the teams you see on television at Indianapolis or Daytona Beach during automobile racing. When the driver guides the race car off the track to make a pit stop, a team of people swarm over the wall and quickly jack up the car to change tires, refuel the tank, and clean the windshield—all operating in a matter of seconds. The performance goals are to have the car back on the track as quickly as possible. The number of seconds of elapsed time—and the driver's place among competitors once back in the race—tells them how well they are doing.

2. Motivation through Mutual Accountability

Do you work harder when you're alone or when you're in a group? When clear performance goals exist, when the work is considered meaningful, when members believe their efforts matter, and when they don't feel they are being exploited by others, this kind of culture supports teamwork.[31] Being mutually accountable to other members of the team rather than to a supervisor makes members feel mutual trust and commitment—a key part in motivating members for team effort. To bring about this team culture, managers often allow teams to do the hiring of new members.

3. Size: Small Teams or Large Teams?

192 Size, which is often determined by the team's purpose, can be important in affecting members' commitment and performance. Whereas in some flat-organization structures groups may consist of 30 or more employees, teams seem to range in size from 2–16 people, with those of 5–12 generally being the most workable and 5–6 considered optimal.[32] A survey of 400 workplace team members in the United States found that the average team consisted of 10 members, with 8 being the most common size.[33]

Small and large teams have different characteristics, although the number of members is, to be sure, somewhat arbitrary.[34]

Small Teams: 2–9 Members for Better Interaction & Morale Teams with 9 or fewer members have two advantages:

- **Better interaction.** Members are better able to interact, share information, ask questions of one another, and coordinate activities than are those in larger teams. In particular, teams with five or fewer offer more opportunity for personal discussion and participation.
- **Better morale.** They are better able to see the worth of their individual contributions and thus are more highly committed and satisfied. Members are less apt to feel inhibited in participating. Team leaders are subject to fewer demands and are able to be more informal.[35]

However, small teams also have some disadvantages:

- **Fewer resources.** With fewer hands, there will be fewer resources—less knowledge, experience, skills, and abilities to apply to the team's tasks.
- **Possibly less innovation.** A group that's too small may show less creativity and boldness because of the effect of peer pressure.
- **Unfair work distribution.** Because of fewer resources and less specialization, there may be an uneven distribution of the work among members.

Large Teams: 10–16 Members for More Resources & Division of Labor Teams with 10–16 members have different advantages over small teams. (Again, the numbers are somewhat arbitrary.)

- **More resources.** Larger teams have more resources to draw on: more knowledge, experience, skills, abilities, and perhaps time. These will give them more leverage to help them realize the team's goals.
- **Division of labor.** In addition, a large team can take advantage of ***division of labor,*** **in which the work is divided into particular tasks that are assigned to particular workers.**

Yet bigness has its disadvantages:

- **Less interaction.** With more members, there is less interaction, sharing of information, and coordinating of activities. Leaders may be more formal and autocratic, since members in teams this size are apt to be more tolerant of autocratic leadership. The larger size may also lead to the formation of cliques.
- **Lower morale.** Because people are less able to see the worth of their individual contributions, they show less commitment and satisfaction and more turnover and absenteeism. They also express more disagreements and turf struggles and make more demands on leaders.
- **Social loafing.** The larger the size, the more likely performance is to drop, owing to the phenomenon known as ***social loafing,*** **the tendency of people to exert less effort when working in groups than when working alone.**[36]

Example

Team Size: And the Magic Number Is . . .

The subject of team size has become a topic of fascination, according to two scholars, because "in the past decade, research on team effectiveness has burgeoned as teams have become increasingly common in organizations of all kinds."[37] What's the right number of people for a team? Various companies have various rules. At Amazon.com, there is a "two-pizza rule"—namely, if a team can't be fed by two pizzas, it's too large.[38] Other companies have their own ideal sizes: Titeflex, 6–10 people; EDS, 8–12; Johnsonville Foods, 12; Volvo, 20. Microsoft Corp. felt the optimal size for a software-development team was 8.[39]

J. Richard Hackman, Harvard professor of social and organizational psychology, thinks there should be no more than 6—the maximum he will allow for students forming project groups.[40] In 1970, Hackman and colleague Neil Vidmar set out to discover the perfect size, asking various teams large and small whether their number was too large or too small for the task. The optimal number: 4.6.[41]

Size is not the only consideration, however. For instance, says Wharton management professor Katherine J. Klein, the nature of the team's task is key because it defines the type of skills you are looking for and the type of coordination necessary.[42]

Your Call

What's been your experience, if any, with team size? At what point does adding members begin to hurt a team's performance as people become less motivated and group coordination becomes more difficult?

4. Roles: How Team Members Are Expected to Behave

Group Exercises: *Identifying Task and Maintenance Roles within Groups*

A *role* is a socially determined expectation of how an individual should behave in a specific position. As a team member, your role is to play a part in helping the team reach its goals. Members develop their roles based on the expectations of the team, of the organization, and of themselves, and they may do different things. You, for instance, might be a team leader. Others might do some of the work tasks. Still others might communicate with other teams.

Two types of team roles are task and maintenance.[43]

Self-Assessment Exercise: *Team Roles Preference Scale*

Task Roles: Getting the Work Done **A *task role,* or *task-oriented role,* consists of behavior that concentrates on getting the team's tasks done.** Task roles keep the team on track and get the work done. If you stand up in a team meeting and say, "What is the real issue here? We don't seem to be getting anywhere," you are performing a task role.

Examples: Coordinators, who pull together ideas and suggestions; orienters, who keep teams headed toward their stated goals; initiators, who suggest new goals or ideas; and energizers, who prod people to move along or accomplish more are all playing task roles.

Maintenance Roles: Keeping the Team Together **A *maintenance role,* or *relationship-oriented role,* consists of behavior that fosters constructive relationships among team members.** Maintenance roles focus on keeping team members. If someone at a team meeting says, "Let's hear from those who oppose this plan," he or she is playing a maintenance role.

Examples: Encouragers, who foster group solidarity by praising various viewpoints; standard setters, who evaluate the quality of group processes; harmonizers, who mediate conflict through reconciliation or humor; and compromisers, who help resolve conflict by meeting others "halfway."

5. Norms: Unwritten Rules for Team Members

194 Norms are more encompassing than roles. ***Norms* are general guidelines or rules of behavior that most group or team members follow.** Norms point up the boundaries between acceptable and unacceptable behavior.[44] Although norms are typically unwritten and seldom discussed openly, they have a powerful influence on group and organizational behavior.[45]

Example

Team Norms: A Steelmaker Treats Workers Like Owners

When the electrical grid at Nucor Corp.'s steelmaking plant in Hickman, Arkansas, failed, electricians drove or flew in from other Nucor plants as far away as Alabama and North Carolina. No supervisor asked them to do so, nor was there any direct financial incentive for them to blow their weekends to help out. The electricians were following team norms. They came because, as a *BusinessWeek* article states, "Nucor's flattened hierarchy and emphasis on pushing power to the front line lead its employees to adopt the mindset of owner-operators."[46]

Nucor's close-knit culture is the outgrowth of former CEO F. Kenneth Iverson's insight that employees would make extraordinary efforts if they were treated with respect, given real power, and rewarded richly. Instead of following the typical command-and-control model typical of most American businesses in recent decades, Nucor executives motivate their front-line people by "talking to them, listening to them, taking a risk on their ideas, and accepting the occasional failure," says *BusinessWeek.*

Good work is rewarded—production of defect-free steel can triple a worker's pay—but bad work is penalized, with employees losing bonuses they normally would have made. Executive pay is tied to team building, with bonuses tied not just to the performance of a particular plant but to the entire corporation's performance. There is not only healthy competition among facilities and shifts but also cooperation and idea-sharing. The result: Nucor is highly profitable, producing a 387% return to shareholders in the past 5 years.

Your Call

Can you think of any kind of businesses in which Nucor's model for strengthening team norms would not work very well? Could American manufacturing companies, automakers, and certain airlines make a comeback if their work and pay rules were made to copy Nucor's?

Why Norms Are Enforced: Four Reasons Norms tend to be enforced by group or team members for four reasons:[47]

- **To help the group survive—"Don't do anything that will hurt us."** Norms are enforced to help the group, team, or organization survive.

  Example: The manager of your team or group might compliment you because you've made sure it has the right emergency equipment.
- **To clarify role expectations—"You have to go along to get along."** Norms are also enforced to help clarify or simplify role expectations.

  Example: At one time, new members of Congress wanting to buck the system by which important committee appointments were given to those with the most seniority were advised to "go along to get along"—go along with the rules in order to get along in their congressional careers.
- **To help individuals avoid embarrassing situations—"Don't call attention to yourself."** Norms are enforced to help group or team members avoid embarrassing themselves.

Special norms. Enterprise Rent-A-Car, the largest and most prosperous car-rental company in the United States (more than Hertz and Avis), operates on the principle that "If you take care of your customers and employees, the bottom line will take care of itself." In a 2006 survey, 80% of customers said they were "completely satisfied" with their Enterprise rental—which *FORTUNE* magazine calls "an extraordinary score."

Examples: You might be ridiculed by fellow team members for dominating the discussion during a report to top management ("Be a team player, not a show-off"). Or you might be told not to discuss religion or politics with customers, whose views might differ from yours.

- **To emphasize the group's important values and identity—"We're known for being special."** Finally, norms are enforced to emphasize the group, team, or organization's central values or to enhance its unique identity.

  Examples: Nordstrom's department store chain emphasizes the great lengths to which it goes in customer service. Every year a college gives an award to the instructor whom students vote best teacher.

6. Cohesiveness: The Importance of Togetherness

Another important characteristic of teams is ***cohesiveness,* the tendency of a group or team to stick together.** This is the familiar sense of togetherness or "we-ness" you feel, for example, when you're a member of a volleyball team, a fraternity or a sorority, or a company's sales force.

Managers can stimulate cohesiveness by allowing people on work teams to pick their own teammates, allowing off-the-job social events, and urging team members to recognize and appreciate each other's contributions to the team goal.[48] Cohesiveness is also achieved by keeping teams small, making sure performance standards are clear and accepted, and following the tips in the following table. *(See Table 13.3.)*

table 13.3

WHAT MANAGERS CAN DO TO ENHANCE TEAM COHESIVENESS

• Keep the team relatively small	• Regularly update and clarify the team's goals
• Strive for a favorable public image to increase the status and prestige of belonging	• Give every group member a vital "piece of the action"
• Encourage interaction and cooperation	• Channel each team member's special talents toward the common goals
• Emphasize members' common characteristics and interests	• Recognize and equitably reinforce each member's contributions
• Point out environmental threats—e.g., competitors' achievements—to rally the team	• Frequently remind group members they need each other to get the job done

7. Groupthink: When Peer Pressure Discourages "Thinking Outside the Box"

Cohesiveness isn't always good. An undesirable by-product that may occur, according to psychologist **Irvin Janis,** is ***groupthink*—a cohesive group's blind unwillingness to consider alternatives.** In this phenomenon, group or team members are friendly and tight-knit, but they are unable to think "outside the box." Their "strivings for unanimity override their motivation to realistically appraise alternative courses of action," says Janis.[49]

The word "groupthink" regained some prominence in mid-2004 when the Senate Intelligence Committee said the U.S. invasion of Iraq had occurred because too many people in the government tended to think alike and failed to challenge basic assumptions about Iraq's weapons capability.[50] It cannot be said, however, that group opinion is always risky. Indeed, financial writer James Surowiecki, author of *The Wisdom of Crowds,* argues that "Under the right circumstances, groups are remarkably intelligent, and are often smarter than the smartest people in them."[51] As evidence, he cites how groups have been used to predict the election of the President of the United States, find lost submarines, and correct the spread on a sporting event.

Symptoms of Groupthink How do you know that you're in a group or team that is suffering from groupthink? Some symptoms:[52]

- **Invulnerability, inherent morality, and stereotyping of opposition.** Because of feelings of invulnerability, group members have the illusion that nothing can go wrong, breeding excessive optimism and risk taking. Members may also be so assured of the rightness of their actions that they ignore the ethical implications of their decisions. These beliefs are helped along by stereotyped views of the opposition, which leads the group to underestimate its opponents.
- **Rationalization and self-censorship.** Rationalizing protects the pet assumptions underlying the group's decisions from critical questions. Self-censorship also stifles critical debate. It is especially hard to argue with success, of course. But if enough key people, such as outside analysts, had challenged the energy giant Enron when it seemed to be flying high, it might not have led to the largest bankruptcy in corporate history.
- **Illusion of unanimity, peer pressure, and mindguards.** The illusion of unanimity is another way of saying that silence by a member is interpreted to mean consent. But if people do disagree, peer pressure leads other members to question the loyalty of the dissenters. In addition, in a groupthink situation there may exist people who might be called *mindguards*—self-appointed protectors against adverse information.
- **Groupthink versus "the wisdom of crowds."** Groupthink is characterized by a pressure to conform that often leads members with different ideas to censor themselves—the opposite of collective wisdom, says James Surowiecki, in which "each person in the group is offering his or her best independent forecast. It's not at all about compromise or consensus."[53]

The Results of Groupthink: Decision-Making Defects Groups with a moderate amount of cohesiveness tend to produce better decisions than groups with low or high cohesiveness. Members of highly cohesive groups victimized by groupthink make the poorest decisions—even though they show they express great confidence in those decisions.[54]

Among the decision-making defects that can arise from groupthink are the following.

- **Reduction in alternative ideas.** The principal casualty of groupthink is a shrinking universe of ideas. Decisions are made based on few alternatives. Once preferred alternatives are decided on, they are not reexamined, and, of course, rejected alternatives are not reexamined.
- **Limiting of other information.** When a groupthink group has made its decision, others' opinions, even those of experts, are rejected. If new information is considered at all, it is biased toward ideas that fit the group's preconceptions. Thus, no contingency plans are made in case the decision turns out to be faulty.

Example

Groupthink: Is Dell a "One-Trick Pony"?[55]

Dell Inc. became a success story through one core idea: becoming a lean, mean, direct sales machine. Using the slogan "Direct from Dell," it made personal computers cheaply by being super-efficient in acquiring and assembling their components (supply chain management) and selling them directly to consumers via the Internet.

In 2006, however, sales began to decline as competitors stepped up their efforts and markets shifted away from some of Dell's key advantages. Instead of adapting, however, Dell stuck to its old way of doing things, cutting costs to the point that, critics say, they compromised customer service and possibly product quality. Said a rival, "They're a one-trick pony. It was a great trick for over 10 years, but the rest of us have figured it out and Dell hasn't plowed any of its profits into creating a new trick." Even back in 2003, Dell revealed the limits of its business model. "There are some organizations where people think they're a hero if they invent a new thing," said CEO Kevin Rollins. "Being a hero at Dell means saving money."

The depth of groupthink at Dell was revealed in the extent to which new ideas were discouraged. Says one former manager, "You had to be very confident and thick-skinned to stay on an issue that wasn't popular. A lot of red flags got waved—but only once." Adds Geoffrey Moore, author of *Dealing with Darwin: How Great Companies Innovate at Every Phase of Their Evolution*, "Dell's culture is not inspirational or aspirational. This is when they need to be imaginative, but [Dell's] culture only wants to talk about execution."[56]

Your Call

The primacy of groups and teamwork "is so ingrained that we seldom stop to think about it anymore," says an *Inc. Magazine* writer. However, he adds, "In many cases, individuals do *much* better on their own. Our bias toward groups is counterproductive."[57] If you were chairman Michael Dell, who originally founded the company in his University of Texas dorm room, what would you do to break the groupthink culture at Dell?

Preventing Groupthink: Making Criticism & Other Perspectives Permissible

Janis believes it is easier to prevent groupthink than to cure it. As preventive measures, he suggests the following:

- **Allow criticism.** Each member of a team or group should be told to be a critical evaluator, able to actively voice objections and doubts. Subgroups within the group should be allowed to discuss and debate ideas. Once a consensus has been reached, everyone should be encouraged to rethink his or her position to check for flaws.

- **Allow other perspectives.** Outside experts should be used to introduce fresh perspectives. Different groups with different leaders should explore the same policy questions. Top-level executives should not use policy committees to rubber-stamp decisions that have already been made. When major alternatives are discussed, someone should be made devil's advocate to try to uncover all negative factors. ●

Fighting groupthink. For a long time, the Coca-Cola Co. had a culture of politeness and consensus that kept it from developing new products, at a time when consumers were flocking to a new breed of coffees, juices, and teas. Under Mary Minnick, who heads marketing, strategy, and innovation, the company is developing new beverages, such as the coffee-flavored Coca-Cola Blak. Do you think Coke can move beyond groupthink and "me-too" products to become cutting edge?

3.5 THE NEW DIVERSIFIED WORKFORCE

What trends in workplace diversity should managers be aware of?

major question

THE BIG PICTURE

One of today's most important management challenges is working with stakeholders of all sorts who vary widely in diversity—in age, gender, race, religion, ethnicity, sexual orientation, capabilities, and socioeconomic background. Managers should also be aware of the differences between internal and external dimensions of diversity and barriers to diversity.

"Coors Cares," says one of the beer company's slogans.

Didn't it always? Actually, in the 1980s the Coors family's funding of right-wing causes—they helped start the conservative Heritage Foundation—gave the brewer such a bad reputation with minorities and unions that it was devastated financially. Today Coors still gives steady support to the political right. Ironically, however, the company goes far beyond government requirements in embracing sensitivity, diversity, and other politically left policies.

Inside Coors, workers get training in sexual harassment and attend diversity workshops. "Employees can choose among eight 'resource councils'—groups representing gays, women, and Native Americans, among others," says a *Time* article. It also claims to offer "the first corporate mammography program in the country." In addition, it sets aside a specific share of purchases for minority-owned firms. Outside, it provides sponsorship of such programs as the Mi Casa resource center for women, a black-heritage festival, and a marathon gay dance party. It is one of the three out of four Fortune 500 companies to have diversity programs to help attract and keep minorities.[83]

Coors and other companies have discovered they can benefit from a singular fact: minority markets buy more goods and services than any country that trades with the United States.[84] In this section, we describe one of the most important management challenges—dealing with diversity.

How to Think about Diversity: Which Differences Are Important?

Diversity **represents all the ways people are unlike and alike—the differences and similarities in age, gender, race, religion, ethnicity, sexual orientation, capabilities, and socioeconomic background.** Note here that diversity is not synonymous with differences. Rather, it encompasses both differences and similarities. This means that as a manager you need to manage both simultaneously.

To help distinguish the important ways in which people differ, diversity experts Lee Gardenswartz and Anita Rowe have identified a "diversity wheel" consisting of four layers of diversity: (1) personality, (2) internal dimensions, (3) external dimensions, and (4) organizational dimensions. *(See Figure 3.2, next page.)*

Let's consider these four layers:

Personality At the center of the diversity wheel is personality. It is at the center because ***personality*** **is defined as the stable physical and mental characteristics responsible for a person's identity.** We cover the dimension of personality in Chapter 11.

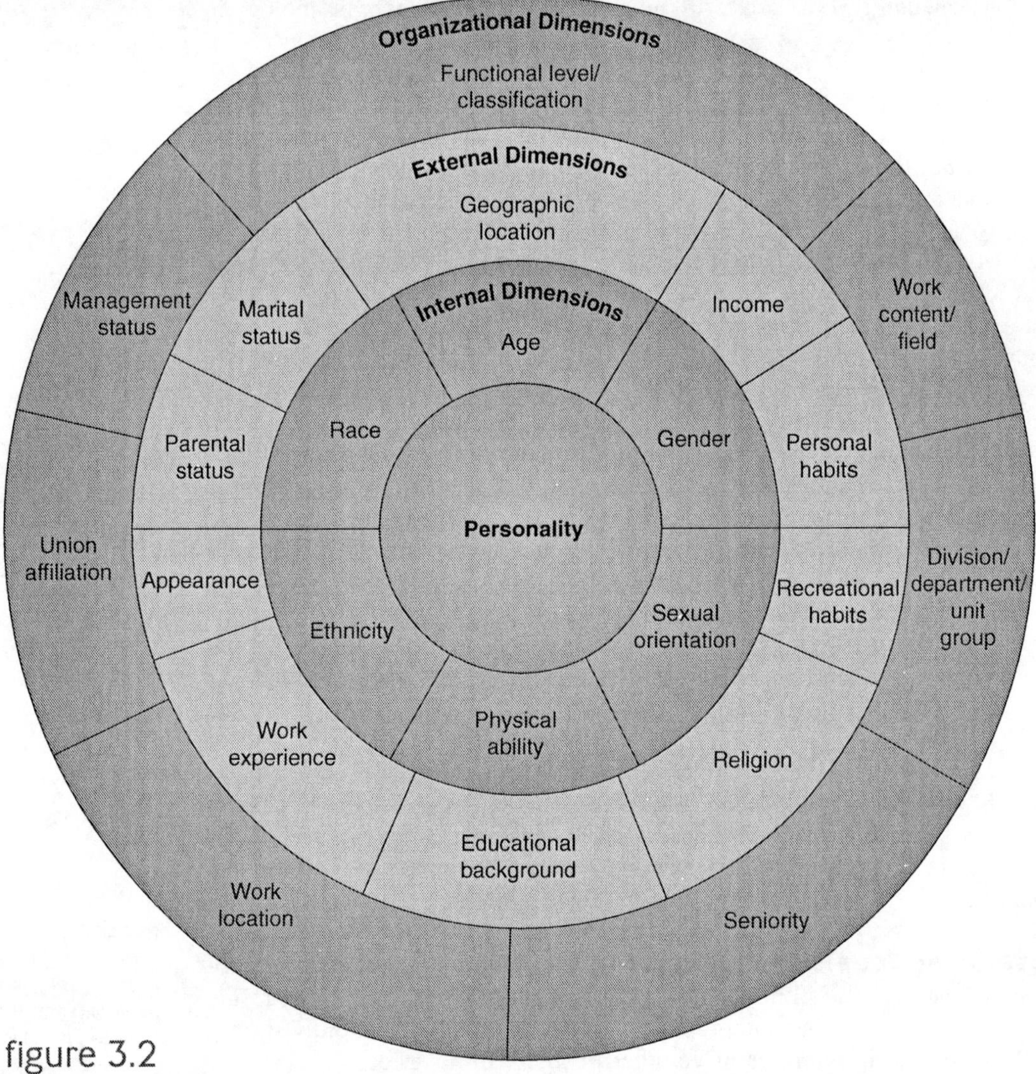

figure 3.2

THE DIVERSITY WHEEL

Four layers of diversity

Source: L. Gardenswartz and A. Rowe, *Diverse Teams at Work: Capitalizing on the Power of Diversity* (New York: McGraw-Hill, 1994), p. 33, © 1994. Reproduced with permission of The McGraw-Hill Companies and by permission of The Society for Human Resource Management via The Copyright Clearance Center. Internal dimensions and external dimensions are adapted from M. Loden and J. B. Rosener, *Workforce America! Managing Employee Diversity as a Vital Resource,* (Homewood, IL: Business One Irwin, 1991).

Internal Dimensions ***Internal dimensions of diversity*** **are those human differences that exert a powerful, sustained effect throughout every stage of our lives:** gender, age, ethnicity, race, sexual orientation, physical abilities.[85] These are referred to as the *primary* dimensions of diversity because they are not within our control for the most part. Yet they strongly influence our attitudes and expectations and assumptions about other people, which in turn influence our own behavior.

What characterizes internal dimensions of diversity is that they are visible and salient in people. And precisely because these characteristics are so visible, they may be associated with certain stereotypes—for example, that black people work in menial jobs. For instance, an African American female middle manager reports that, while on vacation and sitting by the pool at a resort, she was approached by a 50ish white male who "demanded that I get him extra towels. I said, 'Excuse me?' He then said, 'Oh, you don't work here,' with no shred of embarrassment or apology in his voice."[86]

External Dimensions ***External dimensions of diversity*** **include an element of choice; they consist of the personal characteristics that people acquire, discard, or modify throughout their lives:** educational background, marital status, parental status, religion, income, geographic location, work experience, recreational habits, appearance, personal habits. They are referred to as the *secondary* dimensions of diversity because we have a greater ability to influence or control them than we do internal dimensions.

These external dimensions also exert a significant influence on our perceptions, behavior, and attitudes. If you are not a believer in the Muslim religion, for example, you may not perceive the importance of some of its practices—as with some managers at Atlanta-based Argenbright Security Inc., who sent seven Muslim female employees home for wearing Islamic head scarves at their security jobs at Dulles International Airport. Because wearing head scarves in no way affected their job performance, the company had to reimburse the women for back pay and other relief in a settlement negotiated with the Equal Employment Opportunity Commission.[87]

Organizational Dimensions Organizational dimensions include management status, union affiliation, work location, seniority, work content, and division or department.

Trends in Workforce Diversity

How is the U.S. workforce apt to become more diverse in the 21st century? Let's examine five categories on the internal dimension—*age, gender, race/ethnicity, sexual orientation, and physical/mental abilities*—and one category on the external dimension, *educational level.*

Age: More Older People in the Workforce The most significant demographic event, management philosopher Peter Drucker suggested, "is that in the developed countries the number and proportion of younger people is rapidly shrinking. . . . Those shrinking numbers of younger people will have to both drive their economies and help support much larger numbers of older people."[88] In Europe and Japan, births are not keeping pace with deaths. Italy, for example, could drop from 60 million to 20 million by the end of the 21st century. Even China is faced with a nationwide aging gap, which means the country may face a shortage of cheap labor.[89]

Diversity enriches. A diverse population in a company can provide ideas, experience, and points of view that strengthen the business culture.

The United States, suggested Drucker, is the only developed economy to have enough young people, and that is only because immigrants to the United States still have large families. Even so, the median age of the American worker was 36.2 in 2005, up from 34.3 in 1980.[90]

Gender: More Women Working Since the 1960s, women have been flooding into the workplace in great numbers, with about 75% of women ages 25–54 in the workforce, up from about 40% in the late 1950s.[91] (For men in the same age range, participation is about 90%.) Although women's participation in the labor force has declined a bit (in part because of delayed motherhood), today females hold half of all management and professional jobs. In addition, more and more businesses are owned by women—about 30% of all U.S. nonfarm companies.[92]

Traditionally, however, women have earned roughly the same pay as men only in jobs paying $25,000–$30,000 a year. The further up the pay scale and the higher the education level, the wider the earnings gap. Thus, for every dollar a man earns,

African-American success. Police chief Annetta Nunn, the first woman African-American police chief of Birmingham, Alabama, prepares for a press conference. Nunn broke through a glass ceiling of a different sort, taking over the police operations in 2003 for a city known for its racial discrimination only a few decades earlier.

a woman cashier earns 93 cents, an administrative assistant 93 cents, and a registered nurse 88 cents. But for a woman physician or surgeon, it is 59 cents, a woman lawyer or judge 69 cents, a woman college professor 75 cents, and a woman psychologist 83 cents.[93] The obstacles to women's progress are known as the ***glass ceiling*****—the metaphor for an invisible barrier preventing women and minorities from being promoted to top executive jobs.** For instance, women account for only about 8% of executive vice presidents and above at Fortune 500 companies.[94] Females also hold only 14.7% of seats on the boards of directors for these 500 largest companies.[95] (Black, Latina, and Asian women held only 3.4% of such seats.)

What factors are holding women back? Three that are mentioned are negative stereotypes, lack of mentors, and limited experience in line or general management.[96]

Interestingly, however, several studies have suggested that female managers outshine their male counterparts on almost every measure, from motivating others to fostering communication to producing high-quality work to goal-setting to mentoring employees.[97] Indeed, one study, by Catalyst, an advocacy group for women in business, found that companies with more women executives have better financial performance.[98] We discuss this further in a later chapter.

Race & Ethnicity: More People of Color in the Workforce By 2020, people of color are expected to make up 37% of the U.S. adult workforce (Hispanic/Latino 17%, African Americans 13%, Asian Americans 6%, and Native Americans 0.8%).[99] Unfortunately, three trends show that American businesses need to do a lot better by this population.

First, people of color, too, have hit the glass ceiling. For example, African Americans held only 11.3% and Hispanics only 10.9% of all managerial and professional jobs in 2001.[100]

Second, minorities tend to earn less than whites. Median household income in 2004 was $30,442 for African Americans and $33,884 for Hispanics. It was $49,061 for whites. (Asians had the highest median income, at $57,196.)[101]

Third, their chances of success have been hurt by perceived discrimination, as shown, for example, by a study of 200 black managers and 139 Hispanic employees.[102] African Americans also have been found to receive lower performance ratings than whites have.[103] Another study found 44 black managers experienced slower rates of promotion compared with 890 white managers.[104] No wonder the turnover rate is 40% higher for black than for white executives.[105]

Recently employers have had to become aware of another wrinkle in ethnic and race relations—namely, whether the labor they are hiring is legal. Illegal immigrants make up 1 in 20 workers, according to a 2006 Pew Hispanic Center study.[106] They account for nearly 1 in 4 farm workers, 1 in 6 maids and housekeepers, 1 in 7 in construction, and 1 in 8 in food preparation. Companies such as Georgia carpet maker Mohawk Industries depend substantially on immigrants from Mexico and other Latin American countries, many of whom are illegal.[107]

Sexual Orientation: Gays & Lesbians Become More Visible Gays and lesbians make up, by some estimates, 6% of the U.S. population. Between a quarter and two-thirds report being discriminated against at work (with negative attitudes directed toward them held more by men than by women).[108] One 2003 study found that 41% of gay employees said they had been harassed, pressured to quit, or denied a promotion because of their sexual orientation.[109] Homosexual workers report higher levels of stress compared with heterosexual workers, and one source of this may be the fact that in 36 states homosexuality is still a legitimate legal basis for firing an employee. Finally, gay and bisexual male workers were found to earn 11–27% less than equally qualified heterosexual counterparts.[110]

How important is the issue of sexual preference? Once again, if managers are concerned about hiring and keeping workplace talent, they shouldn't ignore the motivation and productivity of 6% of the workforce. Many employers are recognizing this: 430 of the top 500 U.S. companies now offer policies prohibiting discrimination based on sexual preference, and more than half offer domestic partner benefits for same-sex couples.[111]

People with Differing Physical & Mental Abilities One out of six Americans has a physical or mental disability, according to the U.S. Department of Labor. Since 1992 we have had the ***Americans with Disabilities Act,*** **which prohibits discrimination against the disabled** and requires organizations to reasonably accommodate an individual's disabilities. Despite what we've all heard about organizations having to spend hundreds of thousands of dollars building wheelchair ramps and the like, the costs actually aren't that great: half the disability accommodations cost less than $50 and 69% cost less than $500.[112]

Even so, disabled people have difficulty finding work. Although two-thirds of people with disabilities want to work, roughly two-thirds are unemployed. (Among blind adults, for example, about 70% are out of work.)[113] Those who are working tend to be in part-time, low-status jobs with little chance for advancement. Moreover, they earn up to 35% less than their more fully abled counterparts.[114] Here, too, is a talent pool that managers will no doubt find themselves tapping into in the coming years.

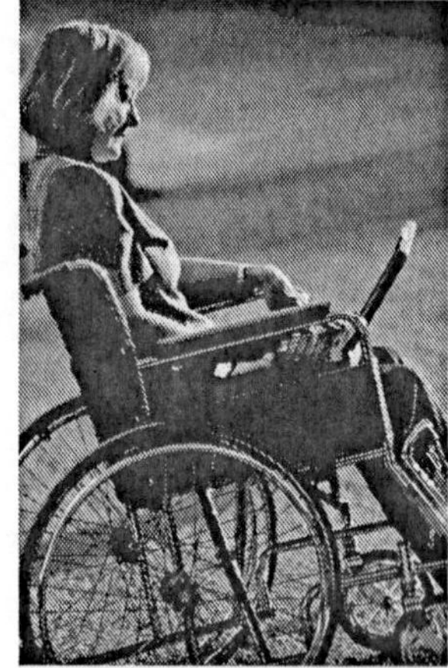

Disability. Everyone recognizes the wheelchair as signifying that a person is disabled, but other disabilities are not easily identified ~~and~~ may not invite understanding. Do you think that mental disabilities, for example, should be accommodated in employment? If you were subject to mood swings, would you think that would prevent you from doing your job effectively?

Educational Levels: Mismatches between Education & Workforce Needs Two important mismatches between education and workplace are these:

- **College graduates may be in jobs for which they are overqualified.** About 27% of people working have a college degree. But some are ***underemployed*** — **working at jobs that require less education than they have**—such as tending bar, managing video stores, or other jobs that someone with less education could do.

  During the period 2000–2004, one national survey of 2,350 college graduates found that 18% were underemployed.[115] It is estimated that for the workforce in general, whether college educated or not, about a quarter is underemployed, a condition associated with higher absenteeism, arrest rates, and unmarried parenthood and with lower motivation, job involvement, and psychological well-being.[116]

- **High-school dropouts and others may not have the literacy skills needed for many jobs.** Among 16- to 24-year-olds in the United States, about 10% were high school dropouts in 2004.[117] In addition, an estimated 90 million adult Americans are functionally illiterate, that is, unable to use "printed and written information to function in society, to achieve one's goals, and to develop one's knowledge and potential."[118] In addition, more than two-thirds of the American workforce reads below ninth-grade level—a problem because about 70% of the on-the-job reading materials are written at or above that level.[119]

Barriers to Diversity

Some barriers are erected by diverse people themselves. In the main, however, most barriers are put in their paths by organizations.[120] When we speak of "the organization's barriers," we are, of course, referring to the *people* in the organization—especially those who may have been there for a while—who are resistant to making it more diverse.

Resistance to change in general is an attitude that all managers come up against from time to time, and resistance to diversity is simply one variation. It may be expressed in the following six ways.

Global diversity vision. Johnson & Johnson publishes this expression of the health products company's desire 'to become the employer of choice" in its employment policies.

OUR GLOBAL DIVERSITY VISION

Johnson & Johnson's Credo sets forth our responsibilities to our employees. It recognizes their dignity and merit, their individuality, and the requirement for equal opportunity in employment, development and advancement for those qualified. From these principles, modified over the years, Johnson & Johnson has fostered and encouraged the development of a diverse workforce - a workforce for the future. ▼ While we can point with pride to a commitment to diversity deeply rooted in our value system, we recognize that our employees, customers and communities, then, were far different from those of today. However, our commitment to these core stakeholders as they have evolved and as Johnson & Johnson has evolved is as strong as ever. ▼ Today's customers and employees come from all over the world and represent different ages, cultures, genders, races and physical capabilities. Through their life experiences, they provide a diversity of thought and perspective that must be reflected in our corporate culture.

Our global diversity vision is to become
THE EMPLOYER OF CHOICE
IN A DYNAMIC GLOBAL ENVIRONMENT.

To achieve this vision, we must build a workforce that is increasingly skilled, diverse, motivated and committed to dynamic leadership. This workforce should reflect our diverse customer base and be knowledgeable of the markets we serve. ▼ Being the Employer of Choice in a Dynamic Global Environment means embracing the differences and similarities of all our employees and prospective employees. It also means the execution of innovative diversity and marketing initiatives to ensure our ability to recruit, develop, retain and promote exceptional talent from an array of backgrounds and geographies, while continuing our pursuit of excellence. ▼ Our goal is to ensure our ability to meet the demands of a changing world with a vision worthy of our values and our commitment to be the leader in health care across the globe. When we achieve our vision, diversity becomes one of our most important competitive advantages.

Johnson & Johnson

1. Stereotypes & Prejudices ***Ethnocentrism* is the belief that one's native country, culture, language, abilities, or behavior is superior to those of another culture.** (An example is embodied in the title of the Wesley Snipes/Woody Harrelson movie about urban basketball hustlers: *White Men Can't Jump.*) When differences are viewed as being weaknesses—which is what many stereotypes and prejudices ultimately come down to—this may be expressed as a concern that diversity hiring will lead to a sacrifice in competence and quality.

2. Fear of Reverse Discrimination Some employees are afraid that attempts to achieve greater diversity in their organization will result in reverse discrimination—that more black or Asian employees will be promoted to fire captain or police lieutenant, for example, over the heads of supposedly more qualified whites.

3. Resistance to Diversity Program Priorities Some companies such as 3M offer special classes teaching tolerance for diversity, seminars in how to get along.[121] Some employees may see diversity programs as distracting them from the organization's "real work." In addition, they may be resentful of diversity-promoting policies that are reinforced through special criteria in the organization's performance appraisals and reward systems.

4. Unsupportive Social Atmosphere Diverse employees may be excluded from office camaraderie and social events.

5. Lack of Support for Family Demands In most families (63%, according to the Bureau of Labor Statistics), both parents work; in 29.5% only the father works, and in 4.5% only the mother works. But more and more women are moving back and forth between being at-home mothers and in the workforce, as economic circumstances dictate.[122] Yet in a great many households, it is still women who primarily take care of children, as well as other domestic chores. When organizations aren't supportive in offering flexibility in hours and job responsibilities, these women may find it difficult to work evenings and weekends or to take overnight business trips.

6. Lack of Support for Career-Building Steps Organizations may not provide diverse employees with the types of work assignments that will help qualify them for positions in senior management. In addition, organizations may fail to provide the kind of informal training or mentoring that will help them learn the political savvy to do networking and other activities required to get ahead. ●

key terms used in this chapter

accommodative approach 90
Americans with Disabilities Act 97
blended value 90
code of ethics 87
competitors 79
customers 79
defensive approach 90
demographic forces 83
distributor 79
diversity 93
economic forces 82
ethnocentrism 98
ethical behavior 84
ethical dilemma 84
ethics 84
external dimensions of diversity 95
external stakeholders 78
general environment 82
glass ceiling 96
government regulators 81
individual approach 85
internal dimensions of diversity 94
internal stakeholders 76
international forces 83
justice approach 85
macroenvironment 82
moral-rights approach 85
obstructionist approach 89
owners 76
personality 93
philanthropy 91
political-legal forces 83
proactive approach 90
Sarbanes-Oxley Act of 2002 86
sociocultural forces 82
social responsibility 88
special-interest groups 81
stakeholders 75
strategic allies 79
supplier 79
sustainability 91
task environment 78
technological forces 82
underemployed 97
utilitarian approach 85
value system 84
values 84
whistleblower 87

summary

3.1 The Community of Stakeholders Inside the Organization

- Managers operate in two organizational environments—internal and external—both made up of shareholders, the people whose interests are affected by the organization's activities. The first, or internal, environment, also includes employees, owners, and the board of directors.

3.2 The Community of Stakeholders Outside the Organization

- The external environment of stakeholders consists of the task environment and the general environment.
- The task environment consists of 11 groups that present the manager with daily tasks to deal with. (1) Customers are those who pay to use an organization's goods and services. (2) Competitors are people or organizations that compete for customers or resources. (3) Suppliers are people or organizations that provide supplies—raw materials, services, equipment, labor, or energy—to other organizations. (4) Distributors are people or organizations that help another organization sell its goods and services to customers. (5) Strategic allies describe the relationship of two organizations who join forces to achieve advantages

4.6 THE IMPORTANCE OF UNDERSTANDING CULTURAL DIFFERENCES

What are the principal areas of cultural differences?

major question

THE BIG PICTURE

Managers trying to understand other cultures need to understand four basic cultural perceptions embodied in language, nonverbal communication, time orientation, and religion.

Americans living near San Jose, California, didn't like it when an Australian company acquired the local Valley Fair shopping center and renamed it Shoppingtown.[68]

"The first time I saw the word Shoppingtown, I nearly choked," complained one letter writer to the local paper. "The more I see it, the more it annoys me."

"We aren't the penny-pinchers this name indicates we are," said another. "What happened to that survey about Valley Fair customers having the area's most upscale lifestyle and money to back it up?"

Said a third: "These are the same people—Australians—who did not get [the U.S. television comedy] *Seinfeld*; the show failed miserably there. 'Shoppingtown' is a brand name in Australia. They are trying too hard to accomplish the same thing here in the U.S. Do you really care that your mall is a 'brand'. . . ? They have not done their homework, and do not understand Americans just yet." (Actually, Westfield's strategy may have been sound; in 2006, with 128 shopping centers in several areas of the English-speaking world, the son of the founder bragged, "We did what others didn't think you can do, which is to brand malls.")[69]

Don't Australians and Americans speak the same language? Could a shopping center risk failing simply because of a name change? And if there can be such misperceptions in English, what might it be like in trying to communicate in a different language? *Training* magazine offers some blunt advice: "The lesson for those [managers] plying foreign markets or hosting business visitors is: Slow down. Shut up. Listen."[70]

The Importance of National Culture

Some of the problems resulting from the experiences of companies such as that described above are the result of cultural differences. A nation's ***culture* is the shared set of beliefs, values, knowledge, and patterns of behavior common to a group of people.**

We begin learning our culture starting at an early age through everyday interaction with people around us. This is why, from the outside looking in, a nation's culture can seem so intangible and perplexing. As cultural anthropologist Edward T. Hall puts it, "Since much of culture operates outside our awareness, frequently we don't even know what we know. . . . We unconsciously learn what to notice and what not to notice, how to divide time and space, how to walk and talk and use our bodies, how to behave as men or women, how to relate to other people, how to handle responsibility. . . ."[71] Indeed, says Hall, what we think of as "mind" is really internalized culture.

And because a culture is made up of so many nuances, this is why visitors to another culture may experience culture shock—the feelings of discomfort and disorientation associated with being in an unfamiliar

Would you shop at 'Shoppingtown'? That was the name new Australian owners gave to a California shopping center known as Valley Fair.

culture. According to anthropologists, culture shock involves anxiety and doubt caused by an overload of unfamiliar expectations and social cues.[72]

Cultural Dimensions: The Hofstede & GLOBE Project Models

Misunderstandings and miscommunications often arise in international business relationships because people don't understand the expectations of the other side. A person from North America, Great Britain, Scandinavia, Germany, or Switzerland, for example, comes from a ***low-context culture* in which shared meanings are primarily derived from written and spoken words.** Someone from China, Korea, Japan, Vietnam, Mexico, or many Arab cultures, on the other hand, comes from a ***high-context culture* in which people rely heavily on situational cues for meaning when communicating with others,** relying on nonverbal cues as to another person's official position, status, or family connections.

One way to avoid cultural collisions is to have an understanding of various cultural dimensions, as expressed in the Hofstede model and the GLOBE project.

Hofstede's Model of Four Cultural Dimensions Thirty years ago Dutch researcher and IBM psychologist **Geert Hofstede** collected data from 116,000 IBM employees in 53 countries and proposed his ***Hofstede model of four cultural dimensions,* which identified four dimensions along which national cultures can be placed: (1) individualism/collectivism, (2) power distance, (3) uncertainty avoidance, and (4) masculinity/femininity.**[73]

- **Individualism/collectivism—how loosely or tightly are people socially bonded?** The United States, Australia, Sweden, France, Canada, and Great Britain have high individualistic values. *Individualism* indicates a preference for a loosely knit social framework in which people are expected to take care of themselves. Costa Rica, Thailand, Mexico, China, Guatemala, and Ecuador have high collectivist values. *Collectivism* indicates a preference for a tightly knit social framework in which people and organizations are expected to look after each other.
- **Power distance—how much do people accept inequality in power?** *Power distance* refers to the degree to which people accept inequality in social situations. *High power distance,* such as occurs in Mexico, India, Thailand, Panama, and the Philippines, means that people accept inequality in power among people, institutions, and organizations. *Low power distance,* such as occurs in Sweden, Germany, Israel, and Australia, means that people expect equality in power.
- **Uncertainty avoidance—how strongly do people desire certainty?** This dimension is about being comfortable with risk and uncertainty. Countries such as Japan, France, Greece, Portugal, and Costa Rica are very high in *uncertainty avoidance,* which expresses people's intolerance for uncertainty and risk. *High uncertainty avoidance* means people feel uncomfortable with uncertainty and support beliefs that promise certainty and conformity. Countries such as Sweden, India, the United States, Singapore, and Jamaica are very low on this dimension. *Low uncertainty avoidance* means that people have high tolerance for the uncertain and ambiguous.
- **Masculinity/femininity—how much do people embrace stereotypical male or female traits?** *Masculinity* expresses how much people value performance-oriented masculine traits, such as achievement, assertiveness, and material success. Countries with strong masculine preferences are Japan, Mexico, Austria, and Germany. *Femininity* expresses how much people embrace relationship-oriented feminine traits, such as cooperation and group decision making. Sweden, Norway, Thailand, Denmark, Costa Rica, and France are high on this cultural dimension.

In general, the United States ranked very high on individualism, relatively low on power distance, low on uncertainty avoidance, and moderately high on masculinity.

The GLOBE Project's Nine Cultural Dimensions Started in 1993 by University of Pennsylvania professor **Robert J. House, the *GLOBE project* is a massive and ongoing cross-cultural investigation of nine cultural dimensions involved in leadership and organizational processes.**[74] (GLOBE stands for Global Leadership and Organizational Behavior Effectiveness.) GLOBE has evolved into a network of more than 150 scholars from 62 societies, and most of the researchers are native to the particular cultures they study. The nine cultural dimensions are as follows:

- **Institutional collectivism—how much should leaders encourage and reward loyalty to the social unit?** *Institutional collectivism,* or *individualism/collectivism,* expresses the extent to which individuals should be encouraged and rewarded for loyalty to the social group as opposed to the pursuit of individual goals. Countries ranking high in individualism: Argentina, Germany, Greece, Hungary, Italy. Countries ranking low: Denmark, Japan, Singapore, South Korea, Sweden. (The United States is rated moderate in individualism, a change from 30 years ago, when it ranked high.)
- **In-group collectivism—how much pride and loyalty should people have for their family or organization?** In contrast to individualism, *in-group collectivism* expresses the extent to which people should take pride in being members of their family, circle of close friends, and their work organization. High: China, Egypt, India, Iran, Morocco. Low: Denmark, Finland, Netherlands, New Zealand, Sweden.
- **Power distance—how much unequal distribution of power should there be in organizations and society?** *Power distance* expresses the degree to which a society's members expect power to be unequally shared. High: Argentina, Morocco, Russia, Spain, Thailand. Low: Costa Rica, Denmark, Israel, Netherlands, South Africa.
- **Uncertainty avoidance—how much should people rely on social norms and rules to avoid uncertainty?** *Uncertainty avoidance* expresses the extent to which a society relies on social norms and procedures to alleviate the unpredictability of future events. Countries high in uncertainty avoidance: Austria, Denmark, Germany, Sweden, Switzerland. Countries low in this dimension: Bolivia, Greece, Hungary, Russia, Venezuela. (The United States is rated moderate.)
- **Gender differentiation—how much should society maximize gender role differences?** *Gender differentiation* expresses the extent to which a society should minimize gender discrimination and role inequalities. High in gender egalitarianism: Denmark, Hungary, Poland, Slovenia, Sweden. Low: China, Egypt, India, Morocco, South Korea.
- **Assertiveness—how confrontational and dominant should individuals be in social relationships?** *Assertiveness* represents the extent to which a society expects people to be confrontational and competitive as opposed to tender and modest. High: Austria, Germany, Greece, Spain, United States. Low: Japan, Kuwait, New Zealand, Sweden, Switzerland.
- **Future orientation—how much should people delay gratification by planning and saving for the future?** *Future orientation* expresses the extent to which a society encourages investment in the future, as by planning and saving. High: Canada, Denmark, Netherlands, Singapore, Switzerland. Low: Argentina, Italy, Kuwait, Poland, Russia.
- **Performance orientation—how much should individuals be rewarded for improvement and excellence?** *Performance orientation* expresses the extent

to which society encourages and rewards its members for performance improvement and excellence. High: Hong Kong, New Zealand, Taiwan, Singapore, United States. Low: Argentina, Greece, Italy, Russia, Venezuela.

- **Humane orientation—how much should society encourage and reward people for being kind, fair, friendly, and generous?** *Humane orientation* represents the degree to which individuals are encouraged to be altruistic, caring, kind, generous, and fair. High: Egypt, Indonesia, Ireland, Malaysia, Philippines. Low: Brazil, France, Germany, Singapore, Spain.

The United States, you may notice, scored high on assertiveness and performance orientation, which is why Americans are perceived as being pushy and hardworking.

Clearly, there is an important lesson in the Hofstede and GLOBE cultural dimensions—namely, knowing the cultural tendencies of foreign business partners and competitors can give you a strategic competitive advantage.

Other Cultural Variations: Language, Interpersonal Space, Time Orientation, & Religion

How do you go about bridging cross-cultural gaps? It begins with understanding. Let's consider variations in four basic culture areas: (1) *language,* (2) *interpersonal space,* (3) *time orientation,* and (4) *religion.*

Note, however, that such cultural differences are to be viewed as *tendencies* rather than absolutes. We all need to be aware that the *individuals* we are dealing with may be exceptions to the cultural rules. After all, there *are* talkative and aggressive Japanese, just as there are quiet and deferential Americans, stereotypes notwithstanding.[75]

1. Language More than 3,000 different languages are spoken throughout the world. However, even if you are operating in the English language, there are nuances between cultures that can lead to misperceptions. For instance, in Asia, a "yes" answer to a question "simply means the question is understood," says one well-traveled writer. "It's the beginning of negotiations."[76]

In communicating across cultures you have three options: (a) You can speak your own language. (The average American believes that about half the world can speak English, when actually it's about 20%.)[77] (b) You can use a translator. (If you do, try to get one that will be loyal to you rather than to your overseas host.) (c) You can learn the local language—by far the best option (as reflected in the *USA Today* headline: "U.S. Firms Becoming Tongue-Tied. Global Trade Requires Foreign Language Skills").[78]

2. Interpersonal Space People of different cultures have different ideas about what is acceptable interpersonal space—that is, how close or far away one should be when communicating with another person. For instance, the people of North America and northern Europe tend to conduct business conversations at a range of 3–4 feet. For people in Latin American and Asian cultures, the range is about 1 foot. For Arabs, it is even closer.

This can lead to cross-cultural misunderstandings. "Arabs tend to get very close and breathe on you," says anthropologist Hall. "The American on the receiving end can't identify all the sources of his discomfort but feels that the Arab is pushy. The Arab comes close, the American backs up. The Arab follows, because he can only interact at certain distances."[79] However, once the American understands that Arabs handle interpersonal space differently and that "breathing on people is a form of communication," says Hall, the situation can sometimes be redefined so that the American feels more comfortable.

3. Time Orientation Time orientation is different in many cultures. Anthropologist Hall makes a useful distinction between monochronic time and polychronic time:

- **Monochronic time.** This kind of time is standard American business practice. That is, ***monochronic time* is a preference for doing one thing at a time.** In this perception, time is viewed as being limited, precisely segmented, and schedule driven. This perception of time prevails, for example, when you schedule a meeting with someone and then give the visitor your undivided attention during the allotted time.[80]

Indeed, you probably practice monochronic time when you're in a job interview. You work hard at listening to what the interviewer says. You may well take careful notes. You certainly don't answer your cell phone or gaze repeatedly out the window.

- **Polychronic time.** This outlook on time is the kind that prevails in Mediterranean, Latin American, and especially Arab cultures. ***Polychronic time*** **is a preference for doing more than one thing at a time.** Here time is viewed as being flexible and multidimensional.

  This perception of time prevails when you visit a Latin American client, find yourself sitting in the waiting room for 45 minutes, and then find in the meeting that the client is dealing with three other people at the same time. (The American variant these days is referred to as "multitasking," as when you talk on the phone while simultaneously watching television and doing a crossword puzzle.)

As a manager, you will probably have to reset your mental clock when doing business across cultures.

4. Religion Are you a Protestant doing business in a predominantly Catholic country? Or a Muslim in a Buddhist country? How, then, does religion influence the work-related values of the people you're dealing with?

A study of 484 international students at a Midwestern university uncovered wide variations in the work-related values for different religious affiliations.[84] For example,

Example

Cultural Differences in Time: A Garment Factory in Mexico

Harry Mehserjian and his brothers own a garment factory near Los Angeles, and they still do the high-fashion work there. However, the T-shirts and other low-budget knitware are sent deep into Mexico, to a factory in a suburb of Guadalajara, where wages are one-seventh those in Los Angeles.[81]

"I never wanted to go to Mexico," Harry says. But since NAFTA removed quotas limiting how much clothing could be brought in from Mexico, that country has shot from sixth place to first place (passing China) in exporting garments to the U.S. The changes caused by NAFTA, along with a rise in minimum wage in California, aggressive unionization, and more regulations, made it difficult for the Mehserjians to continue doing all their business in the United States.

One of the challenges to the Mehserjians is to change their workers' attitudes about time. "If they come on Monday, they're out on Tuesday. If they come on Tuesday, they're out on Wednesday," says a plant manager. To try to overcome absenteeism, the Mehserjians offer a 10% bonus to those who come to work faithfully for the entire week. Even so, their factory is still plagued by absenteeism and turnover. The workplace culture in the interior of Mexico is looser than in the United States—or even in northern Mexico, such as Juarez.

Says one UCLA expert, "These workers don't necessarily see their lives revolving around a job. There's a great deal of informality that they have come to expect from factory employment. You work hard during certain periods of time, and relax during others."[82]

Your Call

A 2006 Associated Press poll found the United States to be an impatient nation, with Americans getting antsy after 5 minutes on hold on the phone and 15 minutes maximum in a Department of Motor Vehicles line.[83] If you were supervising this factory in Mexico, what would you do to adjust?

among Catholics, the primary work-related value was found to be consideration. For Protestants, it was employer effectiveness; for Buddhists, social responsibility; for Muslims, continuity. There was, in fact, virtually *no agreement* among religions as to what is the most important work-related value. This led the researchers to conclude: "Employers might be wise to consider the impact that religious differences (and more broadly, cultural factors) appear to have on the values of employee groups."

Current Followers of the Major World Religions	
Christianity	2.1 billion
Islam	1.3 billion
Hinduism	900 million
Buddhism	376 million
Judaism	15 million
Chinese traditional religions	394 million

After what some World War II veterans have been through, one can sympathize with their outrage over drivers who fly American flags from cars made by their former enemies—Toyotas, Mitsubishis, BMWs, Porsches, and other Japanese and German cars. "I drive all-American," boasts one vet.

But just what *is* an American car nowadays? "Is it a Honda Accord built by Americans in the Midwest," asks a newspaper reader, "or is it a Chrysler built in Mexico with parts from Canada by a company owned by Daimler-Benz?"[85] Perhaps the lesson is this: In a global economy, cultural arrogance is a luxury we can no longer afford. ●

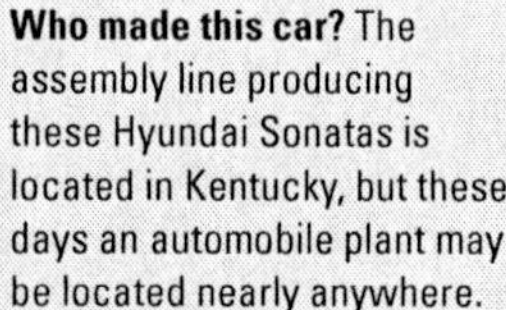

Who made this car? The assembly line producing these Hyundai Sonatas is located in Kentucky, but these days an automobile plant may be located nearly anywhere.

chapter 15

Interpersonal & Organizational Communication

Mastering the Exchange of Information

Major Questions You Should Be Able to Answer

15.1 The Communication Process: What It Is, How It Works
Major Question: What do I need to know about the communication process to be an effective communicator?

15.2 Barriers to Communication
Major Question: What are the important barriers I need to be aware of, so I can improve my communication skills?

15.3 How Managers Fit into the Communication Process
Major Question: How can I use the different channels and patterns of communication to my advantage?

15.4 Communication in the Information Age
Major Question: How do contemporary managers use information technology to communicate more effectively?

15.5 Improving Communication Effectiveness
Major Question: How can I be a better listener, reader, writer, and speaker?

THE MANAGER'S toolbox

Becoming a Better Communicator: Being Telephone Savvy

Some communication doesn't matter much (such as small talk with the latte server). Some matters a lot, as when you're using the phone to try to get a job interview. Indeed, despite e-mail, the phone is still the most used business tool, so you need to become skilled at it.

Ever feel that someone you called (whether a prospective date or prospective employer) is ignoring you because they never call back? Maybe the reason is inadequate telephone skills. Following are some suggestions for becoming phone-savvy, which will give you a practical introduction to the subject of communication.[1]

- **Consider the impression you make on the phone:** Watch out for self-defeating telephone behavior. Talking too fast, for instance, makes what you say seem unimportant. Talking too slowly makes you sound tired or uninterested. Talking too softly makes you hard to understand. Talking too loudly grates on others' ears. Talking too much—giving more details than your listener wants—makes people impatient.
- **When you call someone:** When you make a call to someone you don't know, do you speak briefly and above all *clearly*? When leaving a message, do you *slowly* give your name, organization, and phone number (*twice*)? Do you give the date and time you called? If you want a call back, do you specify a *time when you'll be available*? (Don't say: "Uh, I'll be around maybe later.")
- **When someone calls you:** Do you give a favorable first impression, showing the caller that you're helpful and confident? Do you identify yourself? Do you repeat (and *jot down*) the caller's name? (Don't say: "Um, what'd you say your name was again?")
- **Being courteous:** Do you keep your voice interested, attentive, and friendly? Do you say "please" and "thank you"? Do you ask callers if it's okay to put them on hold or if you should call back in a few minutes? Do you say "Thank you for waiting" when you come back on? Do you let the caller hang up first? (Of course, as a time-starved manager you'll sometimes have to politely terminate the conversation first.)
- **Making difficult calls:** When you have to make a difficult telephone call, such as when you're angling for a job interview, are you prepared? Do you have a script that you wrote out beforehand and practiced? Do you get to the point right away? (Attention spans are shorter on the phone.) Do you repeat the other person's name once in a while to make the conversation more personal?
- **Dealing with phone tag:** You phone. Your caller isn't in. That person calls you back. You're not in. That's "phone tag." To deal with it, you need to be aware of the following tricks. (1) Persistence is important. Four or five calls are fine. More than that and the other person may consider you a pest. (2) Don't just use the other person's answering machine or voice mail. If he or she has a secretary or administrative assistant, leave messages with that person as well. (And get to know that person by name and become allies.) (3) Describe your schedule and your availability. (4) If the other person calls back, note the time, which may be when he or she is always at a desk making calls. (5) When you leave a message, make it clear and complete but not overly long.

For Discussion From this list, can you tell there are some things you do that need improvement? Which ones?

forecast

What's Ahead in This Chapter

This chapter describes the process of transferring information and understanding from one person to another. It also describes three communications barriers—physical, semantic, and personal. It shows how you can use different channels and patterns of communication, both formal and informal, to your advantage. It discusses how star managers use information technology to communicate more effectively. Finally, we talk about how to be a better listener, talker, writer, and reader.

15.1 THE COMMUNICATION PROCESS: WHAT IT IS, HOW IT WORKS

major question What do I need to know about the communication process to be an effective communicator?

THE BIG PICTURE

Communication is the transfer of information and understanding from one person to another. The process involves sender, message, and receiver; encoding and decoding; the medium; feedback; and dealing with "noise," or interference. Managers need to tailor their communication to the appropriate medium (rich or lean) for the appropriate situation.

"Good writing is one of two key abilities I focus on when hiring," says Richard Todd at the Federal Reserve Bank of Minneapolis; "the other is the ability to read critically. I can train people to do almost anything else, but I don't have time to teach this."[2] In another survey of 300 executives, 71% said they believed written communication skills were a critical competency that needed enhancement via training; 68% said they believed the same about interpersonal communications skills.[3]

Because many students have not had sufficient training of this sort and because today's work environment is so fast-paced, faulty communication has become a real problem in the workplace. According to one survey, executives say 14% of each 40-hour workweek is wasted because of poor communication between staff and managers.[4] That's the equivalent of 7 workweeks of lost productivity a year. Thus, there's a hard-headed argument for better communication: It can save money.

Communication Defined: The Transfer of Information & Understanding

***Communication*—the transfer of information and understanding from one person to another**—is an activity that you as a manager will have to do a lot of. Indeed, one study found that 81% of a manager's time in a typical workday is spent communicating.[5]

I hear you. Today some people can work almost anywhere, even more so as the cell phone becomes a more versatile instrument permitting Internet and e-mail access, text messaging, and access to huge databases. Do you think our ability to work outside traditional offices because of today's technology will negatively affect the communication process and employee camaraderie?

The fact that managers do a lot of communicating doesn't mean they're necessarily good at it—that is, that they are efficient or effective. You are an *efficient communicator* when you can transmit your message accurately in the least time. You are an *effective communicator* when your intended message is accurately understood by the other person. Thus, you may well be efficient in sending a group of people a reprimand by e-mail. But it may not be effective if it makes them angry so that they can't absorb its meaning.

From this, you can see why it's important to have an understanding of the communication process.

How the Communication Process Works

Communication has been said to be a process consisting of "a sender transmitting a message through media to a receiver who responds."[6] Let's look at these and other parts of the process.

Sender, Message, & Receiver **The *sender* is the person wanting to share information—called a *message*—and the *receiver* is the person for whom the message is intended,** as follows.

Sender → Message → Receiver

Encoding & Decoding Of course, the process isn't as simple as just sender/message/receiver. If you were sending the message over a telegraph line, you would first have to encode the message, and the receiver would have to decode it. But the same is true if you are sending the message by voice to another person in the same room, when you have to decide what language to speak in and what terms to use.

***Encoding* is translating a message into understandable symbols or language. *Decoding* is interpreting and trying to make sense of the message.** Thus, the communication process is now

Sender **[Encoding]** → Message → **[Decoding]** Receiver

The Medium The means by which you as a communicator send a message is important, whether it is by typing an e-mail traveling over the Internet, by voice over a telephone line, or by hand-scrawled note. This is the ***medium,* the pathway by which a message travels:**

Sender [Encoding] → Message **[Medium]** Message → [Decoding] Receiver

Feedback "Flight 123, do you copy?" In the movies, that's what you hear the flight controller say when radioing the pilot of a troubled aircraft to see if he or she received ("copied") the previous message. And the pilot may radio back, "Roger, Houston, I copy." This is an example of ***feedback*** **—the receiver expresses his or her reaction to the sender's message.**

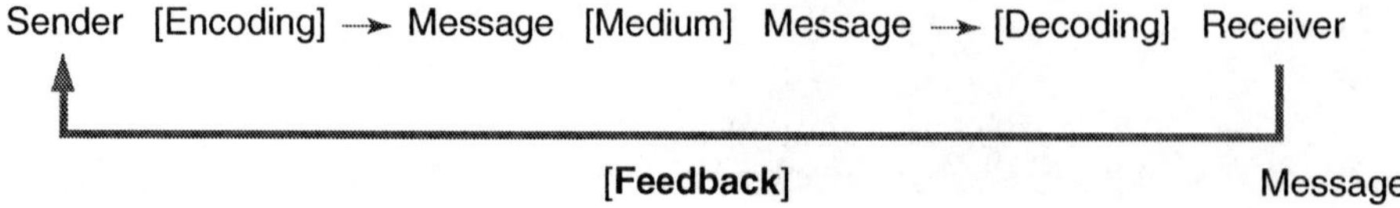

Noise Unfortunately, the entire communication process can be disrupted at several different points by what is called ***noise*** —**any disturbance that interferes with the transmission of a message.** The noise can occur in the medium, of course, as when you have static in a radio transmission or fade-out on a cell phone or when there's loud music when you're trying to talk in a noisy restaurant. Or it can occur in the encoding or decoding, as when a pharmacist can't read a prescription because of a doctor's poor handwriting.[7]

Noise also occurs in *nonverbal communication* (discussed later in this chapter), as when our physical movements send a message that is different from the one we are speaking, or in *cross-cultural communication* (discussed in Chapter 4), as when we make assumptions about other people's messages based on our own culture instead of theirs. We discuss noise further in the next section.

The communication process is shown below. *(See Figure 15.1.)*

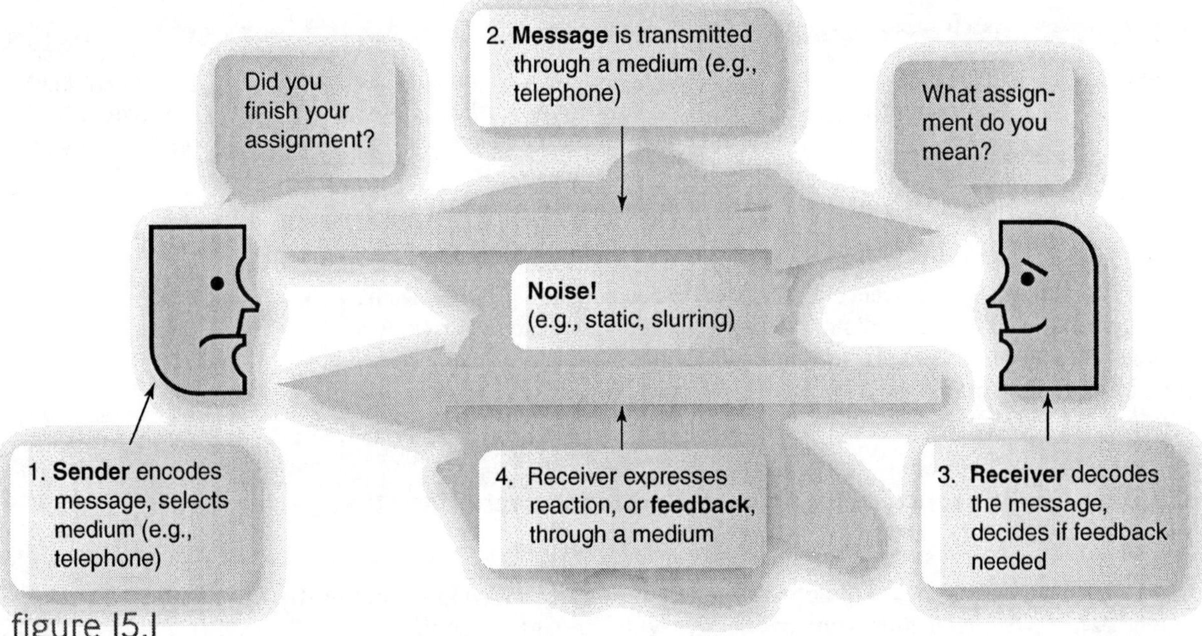

figure 15.1

THE COMMUNICATION PROCESS

"Noise" is not just noise or loud background sounds but any disturbance that interferes with transmission—static, fadeout, distracting facial expressions, uncomfortable meeting site, competing voices, and so on.

Selecting the Right Medium for Effective Communication

There are all kinds of communications tools available to managers, ranging from one-to-one face-to-face conversation all the way to use of the mass media. However, managers need to know how to use the right tool for the right condition—when to use e-mail, when to meet face to face, for example. Should you praise an employee by voicing a compliment, sending an e-mail, posting an announcement near the office coffee machine—or all three? How about when carrying out a reprimand?

Is a Medium Rich or Lean in Information? As a manager, you will have many media to choose from: conversations, meetings, speeches, the telephone, e-mail, memos, letters, bulletin boards, PowerPoint presentations, videoconferencing, printed publications, videos, and so on. Beyond these are the sophisticated communications possibilities of the mass media: public relations; advertising; news reports via print, radio, TV, the Internet.

Media richness **indicates how well a particular medium conveys information and promotes learning.** That is, the "richer" a medium is, the better it is at conveying information. The term *media richness* was proposed by respected organizational theorists Richard Daft and Robert Lengel as part of their contingency model for media selection.[8]

Ranging from high media richness to low media richness, types of media may be positioned along a continuum as follows:

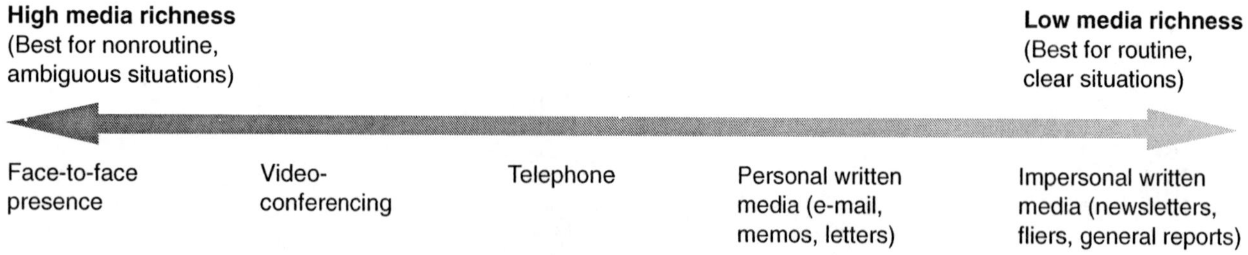

High media richness
(Best for nonroutine, ambiguous situations)

Low media richness
(Best for routine, clear situations)

Face-to-face presence	Video-conferencing	Telephone	Personal written media (e-mail, memos, letters)	Impersonal written media (newsletters, fliers, general reports)

Face-to-face communication, also the most personal form of communication, is the richest. It allows the receiver of the message to observe multiple cues, such as body language and tone of voice. It allows the sender to get immediate feedback, to see how well the receiver comprehended the message. At the other end of the media richness scale, impersonal written media is just the reverse—only one cue and no feedback—making it low in richness.

Matching the Appropriate Medium to the Appropriate Situation In general, follow these guidelines:

- **Rich medium—best for nonroutine situations and to avoid oversimplification.** A *rich* medium is more effective with nonroutine situations.

  Examples: In what way would you like to learn the facts from your boss of a nonroutine situation such as a major company reorganization, which might affect your job? Via a memo tacked on the bulletin board (a lean medium)? Or via face-to-face meeting or phone call (rich medium)?

  The danger of using a rich medium for routine matters (such as monthly sales reports) is that it results in information *overloading*—more information than necessary.

- **Lean medium—best for routine situations and to avoid overloading.** A *lean* medium is more effective with routine situations.

  Examples: In what manner would you as a sales manager like to get routine monthly sales reports from your 50 sales reps? Via time-consuming phone calls (somewhat rich medium)? Or via written memos or e-mails (somewhat lean medium)? The danger of using a lean medium for nonroutine manners (such as a company reorganization) is that it results in information *oversimplification*—it doesn't provide enough of the information the receiver needs and wants. ●

15.2 BARRIERS TO COMMUNICATION

major question What are the important barriers I need to be aware of, so I can improve my communication skills?

THE BIG PICTURE

We describe three barriers to communication. Physical barriers include sound, time, and space. Semantic barriers include unclear use of words and jargon. Personal barriers include variations in communication skills, trustworthiness and credibility, stereotypes and prejudices, and faulty listening skills.

Test Your Knowledge: *Barriers to Effective Communication*

Stand up and give a speech to a group of co-workers? Connecticut businessman Robert Suhoza would prefer to be trampled by elephants, says a news story. "Make small talk at a cocktail party?" it goes on. "Just go ahead and shoot him. Introduce himself to a room full of strangers? Maybe he'll just come back some other time. . . . Even answering the phone seemed at times an insurmountable task: He knew he should pick up the receiver, but he was paralyzed by not knowing who was on the other end, or what the caller wanted."[9]

Suhoza is 53 years old, but all his life he has suffered from social phobia or social anxiety disorder. In this he has plenty of company: One in every eight Americans apparently meets the diagnostic criteria for social anxiety disorder at some point in their lives, making it the third most common psychiatric condition. More women suffer from it than men, although men are more likely to seek treatment.[10]

Social anxiety disorder is an example (though an extreme one) of a communication *barrier*—a barrier being anything interfering with accurate communication between two people. Some barriers may be thought of as happening within the communication

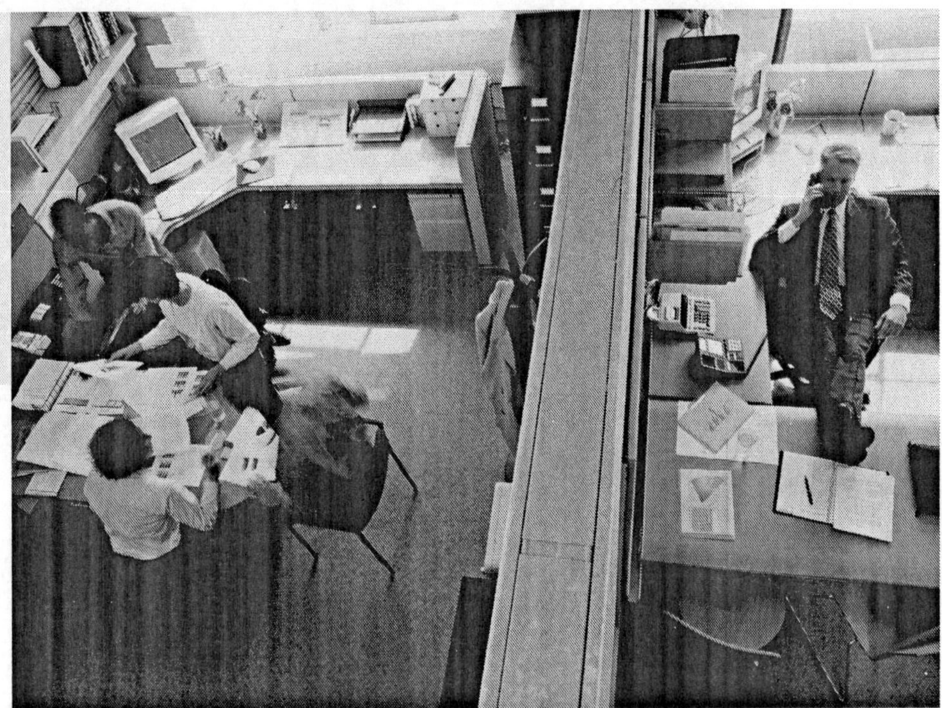

Without walls. Supposedly businesses that have open floor plans with cubicles instead of private offices function better because people can more easily talk across the shoulder-high partitions. But do you think the absence of floor-to-ceiling physical barriers might, in fact, lead to other kinds of barriers—such as others talking making it hard to hear while on the phone?

table 15.1

SOME BARRIERS THAT HAPPEN WITHIN THE COMMUNICATION PROCESS

All it takes is one blocked step in the communication process described in the text for communication to fail. Consider the following.

- **Sender barrier—no message gets sent.** Have you ever had an idea but were afraid to voice it because (like Robert Suhoza) you feared criticism? Then obviously no message got sent.
  But the barrier need not be for psychological reasons. Suppose as a new manager you simply didn't realize (because you weren't told) that supervising your subordinates' expense accounts was part of your responsibility. In that case, it may be understandable why you never call them to task about fudging their expense reports—why, in other words, no message got sent.
- **Encoding barrier—the message is not expressed correctly.** No doubt you've sometimes had difficulty trying to think of the correct word to express how you feel about something. If English is not your first language, perhaps, then you may have difficulty expressing to a supervisor, co-worker, or subordinate what it is you mean to say.
- **Medium barrier—the communication channel is blocked.** You never get through to someone because his or her phone always has a busy signal. The computer network is down and the e-mail message you sent doesn't go through. These are instances of the communication medium being blocked.
- **Decoding barrier—the recipient doesn't understand the message.** Your boss tells you to "lighten up" or "buckle down," but because English is not your first language, you don't understand what the messages mean. Or perhaps you're afraid to show your ignorance when someone is throwing computer terms at you and says that your computer connection has "a bandwidth problem."
- **Receiver barrier—no message gets received.** Because you were talking to a co-worker, you weren't listening when your supervisor announced today's work assignments, and so you have to ask him or her to repeat the announcement.
- **Feedback barrier—the recipient doesn't respond enough.** No doubt you've had the experience of giving someone street directions, but since they only nod their heads and don't repeat the directions back to you, you don't really know whether you were understood. The same thing can happen in many workplace circumstances.

process itself, as the table above shows. *(See Table 15.1.)* It's more practical, however, to think of barriers as being of three types: (1) *physical barriers,* (2) *semantic barriers,* and (3) *personal barriers.*

1. Physical Barriers: Sound, Time, Space, & So On

Try shouting at someone on the far side of a construction site—at a distance of several yards over the roar of earth-moving machinery—and you know what physical barriers are. Other such barriers are time-zone differences, telephone-line static, and crashed computers. Office walls can be physical barriers, too, which is one reason for the trend toward open floor plans with cubicles instead of offices in many workplace settings.

2. Semantic Barriers: When Words Matter

When a supervisor tells you, "We need to get this done right away," what does it mean? Does "We" mean just you? You and your co-workers? Or you, your co-workers, and the boss? Does "right away" mean today, tomorrow, or next week? These are examples of semantic barriers. ***Semantics* is the study of the meaning of words.**

In addition, we may encounter semantic difficulties when dealing with other cultures (as we discussed in Chapter 4). When talking on the phone with Indians

Practical Action

Minding Your Manners: Workplace Etiquette Can Be Crucial to Your Career

Even when you're not talking, you're often communicating—nonverbally (as we discuss elsewhere in this chapter). Manners are a big part of this.

Consider: While at lunch with your business clients, do you eat your soup by swiping the spoon from 12 o'clock to 6 o'clock in the bowl? (It should be the reverse.) Do you order a glass of wine with your meal? (Best not to drink alcohol on someone else's clock.) Do you squeeze lemon into your ice tea with a client across the table? (Best not—you might squirt him or her in the eye.) Do you scratch your back with your fork?

We are talking about a form of communication known as *etiquette* or *manners*. Despite the informality (including not just dress-down Fridays but dress-down everydays) of many offices, managers need to learn business etiquette—manners, politeness, appropriate behavior—if they are to achieve career success. Etiquette is more than table manners; it is the expression of being considerate. If you have to take clients out to dinner a couple times a week, you'll be glad if you know which fork to use. MBA candidates at Daniels College of Business at the University of Denver are required to attend an etiquette dinner, and the Massachusetts Institute of Technology also runs a not-for-credit charm school. These and similar courses provide lessons in dining etiquette, pager protocol, cell phone politeness, and the like. "In climbing the slippery ladder of success," says the founder of an etiquette training firm, "people have to recognize that they will never get promoted if their bosses and customers don't see them as looking and acting the part."

Some matters to be aware of:[11]

- **Handshakes.** The proper manner is to clasp firmly at an angle, then give two or three pumps.
- **Introductions.** When your boss is meeting your client, you should start with the person you want to honor—the client. ("Mr. Smith, I'd like you to meet my boss, Janet Jones. Jan, this is Horatio Smith, vice-president of Associated Success Inc.") Also, you should give some information about each person in order to get a conversation started. ("Jan is head of our Far West Division, and she just got back from a rock-climbing vacation.")
- **Thank-you notes.** When someone prepares an all-day or all-week program in which you've participated, send him or her a thank-you note. When the boss entertains you on her boat, send her a thank-you note. When a client gives you a plant tour, send him a note. And ALWAYS send a thank-you note after a job interview.
- **Dining tips and table manners.** Don't order the most expensive item. Don't start eating before your host. Avoid ordering food you think you might have difficulty handling properly because of splattering (such as soup or pasta). Know what to do with your bread. (Take the bread or roll, hold it over your plate—it's the plate on the left—break off a piece of it, and then put butter on it. If you drop a roll on the floor, don't pick it up; point it out to the waiter.) Don't kick your shoes off under the table. Turn off your cell phone so it won't beep. When you leave the table and plan to return, leave your napkin on your chair; when you're leaving for good, leave it on the table. In the U.S., you should keep your elbows off the table, and it's okay to keep your hands beneath it. In European countries, however, the reverse is considered polite.

working in call centers in India, for example, we may find their pronunciation unusual. Perhaps that is because, according to one Indian speech-voice consultant, whereas "Americans think in English, we think in our mother tongue and translate it while speaking."[12] As our society becomes more technically oriented, semantic meaning becomes a problem because jargon develops. ***Jargon* is terminology specific to a particular profession or group.** (Example: "The HR VP wants the RFP to go out ASAP." Translation: "The Vice President of Human Resources wants the Request For Proposal to go out as soon as possible.") As a manager in a specialized field, you need to remember that what are ordinary terms for you may be mysteries to outsiders.[13]

3. Personal Barriers: Individual Attributes That Hinder Communication

Self-Assessment Exercise: *What Is Your Communication Style under Stress?*

"Is it them or is it me?"

How often have you wondered, when someone has shown a surprising response to something you said, how the miscommunication happened? Let's examine nine personal barriers that contribute to miscommunication.[14]

Variable Skills in Communicating Effectively As we all know, some people are simply better communicators than others. They have the speaking skills, the vocabulary, the facial expressions, the eye contact, the dramatic ability, the "gift of gab" to express themselves in a superior way. Conversely, other people don't have this quality. But better communication skills can be learned.

Variations in How Information Is Processed & Interpreted Are you from a working-class or privileged background? Are you from a particular ethnic group? Are you better at math or at language? Are you from a chaotic household filled with alcoholism and fighting, which distracts you at work?

Because people use different frames of reference and experiences to interpret the world around them, they are selective about what things have meaning to them and what don't. All told, these differences affect what we say and what we think we hear.

Variations in Trustworthiness & Credibility Without trust between you and the other person, communication is apt to be flawed. Instead of communicating, both of you will be concentrating on defensive tactics, not the meaning of the message being exchanged.[15] How will subordinates react to you as a manager if your predecessors in your job lied to them? They may give you the benefit of a doubt, but they may be waiting for the first opportunity to be confirmed in the belief that you will break their trust.

Oversized Egos Our egos—our pride, our self-esteem, even arrogance—are a fifth barrier. Egos can cause political battles, turf wars, and the passionate pursuit of power, credit, and resources. Egos influence how we treat each other as well as how receptive we are to being influenced by others. Ever had someone take credit for an idea that was yours? Then you know how powerful ego feelings can be.

Faulty Listening Skills When you go to a party, do people ever ask questions of you and about who you are and what you're doing? Or are they too ready to talk about themselves? And do they seem to be waiting for you to finish talking so that they can then resume saying what they want to say? (But here's a test: Do you actually *listen* when they're talking?)

Tendency to Judge Others' Messages Suppose another student in this class sees you reading this text and says, "I like the book we're reading." You might say, "I agree." Or you might say, "I disagree—it's boring." The point is that we all have a natural tendency, according to psychologist Carl Rogers, to judge others' statements from our own point of view (especially if we have strong feelings about the issue).[16]

Inability to Listen with Understanding To really listen with understanding, you have to imagine yourself in the other person's shoes. Or, as Rogers and his coauthor put it, you have to "see the expressed idea and attitude from the other person's point of view, to sense how it feels to him, to achieve his frame of reference in regard to the thing he is talking about."[17] When you listen with understanding, it makes you feel less defensive (even if the message is criticism) and improves your accuracy in perceiving the message.

Stereotypes & Prejudices **A *stereotype* consists of oversimplified beliefs about a certain group of people.** There are, for instance, common stereotypes about old people, young people, males, and females. Wouldn't you hate to be categorized according to just a couple of exaggerated attributes—by your age and gender, for example? ("Young men are reckless." "Old women are scolds." Yes, *some* young men and *some* old women are this way, but it's unrealistic and unfair to tar every individual in these groups with the same brush.)

We consider matters of gender communication later in this chapter.

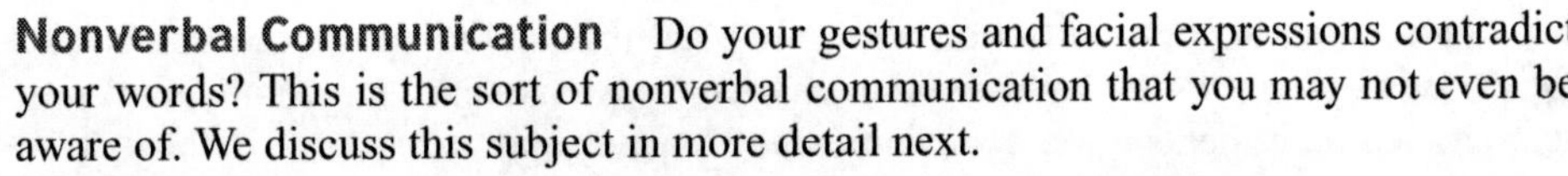

Nonverbal Communication Do your gestures and facial expressions contradict your words? This is the sort of nonverbal communication that you may not even be aware of. We discuss this subject in more detail next.

Group Exercise:
Noverbal Communication: A Twist on Charades

Nonverbal Communication

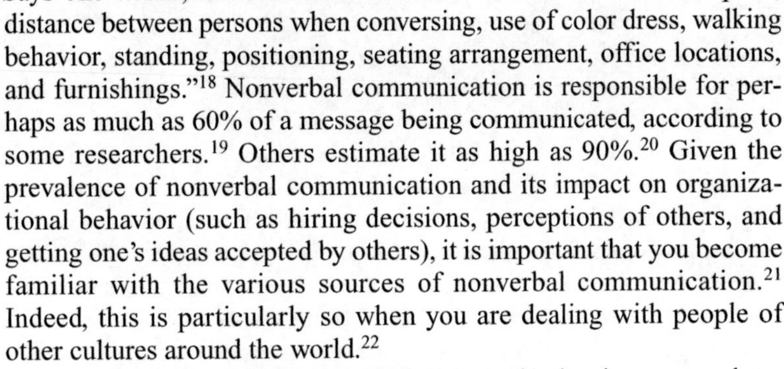

***Nonverbal communication* consists of messages sent outside of the written or spoken word.** Says one writer, it includes such factors as "use of time and space, distance between persons when conversing, use of color dress, walking behavior, standing, positioning, seating arrangement, office locations, and furnishings."[18] Nonverbal communication is responsible for perhaps as much as 60% of a message being communicated, according to some researchers.[19] Others estimate it as high as 90%.[20] Given the prevalence of nonverbal communication and its impact on organizational behavior (such as hiring decisions, perceptions of others, and getting one's ideas accepted by others), it is important that you become familiar with the various sources of nonverbal communication.[21] Indeed, this is particularly so when you are dealing with people of other cultures around the world.[22]

Seven ways in which nonverbal communication is expressed are through (1) *interpersonal space,* (2) *eye contact,* (3) *facial expressions,* (4) *body movements and gestures,* (5) *touch,* (6) *setting,* and (7) *time.*

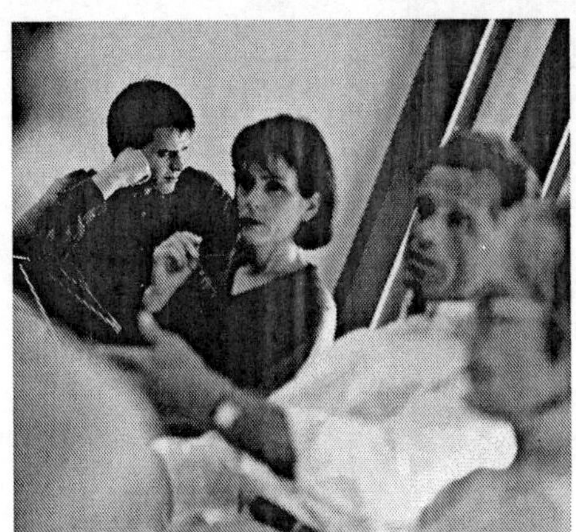

Body language. Who's paying attention and who isn't? If you were a manager speaking at this meeting and you noticed the man at the end of the row looking out the window as you talked, would you continue to speak to those who seem attentive? Or would you try to adjust your remarks and your own body language to try to reach the man who is tuning you out?

1. Interpersonal Space People of different cultures have different ideas about what is acceptable interpersonal space—that is, how close or far away one should be when communicating with another person. For instance, the people of North America and northern Europe tend to conduct business conversations at a range of 3–4 feet. For people in Latin American and Asian cultures, the range is about 1 foot. For Arabs, it is even closer.

This can lead to cross-cultural misunderstandings. "Arabs tend to get very close and breathe on you," says anthropologist Edward Hall. "The American on the receiving end can't identify all the sources of his discomfort but feels that the Arab is pushy. The Arab comes close, the American backs up. The Arab follows, because he can only interact at certain distances."[23] However, once the American understands that Arabs handle interpersonal space differently and that "breathing on people is a form of communication," says Hall, the situation may be redefined so that the American feels more comfortable.

2. Eye Contact Eye contact serves four functions in communication: (1) It signals the beginning and end of a conversation; there is a tendency to look *away* from others when beginning to speak and to look *at* them when done. (2) It expresses emotion; for instance, most people tend to avoid eye contact when conveying bad news or negative feedback. (3) Gazing monitors feedback because it reflects interest and attention. (4) Depending on the culture, gazing also expresses the type of relationship between the people communicating. For instance, Westerners are taught at an early age to look at their parents when spoken to. However, Asians are taught to avoid eye contact with a parent or superior in order to show obedience and subservience.[24]

3. Facial Expressions Probably you're accustomed to thinking that smiling represents warmth, happiness, or friendship whereas frowning represents dissatisfaction or anger. But these interpretations of facial expressions don't apply across all cultures.[25] A smile, for example, doesn't convey the same emotions in different countries.

4. Body Movements & Gestures An example of a body movement is leaning forward; an example of a gesture is pointing. Open body positions, such as leaning backward, express openness, warmth, closeness, and availability for communication. Closed body positions, such as folding one's arms or crossing one's legs, represent defensiveness.

Some body movements and gestures are associated more with one sex than the other, according to communication researcher Judith Hall. For instance, women nod their heads and move their hands more than men do. Men exhibit large body shifts and foot and leg movements more than women do.[26]

We need to point out, however, that interpretations of body language are subjective, hence easily misinterpreted, and highly dependent on the context and cross-cultural differences.[27] You'll need to be careful when trying to interpret body movements, especially when you're operating in a different culture.

5. Touch Norms for touching vary significantly around the world. In the Middle East, for example, it is normal for two males who are friends to walk together holding hands—not commonplace behavior in the U.S.

People tend to touch those they like, and women tend to do more touching during conversations than men do.[28] It needs to be noted, however, that men and women interpret touching differently, and in the United States, at least, sexual harassment claims might be reduced by keeping this perceptual difference in mind.

Still, women clearly have the advantage here, at least in the U.S. One study found that, whereas men are "largely boxed into the formality of a handshake," women are freer to emphasize a point with a brief (nonsexual) touch to the forearm of a man or a woman, give a playful mock push to a man's shoulder, and even place a firm hand on a man's shoulder to signal, if necessary, who is in charge. The risk of touching for a woman, however, is that she may appear flirtatious.[29]

6. Setting How do you feel when you visit someone who sits behind a big desk and is backlit by a window so her face is obscured? What does it say when someone comes out from behind his desk and invites you to sit with him on his office couch? The location of an office (such as corner office with window versus interior office with no window), its size, and the choice of furniture often expresses the accessibility of the person in it.

7. Time When your boss keeps you waiting 45 minutes for an appointment with him, how do you feel? When she simply grunts or makes one-syllable responses to your comments, what does this say about her interest in your concerns? As a manager yourself, you should always give the people who work for you adequate time. You should also talk with them frequently during your meetings with them so they will understand your interest.

The table below gives some suggestions for better nonverbal communication skills. *(See Table 15.2.)*

table 15.2

TOWARD BETTER NONVERBAL COMMUNICATION SKILLS

You can practice these skills by watching TV with the sound off and interpreting people's emotions and interactions.

Do	Don't
Maintain eye contact	Look away from the speaker
Lean toward the speaker	Turn away from the speaker
Speak at a moderate rate	Speak too quickly or slowly
Speak in a quiet, reassuring tone	Speak in an unpleasant tone
Smile and show animation	Yawn excessively
Occasionally nod head in agreement	Close your eyes

Source: Adapted from W. D. St. John, "You Are What You Communicate," *Personnel Journal,* October 1985, p. 43.

Gender-Related Communication Differences

Men are eight times as likely as women to bargain over starting pay. Indeed, says one account, "Women often are less adroit at winning better salaries, assignments, and jobs—either because they don't ask or because they cave in when they do."[30] In other words, women need to hone their negotiation skills, or else they will fall behind.

Some possible general differences in communication between genders are summarized below. *(See Table 15.3.)* Note, however, that these don't apply in all cases, which would constitute stereotyping.

table 15.3

COMMUNICATION DIFFERENCES

How do men and women differ?

Linguistic characteristic	Men	Women
Taking credit	Greater use of "I" statements (e.g., "I did this" and "I did that"); more likely to boast about their achievements	Greater use of "We" statements (e.g., "We did this" and "We did that"); less likely to boast about their achievements
Displaying confidence	Less likely to indicate that they are uncertain about an issue	More likely to indicate a lack of certainty about an issue
Asking questions	Less likely to ask questions (e.g., asking for directions)	More likely to ask questions
Conversation rituals	Avoid making apologies because it puts them in a one-down position	More frequently say "I'm sorry"
Giving feedback	More direct and blunt	More tactful; tend to temper criticism with praise
Giving compliments	Stingy with praise	Pay more compliments than men
Indirectness	Indirect when it comes to admitting fault or when they don't know something	Indirect when telling others what to do

Source: Derived from D. Tannen, "The Power of Talk: Who Gets Heard and Why," *Harvard Business Review,* September–October 1995; and D. Tannen, *You Just Don't Understand: Women and Men in Conversation* (New York: Ballantine Books, 1990).

How useful do you think these specific styles are in a managerial context? (Recall the discussion of men and women with reference to leadership in Chapter 14.)

Author Judith Tingley suggests that women and men should learn to "genderflex"—temporarily use communication behaviors typical of the other gender to increase the potential for influence.[31] For example, a female manager might use sports analogies to motivate a group of males.

Deborah Tannen, by contrast, recommends that everyone become aware of how differing linguistic styles affect our perceptions and judgments. For example, in a meeting, regardless of gender, "those who are comfortable speaking up in groups, who need little or no silence before raising their hands, or who speak out easily without waiting to be recognized are more apt to be heard," she says. "Those who refrain from talking until it's clear that the previous speaker is finished, who wait to be recognized, and who are inclined to link their comments to those of others will do fine at a meeting

Example

Do Female Executives Have an Edge in Business? Women & Communication

Women in business have the edge in two ways, says Chris Clarke, head of an executive search firm with offices in more than 40 countries. "There is increasing evidence," he says, "that women are superior at multitasking, which is needed to handle business complexities, and that they are better at relationships, which is important developing effective teams."[33]

There is another way that women also have an edge, suggests a *BusinessWeek* article: instead of tightly controlling information, they are more willing to share it.[34] A representative of this viewpoint is Anu Shukla, who sold her Internet marketing company for $390 million and made 65 of her 85 employees millionaires. "It's better to overcommunicate," she says. As an example, she made it her policy to share information with all her employees rather than to impart it to selected employees on a need-to-know basis. In addition, she created what she called the "CEO lunch," in which she invited six to eight employees at a time to discuss the business with her.

Your Call

Anne Cummings, professor of business administration at the University of Minnesota at Duluth, suggests there are "masculine" and "feminine" styles in business, in which men tend to be more task-oriented and assertive and to take greater intellectual risks whereas women tend to be more relationship oriented and "democratic" and to be more efficient at solving problems.[35] (Of course, all this behavior operates on a continuum, and most people have a multitude of styles.) Do you think a woman can be successful by taking on the "masculine" style? Can a man be successful taking on the "feminine" style?

where everyone else is following the same rules but will have a hard time getting heard in a meeting with people whose styles are more like the first pattern."[32]

By now most male students and managers know they should avoid the use of masculine wording for jobs or roles that are occupied by both genders, using *police officer* instead of *policeman; supervisor* rather than *foreman.* (Conversely, secretaries, nurses, and babysitters should no longer be referred to as "she.") If you stay alert, it's fairly easy to avoid sentence constructions that are demeaning to women. (Instead of saying "he is," say "he or she is" or "they are.")

But, of course, there's more to effective managerial communication than that. Indeed, there are executive-training programs designed to teach men the value of emotion in relationships—the use of "soft skills" to communicate, build teams, and develop flexibility. "The nature of modern business requires what's more typical to the female mold of building consensus as opposed to the top-down male military model," says Millington F. McCoy, managing director of a New York executive search firm. One program given by London-based James R. Traeger helps participants break down the stereotype of the aggressive, controlling man who always wants to take charge and solve problems and to learn to listen and work in harmony.

Interestingly, although men hold 94% of the top corporate jobs, when they want the advice of an executive coach—a trained listener to help them with their goals and personal problems—they usually turn to a woman. And, in fact, females always want another female as a coach. As a result, 7 out of 10 graduates of Coach U, the largest training school for executive coaches, are women. Because good coaches, says Coach U's CEO Sandy Vilas (who is male), are intuitive communicators and have done a lot of personal development work, "that profile tends to fit women better." Says Susan Bloch, who heads an executive coaching practice, "When a man is asked to coach another, they have a tendency to compete. Man to man, they have to show each other how great they are."[36] ●

15.3 HOW MANAGERS FIT INTO THE COMMUNICATION PROCESS

major question How can I use the different channels and patterns of communication to my advantage?

THE BIG PICTURE

Formal communication channels follow the chain of command, which is of three types—vertical, horizontal, and external. Informal communication channels develop outside the organization's formal structure. One type is gossip and rumor. Another is management by wandering around, in which a manager talks to people across all lines of authority.

If you've ever had a low-level job in nearly any kind of organization, you know that there is generally a hierarchy of management between you and the organization's president, director, or CEO. If you had a suggestion that you wanted him or her to hear, you doubtless had to go up through management channels. That's formal communication. However, you may have run into that top manager in the elevator. Or in the restroom. Or in a line at the bank. You could have voiced your suggestion casually then. That's informal communication.

Formal Communication Channels: Up, Down, Sideways, & Outward

Formal communication channels **follow the chain of command and are recognized as official.** The organizational chart we described in Chapter 8 (page 257) indicates how official communications—memos, letters, reports, announcements—are supposed to be routed.

Formal communication is of three types: (1) *vertical*—meaning upward and downward, (2) *horizontal*—meaning laterally (sideways), and (3) *external*—meaning outside the organization.

I. Vertical Communication: Up & Down the Chain of Command Vertical communication is the flow of messages up and down the hierarchy within the organization: bosses communicating with subordinates, subordinates communicating with

Upward bound. How do you communicate with a manager two or three levels above you in the organization's hierarchy? You can send a memo through channels. Or you can watch for when that manager goes to the water cooler or the coffee pot.

bosses. As you might expect, the more management levels through which a message passes, the more it is prone to distortion.

- **Downward communication—from top to bottom.** ***Downward communication* flows from a higher level to a lower level (or levels).** In small organizations, top-down communication may be delivered face to face. In larger organizations, it's delivered via meetings, e-mail, official memos, and company publications.
- **Upward communication—from bottom to top.** ***Upward communication* flows from a lower level to a higher level(s).** Often this type of communication is from a subordinate to his or her immediate manager, who in turn will relay it up to the next level, if necessary. Effective upward communication depends on an atmosphere of trust. No subordinate is going to want to be the bearer of bad news to a manager who is always negative and bad-tempered.

Types of downward and upward communication are shown below. *(See Table 15.4.)*

table 15.4

TYPES OF DOWNWARD AND UPWARD COMMUNICATION

Downward communication

Most downward communication involves one of the following kinds of information:

- Instructions related to particular job tasks. Example (supervisor to subordinate): "The store will close Monday for inventory. All employees are expected to participate."
- Explanations about the relationship between two or more tasks. Example: "While taking inventory, employees need to see what things are missing. Most of that might be attributable to shoplifting."
- Explanations of the organization's procedures and practices. Example: "Start counting things on the high shelves and work your way down."
- A manager's feedback about a subordinate's performance. Example: "It's best not to try to count too fast."
- Attempts to encourage a sense of mission and dedication to the organization's goals. Example: "By keeping tabs on our inventory, we can keep our prices down and maintain our reputation of giving good value."

Upward communication

Most upward communication involves the following kinds of information:

- Reports of progress on current projects. Example: "We shut down the store yesterday to take inventory."
- Reports of unsolved problems requiring help from people higher up. Example: "We can't make our merchandise count jibe with the stock reports."
- New developments affecting the work unit. Example: "Getting help from the other stores really speeded things up this year."
- Suggestions for improvements. Example: "The stores should loan each other staff every time they take inventory."
- Reports on employee attitudes and efficiency. Example: "The staff likes it when they go to another store and sometimes they pick up some new ways of doing things."

Sources: D. Katz and R. Kahn, *The Social Psychology of Organizations* (New York: Wiley, 1966); and E. Planty and W. Machaver, "Upward Communications: A Project in Executive Development," *Personnel* 28 (1952), pp. 304–318.

2. Horizontal Communication: Within & Between Work Units ***Horizontal communication* flows within and between work units; its main purpose is coordination.** As a manager, you will spend perhaps as much as a third of your time in this form of communication—consulting with colleagues and co-workers at the same level as you within the organization. In this kind of sideways communication, you will be sharing information, coordinating tasks, solving problems, resolving conflicts, and getting the support of your peers. Horizontal communication is encouraged through the use of committees, task forces, and matrix structures.

Horizontal communication can be impeded in three ways: (1) by specialization that makes people focus just on their jobs alone; (2) by rivalry between workers or work units, which prevents sharing of information; and (3) by lack of encouragement from management.[37]

3. External Communication: Outside the Organization ***External communication*** **flows between people inside and outside the organization.** These are other stakeholders: customers, suppliers, shareholders or other owners, and so on. Companies have given this kind of communication heightened importance, especially with customers or clients, who are the lifeblood of any company.

Informal Communication Channels

Informal communication channels **develop outside the formal structure and do not follow the chain of command**—they skip management levels and cut across lines of authority.

Two types of informal channels are (1) the *grapevine* and (2) *management by wandering around.*

The *grapevine* is the unofficial communication system of the informal organization, a network of gossip and rumor of what is called "employee language." Research shows that the grapevine is faster than formal channels, is about 75% accurate, and is used by employees to acquire the majority of their on-the-job information.[38]

Management by wandering around (MBWA) **is the term used to describe a manager's literally wandering around his or her organization and talking with people across all lines of authority.**[39] Management by wandering around helps to reduce the problems of distortion that inevitably occur with formal communication flowing up a hierarchy. MBWA allows managers to listen to employees and learn about their problems as well as to express to employees what values and goals are important. ●

MBWA. Management by wandering around is sort of the reverse of employees exchanging informal views with top managers at the water cooler. That is, by wandering around the organization, top managers can stop and talk to nearly anyone—and thus perhaps learn things that might be screened out by the formal up-the-organization reporting process. If top managers can do MBWA, do you think mid-level managers can as well?

15.4 COMMUNICATION IN THE INFORMATION AGE

How do contemporary managers use information technology to communicate more effectively?

major question

THE BIG PICTURE

We discuss seven communications tools of information technology: (1) the Internet and its associated intranets and extranets, (2) e-mail, (3) videoconferencing, (4) group support systems, (5) telecommuting, (6) handheld devices, and (7) blogs. We also discuss impediments to productivity: (1) misuse of technology, (2) fussing with computers, and (3) information overload.

"I'm dangerous," jokes Gregory Summe between runs at a Utah ski resort, as he pulls out his tiny cell phone and his electronic organizer with its 12,000-name contact list. With this kind of portable information technology, Summe, CEO of EG&G Inc., is able to work anywhere and contact anyone. "There's an expectation for CEOs to be much more in touch with customers, employees, and investors than in the past," he says. "A big part of the reason may be [portable information] technology."[40]

Communications Tools of Information Technology: Offspring of the Internet

Here we explore some of the more important aspects of information technology: (1) the Internet along with intranets and extranets, (2) e-mail, (3) videoconferencing, (4) group support systems, (5) telecommuting, (6) handheld devices, and (7) blogs.

1. The Internet, Intranets, & Extranets The Internet, or more simply "the Net," is more than a computer network. As we said in Chapter 1, it is a network of computer networks. The Internet is a global network of independently operating but interconnected computers, linking hundreds of thousands of smaller networks around the world. The Internet connects everything from personal computers to supercomputers in organizations of all kinds.[41]

Two private uses of the Internet are as intranets and extranets.

- **Intranets. An *intranet* is nothing more than an organization's private Internet.** Intranets also have *firewalls* that block outside Internet users from accessing internal information. This is done to protect the privacy and confidentiality of company documents. The top four uses for intranets are information sharing, information publishing, e-mail, and document management.[42]
- **Extranets. An *extranet* is an extended intranet in that it connects internal employees with selected customers, suppliers, and other strategic partners.** Ford Motor Co., for instance, has an extranet that connects its dealers worldwide. Ford's extranet was set up to help support the sales and servicing of cars and to enhance customer satisfaction.

No rigorous studies have demonstrated productivity increases from using the Internet, intranets, or extranets. However, research reveals some other organizational benefits. For example, Cisco Systems used the Internet to recruit potential employees, hiring 66% of its people and receiving 81% of its résumés from the Net.[43] General Mills used to send researchers across country to conduct focus groups or poll consumers on prospective products, but now it conducts 60% of its consumer research online, reducing its costs by half.[44]

2. E-mail E-mail, short for *electronic mail,* uses the Internet to send computer-generated text and documents between people. E-mail has become a major communications medium because of four key benefits: (1) reduced cost of distributing information, (2) increased teamwork, (3) reduced paper costs, and (4) increased flexibility. On the other hand, it has three drawbacks: It can lead to (1) wasted time, as in having to deal with ***spam,* or unsolicited jokes and junk mail;** (2) information overload; and (3) neglect of other media. *(See Table 15.5.)*

table 15.5

E-MAIL: BENEFITS, DRAWBACKS, AND TIPS FOR DOING BETTER

Benefits

- *Reduced cost of distributing information.* One software developer found that its telephone bill dropped by more than half after its employees and dealers were told to use e-mail instead of the phone.
- *Increased teamwork.* Users can send messages to colleagues anywhere, whether in the office or around the world.
- *Reduced paper costs.* E-mail reduces the costs and time associated with print duplication and paper distribution.
- *Increased flexibility.* Employees with portable computers, PDAs, and cell phones can access their e-mail from anywhere.

Drawbacks

- *Wasted time.* E-mail can distract employees from critical job duties. Employees now average nearly an hour a day managing their e-mail.
- *Information overload.* E-mail users tend to get too much information—in some cases, only 10 of 120 daily inbox messages may be worthwhile.
- *Neglect of other media.* Increased use of e-mail can be found to be associated with decreased face-to-face interactions and decreased overall organizational communication, with lessened cohesion.

Tips for better e-mail handling

- *Treat all e-mail as confidential.* Pretend every message is a postcard that can be read by anyone. (Supervisors may legally read employee e-mail.)
- *Be careful with jokes and informality.* Nonverbal language and other subtleties are lost, so jokes may be taken as insults or criticism.
- *Avoid sloppiness, but avoid criticizing others' sloppiness.* Avoid spelling and grammatical errors, but don't criticize errors in others' messages.
- *When replying, quote only the relevant portion.* Edit long e-mail messages you've received down to the relevant paragraph and put your response immediately following.
- *Not every topic belongs on e-mail.* Complicated topics may be better discussed on the phone or in person to avoid misunderstandings.

Sources: R. F. Federico and J. M. Bowley, "The Great E-Mail Debate," *HR Magazine,* January 1996, pp. 67–72; M. S. Thompson and M. S. Feldman, "Electronic Mail and Organizational Communication: Does Saying 'Hi' Really Matter?" *Organizational Science,* November–December 1998, pp. 685–698; J. Yaukey, "E-Mail Out of Control for Many," *Reno Gazette-Journal,* May 7, 2001, p. 1E; D. Halpern, "Dr. Manners on E-Mail Dos and Don'ts," *Monitor of Psychology,* April 2004, p. 5; and B. K. Williams and S. C. Sawyer, *Using Information Technology,* 7th ed. (New York: McGraw-Hill/Irwin, 2007), p. 91.

3. Videoconferencing Also known as *teleconferencing, videoconferencing* uses video and audio links along with computers to enable people located at different locations to see, hear, and talk with one another. This enables people from many locations to conduct a meeting without having to travel. Videoconferencing can thus significantly reduce an organization's travel expenses.

Many organizations set up special videoconferencing rooms or booths with specially equipped television cameras. More recent equipment enables people to attach small cameras and microphones to their desks or computer monitors. This enables employees to conduct long-distance meetings and training classes without leaving their office or cubicle.[45]

Videoconferencing. In this arrangement, three people in different locations can computer-conference~~view~~ and interact with one another—while studying a layout on-screen. Videoconferencing offers considerable savings in time and money over the cost of travel. Do you think you would feel inhibited working with people in this way?

4. Group Support Systems *Group support systems* **(GSSs) entail using state-of-the-art computer software and hardware to help people work better together.** They enable people to share information without the constraints of time and space. This is accomplished using computer networks to link people across a room or across the globe. Collaborative applications include messaging and e-mail systems, calendar management, videoconferencing, and electronic whiteboards. GSS applications have demonstrated increased productivity and cost savings. In addition, groups using GSSs during brainstorming experienced greater participation and influence quality, a greater quantity of ideas generated, and less domination by individual members than did groups meeting face to face.[46]

Organizations that use full-fledged GSSs have the ability to create virtual teams (described in Chapter 13), who tend to use Internet or intranet systems, collaborative software, and videoconferencing to communicate with team members anytime.

It is important to keep in mind that modern-day information technology enables people to interact virtually, but it doesn't guarantee effective communications. Indeed, there is a host of unique communication problems associated with using information technology to operate virtually.[47]

5. Telecommuting *Telecommuting* involves doing work that is generally performed in the office away from the office, using a variety of information technologies. Employees typically receive and send work from home via phone and fax or by using a modem to link a home computer to an office computer. Among the benefits are (1) reduction of capital costs, because employees work at home; (2) increased flexibility and autonomy for workers; (3) competitive edge in recruiting hard-to-get employees; (4) increased job satisfaction and lower turnover; (5) increased productivity; and (6) ability to tap nontraditional labor pools (such as prison inmates and homebound disabled people).[48]

Telecommuting is more common for jobs that involve computer work, writing, and phone or brain work that requires concentration and limited interruptions. A 2006 Deloitte report states that by 2008 41 million corporate employees globally may spend at least 1 day a week teleworking and that 200 million will work from home at least 1 day a month.[49] A report by the Reason Foundation, a California-based think tank, found that telecommuters presently outnumbered actual mass-transit commuters in 27 of the largest U.S. metropolitan areas, and that two-thirds of Fortune 1000 companies now have telecommuting programs.[50]

Although telecommuting represents an attempt to accommodate employee needs and desires, it requires adjustments and is not for everybody. People who enjoy the social camaraderie of the office setting, for instance, probably won't like it. Others lack the self-motivation needed to work at home.

6. Handheld Devices Handheld devices such as personal digital assistants (PDAs) and smartphones offer users the portability to do work from any location. PDAs, for example, are used to track appointments, work spreadsheets, manage e-mail, organize photos, play games, and watch videos. Multimedia smartphones, which combine some of the capabilities of a personal computer with a handset, offer a wealth of gadgetry: text messaging, cameras, music players, videogames, e-mail access, digital-TV viewing, search tools, personal information management, GPS locators, Internet phone service, and even phones doubling as credit cards (which, among other things, can be used to pay for parking time on a new generation of wireless parking meters).[51] As one newspaper headline put it, "It's Not Just a Phone, It's an Adventure."[52]

7. Blogs **A *blog* is an online journal in which people write whatever they want about any topic.** According to a study from the Pew Internet and American Life Project, in 2006 there were an estimated 12 million adult bloggers in the United States, a threefold increase in 2 years.[53] Four million teens are also blogging.[54]

The benefits of blogs include the opportunity for people to discuss issues in a casual format, serving much like a chat group and thus providing managers with insights from a variety of employees and customers. Thus, managers such as Paul Otellini, CEO of Intel, who was one of the first executive bloggers, use blogs to discuss matters of importance.[55] Blogs also give people the opportunity to air their opinions, grievances, and creative ideas. In addition, blogs can be used to obtain feedback.

But blogs also have some drawbacks. One is the lack of legal and organizational guidelines about what can be posted online, resulting in some people being fired after posting information online (such as suggestive pictures or information about company finances).[56] Another problem is that employees can use blogs to say unflattering things or leak confidential information about their employers. There is also the problem of believability; can you trust what you read on blogs when, for example, bloggers are being paid to push products without disclosure?[57]

Workplace Problems: Impediments to Productivity

First the mainframe computer, then the desktop stand-alone personal computer, and then the networked computer were all brought into the workplace for one reason only: to improve productivity. But there are several ways in which information technology actively interferes with productivity. We consider (1) *misuse of technology,* (2) *fussing with computers,* and (3) *information overload.*

1. Misuse of Technology Employees may look busy, as they stare into their computer screens with brows crinkled, but sometimes they are just hard at work playing video games. Or browsing online malls, or looking at their investments or pornography sites. Indeed, one study found that recreational Web surfing accounts for nearly one-third of office workers' time online.[58] In 2006, one survey found the average U.S. worker fritters away 1.86 hours per 8-hour workday and that the biggest time killer was personal use of the Internet (52% said they wasted more time online than any other way).[59]

2. Fussing with Computers Most computer users at some point have to get involved with making online connections work or experience the frustrations of untangling complications caused by spam, viruses, and other Internet deviltry.

A Stanford study found that junk e-mail and computer maintenance take up a significant amount of time spent online each day. Indeed, people surveyed said they spent 14 minutes daily dealing with computer problems, which would add up to a total of 10 days a year. [60]

3. Information Overload ***Information overload*** **occurs when the amount of information received exceeds a person's ability to handle or process it.** Clearly, information technology is a two-edged sword. The average businessperson sends and receives 84 email messages a day, according to some research, and that average will increase to 110 messages a day by the end of 2008.[61] Cell phones, pagers, and laptops may untether employees from the office, but these employees tend to work longer hours under more severe deadline pressure than do their tethered counterparts who stay at the office, according to one study.[62] Moreover, the devices that once promised to do away with irksome business travel by ushering in a new era of communications have done the opposite. They have created the office-in-a-bag that allows businesspeople to continue to work from airplane seats, hotel desks, and their own kitchen tables. The diminishing difference between work and leisure is what Motorola calls the "blurring of life segments."[63]

Makers of handheld devices claim that the combination of portability and multitasking features makes people more productive, but David Greenfield, director of the Center for Internet Studies, thinks this idea "is a scam and illusion," because multitasking can easily become "multislacking" and in fact may make us take more time to accomplish basic tasks.[64] Probably a better information-management strategy is to reduce your information load and increase your information-processing capacity. *(See Table 15.6.)* ●

table 15.6

INFORMATION MANAGEMENT STRATEGY

Reducing information load and increasing information-processing capacity

Reducing your information load

- *Preview and ignore messages.* When going through your e-mail, quickly glance at the subject line and immediately delete anything that looks like spam or (if you can) messages from people you don't know. Do the same with voice mail or phone slips.
- *Filter messages.* Many e-mail programs have message filtering, so that an urgent message from the boss, for example, will go to the top of your e-mail queue. Spam-killer software is available to help eliminate junk mail. Some executives put all "cc" e-mails in a special file and rarely read them.
- *Organize your e-mail inbox.* Set up a folder for e-mails you want to keep. Don't use your e-mail inbox for general storage.

Increasing your information-processing capacity

- *Use discipline.* Check e-mail only three times a day. Handle every message only once. When an e-mail message arrives, deal with it immediately—read it and then either respond to it, delete it, or file it away in a folder.
- *Get a unified messaging site.* It's possible to get one unified messaging site to which all your e-mails, faxes, and voice mails are delivered. Voice mails arrive as audio files that you can listen to, while e-mails are read to you over the phone by a virtual (robot) assistant.
- *Use your company address for work-related e-mails only.* Have personal messages go to a separate account.

Sources: C. Hymowitz, "Taking Time to Focus on the Big Picture Despite the Flood of Data," *The Wall Street Journal,* February 27, 2001, p. B1; R. Strauss, "You've Got Maelstrom," *The New York Times,* July 5, 2001, pp. D1, D9; C. Canabou, "A Message about Managing E-mail," *Fast Company,* August 2001, p. 38; C. Cavanagh, *Managing Your Email: Thinking Outside the Inbox* (New York: John Wiley & Sons, 2003); and J. Zaslow, "Hoarders vs. Deleters: How You Handle Your Email Inbox Says a Lot About You," *The Wall Street Journal,* August 10, 2006, p. D1.

15.5 IMPROVING COMMUNICATION EFFECTIVENESS

How can I be a better listener, reader, writer, and speaker?

THE BIG PICTURE

We describe how you can be a more effective listener, as in learning to concentrate on the content of a message. We also describe how to be an effective reader. We offer four tips for becoming a more effective writer. Finally, we discuss how to be an effective speaker, through three steps.

Self-Assessment Exercise: *Active Listening Skills Inventory*

The principal activities the typical manager does have to do with communication—listening, 40%; talking, 35%; reading, 16%; and writing, 9%.[65] Listening and speaking often take place in meetings (see the Practical Action box "How to Streamline Meetings" in Chapter 5), although they are not the only occasions. Regardless of the environment, let's see how you can be more effective at these four essential communication skills.

Being an Effective Listener

Is listening something you're good at? Then you're the exception. Generally, people comprehend only about 35% of a typical verbal message, experts say.[66] Two-thirds of all employees feel management isn't listening to them.[67] Interestingly, the average speaker communicates 125 words per minute, while we can process 500 words per minute. Poor listeners use this information-processing gap to daydream. They think about other things, thus missing the important parts of what's being communicated.[68] Good listeners know how to use these gaps effectively, mentally summarizing the speaker's remarks, weighing the evidence, and listening between the lines.

How do you become the kind of manager who others say is a good listener? Following are some suggestions (you can practice them in your college lectures and seminars).[69]

Concentrate on the Content of the Message Don't think about what you're going to say until the other person has finished talking.

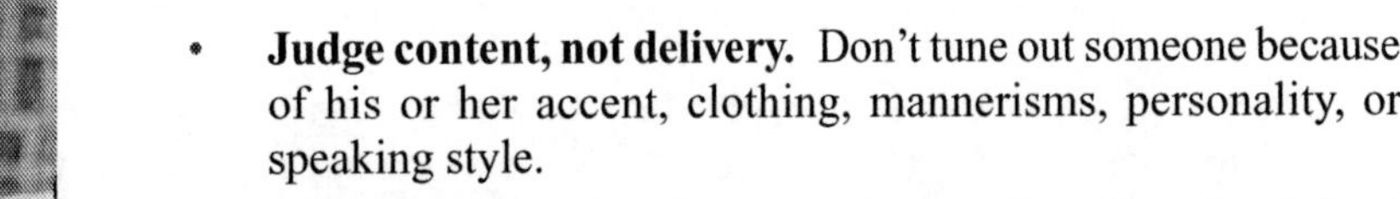

- **Judge content, not delivery.** Don't tune out someone because of his or her accent, clothing, mannerisms, personality, or speaking style.
- **Ask questions, summarize remarks.** Good listening is hard work. Ask questions to make sure you understand. Recap what the speaker said.
- **Listen for ideas.** Don't get diverted by the details; try to concentrate on the main ideas.
- **Resist distractions, show interest.** Don't get distracted by things other people are doing, paperwork on your desk, things happening outside the window, television or radio, and the like. Show the speaker you're listening, periodically restating in your own words what you've heard.

Understand me. What's the recipe for effective listening-~~for~~ really finding out what someone has to say? Probably it is *listen, watch, write, think, question.* What do you do to fight flagging concentration if you're tired or bored? You suppress negative thoughts, ignore distractions about the speaker's style of delivery or body language, and encourage the speaker with eye contact, an interested expression, and an attentive posture. This will make you more involved and interested in the subject matter.

Practical Action

Communication by Listening

Often the reason that people act subversively against their employers is that they can't or are afraid to communicate with their managers.

Resistance may take the form of "malicious compliance" (following supervisors' instructions to the letter while ignoring the real goal), withholding crucial data, or sabotaging projects that reflect directly on the manager.

One bookstore employee sabotaged his nonlistening, always-angry boss by going through the store and discreetly pocketing any pens, pencils, even crayons, then hiding them in a backroom cabinet. "My already preternaturally enraged boss," he reported later, "reached glorious heights of apoplexy."[70]

As we discuss in the text, effective communication begins with listening. There is a technique for doing this. "To begin with, listen to people as if you don't know the answer," suggests Meg Price, a Reno, Nevada, human resource professional. "This means that you will ask more questions to try to understand the situation from the other person's perspective. When you think you've got it, make a statement to the speaker summarizing what you believe they have told you. Only when they agree that indeed you do 'get it' should you begin to offer potential solutions or answers."[71]

Of course, sometimes there are true disagreements, and no amount of listening on your part is going to change that fact. Here, according to David Stiebel, author of *When Talking Makes Things Worse! Resolving Problems When Communication Fails,* is how to identify the nature of a dispute:

- If you only listened to the other person, would she feel satisfied and stop opposing you?
- If you succeed in explaining yourself, would you really change the other person's mind?
- If the other person explained himself more, would you change your mind?

When true disagreements occur, one person ultimately must be willing to change so that negotiations can begin.[72]

- **Give a fair hearing.** Don't shut out unfavorable information just because you hear a term—"Republican," "Democrat," "union," "big business," "affirmative action," "corporate welfare"—that suggests ideas you're not comfortable with. Try to correct for your biases.

Hot Seat DVD Application:
Listening Skills: Yeah, Whatever

Being an Effective Reader

Reading shares many of the same skills as listening. You need to concentrate on the content of the message, judge the content and not the delivery, and concentrate on the main ideas. But because managers usually have to do so much reading, you also need to learn to apply some other strategies.

Realize That Speed Reading Doesn't Work Perhaps you've thought that somewhere along the line you could take a course on speed reading. By and large, however, speed reading isn't effective. Psychologists have found that speed reading or skimming may work well with easy or familiar reading material, but it can lead to problems with dense or unfamiliar material. For instance, in one study, when questioned about their reading of difficult material, average readers got half the questions right, while speed readers got only one in three.[73]

Learn to Streamline Reading Management consultant and UCLA professor Kathryn Alesandrini offers a number of suggestions for streamlining your reading.[74]

- **Be savvy about periodicals and books.** Review your magazine and newspaper subscriptions and eliminate as many as possible. You can subscribe to just

Speed-read this? Maybe you could—if it's easy or familiar material. But lots of things managers are required to read take patient study. How are you going to manage such reading day after day?

a few industry publications, scan and mark interesting material, later read what's marked, and pitch the rest. Read summaries and reviews that condense business books and articles.

- **Transfer your reading load.** With some material you can ask some of your employees to screen or scan it first, then post an action note on each item that needs additional reading by you. You can also ask your staff to read important books and summarize them in four or five pages.
- **Make internal memos and e-mail more efficient.** Ask others to tell you up front in their e-mails, memos, and reports what they want you to do. Instruct them to include a one-page executive summary of a long report. When you communicate with them, give them specific questions you want answered.

Do Top-Down Reading—SQ3R "The key to better reading is to be a productive rather than a passive reader," writes Alesandrini. "You'll get more out of what you read if you literally produce meaningful connections between what you already know and what you're reading."[75] This leads to what she calls a "top-down" strategy for reading, a variant on the SQ3R (Survey, Question, Read, Recite, Review) method we discussed in the box at the end of Chapter 1.

The top-down system has five steps:

- **Rate reasons to read.** Rate your reasons for reading ("Why should I read this? Will reading it contribute to my goals?").
- **Question and predict answers.** Formulate specific questions you want the reading to answer. This will give you reasons for reading—to get answers to your questions.
- **Survey the big picture.** Survey the material to be read so you can get a sense of the whole. Take a few minutes to get an overview so that you'll be better able to read with purpose.
- **Skim for main ideas.** Skimming the material is similar to surveying, except it's on a smaller scale. You look for the essence of each subsection or paragraph.
- **Summarize.** Summarize as you skim. Verbally restate or write notes of the main points, using your own words. Visualize or sketch the main points. Answer your initial questions as you skim the material.

Being an Effective Writer

Writing is an essential management skill, all the more so because e-mail has replaced the telephone in so much of business communication. In addition, downsizing has eliminated the administrative assistants who used to edit and correct business correspondence, so even upper-level executives often write their own letters and e-mail now.[76] A lot of students, however, don't get enough practice in writing, which puts them at a career disadvantage. Taking a business writing class can be a real advantage. (Indeed, as a manager, you may have to identify employees who need writing training.)

Following are some tips for writing more effectively. These apply particularly to memos and reports but are also applicable to e-mail messages.

Don't Show Your Ignorance E-mail correspondence has made people more relaxed about spelling and grammar rules. While this is fine among friends, as a manager you'll need to create a more favorable impression in your writing. Besides using the spelling checkers and grammar checkers built in to most word processing programs, you should reread, indeed proofread, your writing before sending it on.

Understand Your Strategy before You Write Following are three strategies for laying out your ideas in writing.

- **Most important to least important.** This is a good strategy when the action you want your reader to take is logical and not highly political.
- **Least controversial to most controversial.** This builds support gradually and is best used when the decision is controversial or your reader is attached to a particular solution other than the one you're proposing.
- **Negative to positive.** This strategy establishes a common ground with your reader and puts the positive argument last, which makes it stronger.[77]

Start with Your Purpose Often people organize their messages backward, putting their real purpose last, points out Alesandrini. You should *start* your writing by telling your purpose and what you expect of the reader.

Write Simply, Concisely, & Directly Keep your words simple and use short words, sentences, and phrases. Be direct instead of vague, and use the active voice rather than the passive. (Directness, active voice: "Please call a meeting for Wednesday." Vagueness, passive voice: "It is suggested that a meeting be called for Wednesday.")

Telegraph Your Writing with a Powerful Layout Make your writing as easy to read as possible, using the tools of highlighting and white space.

- **Highlighting.** Highlighting consists of using **boldface** and *italics* to emphasize key concepts and introduce new concepts, and bullets—small circles or squares like the ones in the list you're reading—to emphasize list items. (Don't overuse any of these devices, or they'll lose their effect. And particularly don't use ALL CAPITAL LETTERS for emphasis, except rarely.)
- **White space.** White space, which consists of wide margins and a break between paragraphs, produces a page that is clean and attractive.[78]

Being an Effective Speaker

Speaking or talking covers a range of activities, from one-on-one conversations, to participating in meetings, to giving formal presentations. In terms of personal oral communication, most of the best advice comes under the heading of listening, since effective listening will dictate the appropriate talking you need to do.

However, the ability to talk to a room full of people—to make an oral presentation—is one of the greatest skills you can have. A study conducted by AT&T and Stanford University found that the top predictor of success and professional upward mobility is how much you enjoy public speaking and how effective you are at it.[79]

The biggest problem most people have with public speaking is controlling their nerves. Author and lecturer Gael Lindenfield suggests that you can prepare your nerves by practicing your speech until it's near perfect, visualizing yourself performing with brilliance, getting reassurance from a friend, and getting to the speaking site early and releasing physical tension by doing deep breathing. (And staying away from alcohol and caffeine pick-me-ups before your speech.)[80] As for the content of the speech, some brief and valuable advice is offered by speechwriter Phil Theibert, who says a speech comprises just three simple rules: (1) Tell them what you're going to say. (2) Say it. (3) Tell them what you said.[81]

Predictor for success. Enjoying public speaking and being good at it are the top predictors of success and upward mobility. Do you think you could develop these skills?

1. Tell Them What You're Going to Say The introduction should take 5%–15% of your speaking time, and it should prepare the audience for the rest of the speech. Avoid jokes and such phrases as "I'm honored to be with you here today . . ." Because everything in your speech should be relevant, try to go right to the point. For example:

"Good afternoon. The subject of identity theft may seem far removed from the concerns of most employees. But I intend to describe how our supposedly private credit, health, employment, and other records are vulnerable to theft by so-called identity thieves and how you can protect yourself."

2. Say It The main body of the speech takes up 75%–90% of your time. The most important thing to realize is that your audience won't remember more than a few points anyway. Thus, you need to decide which three or four points must be remembered.[82] Then cover them as succinctly as possible.

Be particularly attentive to transitions during the main body of the speech. Listening differs from reading in that the listener has only one chance to get your meaning. Thus, be sure you constantly provide your listeners with guidelines and transitional phrases so they can see where you're going. Example:

"There are five ways the security of your supposedly private files can be compromised. The first way is . . . "

3. Tell Them What You Said The end might take 5%–10% of your time. Many professional speakers consider the conclusion to be as important as the introduction, so don't drop the ball here. You need a solid, strong, persuasive wrap-up.

Use some sort of signal phrase that cues your listeners that you are heading into your wind-up. Examples:

"Let's review the main points . . . "

"In conclusion, what CAN you do to protect against unauthorized invasion of your private files? I point out five main steps. One . . . "

Give some thought to the last thing you will say. It should be strongly upbeat, a call to action, a thought for the day, a little story, a quotation. Examples:

"I want to leave you with one last thought . . . "

"Finally, let me close by sharing something that happened to me . . . "

"As Albert Einstein said, 'Imagination is more important than knowledge.'"

Then say "Thank you" and stop talking. ●

key terms used in this chapter

summary

15.1 The Communication Process: What It Is, How It Works

- Communication is the transfer of information and understanding from one person to another. The process involves sender, message, and receiver; encoding and decoding; the medium; feedback; and dealing with "noise." The sender is the person wanting to share information. The information is called a message. The receiver is the person for whom the message is intended. Encoding is translating a message into understandable symbols or language. Decoding is interpreting and trying to make sense of the message. The medium is the pathway by which a message travels. Feedback is the process in which a receiver expresses his or her reaction to the sender's message. The entire communication process can be disrupted at any point by noise, defined as any disturbance that interferes with the transmission of a message.
- For effective communication, a manager must select the right medium. Media richness indicates how well a particular medium conveys information and promotes learning. The richer a medium is, the better it is at conveying information. Face-to-face presence is the richest; an advertising flyer would be one of the lowest. A rich medium is best for nonroutine situations and to avoid oversimplification. A lean medium is best for routine situations and to avoid overloading.

15.2 Barriers to Communication

- Barriers to communication are of three types:

  (1) Physical barriers are exemplified by walls, background noise, and time-zone differences.

  (2) Semantics is the study of the meaning of words. Jargon, terminology specific to a particular profession or group, can be a semantic barrier.

  (3) Personal barriers are individual attributes that hinder communication. Nine such barriers are (a) variable skills in communicating effectively, (b) variations in frames of reference and experiences that affect how information is interpreted, (c) variations in trustworthiness and credibility, (d) oversized egos, (e) faulty listening skills, (f) tendency to judge others' messages, (g) inability to listen with understanding, (h) stereotypes (oversimplified beliefs about a certain group of people) and prejudices, and (i) nonverbal communication (messages sent outside of the written or spoken word, including body language).
- Seven ways in which nonverbal communication is expressed are through (1) interpersonal space, (2) eye contact, (3) facial expressions, (4) body movements and gestures, (5) touch, (6) setting, and (7) time.

15.3 How Managers Fit into the Communication Process

- Communication channels may be formal or informal.
- Formal communication channels follow the chain of command and are recognized as official. Formal communication is of three types:

  (1) Vertical communication is the flow of messages up and down the organizational hierarchy.

  (2) Horizontal communication flows within and between work units; its main purpose is coordination.

  (3) External communication flows between people inside and outside the organization.
- Informal communication channels develop outside the formal structure and do not follow the chain of command. Two aspects of informal channels are the grapevine and management by wandering around.

  (1) The grapevine is the unofficial communication system of the informal organization. The grapevine is faster than formal channels, is about 75% accurate, and is used by employees to acquire most on-the-job information.

  (2) In management by wandering around (MBWA), a manager literally wanders around his or her organization and talks with people across all lines of authority; this reduces distortion caused by formal communication.

15.4 Communication in the Information Age

- This section considers seven communications tools of information technology:

  (1) The Internet is a global network of independently operating but interconnected computers, linking smaller networks. Two private uses of the Internet are for intranets, organizations' private Internets, and for extranets, extended intranets that connect a company's internal employees with selected customers, suppliers, and other strategic partners.

  (2) E-mail, for electronic mail, uses the Internet to send computer-generated text and documents between people. E-mail has become a major communication medium because it reduces the cost of distributing information, increases teamwork, reduces paper costs, and increases flexibility. However, e-mail has three drawbacks: wasted time; information overload, in part because of spam, or unsolicited jokes and junk mail; and it leads people to neglect other media.

  (3) Videoconferencing uses video and audio links along with computers to enable people located at different locations to see, hear, and talk with one another.

  (4) Group support systems entail using state-of-the-art computer software and hardware to help people work better together.

  (5) Telecommuting involves doing work that is generally performed in the office away from the office, using a variety of information technologies.

  (6) Handheld devices such as personal digital assistants and smartphones offer users the portability to work from any location.

  (7) Blogs are online journals in which people write whatever they want about any topic.
- Three impediments to productivity of information technology are (1) the technology is misused, as for video games; (2) it requires a lot of fussing with, as in untangling complications caused by spam and viruses; and (3) it can produce information overload—the amount of information received exceeds a person's ability to handle or process it.

15.5 Improving Communication Effectiveness

- This section describes how to be more effective at listening, reading, writing, and speaking.
- To become a good listener, you should concentrate on the content of the message. You should judge content, not delivery; ask questions and summarize the speaker's remarks; listen for ideas; resist distractions and show interest; and give the speaker a fair hearing.
- To become a good reader, you need to first realize that speed reading usually doesn't work. You should also be savvy about how you handle periodicals and books, transfer your reading load to some of your employees, and ask others to use e-mails and reports to tell you what they want you to do. A top-down reading system that's a variant on the SQ3R system (survey, question, read, recite, review) is also helpful.
- To become an effective writer, you can follow several suggestions. Use spelling and

grammar checkers in word processing software. Use three strategies for laying out your ideas in writing: go from most important topic to least important; go from least controversial topic to most controversial; and go from negative to positive. When organizing your message, start with your purpose. Write simply, concisely, and directly. Telegraph your writing through use of highlighting and white space.

- To become an effective speaker, follow three simple rules. Tell people what you're going to say. Say it. Tell them what you said.

management in action

Boeing Co. Uses Blogging to Improve Communication Both Inside & Outside the Organization

Defense contractors and aerospace companies aren't known for their openness. After all, this is an industry built on security clearances and classified government projects. But today Boeing Co. is embracing a kind of management *glasnost* that would have been unthinkable a few years ago.

The evidence? Boeing's use of blogs. The Chicago aerospace giant—no stranger to recent and well-publicized ethical and political scandals—is among a small but growing group of large non-tech companies such as Walt Disney, General Motors, and McDonald's that are embracing the power of blogging. That means Boeing has learned to cede some control and expose itself to stinging criticism in exchange for a potentially more constructive dialogue with the public, customers, and employees. "Companies are nervous about creating external blogs because they fear the negative comments," says Charlene Li, an analyst at Forrester Research Inc. "But negative comments do exist. A company is better off knowing about them."

Boeing's early results suggest that the rewards outweigh the risks. The company's two public blogs give Boeing a direct link to the public, something the 91-year-old company has never had before. And executives are starting to use internal blogs to get conversations going and allow employees to raise issues anonymously. "I've always been a big believer in open and honest dialogue that gets the issues on the table," says James F. Albaugh, the chief executive of Boeing Integrated Defense Systems (IDS). He championed using blogs at the defense unit's meeting of 1,000 executives in February. "I was a little concerned and I had no idea how it would turn out, but I'm sold on it."

Boeing's entry into the blogosphere got off to a rocky start. Eighteen months ago, Randy Baseler, vice-president for marketing at Boeing Commercial Airplanes, started a Web log to talk about the company's view of the commercial airplane world. Almost immediately, he was blasted by the blogerati for not allowing comments, considered to be a key component of blogging. And he was dinged for the perception that his posts gave more of a marketing spin than an inside perspective. In one e-mail, an outside reader wrote: "Take down your blog. You embarrass us, everyone who reads it, and you make the world a dumber place."

Instead of backing down, Baseler responded. As the blog evolved, he found his voice. He began to offer insights into the industry that would be hard to find elsewhere, such as a post about emerging airplane markets in Latin America, called "Latin Rhythm." His explanation of the differences between Boeing's and Airbus' strategy, particularly an ongoing controversy about how they handle seat width, has been light on emotion and heavy on facts. The site drew 30,000 visitors in April, a new high for a blog that started with low expectations. . . .

Boeing's latest experiments have focused inward. In February, Boeing's senior IDS leaders set up blog kiosks at the annual strategy meeting in Los Angeles for the company's top 1,000 defense executives. During a series of briefings, managers went over new company policies and the division's top strategic and business priorities for the year. While Albaugh and his team discussed hot topics such as ethical compliance rules and a new management compensation plan, executives responded at the kiosks located outside the conference room. "As each exec talked, they would talk about comments from the blog," says DL Byron, a blogging consultant to Boeing.

In the end, the blog helped air questions about the unit's strategy and made sure everyone understood the human resources and diversity policies. It also let Albaugh understand what his top people knew or didn't know. For instance, he asked how many executives were actively using the division's Vision Support Plan software that helps managers track how their units are doing. About 30% said they weren't. Thanks to the blog, Albaugh can now try to create converts.

Questions for Discussion

1. To what extent are blogs helping Boeing to provide better customer service? Explain.
2. How would you rate blogs in terms of their media richness? Given this conclusion, was Boeing's senior IDS leader's use of blogs consistent with the recommendations for matching the appropriate medium to the appropriate situation? Discuss your rationale.
3. What are the pros and cons of Boeing's use of blogs? Provide your rationale.
4. Which of the three key barriers to communication are most likely to influence the effectiveness of blogs? Discuss.

Source: Excerpted from Stanley Holmes, "Into the Wild Blog Yonder," *BusinessWeek,* May 22, 2006, pp. 84, 86.

self-assessment

What Is Your Most Comfortable Learning Style?

Objectives

1. To learn about your visual, auditory, and kinesthetic learning/communication style.
2. To consider how knowledge about learning/communication styles can be used to enhance your communication effectiveness.

Introduction

The purpose of this exercise is to find out what your most prominent learning style is—that is, what forms of communication can you best learn from. You should find the information of value for understanding not only your own style but those of others. Knowing your own style should also allow you to be a much more effective learner.

Instructions

Read the following 36 statements and indicate the extent to which each statement is consistent with your behavior by using the following rating scale: 1 = almost never applies; 2 = applies once in a while; 3 = sometimes applies; 4 = often applies; 5 = almost always applies.

1. I take lots of notes.	1 2 3 4 5
2. When talking to others, I have the hardest time handling those who do not maintain good eye contact with me.	1 2 3 4 5
3. I make lists and notes because I remember things better when I write them down.	1 2 3 4 5
4. When reading a novel, I pay a lot of attention to passages picturing the clothing, scenery, setting, etc.	1 2 3 4 5
5. I need to write down directions so that I can remember them.	1 2 3 4 5
6. I need to see the person I am talking to in order to keep my attention focused on the subject.	1 2 3 4 5
7. When meeting a person for the first time, I initially notice the style of dress, visual characteristics, and neatness.	1 2 3 4 5

(continued)

8. When I am at a party, one of the things I love to do is stand back and "people watch."	1 2 3 4 5
9. When recalling information, I can see it in my mind and remember where I saw it.	1 2 3 4 5
10. If I had to explain a new procedure or technique, I would prefer to write it out.	1 2 3 4 5
11. With free time I am most likely to watch television or read.	1 2 3 4 5
12. If my boss has a message for me, I am most comfortable when he or she sends a memo.	1 2 3 4 5
Total A (the minimum is 12 and the maximum is 60)	________
1. When I read, I read out loud or move my lips to hear the words in my head.	1 2 3 4 5
2. When talking to someone else, I have the hardest time handling those who do not talk back with me.	1 2 3 4 5
3. I do not take a lot of notes, but I still remember what was said. Taking notes distracts me from the speaker.	1 2 3 4 5
4. When reading a novel, I pay a lot of attention to passages involving conversations.	1 2 3 4 5
5. I like to talk to myself when solving a problem or writing.	1 2 3 4 5
6. I can understand what a speaker says, even if I am not focused on the speaker.	1 2 3 4 5
7. I remember things easier by repeating them again and again.	1 2 3 4 5
8. When I am at a party, one of the things I love to do is have in-depth conversations about a subject that is important to me.	1 2 3 4 5
9. I would rather receive information from the radio than a newspaper.	1 2 3 4 5
10. If I had to explain a new procedure or technique, I would prefer telling about it.	1 2 3 4 5
11. With free time I am most likely to listen to music.	1 2 3 4 5
12. If my boss has a message for me, I am most comfortable when he or she calls on the phone.	1 2 3 4 5
Total B (the minimum is 12 and the maximum is 60)	________

(continued)

1. I am not good at reading or listening to directions.	1 2 3 4 5
2. When talking to someone else, I have the hardest time handling those who do not show any kind of emotional support.	1 2 3 4 5
3. I take notes and doodle, but I rarely go back and look at them.	1 2 3 4 5
4. When reading a novel, I pay a lot of attention to passages revealing feelings, moods, action, drama, etc.	1 2 3 4 5
5. When I am reading, I move my lips.	1 2 3 4 5
6. I will exchange words and places and use my hands a lot when I can't remember the right thing to say.	1 2 3 4 5
7. My desk appears disorganized.	1 2 3 4 5
8. When I am at a party, one of the things I love to do is enjoy activities, such as dancing, games, and totally losing myself.	1 2 3 4 5
9. I like to move around. I feel trapped when seated at a meeting or desk.	1 2 3 4 5
10. If I had to explain a new procedure or technique, I would prefer actually demonstrating it.	1 2 3 4 5
11. With free time, I am most likely to exercise.	1 2 3 4 5
12. If my boss has a message for me, I am most comfortable when he or she talks to me in person.	1 2 3 4 5
Total C (the minimum is 12 and the maximum is 60)	________

Scoring & Interpretation

Total A is your Visual Score ________; Total B is your Auditory Score ________; and Total C is your Kinesthetic Score ________. The area in which you have your highest score represents your "dominant" learning style. You can learn from all three, but typically you learn best using one style. Communication effectiveness is increased when your dominant style is consistent with the communication style used by others. For example, if you are primarily kinesthetic and your boss gives you directions orally, you may have trouble communicating because you do not learn or process communication well by just being told something. You must consider not only how you communicate but also how the people you work with communicate.

Questions for Discussion

1. Do you agree with the assessment? Why or why not? Explain.
2. How valuable is it to know your learning style? Does it help explain why you did well in some learning situations and poorly in others? Describe and explain.
3. How important is it to know the learning style of those you work with? Explain.

Source: www.nwlink.com/~donclark/hrd/vak.html. Used by permission.

How Well Does Your Group Swim in a Fishbowl?

Objectives

- To see how you communicate in a fishbowl setting.
- To assess how you communicate when under pressure.

Introduction

You can learn a great deal about your communication style by receiving feedback from others. Although we communicate all day long, we do not always stop to check whether we are actually communicating the intended message. By practicing our communication skills and receiving feedback, this exercise helps you become a more effective communicator. The purpose of this exercise is twofold: to see how you communicate in a group and to see how others communicate—and to learn how to develop your skills from both experiences.

Instructions

The fishbowl technique has been used for many years as a vehicle for providing feedback to individuals or groups. The class should first divide into groups of five or six people. Next these subgroups are formed into teams comprised of two groups of five or six people. Once the groups/teams are formed, one group is selected to be the discussion group, the other group will form the observing group. The seats should be arranged so that members of one group sit in the middle and members in the second group arrange their desks to form a circle around this group. The center group is the discussion group. This group will discuss a topic from the list below for approximately 10 minutes. The group surrounding the center group will observe and take notes on the center group's discussion and interaction with one another.

After time is up, the groups switch—the outer group moves to the center and begins discussion on a topic while the center group moves to the outer circle and begins observing and taking notes.

Once all of the groups have had a chance to observe and discuss, all of the two groups/teams should share their observations with one another. The feedback you receive from the group can be used or discarded by you. It is often hard to hear that we are different from how we think we are in terms of how others see and hear us, but this is an opportunity to learn both.

Topics for Discussion

1. Paris Hilton and Bono should be UN Ambassadors for the United States.
2. The Internet should be regulated.
3. Gnutella and other Web sites that allow you to download free music should not be regulated, and it is okay to burn CDs with music downloaded from these sites.
4. Chief executive officers who make over $10 million a year are overpaid.
5. The minimum wage should be $10 an hour.
6. All U.S. citizens should be allowed to attend college at the taxpayers' expense.

Observation Guidelines

Use the form shown below to take notes on how the center group communicates. Use the following guidelines.

What personal barriers to communication do you see in this group? That is, do any of the members have a tendency to judge others' messages? Do any of the members exhibit faulty listening skills? What types of communication styles do you see? Do some members appear to be better communicators? Do any members seem to have "the gift of gab"?

How well does this group communicate nonverbally? Do any group members look away from the speaker? Do any of the members speak too quickly or too slowly? Is there a group member that smiles and is animated? Do any of the members yawn excessively?

Questions for Discussion

1. Were you surprised at some of your behavior that your classmates noted? Explain.
2. Based on the feedback from your classmates, what are some things you can do to work on your communication style?
3. During your observation role, did you notice any gender-related communication differences? Explain.
4. Do you think the fishbowl technique is a valuable tool for obtaining feedback on interpersonal skills? Why or why not?

Group One:	Communication Styles Noted:
Student Name:	
Student Name:	
Student Name:	
Student Name:	
Student Name:	
Student Name:	

ethical dilemma

Are Camera Cell Phones Creating Ethical Problems?

Although camera phones have been broadly available for only a few months in the United States, more than 25 million of the devices are out on the streets of Japan. . . .

Now that the use of cell phones with little digital cameras has spread throughout Asia, so have new brands of misbehavior. Some people are secretly taking photos up women's skirts and down into bathroom stalls. Others are avoiding buying books by snapping free shots of desired pages.

"The problem with a new technology is that society has yet to come up with a common understanding about appropriate behavior," said Mizuko Ito, an expert on mobile phone culture at Keio University Tokyo.

Samsung Electronics is banning their use in semiconductor and research facilities, hoping to stave off industrial espionage. Samsung, a leading maker of cell phones, is taking a low-tech approach, requiring employees and visitors to stick tape over the handset's camera lens.

Solving the Dilemma

You are the manager of a large bookstore. You have seen customers use their camera phones to take pictures of one another in the store. Yesterday, for the first time, you observed a customer taking photos of 10 pages of material in a cookbook (and not buying the book). Although you did not say anything to this customer, you wonder what to do in the future. Which of the following options would you select?

1. Place a sign on the door asking customers to mind their "cell phone manners." This way you don't have to prevent people from using their phones; you can rely on common decency.
2. Ask customers to leave their camera cell phones with an employee at the front of the store. The employee will give the customer a claim check, and they can retrieve their phones once they finish shopping.
3. Station an employee at the front of the store who places tape over the lens of camera phones as customers come in.
4. Don't do anything. There is nothing wrong with people taking pictures of materials out of a book.
5. Invent other options. Discuss.

Source: *Excerpted from Yuri Kageyama, "Cellphones with Cameras Creating Trouble: Concerns Include Voyeurism,"* The Arizona Republic, *July 10, 2003, p. A18.*

Wolinsky & Williams

Wolinsky & Williams, Inc. (W&W) is an international architectural firm employing over 400 individuals in nine countries. They primarily specialize in office parks and corporate high rises. The company has grown quickly over the past 8 years—so quickly, in fact, that changes have occurred inefficiently and without proper planning. For instance, new offices were opened without any sense of continuity of process or corporate culture. Each of the offices is using different levels of computerization and different technologies for different tasks. The lack of consistency increases the complexity of all processes, from collaboration and revisions to cost and time management.

Recently, however, business has hit a plateau, and senior management now sees the opportunity to assess practices and make across-the-board improvements.

A committee has been appointed to formulate a proposal for streamlining the antiquated blueprint-generation process. Currently, the committee consists of four account managers. Joe Tanney has been employed at W&W for 6 years, working his way up from assistant to account manager and has held his current position for 1 year. Joe is a diligent and motivated worker, eager to move up the corporate ladder. Simon Mahoney has been with the company for over 15 years. Although his job performance is more than adequate, it's clear that he's running on "auto pilot" most of the time. His passion for his job is no longer there. In fact, he seems jaded, tired, and reluctant to step outside his comfortable routine. Cheng Jing has 2 years' experience as an account manager, but his true passion is designing. He will finish his graduate degree within the next few months and expects to be transferred to a position in the design department. Needless to say, his heart is not in account management. Rosa Denson transferred to her current location from the Dallas office about 3 years ago. She is known for her enthusiastic attitude and quality work. However, she has a reputation for letting difficulties in her personal life distract her from the work at hand.

For several weeks the team has been trying but unable to agree on a meeting date. In the meantime, all members agreed to individually generate ideas and identify necessary tasks. When the first meeting is finally convened, only Joe Tanney has completed this assignment. In fact, he has created a thorough analysis of the project. All others have come to the first meeting completely unprepared. During this meeting, it is clear that the committee needs to plan a course of action, assign tasks, and set deadlines. Because Simon Mahoney is the most senior manager, everyone, including senior management, assumes that he will assume the role of team leader.

At the second meeting, however, again nobody except Tanney has met a single deadline or shared a single memo. It's clear that Mahoney is not leading the committee; in fact, he's barely even participating. Cheng Jing would like to be more helpful, but committee tasks are still low on his priority list. Rosa Denson realizes the committee will have difficulty meeting deadlines, yet she is willing to work nights and weekends even in the face of continued hardship in her family life.

Discussion Questions

1. It's important to select the right medium for effective communication. Evaluate the richness of the communication media used by the committee. Are these media appropriate for the situation? Why or why not?
2. Identify the three types of barriers to effective communication. Which type is evident in the interactions among committee members?
3. Formal communication comes in three types: vertical, horizontal, and external. Explain each of these types. Which is/are being used by the committee at W&W?